# The Nine Pillars of History

## A Guide For Peace, A Personal Perspective
## 7th Edition

GUNNAR SEVELIUS MD

authorHOUSE®

AuthorHouse™
1663 Liberty Drive
Bloomington, IN 47403
www.authorhouse.com
Phone: 1 (800) 839-8640

Published by AuthorHouse  05/20/2016

ISBN: 978-1-5246-0185-0 (sc)
ISBN: 978-1-5246-0184-3 (hc)
ISBN: 978-1-5246-0186-7 (e)

Library of Congress Control Number: 2016905640

Print information available on the last page.

This book is printed on acid-free paper.

# Other Books by the Author

**In English:**
*Add Years to Your Life and Life to Your Years*
*Part I. Heart Attack Prevention*

*Add Years to Your Life and Life to Your Years*
*Part II. Family and Work Enhancement*

*You Are It: First Aid*

*Radioisotopes and Circulation, Editor*

**In Swedish:**
*Historiens Nio Grundstenar*
*Även en Guide för Världsfred*

# Contents

# Comments about the Seventh Edition
# of the Nine Pillars of History

Hardly any manuscript is finished when it is published. Authors will always want to change or add new thoughts. This has now happened to me for the seventh time in the regard to the *Nine Pillars of History.*

After I had done the fifth edition, I was able to summarize 200,000 years of human history on just one page. This was published on the World Wide Web and on the homepage of the American Anthropological Association. It had to be celebrated with a special edition; a special printing, where I highlighted paragraphs that have helped me identify the cause of war. This bold text becomes a book within the book so that busy readers may skim through some well-known text and still get the essence of the *Nine Pillar* message.

In this revised text, the first pillar need with its five modalities (food, water, air, energy and sex) has simply been named the "Survival

Pillar." I use more functional names for each pillar, such as "Dwelling" instead of the "Second" pillar. There are also some editorial changes in the table of contents and the title of the book has been shortened.

Each paragraph is numbered in order to encourage readers to comment and communicate.

The purpose of the *Nine Pillars of History* to society is to secure our living and to leave this life with some dignity for the next generation to follow.

Gunnar Sevelius MD

# Dedication

This work is dedicated to:

The one million Estonians, living free and in peaceful co-existence with their neighbors in 1939;

The almost 200,000 people, mostly married with families, who were rounded up, separated into men and women, and packed into animal boxcars, for a week-long transportation to slave camps in Siberia.

The one who got away and who has filled my life with continuous happiness.

I started to work on this manuscript on February 1, 2001. I am completing it in celebration of our 60th year marriage. The work is totally dedicated to you.

*I loved you on our first date.*
*I loved you even more after the birth of our son.*
*I loved you even more after the birth of our daughter.*
*I love you even more after 60 years of happiness.*

# The Problem

*"Don't you know, my son, with which little
wisdom the world is ruled?"*[*]

Many leaders of society want the best for their people, but not many have the historical insight to recognize what is "best."

[*]Axel Oxenstierna (1583-1654), Swedish Prime Minister during the Thirty-Year War.

# The Goal

## From a Political Standpoint

*"Truth has not the name of a political party."*

Francois Voltaire (1694-1778), the French author, stated this before the French Revolution 1789 and was banished from France. He settled just outside the border and continued to criticize the Sumeric French politics. After the revolution he returned to France and was given a hero's monument in Paris' Pantheon.

Different political parties promote different "good" ideas for our society. What is considered "good" for citizens depends on the values of different political parties. I have identified and suggest that "The Nine Pillars of History" have covered pillar needs for 200,000 years and would therefore be a good bet for norm settings.

## From an Anthropological Standpoint

In the 1000-page anthology, with 56 contributors devoted to the memory of the prominent anthropologist, Paul Radin, one contributor, Gene Weltfish from the University of Nebraska, names his manuscript: *The Anthropologist and the Question of the Fifth Dimension.* He ends his dissertation with: *"Human culture in which man's cumulative knowledge is summarized is a major dimension of our universe, and it is one of the primary tasks of the anthropologist to search for it and determine its common basis."*

I hope the *Nine Pillars of History* is this common basis.

In the same anthology, Kurt Goldstein, M.D., quotes Paul Radin: *"No progress in ethnology will be achieved until scholars rid themselves once and for all of the curious notion that everything possesses history, until they realize that certain ideas and concepts are ultimate for man."*

I hope that *The Nine Pillars of History* are these certain ideas and concepts ultimate for man.

## From a Religious, Philosophical Standpoint

Alfred North Whitehead (1881-1947) wrote in his *Adventures of Ideas*: *"The very purpose of philosophy is to delve below the apparent clarity of common speech."*

I have used philology to arrive at a generic religion and have used the eternal Golden Rule as the guiding rule for a revealing assessment of five world religions in order to clarify the religious concepts of each one.

## From an Economical Standpoint

Both *Economy* and the *Nine Historical Pillars* address individual and family security.

Economy was found to have a floating value while the *"Nine Pillars of History"* together have an eternal value. Our analysis may bring new light to some pressing economical problems.

## My Overall Goal—
## Peace.

After we have given our generation peace, we need to give it **Security** and bid them farewell from a platform of **Dignity**.

Gunnar Sevelius MD

# Preface

As a high school student in Sweden, I was surrounded by World War II and asked myself: "Is war really necessary? Do governments have a flaw in the way they are built or how they work? Maybe a common denominator, a common goal for humanity exists that, when given to all, would prevent war."

In the fifth printing I reported on very pragmatic explanations to the causes of war. In my fifth printing I am now raising my goal from not only achieving peace but also adding security for each generation and leaving each generation from a platform of dignity.

My medical studies put these questions on the shelf. In my later "philosophical" years, fortunately still youthfully naïve and now with 55 years of experience living and farming in both Sweden and the USA, I took up the questions again and began an informal study.

I was not looking for details; I was looking for fundamental rights or wrongs. History texts and their varied interpretations of history gave me no clue. A breakthrough of sorts came when I started to study history based on anthropological, philological and generic medical evidence. Here my medical background complemented my interest in history.

Genetic evidence is particularly useful providing new tools for the study of the early Hunting and Gathering (H/G) period.

The background history for this study is immense; no one person can be expected to know it all. Professional historians usually make an effort to be very detailed in describing past events. Will Durant's *The Story of Civilization,* for instance, consists of 11,000 pages, took a lifetime to write, and did not reach beyond Napoleon. Details of history are not the purpose of this short review. History in this text is only the background to the anthropological evolution of the "Nine Pillars of History" through time.

Professional historians have been consulted in order to narrate history correctly. I have left out a reference list because the basic historical background I use is very simple; you'll probably remember it from high school or college world history classes.

I have named a source in the text if it is an unusual specific reference. Other resources that I found helpful for a general interest of history are listed at the end of each major part.

History is memory. I feel a clean written number with numerals gives a better memory picture than a description of a number with letters. The book covers 2000 centuries. I have sometimes used a year preceded by a minus sign (for instance -250) to express that the year is BCE (before the Common or Christian Era) and the positive number 250 if the year is after BCE. I try to avoid the word "century" and write instead 1400s when I am referring to the years 1400-1499 or the 15th Century.

I offer this book as a synthesized analysis of the past, using the Nine Historical Pillars as common, non-political and non-religious denominators. From this, I deduct as logically as possible a commentary on the present and future. Whether I am "right" or "wrong," I hope to stimulate an interest in history and constitutional, democratic governments.

In the first printing of *The Nine Pillars of History, A Guide to Peace*, I set out to explain why humans have struggled with 7,000 years of war. After reviewing political history, five world religions, human sexuality, and finally the history of economics, **the answer was simply that self-focused dogmatic leaders would choose to go to war when they had garnered sufficient community resources to use to their advantage.**

I promised my "one-page" summary (really 2+ pages in this printing) of world history for this, the seventh printing. This summary reflects the forces at work in countries, corporations, governments, stock market mutual funds, farm-cooperatives and also the forces that work within the field of medicine. Keep this summary in mind as you plow through the total text. Look back at the same text after you are through. Ask yourself: Does this "one-page" summary of history describe the ultimate truth of society? I think it does, but you have to be the judge.

Website: www.ninepillars.com

The discovery of nine common denominators through 200,000 years of history yields compelling hypotheses for their anthropological scope and present social relevance.

### The Nine Pillars of History are:

1) Survival (food, water, air, energy, sex)
2) Shelter
3) Cleanliness
4) Art
5) Communication
6) Community (freedom to assemble for group support)
7) Religion
8) Medicine
9) Trade

**Food transport defines three historical time periods:**

- **Hand** food transport for tribal time: 200,000 - 10,000 years.
- **Animal** food transport for agricultural time: 10,000 years - 1826 (steam-engine).
- **Machine** food transport for industrial time: 1826 - forward.

**The female role in society parallels the periods of food transport:**

- In tribal time, she was as important as the male, contributing 70% of calories.
- In agricultural time, she was essentially politically powerless.
- In industrial time, she is recovering her individual and political identity.

**The Nine Pillars of History recognize only two kinds of social leadership**, one leading to conflicts:

- Democratic, based on the also 200,000 year old Golden Rule (no society is sustainable without the Golden Rule).
- Dogmatic, based on political or religious dogma, **often connected with conflicts.**

**The Nine Historical Pillars have three inevitable traits:**

- The Nine Pillars of History are: 1) eternal, 2) must be sustainable, and 3) their cost can only be controlled through free market forces.

**The present social fallout of the Nine Pillars of History:** The Tragedy of the Commons (what many own, nobody owns) from agricultural time will usually lead to selfish goals instead of for the public good with predictable results:

- For countries: royal, church or political dogmatism leading to 10,000 years of war conflicts. **Democracy is the key to peace.**
- For corporations: capital drifts to the top **and stockholders lose control.**
- For federal, state and local government: personal agendas may lead to tax-waste **and the public loses control.**

**Medical cost, the 8ᵗʰ Pillar, compared to GNP is presently unsustainable:**

- Medical cost in the U.S. is 17% of the GNP and unsustainable.
- Medical cost in the in EU is 9% of the GNP but still unsustainable.
- Medical cost limits access to the remaining eight Pillars of History.

**The Nine Pillars of History might have a solution for runaway medical cost control:**

- Analyzing computerized medical records for medical efficacy.
- Comparing for-profit and not for-profit medical delivery systems for cost and medical efficiency.
- Mitigating medical conflicts through peer reviews instead of through litigations.
- Single and local control of payer system is likely to be the most efficient insurance system.

My wish is that the observation of the "Nine Historical Pillars" gives you, dear friend and reader, peace, security, dignity and hope for freedom. So, if I may respectfully borrow President Lincoln's words, *"that governments of the people, by the people and for the people, shall not perish from the earth."*

Gunnar Sevelius MD

# Acknowledgements

No one can be expected to know or even read everything in history. I have therefore had the manuscript criticized by historians with expertise of different parts of history, religion and economy. My main mentor has been James Sheehan, Professor of European History in the Department of History at Stanford University, California. Professor Sheehan was the first to point out to me that I had done something unique in the study of history in that I had summarized history from its beginning in the Hunting and Gathering time to present. He directed me to Chairman John Rick at the Department of Anthropological Science. Professor Rick helped me with references for the hunting and gathering time and made sure my interpretation of that time period was according to present knowledge. Nuclear Anthropologist Charles Roseman checked that my description of the human cell and its chromosomes was correct and Archeologist Tim King added Jared Diamond's book *Guns, Germs and Steel: The Fates of Human Societies* to my references. Professor Dick Harrison of the Department of History at University of Lund, Sweden helped me with early Scandinavian history and recommended Martin Alm, Ph.D. in the same department to review the whole manuscript for historical facts. Martin also helped with the Swedish translation.

Since my treatise touches on macroeconomics, Professor Edward Ericson, Chairman of Department of Management and Professor of Management & Economics at the San Francisco State University, reviewed the manuscript from the standpoint of economics and contributed with a reference on this subject. Professor Edward Ericson is my next-door neighbor. We take daily 2 miles walks. The subject "Nine Pillars" is often our agenda. Ed was very instrumental in formulating the "one-page" summary of world history. Professor Emeritus Assar Lindbeck at the University of Stockholm checked my comments on the Swedish economy and offered the comparison of Sweden's economy to that of the Swiss.

The Standing Committee on Cultural Affairs provided the official information about the Swedish mass media.

Wesley Alles, Ph. D., Coordinator for Health Improvement Program (HIP) at Stanford University, reviewed my first manuscript and gave me valuable suggestions for the outline as well as my formatting of the writing of Part IX. Wes also gave me the idea of describing the timeline of history as a movie with one frame after the other. Wes also helped me with describing health delivery in the U.S. in Part IX. The late Joseph Reagan, Ph. D., read the early manuscript and added that defense was an important community effort. Marianne Ihse, Teacher of Computer Applications at the local high school in Eksjö, Sweden, volunteered and helped me with computer applications. Daniela Castillo, Multimedia Teacher at Canada College in California, volunteered and designed the website (www.ninepillars.com). Daniela became interested in the whole manuscript and has continued to contribute editing remarks to the manuscript.

As in my previous works, Cheryl Cooper and her daughter, Wendi Freeman, have been dedicated secretaries in the formulation of the manuscript.

Without the backup of all this academic expertise and the many, always-volunteering friends, this treatise would have remained just a childhood fantasy. I am eternally thankful for everybody's contribution.

I, and only I, am responsible for the ideas presented. An individual nation's history may look small and naked when placed in a summary of 200,000 years of world history. The purpose of this treatise is neither to glorify nor to criticize the history of any particular nation, religion, and certainly not nationalities or races, but to find the best basis for individual human rights and respect in a world, one day with peace among nations.

# Introduction

The human species, *Homo sapiens*, was genetically established some 200,000 years ago and has physiologically changed very little throughout its history. The needs of the *Homo sapiens* that appeared very early suggested the needs essential for humanity. Nine pillar needs are identified from the 190,000-year-long Hunting and Gathering (H/G) or tribal time. How these needs fared in different historical époques would demonstrate their pertinence. Early in history, some of the needs were just preferences, but as societies grew during the agricultural era and further into multicultural large industrial societies, these needs became more than preferences, they became necessary pillars for human society.

After the "Nine Pillars of History" had been identified in the H/G time, it became clear that history could be divided into just three time periods. Each time period is here based on the main means of food transport: a **human transport** during the Hunting and Gathering (H/G) time, an **animal transport** during the agricultural time, and an **engine transport** during the industrial time. Each period offers fundamentally different possibilities for human survival.

The "Nine Pillars of History" only recognize two types of government leaderships—democratic or dogmatic. During the 190,000-year-long H/G-time, leadership was member-ruled or democratic. The democratic system is dependent on peace and free trade, first within the family, then between clans, and later between countries. After the H/G-time, democracy was formally re-introduced in antique Greece, when Greece had become a major trading country under an aristocratic business leadership. Democracy was lost after the death of Alexander the Great, but again revived in the Renaissance trade cities of Italy. Dogmatic governments destroyed these cities, but democracy moved on and reconfirmed itself slowly in Holland and England as these nations started to reach out for world trade. Finally, democracy matured during the industrial era and is now reaching out to a larger and larger world family of democratic nations.

The dogmatic type of leadership evolved early in Sumeria (historical Mesopotamia or present Iraq) and has dominated 10,000 years of agricultural time. The Sumerian type of government consisted of a dictatorial leader, supported by a dogmatic, religious, or later, a political belief system. I will use the word "Sumeric" as a generic term to describe any dogmatic leadership—dogmatic religious or dogmatic political. My historical review points to the conclusion that most major wars throughout history involved a dogmatic government system. As nations become industrialized, they become dependent on trade, which in turn, is dependent on peace. **I propose that democratic industrialization and world trade is indeed the best assurance for world peace.**

# Part I

## The Hunting and Gathering Period from 200,000 to 10,000 Years Ago with Handheld (Tarp) Food Distribution and Defining the Nine Pillars for Humanity

Dear Reader,

(1) I offer you a challenge. In the following pages I will send you traveling at a racing speed through history. You will start from the very dawn of civilization until today and follow the human evolution from a grunting animal walking on two legs to a modern citizen of a democratic, open society, with freedom and equal rights for all.

(2) I will start with a description of the genetically coded instincts of the human cell in order to explain nine fundamental human rights derived from these instincts. These nine pillars of humanity will be defined from the hunting and gathering period, even if some of them can just be discerned at this time. The "Nine" will be followed through history, how they fared under different governments and how eventually they evolved to become necessary for all modern societies.

(3) The government in Sumeria, historical Mesopotamia, or modern Iraq, will be described first. After Sumeria I will not dwell on the history of each Sumeric-like nation. The Sumeric-like countries in Africa, Early America, China and Japan, despite their long and interesting history, are, from this standpoint, not pertinent. Only when they deviate from the first Sumeric Government formula are they germane.

(4) Brace yourself! I will challenge any prejudices you might have. This has been fun for me to write; I hope it will be equally fun for you to read.

(5) I have to start with some technical medical talks but don't panic. It will be very short.

(6) Much of what everybody wants to accomplish in life comes from two basic instincts baked into our genes: the urges for the self-preservation and propagation, with the best possible chance of survival for the offspring. These two fundamental instincts, we—human beings, the species *Homo sapiens*—have in common with all animals and even plants. It has been postulated that the original mitochondrial DNA, for short mtDNA or the mitochondrial organ, was a bacteria that many millions of years ago invaded a cell and has promoted its own survival by its evolutionary mutations just like

2

any modern virus invades cells, takes over and directs a cell's life. Evolutionary changes in the mitochondrial organ create new species or adaptation of the species to its environment. If a new species is efficient within its environment, the species will survive, if not, it will die. If a new species is unable to adapt to changes in its environment, the species will die out over time. Evolution can therefore take two directions: lead to totally different species or lead to different kinds of closely related species, like to different ape forms.

(7) The mitochondrial organ forms a rugby ball shaped membrane that floats in the cell fluid around the nucleus of every living cell. Protein in the mitochondrion and proteins in the nucleus form genes that are chains of four amino acids: adenine, cytosine, guanine, and thiamine. The order in which these amino acids stack up within genes determines the chemical message for the activities in the cell. The mitochondrion is the organ that is transferred from one cell to another in order to grow specific tissues for transplants, for in vitro fertilization, or to create clones.

(8) The main portion of the mitochondrion has remained unchanged since 200,000-150,000 years back, unchanged from generation to generation for at least some 6000 generations (allowing 25 years for each generation) (Rebecca Cann et al: *Nature* 329, 1987). It can with confidence be stated that the basic physiological and psychological security) needs of humans have remained the same since that time.

(9) The mitochondrion ring has a neutral zone within which mutations can occur without causing new species or diseases. These mutations occur more often and with some statistical regularity, on average, one every 10,000 years. This has been established by several different methods, but one is by simply counting mutations in archeological finds of a known age, as in the 12,000-year-old find from the Gough's cave in Bath, England.

(10) The female chromosome (X) is part of both the male (XY) and female (XX) sex chromosome in the cell nucleus. The female X chromosome is found in the mitochondria and controls the eventual

species of the germ cell. A germ cell is a fertilized egg during its first twenty-four divisions, before an embryo has been defined.

(11) The neutral mitochondrial area can be used to identify family-clans, that is, to determine both when the mutation first occurred in that clan and where the original mother for that clan lived. The more mutations, the older is the clan with a given pattern; the more present inhabitants with that mother's certain pattern of mutations that live within a certain area, the more likely the original clan-mother also used to live there, some thousands of years ago.

(12) Bryan Sykes, Professor of Human Genetics and his colleagues at the Oxford University, have mapped out the origin and present distribution of the world population based on information from the neutral mitochondrial area in his fascinating book, *The Seven Daughters of Eve* (2001, ISBN 0-393-32314-5). He has identified the universal mother, the "Mitochondrial Eve," for the clan that eventually populated the whole world. She might have lived somewhere in Kenya or Ethiopia some 150,000 years ago. Of the 13 clans that have survived in present Africa, only one moved out of Africa by Sinai 50,000 years ago, and formed new clans: seven for Europe between 45,000 and 15,000 years ago, four for America 12,000 years ago, and nine for the rest of the world. The Nine Pillars of Humanity will be tested from the time of Mitochondrial Eve, through history, until today.

(13) The evolutionary hominid species (human-like individuals walking on two legs) was created some five to seven million years ago. Four fundamental pillars or primary instincts of any hominid species may be established already from this time: to live close to water and food resources, to build shelters for their offspring, to communicate by simple sounds, and to live in groups for security and common defense (Richard Klein). All four of these needs we, Homo sapiens, have in common with all ape-like societies.

(14) The genome-mapping project has identified a gene for speech. When this female mutation occurred is not known but now a human being could name things, name things to do, develop systematic thoughts, transfer experiences from one generation to another, build a first memory bank, and form a social culture. This was the birth of

the human society and the birth of the Nine *Historical* Pillars. The original generic instinct, the instinct for sexual propagation that we have common with anything living, has to be reviewed separately.

(15) The male sex (Y) chromosome has also a neutral zone that can be used for markers from generation to generation. The first settlers left descendants at each place they populated, or, maybe more often, children from the first settlement moved on to form new ones. A marker from the first male settlers can still be found in present day male populations. The frequency of markers in the present population can be used to estimate the time for the original settlement and also to follow the whereabouts of the earliest *Homo sapiens* bands. Professor Sykes suggests that people from 33 clans have populated the whole world of today.

(16) The personal identification based on genes makes nonsense of racial and national classifications. Professor Sykes suggests a first name, a surname, and a 'matriname' based on the individual gene-pattern as a specific, personal ID. Using this system for the routine issuing of international passports would be useful in tracking international terrorists, drug dealers, and repeat law offenders. It would be more specific than fingerprints. Done as a routine procedure it would not interfere with privacy conflicts; only persons with bad intentions would have reason to refuse.

(17) I am postulating that the invention that allowed the formation of an organized communal band-society was the "tarp." The word "tarp" is used for lack of a better word, with the understanding that the tarp, at this time, might have been a hide or a fiber-woven mat or maybe even a basket (www.mnsu.edu/emuseum, Olga Soffer). There were definitely other stone and bone tools, but the tarp allowed the band to collect and transport enough food for family meals for several days and even for several families; in other words, to trade and to divide food between the members of the band. The invention of the tarp could be the reason for the successful behavioral change that took place around 40,000 years ago, and became the social basis for Late Stone Age and the world migration of the bands. A hide or

basket is very fragile for time exposure. Archeological support for this postulate is equally fragile, but still, a reasonable assumption.

(18) The hide, or material replacing the hide, eventually became not only a carrying tool, but, when the environment called for it, also bedding, extra clothing, shoes, tent, rope and so on, just as the hide or woven material is being used in modern times by such hunting societies as the Eskimos in the north and the ancient !Kung San tribes in South Africa. (The "!" sign in front of the letter expresses a clicking sound of the tongue.) One should look at this ancestral life not as brutal, but as satisfying, with intelligent people making the most of their knowledge and their environment.

(19) We can establish the first basic pillar of our ancestors. They needed food, clean water, and clean air. These are physiological needs and cannot be compromised for long periods of time. The sun provides the ultimate energy for all food production throughout all of history. They had a need for propagation and developed social rules for the best survival of their tribe. Here the morality of the Golden Rule, "you shall love your neighbor as yourself" starts to evolve.

(20) The second basic pillar need was a shelter with protection for the family from the weather, hostile tribes, and animals. Some used caves, if available, but more commonly simple huts covered with hides or leaf. Eventually, the huts were enhanced with fire for warmth and cooking. The frame of the huts had to be built from local materials. A village with house frames entirely of mammoth bone has been found in Ukraine and dated to be 25,000 years old.

(21) During the Late Stone Age or Bronze Age, one often finds designated areas for waste. This points to a third, maybe not yet a pillar need, but at least a preference for cleanliness. Cleanliness will eventually develop into a third pillar need.

(22) Among early tools were combs carved from bones. An ivory carving of a woman's head from Brassempouy shows a sophisticated hairstyle. The carving is exquisite. The fine hair-do shows there was a desire for the woman to look, what she and her friends possibly perceived as, beautiful. Individual beauty may be a sex signal and a

sign of good physical health for propagation. The carving is 25,000 years old.

(23) From about 40,000 years back there was a flourishing trend to decorate the cave walls with paintings, to make stone-carved forms of the female body, and to design musical instruments. Whether this art was created for enjoyment, or to emphasize religious or hunt rituals is not clear. In any case, it is still beautiful art. Art may not be a life essential need, but it is a working force already among these early people. We now have another pillar need for human society, a fourth: a perception of art in the beauty of both body and surroundings.

(24) The spread of the *Homo sapiens* bands across the world started 50,000 years ago. It has to be considered the most successful land conquest in history. The conquest was completed some 12,000 years back. Its success was due to human's ability to communicate and assemble into groups for hunting, defense, or for a goal of the H/G bands. To communicate and assemble into a group became the fifth and sixth basic pillars for the success of human society.

(25) The earth's population was only four or five million people at this time. It stayed fairly stable at this number during the 190,000-year-long H/G-time because of the limited food supply and limited food transport. Rapid population growth belongs to the coming agricultural and industrial eras, both with more food and better food transport.

(26) Hunting and gathering (H/G) bands never had, and even now living H/G-bands never have, elective leaders in the modern sense. The band could grow to a maximum of 40 to 50 individuals, but no one was allowed to dominate. This is the ultimate description of local control and individual freedom, the ultimate and original democracy.

(27) The yearly rebirth of nature impressed the early humans. In the regularity of nature, they saw a higher power in charge. The H/G-people tend to be monotheistic and according to Collin Turnbull's book *The Forest People* in 1961 the illiterate pygmies in Africa still believed an inactive (otiose) god had created the surrounding jungle. Typically, H/G people don't have priesthood or worry about an afterlife in heaven or hell.

(28) In the random irregularity of nature people saw opposing powers fighting it out. A multi-spiritual world was born. This belief became particularly strong during the agricultural period. Natural events were identified as spirits or gods influencing the outcome of harvest, or eventually, for the protection of any other means of making a living. In later time different saints protecting specific trades are an expression of this trend.

(29) Mythical stories were spun to support social rules, often important to that particular society. The Indians in the jungle of Uruguay still have a rule that the hunter cannot eat his own kill; it would bring him bad luck. His own food had to come from his comrades. By this holy rule the whole band was always assured of food.

(30) Early humans asked themselves: "Could the weather or animal gods be swayed to assure good food supply by gifts?" The Aztecs thought the sun got tired each evening and must be fed hearts and blood to recover for its work the next day. Leaders or shamans pronounced how the gods' needs could be satisfied with offers and ceremonies. Ceremonies were an important part of the offer; professionals, "priests" (generic term), performed them according to a given script in a given place, a "temple" (generic term). Offer-ceremonies have therefore been defined and given a special generic term—dogmas.

(31) The priesthood was the messenger between the super powered spirit, "the transcendent" (Joseph Runzo), and the people. The priesthood became very influential and was closely connected with leadership. A community or state mythical religion became an integral part of the society as it slowly transformed itself from an H/G to an agricultural society.

(32) The need for religion seemed to appear early in humanity, maybe soon after humans had learned to speak. What seemed a logical story to the benefit of both the individual and society was created. "Religion" as a generic term for a "belief system" has remained an essential "Seventh Pillar" all through humanity.

(33) "Gods" and "religious administrations" have varied with people's insight and education. The gods may have different names in different cultures, sometimes only due to different languages. In modern times, the 3000-year-old Jewish "YHWH" gave ideas to the 2000-year-old Christian "God" and the 1500-year-old Muslim god "Allah." All three churches pray to a one, same, single creator. Relative to society, all major world religions, from the oldest 4000 to 5000-year-old Hinduism to the youngest 1500-year-old Islam, claim to hold to the original, moral social truth of the Golden Rule:

(34) **Hinduism:** *One should not behave towards others in a way that is disagreeable to oneself.* Anusasana

(35) **Confucianism:** *Do not do to others what you do not want them to do to you.* Analects

(36) **Buddhism:** *A state that is not pleasing to me, how should I inflict that upon another.* Samyutta Nikaya

(37) **Judaism:** *You shall love your neighbor as yourself.* Leviticus

(38) **Christian:** *You shall love your neighbor as yourself.* Mathew

(39) **Islamism:** *Not one of you is a believer until he loves for his brother what he loves for himself.* According to early traditions the books of Hadith were first written down in the 900s when Islam had conquered large areas of land with jihad and Islam needed a perpetual social rule to live by.

(40) **All religions have to relearn from the ancient Golden Rule what is originally meant with brother, neighbor and democracy. The Golden Rule is a much older concept than any religion. The Golden rule is the original concept for any social life. A democratic society can only survive with the Golden Rule in its nucleus. Without the Golden Rule all societies have to be Sumeric and live off beliefs with made up church dogma. This was of course easier in old time when few could read. Nowadays, with an educated reality, the Public is different in much of the world.**

(41) The separation into exclusive, non-tolerant religions and considering members of other religions as infidel, barbaric, heathen or pagan, is the invention of priesthood. In modern times, in 1925, the archbishop of Sweden, Nathan Söderblom started the inclusive

ecumenical movement of churches. He succeeded in joining only the Protestant and Greek Orthodox Churches. The World Council of Churches followed in 1948. At its first meeting in Chicago, members from 163 churches were represented. **An all-inclusive and tolerant church movement, possibly sponsored by the U.N., would do a lot of good towards world peace.**

(42) Foraging and hunting had daily physical challenges with many opportunities for bodily injury or diseases. The care for childbirth and the care for fever or injuries were learned through experience. Soon, someone in the tribal group became known for being particularly good at treating medical problems. The medicine man and/or woman became for this reason a trusted and important individual in the group. Access to healing became an "Eighth Pillar" for the society.

(43) *Homo sapiens* spread all through the known habitable world. People lived in small kinship bands, where members had specific work assignments. Primarily women gathered vegetables and fruits, and cooked and cared for the children. Only men hunted, but men helped with the gathering and with the childcare. They all brought food back to the home camp with the first transport tool and divided the food between its members. The gathered food for H/G bands and usually supplied more than half (70%) of the caloric intake; the male hunters supplied the rest.

(44) By dividing the food between the band members and eating the food together, the first humans started the most elementary trade, the one between family members and kinfolk, each individual providing his or her special services to the band in exchange for partaking in the family or community meal. The tarp thereby contributed both to community support and trade.

(45) Many still active H/G societies are only physically active for 600 to 1000 hours of the year in the work of collecting food and building shelter for the family. By comparison, a forty-hour workweek represents 2000 hours per year. It is interesting to note that the free time was not used to improve tools for collecting and hunting, nor for the building of more sophisticated shelters. The H/G societies of

today still use the same tools they have used for thousands of years. Intensive tool-invention belongs to the agricultural and industrial time, or to the last ten thousand years of history, when the time factor was introduced as an important integral in the production of food.

(46) The H/G society never used slaves. To feed and control slaves would be an extra burden on the group. The seasonal work of agriculture required timely execution of sowing and harvesting. Here extra help was needed within a given time window. Agriculture introduced subordinates and advanced tool invention to history.

(47) The H/G life was, and still is, nomadic with only an informal, but still enforced, community ownership to a certain H/G area. Everything in H/G life had to be mobile and therefore did not easily lend itself to the accumulation of fortunes. Accumulation of personal, larger fortunes first became possible in the stationary life of agricultural time.

(48) In time, small trade started between different bands. The early trade consisted of tools and food. An area could be close to a mineral that was suited for tools. The people living here traded minerals for other things they wanted. Some signs indicate the earlier *Homo Neanderthal* would trade over a 30-mile (50 km) area while the *Homo sapiens* would trade over an area seven times larger and grew from within the family to between different clans and areas. This early trade was the first evolution of the "Ninth Pillar," the pursuit of a better life through trade.

(49) The foraging of fruits and vegetables developed into small plots of plantings, leading to the early domestication of the first grains such as wheat, rice, sorghum, millet, maize, and barley. Early domesticated animals were cattle, sheep, goats, poultry, dogs, and later horses, camels and llamas. In other words, it was the beginnings of agriculture. The agricultural society could feed more people than the H/G society but, being stationary, it could not adjust to weather with the same ease. Weather has always threatened the stationary agricultural society with starvation.

(50) The speaking human being expanded the genetically established pillar needs to include socially important pillars that collectively comprise the nine pillar needs for humanity.

(51) The designated "Nine Pillars of History" for Humanity from the H/G period are:

(52) **Survival (Food, Water, Air, Energy and Sex):** These needs are essential for humanity to survive: This pillar need eventually develops into a full second age of humanity, the period dominated by the agriculture. As the population grows so will industries for food, water, air, energy and even sex appeal distribution.

(53) The remaining eight pillar-needs are necessary for the human society to pursuit happiness.

(54) **Shelter:** This pillar need eventually develops into a building industry controlled by building codes, to laws for property rights and to social legislation to secure the life of the family.

(55) **Cleanliness:** This pillar need eventually develops into a full industry charged with keeping the distribution of food, air and water supplies, and living areas free of harmful contamination.

(56) **Art:** This pillar need eventually matures into an industry of professional artists and an entertainment industry beautifying life experiences. Community planning may be included in this need.

(57) **Communication:** This pillar need develops into an unrestricted mass media industry, capped off by today's Internet and social media.

(58) **Community (Freedom to Assemble for Group Support):** The pillar need for community support developed into trade unions, political parties, and thousands of other organizations for a variety of purposes. The care for children and elders has led to schools and a social support system for the handicapped, sick, and elderly.

(59) Community support also leads to equal treatment of the individual before the law with an independent court system, in Anglo-Saxon countries watched over by a jury of community peers.

(60) Community support has also led to the organization of a common defense.

(61) **Religion:** The pillar need for a moral belief system is general. The moral belief system has to be in agreement with the knowledge of the individual and has, therefore, to be of free choice. The free choice has led to numerous religious movements, each based on different teachings. Belief systems through their brotherhood often fill some need of community support. Some people claim they do not believe in a specific religion and that is part of free choice. **The overriding morality of a belief system still remains through the ancient social rule of the Golden Rule.**

(62) **Medicine:** The pillar need for medical access has evolved into a continuously improving medical care and a medical insurance system to make access available to all. Educational, preventive, and behavioral medical programs can also be included here.

(63) **Trade:** The pillar need for free trade has led to the modern industrialized society. With only a small percentage of the industrial population involved in food production, trade is fundamental for earth's ever-increasing population to survive.

(64) At this point, I have now to add what I have learned what is characteristic for each pillar need: **Each nine pillar need is eternal, interdependent and the social cost of each pillar cannot be controlled but for competition. This observation is fundamental for social planning of any modern society.**

(65) Agriculture entered society after 190,000 years. With agriculture-entered economics and with economics entered also "Tragedy of Commons" or what many own, nobody owns or is responsible for. **The social consequences of the "Commons" to the modern society are indeed very great and described separately in part IX.**

(66) I have distilled and followed the "Nine Pillars" through history, how the "Nine" have fared during different time periods and under different types of governments in some typical countries. Examining the Nine Pillars of History we can indeed find a way to view and resolve some of today's problems!

(67) For further studies of H/G period consult the Internet with key words: Paleolithic archeology, human evolution, and modern human origin and philosophy.

**For Further Reading:**

(68) *Guns, Germs and Steel: The Fates of Human Societies* by Jared Diamond, W.W. Norton & Company. ISBN 0-393-31755-2.

(69) *The Dawn of Human Culture* by Richard G. Klein, 2002, Nevraumont Publ, ISBN 0-471-25252-2.

(70) *Mapping Human History, Discovering the Past through Our Genes* by Steve Olsen, Houghton Mifflin Company, ISBN 0-618-09157-2.

(71) *Hunting and Gathering Period: The !Kung San, Men, Women, and Work in a Foraging Society* by Richard Borshay Lee, Cambridge University Press 1979, ISBN 0 29561 0.

(72) *Hunters and Gatherers Today*, published 1972 by Holt, Rinehart and Winston, Inc, ISBN: 0-03-076865-9.

(73) *Dawn of Man, the Story of Human Evolution* by Robin McKie, published in 2000 by Dorling Kindersley Inc. ISBN 0-7894-6262-1. Originally the book was to accompany the BBC television program in 2000 *The Apeman*, televised in the U.S. as *The Dawn of Man* by TLC, The Learning Channel, in the same year. The book by Robin McKie gave me the original inspiration for *The Nine Pillars of History*.

(74) *The Eliade Guide to World Religions*, 1991, by Mircea Eliade & Ioan P. Couliano, ISBN 0-06-062145-1.

(75) *The World's Great Religions* by Time Inc., The Swedish translation 1957 by Elisabeth Åkesson is without registrerad ISBN.

(76) *Global Philosophy of Religion* by Joseph Runzo, 2001, ISBN 1-85168-235-X.

(77) *Nathan Söderblom and the Study of Religion* by Eric J. Sharpe, 1990, ISBN 0-8078-1868-2.

(78) *The Power of Myth* by Joseph Campbell, 1988, ISBN 0-385-24773-7.

*(79)* *World Scripture: A Comparative Anthology of Sacred Texts* by International Religious Foundation, 1995, ISBN 1-55778-9.

*(80)* *The Dawn of Human Culture* by Richard Klein, 2002, John Wiley & Sons, New York, ISBN 0-471-25252-2.

# Part II

# The Agricultural Period
## from 10,000 Years Ago to the Year of 1826.
## Animal Drawn (Cart) Food Distribution:
## The First Central Governments

# Introduction to Agricultural Time

(81) The "Nine Pillars" identifies basically only two types of state governments: a dogmatic type and a democratic type. The dogmatic type emerged in the Sumerian State some 7000 years ago. The democratic type government was a natural outgrowth of the Hunting and Gathering band (H/G-band) but was first historically documented and formally implemented in antique Athens only 2400 years ago. Democratic government had probably

**been present in many cultures informally a lot earlier. How the two types of governments have served humanity relative to its "Nine Pillars" will be described here in part II.**

(82) The Roman Empire will be followed on its way from democracy back to the Sumerian type of government. I will describe how Charlemagne gave the Medieval Church an economic base for a Sumeric, dogmatic type of dominance and how the Renaissance broke that religious dogmatic dominance. I will discuss how democracy from tribal life in Scandinavia slowly made headway in a Sumeric England and Holland and how that system has been challenged by different Sumerian kinds of governments in both old clothing—a leadership supported by religious dogma; and in modern clothing—a leadership supported by political dogma. A dogmatic government sets its own religious or political dogma as the basis for laws; a democratic government defines human freedom and rights and uses these as the basis for laws. The study concludes that a Sumerian type of government has been the cause of most wars for the last 10,000 years. The history of a few influential countries will be described in order to illustrate my thoughts.

(83) The agricultural time is not the longest period of human history—that was the preceding 190,000-year-long hunting and gathering era—but compared to the industrial period of only two hundred years, it still lasted for a long time. The agricultural period started probably independently in nine different areas of the world: Mesopotamia (-8500) and by diffusion to Indus Valley (-7000), Egypt (-6000) and Western Europe (from -6000 to -4000). Independent from Mesopotamia, agriculture developed in China (-7500), New Guinea (-7000), West Africa (-5000), Mesoamerica (-3500), Andes and Amazonia (-3500), Eastern USA (-3500), Sub-Saharan Tropical West Africa (-3000). The very first agricultural societies evolved in the so-called Fertile Crescent, that is, in the area of present day Iraq, Syria, Jordan, and southeast Turkey.

(84) Agriculture is today still the basic industry, producing the food for humanity, but it is now part of other large industries that fill

the need for dwellings, cleanliness, art, communication, community support, religion, medical support, and trade/transport.

## Life in Sumerian Mesopotamia

(85) Wheat and barley, peas and olive plants grew wild in the Fertile Crescent. The earliest farmers started to cultivate these plants near their dwellings some 10,500 years ago. Food was now produced instead of gathered. The grains could be stored, thereby producing food surplus for the whole year. People became stationary farmers bound to their fields. By cultivating larger lots, farmers could trade surplus grain for other needs. For the next 10,000 years, agriculture became increasingly popular.

(86) The first large animals, sheep and goats were domesticated at about the same time as the first plants and complemented people's need for food and other products. The demand for food grew as the population grew. With the increasing demand for food, the technique of domestication has over time been tried on all known plants and animals. Only a few were found suitable, and they are the ones that still dominate agriculture. The east-west wide and large Eurasian landmass had a multitude of both vegetation and animals to offer as food for future population growth. Agriculture spread easier along similar east-west climate zones than through dissimilar south-north climate zones.

(87) Populations based on early agriculture lived in a crowded, stationary society in close contact with its domesticated animals. Diseases of domesticated animals spread to humans and caused widespread epidemics. These diseases, called crowd diseases, came to play a major part in the history of humanity. The most important of these crowd diseases were measles, tuberculosis, and smallpox received from cattle, flu from pigs and ducks, whooping cough from pigs and dogs, and malaria from birds. Other crowd diseases, such as typhus, cholera and plague, found fertile ground in animals and bacteria that grew in the waste from the unclean human crowd. HIV from African monkeys and Chinese chicken flu are modern

examples of such epidemics. The bird flu of 1918 killed 15 million people all over the world. It was a major factor in ending WW I. The soldier fought in crowded trenches and died in droves from the flu rather from the fighting. (Looking back from todays intermingled population in Europe the picture from that time of Europe feels almost like a living fantasy and probably was.)

(88) Epidemics of crowd diseases could infect and kill 95% of their target population before the epidemic died out. The epidemic returned when the crowded population grew back. Over thousands of years, the 5% surviving humans developed into populations resistant to these epidemic circles. When disease-resistant humans moved to an area of the globe where humans still lived in dispersed non-crowded H/G societies or had agriculture based on different domesticated animals, the crowd diseases killed 95% of the natives. This happened when Europeans arrived for the first time in America, Australia and the Pacific Islands.

(89) On the other hand, Europeans were unable to live in the tropics before malaria was stamped out. All this has been described in detail by Jared Diamond in his epoch-making history book *Guns, Germs and Steel: The Fates of Human Societies.*

(90) The population of the Fertile Crescent grew despite all diseases; it grew many times faster than the population living as hunters and gatherers. Women in farm societies could have children once a year while women in the H/G society had to wait for children to be able to walk with the band before the next child could be cared for.

(91) When the land in the hills was fully populated, farmers looked to the low land below the foothills, to the valley between the river Euphrates and Tigris, Mesopotamia, for food production. The climate here is very warm and dry. Water was needed for the people, their domesticated animals and crops. Diverting the two rivers' water into canals provided the needed irrigation and allowed for the further expansion of agriculture. A surplus of food was produced exclusively for trade.

(92) The first artificially watered farmland in history was introduced. Agriculture changed the environment in order to secure life for humans. Water for both drinking and crops became crucial for the survival of humanity.

(93) The land between the two rivers proved to be a fertile land. Farmers domesticated other large animals such as the ox, dog, sheep, and poultry. The ox was first used to help carry things. Later, the people who lived here, the Sumerians, invented the wheel and built a wagon. A wagon drawn by an ox could transport three times as much as an ox could carry on its back, easing transportation and trade. The Chinese agricultural society invented the wheelbarrow. The Aztecs used slaves. Wheels were used for toys and no animals were domesticated for carrying or pulling. The Incas domesticated llamas for carrying.

(94) The oxcart became the prerequisite for making use of surplus food production. Surplus food and the oxcart led to the formation of local trading markets, that is, the building of cities and the formation of organized states. The oxcart allowed some citizens not to take physical part in food production but to have time for and be involved in the support work for an agricultural society. This happened around -3700.

(95) The oxcart was an evolution from the foraging tarp for food transport. The oxcart became the basis for the new agricultural society. The oxcart put food on the table, not just for the family farmer, but for unrelated families connected by a trade market. Trade grew from within the band to within a state and beyond. Cities and states with animal drawn carts would eventually dominate the world's all agricultural societies until machine driven carts were invented and became the basis for mega-sized cities and states.

(96) The king of the Mesopotamian State and his nobility working for him owned most of the land. The religious organization also owned land as an institution. The religious administration reported to the king. This meant the king indirectly also controlled the "church" property. The remaining smaller portion of farmland was held in private ownership. The "nobility" worked as officers and

administrators. Males dominated the society, as men worked the fields and represented the family in the community. Women worked at home cooking, taking care of the children and the domestic animals. Domesticated animals now included horses imported from the Asian plain and pigs imported from China.

(97) The soldiers consisted of farmers called upon at times of emergency. The king later paid for a standing mercenary army, consisting of cavalry, charioteers, archers and lancers. Sumerian mercenary armies developed strategic military maneuvers.

(98) New in history was that the soldiers attacked an enemy not as a horde, but in disciplined lines. An army was born. The new society used an army to enlarge the area it controlled. A defensive military strategy developed in response to the offensive army. The most important community leader was the one who would lead the offense/defense work. The professional offense/defense worker assisting the leader became nobility with a special standing in the society. The administrators of the belief system engaged the gods in helping the leader in his efforts and wrote about his successes.

(99) The king, controlling most of the food used for trade, had a need for record keeping. The Sumerians invented the very first written language and number system. Pictures, also called hieroglyphs, marked in moist clay tablets, were the first written permanent records. More than 30,000 of these tablets have been found. Through time, the Sumerians exchanged the hieroglyphs for small cuneiform triangles to simplify the writing. Still later, the triangles evolved to represent phonetic words. The early writings developed into our modern alphabet and number system. A point of interest is that music was also written with the same lettering process.

(100) A farmer's almanac was required by structured agriculture. Sumerians studied the moon and the stars extensively. The seasons were divided into twelve modified lunar months. They made the zodiac calendar and gave each star constellation names still in use. Astrology for telling the future was as popular then, as it is today. Time and angles were divided into units of 60, which of course, we still do for hours and circles.

(101) The Sumerians were able to keep records, write contracts, and write laws. Contracts were sealed with a stamp. The first codes of law in history were written, based on examples of past precedent. Punishment was based on "an eye for an eye; a tooth for a tooth," but developed later into a punishment of fines.

(102) Handbooks were written for farmers along with instructions for other occupations, including physicians. Schools were started—closely connected to the religious centers—with temple priests serving as the teachers. The civil support system started to look much like it does in some modern states.

(103) The Sumerian religion had many gods, one for each element of nature that affected people's lives, such as the sun, moon, water and earth. The gods lived a life similar to humans, but they were eternal in mythical stories. The king's family came from and communicated with the gods according to the myths. The gods could be happy or angry and had to be made content by offerings. The good god's realm was above the earth, the bad god's below. The earth was flat, surrounded by a sea of water. When people died they would enter the underworld by crossing a river and be assigned to an eternal life dependent upon their importance or deeds done in this world. Similar descriptions of gods are found in Egyptian, Greek, Roman, Scandinavian, Aztec and Mayan mythology. Each family usually had a house-god to protect the household and had a part of their house devoted to it.

(104) The Sumerian people have been given credit for inventing building bricks, glass, bronze, the plow, the pickax, and iron weapons. They made jewelry from silver, gold and precious stones among other beautiful things, in order to enhance their person or their dwellings.

(105) Small villages grew into sizable towns. Babylon, the largest city, had a population of over 100,000. It required an effective system of roads and community support structures. The government consisted of the king and two chambers of representatives. The king was in the beginning selected from the chambers, but later the kingship was inherited. **The inherited king was always closely connected to the priesthood, anointed, and ruled by a decree from heaven.**

**Eventually the king made himself one of the gods. The Sumerian type of government was born.**

(106) A Sumerian type of government means a government with a leader supported by a belief system and its administration. In history, the belief system will vary between different religions or politics. In early times, the belief system was always religious, enforced by church dogmas and with church controlled education, often with police or military enforcement. **The Sumerian type of governments in modern times maintain their power by controlling mass media and education, and enforce their power by police and military means. A Sumerian type government, contrary to a democratic government, systematically suppresses any question of its authority.**

(107) Kings of different towns competed within the same agricultural business. Eventually one king dominated and had other towns pay him tributes or, in modern terms, taxes.

(108) **A ruler's incentive formula for war all through 10,000 years of agricultural time was born: taking more land for more taxes allowed for a bigger army and a chance for more land and more taxes and war for 10,000 years.**

(109) Nebuchadnezzar II, one of the mightiest kings of Babylon, destroyed Jerusalem in the year -586 (BC) and took the surviving Jewish population to Babylon as slaves. The Jews eventually were allowed to return to Palestine 50 years later in the year –538 by the great warrior Cyrus I. The Jews took with them the knowledge of written language and accounting, important knowledge for their future livelihood.

(110) The king of Babylon ruled the then known civilized world from Egypt and Palestine to the Persian Gulf. All the different conquered kingdoms had to pay taxes to the king of Mesopotamia. Babylon grew with larger and larger palaces and temples. Riches were accumulated. The king built big temples called ziggurat, to praise his gods for his luck. The ziggurat was a tall stepwise base for a temple placed on the top close to "heaven" similar to those built for the Aztec gods. The ziggurats looked like pyramids but were not graves; the tallest reached up 300 feet from a base 300 feet square.

(111) Babylon was admired but also envied by the then civilized world. The Persian King, Cyrus I conquered and destroyed Babylon in the year -539 and built the Persian Empire with a new capital, Persepolis. Persia eventually stretched from present-day Turkey around the entire eastern Mediterranean Coast to the Indian Ocean.

(112) The Persian Empire was overtaken by the Greeks through the leadership of Alexander, called the "Great" in history books. Charles I of France and Peter I of Russia/Soviet Union were both successful warriors and have also been called "Great." **The historic time of agriculture is full of "great" warriors as seen from the standpoint of the history of their home country. They were the "sports heroes" of the "home team." Most of these great warrior kings have contributed little to humanity. They usually used most of their new extra booty and income to build big palaces, which are now mostly spectacles for tourist money and history buffs.**

(113) In the meantime, the surviving farmer continued to raise his crops and pay tax to one king or the other. Attending his crops, he had no time to do anything else. We still need to describe some of these warriors, because they changed the borders of nations and how money was distributed.

(114) At this time Mesopotamia as an agricultural area had lasted for about 5700 years. It had been ruled by many different kings and gone through probably hundreds of wars. At times, Mesopotamian states conquered surrounding kingdoms; at other times its neighbors conquered them. This trend has continued up to modern times when Iraq tried to invade first Iran (old Persia) and then Kuwait. The time and names of the kings of the different countries for the purpose of this historical review are not important.

(115) Important to note is that already 5000 years back, a model for an agricultural civilization both in war and in peace had fully matured.

(116) Cultures similar to the Sumerian grew up in major river valleys around the world in the specific areas mentioned above. **The states that were formed in all these areas were all of the Sumerian type, that is, a hereditary king, who was supported by a belief**

**system and its religious administration.** This was true for Africa with Egypt, for Europe with the Roman Empire, for India, China, Japan, and for early America, all with their "great" dynasties and empires.

(117)  Some empires lasted for a long time. The God/king/religion connection was synonymous with the best knowledge for staying alive with agriculture. The ruler and the religious administrators had the monopoly of a link with the most important god or gods.

(118)  In India and Egypt, the food grains were similar to those of Mesopotamia. In China, rice was the main grain and in the Americas maize and potato ruled the fields.

(119)  The agriculture spread from the original centers in the Middle East to the other valleys. In Europe, it spread along the Mediterranean coast and along the Danube and Rhine rivers. The strongest, most energetic and adventurous of the children led the way through the new land.

(120)  The population all over the world continued to grow with the increase of food. Villages and towns were formed along the cultured farmland. Cities became centers for trading farm products for what farmers needed. Over 90% of every area's economy depended directly on the farm. This became true for all countries except for the ones acting as middlemen in trade.

(121)  The first really great world traders in agricultural time were the Greek City States, the Italian Renaissance City States, the Netherlands, England and Scandinavia that for a long time inspired and held on to the old time tribal democracy. **All four of these areas became pioneers of democracy.**

# Greece

(122)  Athens, 2700 years ago, was just another farming community, a city-state, living off the surrounding land. Greece as a whole is not very fertile. Soon, the land could not support its population and the people had to look to the sea and trade for food. Trade spread to the main islands outside Athens and later to the entire Mediterranean

coast and the Black Sea. Trade is dependent on personal contacts and knowing markets. **Trade is done one trade at a time. The individual entrepreneur became important.** The free men of Athens involved in trade required each one to have his say in the state administration. The natural evolution of such needs was democracy. The single godlike ruler of the agricultural society would never lower himself to personally participate in trades.

(123) **The first democratic ideas evolved in the city-state of Athens in the year -507 (BC) by a brilliant king and reformer Cleisthenes. He succeeded in making it a basic law that all free, adult males had equal rights before the law, equality of power in the administration of the city and freedom to express their opinion in a rule called "freedom of speech."** This was officially posted on a wall in the city. Women and slaves were not allowed these freedoms. The freedom was based on what the Greek philosopher Plato (-427 to -347) defined as "democracy." The constitution of Athens met more of the **tribal** "Nine Pillars" than any leadership since the H/G time. It broke with the prevailing Sumerian way of god-connected ruling regimes, even if it was not the sort of democracy we think of today, but rather a family based aristocracy.

(124) At first Athens was an independent city-state, one of many in Greece. King Philip of Macedonia managed through diplomacy, war and six marriages to unite most of the different city-states on the Greek peninsula. He formed a federation (of tribes) that he called the League of Corinth.

(125) King Philip was murdered in -336. His son Alexander became king at age of twenty. Alexander thought the Greek colonies on the coast of Turkey ought to be included in the Greek State. These colonies had been the subject of a recent war between Greek and Persian interests. He succeeded in convincing the League to help with a fleet and army and sailed across the channel to Turkey. Turkey was part of the Persian Empire and was at this time ruled by a very weak Sumerian-type sultan. Soon, the Greek army had destroyed the Persian. The very young and exuberant Alexander decided to take all of Persia.

(126) Alexander marched on with his army to the capital of Persia, Persepolis. There he took over the sultan's entire accumulated treasury. It took 20,000 mules and 5000 camels to remove the treasure. From this gold, Alexander der minted coins that became the common coin across his Greek Empire and its colonies. This made Greece the first trading Empire. Alexander burned Persepolis and marched on to Egypt and India.

(127) Alexander was now so successful, he felt he had something in common with the Greek gods. He required his generals to address him as a god. This was in tune with all the eastern kingdoms.

(128) On his way back from India, Alexander became ill and died. Each of his four generals grabbed a piece of his empire and split it into four major areas: Egypt, Syria, Carthage (now Tunisia), and Greece. The Athenian ideas of democracy sank into oblivion. It was not of importance to the new rulers, who were not "simple" traders, but successful warriors. They all wrapped themselves in the Sumerian kingdom cape and ruled with anointed authority.

(129) The Greek cultures and trades involving the entire empire continued for some time after Alexander's death and were eventually inherited by the Romans.

(130) The Greeks left for humanity the knowledge of the value of a common currency in a large, common, free trade area. The Greeks also left us the idea of electing officials in a general election and laws that are equal for all, written down and posted on stones for the public to know. The idea of democracy still became forgotten, but it was documented and was brought to new life, when great trade centers evolved in Renaissance Italy from 1300-1600. Greece is considered the birthplace of modern democracy, or as it is taught at western universities as a "Grand Narrative of the West" (*From Plato to Nato* by David Gress, ISBN 0-684-82789-1). Professional historians usually exclude the H/G society, the informal form of democracy for the previous 190,000 years. **Tribal democracy still lived on around the edges of the Greek/Roman Empire. Groups of Vikings still met in "Tings" at Uppsala, elected leaders and decided what was right or wrong behavior.**

(131) The democratic Greek culture became very rich with architects, artists, philosophers, authors, and orators who have been admired throughout history ever since. The schools in Athens were considered the best in the then-civilized world for 500 years forward. The teachings and writings of Homer, Socrates, Plato and Aristotle are the starting points for much of modern art, science, and philosophy.

## Rome

(132)  In the year -509 King Tarquin in the city-state of Rome was deposed and Rome became a republic. The power of the republic was placed in the hands of two consuls elected for one year. In the year -287, the Roman leadership was placed with a Tribunal elected by two-chamber representatives: a Senate consisting of older patrician families and an Assembly consisting of simpler plebian men. All the free men participated in governing the city. The Assembly made laws and elected the Tribunal to execute power for one year. The Assembly maintained veto power. This was a system of power of the rich people for the rich people, similar to the early democracy or aristocracy in Athens at about the same time.

(133)  Rome at this time consisted of farmers, always ready to expand their cultivation. When opportunities opened, the Romans would attack their neighbors. The Romans became recognized as furious warriors. When the Greek General Pyrrhus defended the Greek colonies in southern Italy, he said, "another victory like this and I am lost" (a victory later recognized as a "Pyrrhic victory"). He did lose the next battle. After about 27 years of war, the Romans had conquered the entire Italian peninsula.

(134)  The generals usually retained one to two thirds of the land they conquered. This was the incentive for war according to the old Sumerian growth formula. A few who did more than expected felt they should have more to say. Octavius, alias Augustus the Great, became Principal Citizen after several palace coups.

(135)  The Augustus reign was a time of peace and consolidation for the Roman Empire. The Empire encompassed the entire western

civilized world stretching from York in England, across Europe along the Rhine and Danube Rivers, and around the Mediterranean Sea including Mesopotamia to the Persian Sea. It had fairly natural land borders. In the south and east were the Sahara and the Arabian deserts. In the north were the Caucasus Mountains and the Alps. The Rhine and the Danube were big enough rivers to provide some defense and certainly a defined border. Where there were no natural borders, the Romans built big walls and fortresses. Hadrian's wall, which partly still exists, stretched 75 miles across the island between England proper and Scotland.

(136) The Mediterranean Sea was located in the middle of the Roman Empire. All its contributors—the Black Sea, the East Coast of the Atlantic and all the rivers feeding these waters—formed an enormous water system for transport.

(137) A country can be likened to a human body, where the brain is its leadership, the nervous system its bureaucracy, the white blood cells and skin its military defense, and the blood circulation its transport system. It is therefore common to speak about a state-body. We will use this analogy when we analyze the Roman regime.

(138) Augustus used his long peacetime to build a bureaucracy for the administration of his empire. Administrators reported directly to him. The Senate and the Assembly were essentially excluded from the governing.

(139) Augustus was a good administrator for the Empire. He built roads for overland transport all throughout the land. It has been estimated that the Romans built enough roads to reach 10 times around the world. Augustus built a fleet to control the shipping and a strong army. The army reported to him and he paid its salary. The army consisted of some half-million men.

(140) By declaring himself head of state with veto power over the Senate, Augustus made himself a dictator. He also declared himself governor of the important provinces. He treated Egypt, the breadbasket for the city of Rome, as his personal estate. Augustus ruled for 41 years, until the year 14.

(141)  With the Mediterranean Sea in the middle of its body, it was like an athlete having an extra large blood volume with boats busily shipping foods and products all around the state-body. All orders came from Augustus and were carried out by his bureaucrats. The army defended and even extended its borders.

(142)  One official language, Latin, and one coinage helped to expand and ease trade and record keeping.

(143)  Civil laws were written. Rules for contracts and criminal laws for civil obedience were established across the empire. **The laws established by Emperor Justinius in the 500s became models for the Napoleonic laws in many European countries, and the state of Louisiana. In the 900s it even influenced Sharia law within Islamic countries.**

(144)  **The Justinian laws are written for the public by the ruling authority. Such laws can easily be outdated or politically slanted by the rulers, particularly in laws for civil rights. The Anglo-Saxon countries, England and USA base their laws on preceding case experiences. This is a living law, which changes with the assessment from the community.**

(145)  Many Roman boys were educated in reading, writing and arithmetic and, after age 16, in warfare or postgraduate education in Greek culture. Roman families owned much property. Marriages were therefore often arranged.

(146)  Occupations and positions in government were not formally inherited but often transferred from father to son through influence. There were no questions of what the sons and daughters would do as adults. It was a male-dominated society with all women working or supervising slaves in the homes.

(147)  The Greeks were very much admired for their buildings, art, and writings. Augustus, with greater resources than Athens, wanted to outdo it with a much more splendid Rome. Rome grew to a city of about one million people.

(148)  The Romans had similar gods as the Greeks, but with Roman names. All gods had beautiful temples built for them. The Romans had seen so many different gods in their far-reaching empire that

they tolerated most religions, provided they were not a threat to the government.

(149) The emperor himself was a Sumerian type anointed god/ruler. This was a problem for the Jewish people and also for the Christians, who both believed in only one god. When Jews were asked to acknowledge the emperor as a god, they refused. The Jewish temple in Jerusalem was destroyed in the year 70. After several uprisings, the Jewish people were driven from their homeland for the third time in 135. The Jewish people were assigned to jobs the proud Romans refused to do. They became loan brokers and bookkeepers for the Romans. Jews were assigned to live within walled, designated parts of towns. Within these walls, the Jews maintained their religious belief. The Jewish living area in Venice was an ironsmith area called the Ghetto. The name "Ghetto" became synonymous with Jewish living areas within the Roman Empire.

(150) The early Christians were a new occurrence. When they refused to recognize the Roman emperor as a God, they were punished. Thousands of Christians were thrown to the animals in the Coliseum. Their bravery was impressive and soon people started to listen to what they preached. Christianity appealed to the thousands oppressed.

(151) Eventually, Christianity was permitted and finally the Emperor, Constantine, left Rome and built a new capital in the 300s that he name Constantinople for himself. He educated his children in the Christian religion and all administration in the new capital was Christian. The Emperor himself was baptized in the year 337, on his deathbed.

(152) **Constantinople became now both the seat for government and the Christian Church administration. The Christian Church became tax-exempt. The head of the church called himself Ecumenical Patriarch (Universal Father). The word ecumenical should put him in charge of Rome. The head of the Christian church administration in Rome took the title Pontifex Maximus, the successor of Saint Peter, the Prince of the Apostles, or for short Pope. The Pope refused to submit himself to the Patriarch.**

**The original Roman Empire split into two, one Eastern and one Western half, one communicated in Greek and one in Latin.** (When I started public high school in Sweden in the 1930s, both Greek and Latin were offered as official language to learn before eventual further higher education.)

(153) With the success of the Roman state, there were only a few occupations a Roman gentleman citizen could allow himself to participate in: politics, law, farming, and the army. In the beginning, farming was an occupation for all. With the cheap food imports from the colonies, the local farmers could not compete and lost their land to the aristocrats owning the large estates that they had received in war campaigns. If not your own slaves, contractors of slaves did all other chores in the city, in the country or in the home. In time, the aristocracy ran out of men for the administration. The state grudgingly allowed first other Italians and later men from the provinces to become Roman citizens, particularly if they had served in the army. Once citizens, they could perform important tasks in the government.

(154) The meeting place for the Romans was the Grand Forum Romania. This was an Open Square surrounded by splendid buildings and statues. Most popular were the big public hot baths, one accommodating 1600 customers for free every day. This certainly kept the Romans clean. Not free but still popular were the many theaters. Here, Greek and now also Roman authors had their plays performed. During Augustus' time, they sang praises to the emperor, but later, they could also criticize the establishment.

(155) **This entire splendor was built essentially with one power machine, slave labor.** Contractors provided slaves walking in big squirrel wheels to raise stones and concrete for the tall buildings. Shiploads of slaves, animals, and products were delivered daily from all the conquered regions, either as loot, taxes or, as a last resort, as purchases.

(156) The Roman constitution had many laws, but no laws on how succession was to be accomplished when the Princep died. When Augustus died, he had arranged for his stepson Tiberius to

be Princep. The Princep seat had by now become an inherited, god connected dictatorship. **The Sumerian State form was complete. It had taken 500 years to build the Roman Empire. Now, slowly, it started the decline.**

(157) Tiberius became very paranoid. Often he had somebody executed, whom he imagined was against him. After eleven years of this terror, the palace guards had Tiberius killed.

(158) Tiberius' grandnephew Caligula took his place. He also required to be addressed as a god. He once insisted on his horse to be elected consul. The palace guard again took the initiative and killed Caligula.

(159) Trying to find a timid successor, the palace guard found Claudius, a 50-year-old, stuttering uncle to be the emperor. The Senate was now just a yes-saying institution to the will of the palace guard. The palace guard as a history-making institution became now customary and went on for the next four hundred years. With each coup, the army and the bureaucracy required more pay. Actually the guards held the emperor post up for auction and had it go to the one who promised them the biggest pay increase. Some emperors were terrible, some acceptable.

(160) **The state-body now had two malignant tumors growing: one in the nervous system, its bureaucracy, and one in its defense system, the army. Both sucked the rest of the body with unlimited selfishness. Monetary theories were not known. Inflation started. The government minted more and more coins. Coins used to be made of gold and silver. Now they were diluted with copper dipped in silver. Soon there was no metal cheap enough to mint because the Romans did not know how to print paper money. Finally, cumbersome bartering was the only way to trade.**

(161) The Roman general, Constantine, became emperor in the year 324. He was disappointed with Rome and its corrupt lifestyle. The only way out was to start a new Rome. With Roman grandeur, he had a new Rome built on the shore of northern Greece in a little town called **Byzantium** and named it Constantinople. To his new town, Constantine moved what he felt was the best of Rome—its

Christian people and art. Constantine made himself head of both the political Empire and the Christian Church. The Church as part of the state remained tax-exempt. The Empire still reached all around the Mediterranean Sea.

# Constantinople

(162) The new town, Constantinople became the capital of the original Roman Empire. Constantinople had a terrific location on the shore of the channel between Greece and Turkey. Here trade routes crossed from both the sea and the land from any direction in the Empire. The town grew rapidly to 600,000 people.

(163) Constantinople was built according to the city plan of Rome but even more majestic with big palaces and now only Christian churches. The largest and most splendid church in the empire became the Hagia Sophia Cathedral. The cathedral was built next to the emperor's palace.

(164) The head of the church and the state was the emperor. The emperor selected the head of the church. **The Sumerian State form already established in Rome continued in Constantinople.**

(165) The emperor Theodosius divided the Empire between his two sons: Arkadius ruled the eastern part with its seat in Constantinople and Honorius the Western part with its seat in Rome. This was the end of an undivided empire. Soon centuries of rivalry between the Pope in Rome and the Patriarch in Constantinople started. In 1053, the emperor of Byzantium ordered all churches that adhered to the Roman liturgy closed. Citizenship was given only to those who spoke Greek and adhered to the Byzantine Orthodox Church. Constantinople and the Byzantine Church controlled mainly the land around the eastern and southern part of the Mediterranean Sea.

(166) A new non-Christian religious, missionary movement came out of Mecca on the Arabian Peninsula, Mohamed's Islam. Constantinople and the Orthodox Church's authority were challenged around the Eastern and Southern Mediterranean Sea

and the Roman Catholic Church on the Balkan Peninsula. This was not only missionary message challenge but also a mission by sword.

(167) The land route to India across the Middle East had become less important since Vasco da Gama in late 1400 sailed around Cape Horn of Africa and opened a sea route around Africa to India.

(168) In 1869, the vice sultan in Egypt and French businessmen formed a company to build the Suez Canal. Since the sultan needed money after large gambling losses, he sold his shares in the canal to England. Turkey was on the loosing side in WW I. England made Egypt and Palestine into a British protectorate after WW I. Egypt and Palestine became free after WW II. Egypt's president Gamel Nasser nationalized the Suez Canal 1956.

(169) After WW I and further after WW II, the different Balkan nationalities were declared free from the Ottoman Empire. A mixture of community remnants from Roman, Byzantine and Islamic time remained and has been difficult to keep apart peacefully. Hopefully, the final chapters for the Balkans are being formulated with help from the USA and the European Community. Many Islamic nations maintain the Koran as a rule both for law and religion. After WW I, modern rulers in Turkey have combined Islamic religion with Western European law with civil liberties. Such religious/political movements are presently challenging status quo.

(170) Different Germanic tribes conquered the Western Roman Empire. The Ostrogoths entered the Italian peninsula from the north and plundered Rome in 410. Vandals had warred their way through southern Europe, Spain and North Africa, and, after building a fleet, plundered Rome from the sea in 455. Western Empire was slowly falling apart into many more or less independent Gothic kingdoms.

(171) In the beginning, the Gothic kings admired the Roman system and felt flattered to be part of the Empire. As time went by, they became more independent and finally an Ostrogoth king, Odovacar, had the Emperor removed and placed himself on the throne in 476. This was, after 1000 years, the end of the Western Roman Empire.

(172) Some Gothic kings and their people became more dominant in history than others did. The Visigoths ruled Spain until the Islamic invasion of the Hispanic Peninsula via North Africa. The Franks ruled the French realm. The Anglo-Saxons dominated the English island except for the Welsh area. The Celts settled in Wales, as well as in Ireland and on the Brittany Peninsula of France. The Ostrogoth and later the Lombards ruled much of the Italian Peninsula.

(173) Rome has remained the seat for of the Roman Catholic Church, except for the short time when French rulers ordered the Pope to live close to France and support its agenda.

## Roman Life Versus the "Nine Pillars"

(174) **Survival:** Food and water were abundant, particularly if you lived in Rome, Constantinople or in one of the other major centers. Aqueducts transported water into these centers if local wells did not provide enough water. The land around the Mediterranean Sea became a common market for food. With Egypt harvesting several times a year, food was well provided for. Air and energy were seldom affected until industrial times and will not be commented on for these early cultures. Water for human consumption was small relative to that for agricultural consumption. A water shortage could affect agriculture but would seldom affect an individual's life. The "First Pillar" was met, at least for the Roman citizens. Females formed submissive parts in most areas of societies and had now voting rights. The female played her influence through being a wife and mother to influential men. A male dominated society lasted until the early 1900s and will be commented on specifically in Part VIII.

(175) **Shelter:** Safety in the home was up to the whims of the Emperor as he was a dictator/god. The machinery that built the structures of the towns, the roads and other means of transportation, as well as the machinery for service and production in both factories and the homes, was slave-powered. The Romans must have been excellent engineers because many structures have survived to present day. The slaves had a difficult time under many masters. If you were

a Roman citizen, you were usually safe in your home. The "Second Pillar" was met for the Romans with citizenship.

(176) **Cleanliness:** Cleanliness was important in antique Rome and Constantinople. The Roman aqueducts supplied the city with plenty of water for sewage, bathing, and drinking. The beauty of the homes induced a desire to keep them clean. The "Third Pillar" was met.

(177) **Art:** Romans, with unlimited power and resources, indulged themselves in the beautification of their houses, clothing, and surroundings. The style of the buildings was not only structurally sturdy but also beautiful. Roman art and architecture is still admired, copied, and subject to an enormous tourist business. The "Fourth Pillar" was met with great success.

(178) **Communication:** Communication and gossiping was a popular pastime. Latin was the common language in the whole empire until Byzantine split from Rome and insisted on Greek in its part of the empire. The two languages for communication split the empire totally into two. Latin still lived on in the west as the premier academic language until industrial times. For several hundred years, Latin allowed leaders, businessmen, and scientists from different parts of the world to communicate independently of their mother language. Latin gave many of its words to all major modern languages. Science in industrial time eventually outgrew its vocabulary. The content of news and science was, however, much of the time controlled by the emperor and his church administration. The "Fifth Pillar" was not met.

(179) **Community:** Community support expressed itself in a widespread mentor program for all young Romans. All Roman citizens were equal before the law. Slaves were treated as property both in the Byzantine and Roman parts of the empire and could be well cared for or not. Community support, the "Sixth Pillar," was met for the Roman citizen but not for their slaves and many women.

(180) **Religion:** Religion was not free; it depended on whether a religion was considered a threat or not to the belief system of the Emperor. The Jews were locked up in ghettos and strictly controlled.

Christians were persecuted until the Emperor Constantine himself became christened in the 300s. Now Christianity became the favored state religion, both in Rome with Roman Catholicism and in Constantinople with Byzantine or Greek Orthodox Christianity. **The state and the religious leadership supported each other in a Sumerian, theocratic state form. From then on, there was no religious freedom. The two Christian denominations did not tolerate each other or any other religion. The "Seventh Pillar" was not met.**

(181) **Medicine:** Access to medicine was good, but limited knowledge had limited success. Epidemics ravaged, at times, wiping out two thirds of the populations. Access to the "Eighth Pillar" was met according to the knowledge of the time.

(182) **Trade:** Both the Western and the Eastern Roman Empire flowered under separate but common languages, common coinage, and established contract laws. Pursuit of happiness was a full-time preoccupation for the privileged both in Rome and Constantinople. This grew to a tumor that eventually smothered the both empires. Trade in both Rome and Constatinople consisted of slaves and products going to each Capitals; demands for more taxes coming from it. No theories of economics were known. Rampant inflation sunk to just bartering, because money lost its value. Eventually, any savior from outside their borders was welcomed both from the outnumbered Romans and the many slaves. A Lombard king, **Odovocar, took over much of the Italian Peninsula by promising no further taxes.** An Islamic Sultan conquered Constantinople in 1493. The "Ninth Pillar" was not met. A lack of will and little ability to defend itself led to both the Roman and the Byzantine demise. Its bureaucracy, however, was admired and lived on for several hundred years.

(183) Of the "Nine Pillars" only three—those for communication, religion and trade—were not met satisfactorily. **These three allowed for a selfish and unchecked access to the public money through unreasonable salary compensation or imaginative bookkeeping.** Today, it would correspond to having hundreds of Enron's grabbing for the tax money. Any outside help to relieve the taxpayer was

welcomed. Odovacar's success was in part due to the promise of no more taxes. **This reminds me of the present day "physical cliff" as the only means of holding back taxing of the public. Something radical had to happen before it could be stopped and should be a lesson for present day USA.**

## Feudal Time, 300-1500

(184)  The Roman Empire becoming christened marked the early part of the Millennium. Different "barbarian," mostly non-christened warrior tribes roaming the Euro-Asian continent challenged the outer border of the Empire. After the year 400, the warrior tribes succeeded in plundering Rome and establishing their own kingdoms. The fragment states all had the Sumerian state form, that is, a dynasty king supported by a belief system. In the western part of the Roman Empire, the belief system was the Catholic Church. In Sumerian style, each state fought for control of more land and more people. Some states, such as the Franker State (France) and the Lombard State (Italy), grew into major empires by themselves.

(185)  In Scandinavia, which was outside the Roman Empire, the tradition to rule was through the "Ting." The Ting was simply an assembly in which every free man (not slaves and usually not women) took part and voted. A Ting could be for a local area for a judicial decision, that is, to be a jury, or for larger areas to choose a king, that is, to be a parliament. In the beginning, there were no written laws, but rather a given one, that every one had one vote and that the majority ruled.

(186)  **Majority rule is the natural rule of a free assembly of people, for the people. The leader was selected on the merits of representing the wishes of the group. This was just as it was in the Greek city-states. If one could not participate in a Ting, one would send an "ombudsman" (representative). The title ombudsman still lives in Anglo-Saxon countries as a left over from early Viking colonization and administration.**

(187) Eventually some traditions were written down in Iceland in the old scriptures "Eddan" and "Hafvamal." Like the Old Testament these books describe mythical stories and give examples for a good and honest life.

(188) Early written documents were cut with runes in wooden boards or on birch bark. Such documentation is usually destroyed by time. Recently many family letters have been found preserved in marshland along the Viking trade routes through Russia/Soviet Union.

(189) The square letters of runes were a practical solution to cut letters in wooden boards. Modern law books in Sweden are still divided up into what is called "balks" (Swedish: *balkar*). For instance, there is a "family balk" for laws affecting family relationships. Personal relationships and kinship were the bonds that held the Viking group together, just as in the H/G society. Ting has continued in Iceland and is by now the oldest continuous, democratic assembly in the world.

(190) The religion of the Germanic tribes was very similar to that of the Greeks and the non-Christian Romans. Gods lived a very human life on the Asa-estate in Valhalla except that their life was eternal. Men who died in war would be accepted into Valhalla and served by pretty Valkyries maids just like Aztecs and promised their warriors, Christianity promised its crusaders, Japan promised its Kawasaki volunteers, and Islam now promises its young suicide bombers. The Gods were admired for their freedom-loving bravery, fairness, and trustworthiness, all-important values in any culture.

(191) The kings, particularly in Germany, would divide their domains between their sons. These domains would therefore get smaller and smaller with each generation. People would be bound to the area where they were born because travel was expensive and troublesome. Different domains would develop its cultural and language characteristics and eventually develop into national states both on the continent and in England. It all led to the feudal époque in history.

(192) **The mature feudal époque was based on the fief, the land grant that the king gave to his sons or his aristocracy.** The

term "fief" came from the Gothic term "faihu" (Swedish: *fähus*), which means cattle house and may eventually have turned into the American word "farm." The family inheritance and feudal fights made much of the history of this period. Gothic kings dominated much of Western Roman Empire between 410 and 553. Visigoths ruled Spain; Vandals and Allemandes ruled North Africa; Ostrogoth ruled the Balkan Peninsula. Rusers from Sweden colonized Russia/ Soviet Union during 800-900, Danes ruled England and part of France, and the Norwegians ruled on Ireland, in part of Scotland, Iceland, Faire Islands, Greenland and explored Newfoundland in North America. Many Gothic kings encouraged their bloodlines to stay within their Gothic inheritance.

(193) Established countries in Europe were the large states of the Franks (France), Lombardy (Italy), Visigoths (Spain) and Ostrogoths (Southeast Europe). The Emperor in Constantinople was in the beginning recognized as the rightful super ruler. The old Justinian Roman administrative and legal systems were adopted across the whole realm.

(194) Power in conquered countries rested with its Germanic king but the Roman bishops and bureaucrats were used for administration. Eventually the Christian bishops set moral standards for the country and worked tirelessly to influence and hopefully to convert the kings to Christianity. They found interest in one warrior, Clovis, who became king for the Franks in 481. Clovis had married a Catholic princess, Clothilda. After Clovis had converted to Christianity eventually all his Frank people had to, too. In the name of God, Clovis took on the Visigoths, beat them in 507, and established Paris as his new capital. Clovis's wars were successful and he extended his domain to include much of Germany.

(195) Clovis' descendants ruled the Franks until 638 when Karl Martel in a palace coup declared himself king. History has called his descendants Carolingians. Karl Martel stopped the Arabic influx on the Spanish peninsula.

(196) Because Karl had come to power in a coup, the Pope never recognized him as a justified king. His son Pepin consolidated

southern France and gave a large land area in northern Italy to the Pope. In return, Pepin became anointed as "king by the grace of God."

(197) Pepin's son was Charlemagne, Karl the Great. On Christmas day in the year 800, he was crowned as Emperor of the Roman Empire (in the west). He had by then been a very successful warrior and conquered all of Western Europe except England, Scandinavia, and what was then Moslem Spain. He made the city of Aachen in West Germany his capital.

(198) Charlemagne was a smart administrator. He assigned a governor as well as a bishop for each part of his domains. He also had two inspectors travel between each area and to report to him on its condition. He started a small letter alphabet to ease the writing of the reports. Much of early western history is written with this alphabet. To fill the need for administrators, he founded schools that became the best in Europe.

(199) Charlemagne instituted a common coinage for the large area of Europe that was ruled by him. This helped trade within his domain, as it had done within the Roman and the Greek Empires, and led to a better standard of living for a regular family, not just for nobility. France flourished during Charlemagne's 46-year rule.

(200) **Charlemagne decided that farmers had to give 10% of their produce to the Catholic Church.** This legislation was to become significant for at least the next 700 years. Both the king and the church had as before a common interest for land and people but it would make the Catholic Church less dependent on the king. The administration for the Catholic Church became a super national administration. Eventually it would lead to challenges between the power of the local king and the power of the Pope.

(201) Charlemagne made sure that his only son Louis inherited the empire. Louis had three sons. Louis divided the empire between his three sons, one essentially French, one German and one Italian. On the continent, generation shifts split the land into smaller and smaller units. They would all fight over inherited rights, forming the history of the continental Western Europe up to the present day.

The population in France at this time was about twenty million the most populated country in Western Europe. England had only five million and Scandinavia about two. Scandinavia was geographically the largest land. The populations of Europe varied with wars and epidemics, but stayed essentially constant or grew very slowly.

(202) Hordes of Vikings swarmed over Europe between 800 and 1000. They came in small or longer so called "long ships" that turned out to be very seaworthy. The small ones were also easy to roll over land. The trips were in the beginning only robbing raids. Monasteries were easy and popular targets. The Viking Rolf was given Normandy at the outlet of the River Seine in order to defend Paris, situated farther up the river.

(203) The Gothic kings ruled their land as their own property. Many had an advisory counsel and some even had representatives from the three social groups—nobility, church and commoners. **In Scandinavia on the edge of Roman culture and still with many free farmers, the commoners were divided into farmers and burgers.** However, there were no rules for when to get together. The king could call people together and listen to complaints but most avoided. **Essentially the Sumeric State, dynasty-king/religion lived on.**

(204) A kingdom could grow either by marriage or by war. A successful general would keep two thirds of the land he conquered; the king kept the rest. The king gave privileges in the form of land to people he trusted in the administration. The selected people, the nobility, swore devotion to the king. In return, the nobility could collect taxes. For part of the taxes, the nobleman was expected to provide warriors to the king.

(205) **Between land owned by the king, the nobility, and the church there was not much land left for a simple farmer. Many farm workers on the continent worked for the privileged nobility and the Church and lived in serfdom, bound to the land on which they were born.**

(206) The farm workers got a little better living conditions after the first plague epidemic 1348. The first plague epidemic stopped much of commerce. More than half of Europe's population died

within seven years. The plague epidemics repeated themselves one or several times within each generation for the next 300 years, slowly becoming less devastating. Workers for the farms from this time were very much in demand. Their salaries increased, but surviving farm workers were anyway so few that the general population starved.

(207) The nobility's devotion to the king had nothing to do with the land that belonged to the church. The church land belonged to the Pope in Rome. The king's and the Pope's interest would collide and would later lead to the reformation wars. In the beginning, the Pope had the upper hand. **In the year 1075, Pope Gregorious VII issued a decree, "Dictatus Papae." He declared that the Pope's spiritual authority is total and can never be questioned by anybody on earth. All secular powers must obey him. As Pope, he can dispose of both king and emperor. The Sumerian leadership would now best be described as "religion/royalty" ruled.**

(208) A particular embarrassment for the Roman Church was the Muslim occupation of Palestine and Jerusalem, a part of the Roman Empire since before Christ and so much the scene of Jesus' life. The Pope called on the Christian kings to make a Crusade and recover the Holy Land. There were at least six major military crusades.

(209) On July 15, 1099, Jerusalem succumbed to mainly French crusaders. On Christmas Day 1100, the Kingdom, "Outremer," with Jerusalem as capital, was recognized. This state lasted till 1187, when it was taken back in a jihad by the sultan of Egypt, Saladin. **Today Sumerian type interests still fight over Jerusalem.**

## Renaissance, 1300-1600

(210) An interesting period of history took place in Italy between 1300 and 1600, the Renaissance time, the time for re-recognition of the antique Greek culture.

(211) During this time, the Italian Peninsula was divided into at least 13 kingdoms plus the papal state. The papal state had Rome as the capital. Genoa, Florence, and Venice were the most influential states. In Florence, the Medici family established a bank that became

the papal bank. It became the largest bank in Europe with offices in all major cities, thereby making Florence a major financial center in Europe.

(212) Venice took part in the Fourth Crusade. Instead of going to Jerusalem, the crusaders turned on Christian Constantinople, sacking and plundering the town. Venice took over the eastern trade from Constantinople and became the major Mediterranean Sea power.

(213) Another free state of importance was Genoa. Its citizens supported their bank of credit. Many kings would come to borrow money for their war expeditions. The citizens of Genoa became very rich from their "venture capital." It is said that much of the Inca gold eventually landed in Genoa.

(214) The lively trade of Florence and Venice had brought them in contact with Islamic Spain and Arabian translations of the non-Christian Greek culture from 1700 years before. Also, many Greek scholars had fled from Greece to Italy when the Turks conquered the Balkan Peninsula in 1453. The historical texts told about the old Greek culture and its early democracy. A feverish study of the democratic city-state of Athens, its artists, philosophers, and writings started. The message was quite a break from the previous very religious period, dominated by the teachings of the Catholic Church.

(215) In trade the individual plays a more important role than a king too proud to deal with money. As in early Athens, both Florence and Venice started with elected representative governments. Both cities were small enough for most of the important citizens to take part in the decisions. Greek art and literature were studied. In the next fifty years, Florence produced some of the world's greatest painters, sculptors and architects, including such names as Giotto, Michelangelo, Leonardo da Vinci, Raphael, Titian and Donatello. Most of them came from very simple backgrounds but flourished in the free society—the same exceptional development of art that had happened in the free city of Athens.

(216) A new, more realistic knowledge emerged from secular science and teaching. The artists would study the human body at

autopsy in order to be able to present it accurately. The architect would develop mathematical formulas to achieve the most harmonious proportions. Composers would experiment with new instruments. Schools preached that God created everything and now, we humans had to add what we could do and do the best we could with our lives.

(217)  Before this time, people had been preoccupied with the after life. When the first plague appeared in 1348, the church blamed the immense death numbers on people's sinful life. People had not dared to question the church's preaching of heaven and hell. When the plague came back over and over again, people started to question old church knowledge. Doctors started to seek for other possibilities to explain and stop the epidemics. Medical quarantines were introduced in Venice. A school of humanism started. The new teachings were so explosive that essentially a new modern man emerged.

(218)  The political freedom ended suddenly in 1494, when the French King Charles VIII invaded Italy from the north and conquered most of the states down to Naples. The Spanish Monarchy of Ferdinand and Isabella and their relative, the king of Austria, Maximilian I of Hapsburg joined Charles. Maximilian took Venice. France and Spain split the rest of the peninsula between themselves. The Pope became just a puppet to the French king just as he had been between 1309 and 1377. The Pope was also ordered to live in France, in Avignon. The international Catholic Church became the economic and political supporter of the national policy of France, making France into a **royal/religious Sumeric** type state.

(219)  **The Sumeric kings competed for the control of the production machine of the farm industry, the land. Ever since the beginnings of Sumeric time, royal/theocratic or theocratic/royal but always-dogmatic states have been in wars with their neighbors**. Watching what was taking place in Italy, one of the most influential authors in history, Machiavelli wrote a book on practical diplomacy titled *The Prince*. It was a handbook for rulers. He maintained that a state must have a citizen army and not rely on mercenaries (non-national, paid soldiers). It must be resolute in its policy and back it up with cash and military might. The unarmed neutrality of Venice,

Genoa and Florence had been suicide. A country was only respected if it was strong; money and arms alone counted. **This was and is certainly true as long as Sumerian type of countries exist.**

(220) The Catholic Church had declared that the earth was the center of the Universe. The earth was a flat continent with three known parts: Europe, Asia and Africa and possibly something-called Terra Incognita. Jerusalem was its center. The sea surrounded the known lands. The intelligentsia of the renaissance time questioned the scientific authorities approved by the church.

(221) An early Greek astronomer, Ptolemy, living in Alexandria, Egypt in year 200 had concluded that the Earth must be round. Current Arabic astronomers agreed. This knowledge had been forgotten or suppressed by the Catholic Church. When the idea now was brought forward, it challenged the thoughts of young adventurers.

## Land Exploration, 1400-1600

(222) Europe's trading grew but was hindered by shortages of metals, gold and silver, for coins. Paper money was not yet invented. Arabian dealers imported gold from somewhere on the west cost of Africa. There were stories of Solomon's wealth hidden in Africa. Europeans had been scared of traveling south of the Equator; scared it would make them black.

(223) With skepticism of the old sea-stories, Prince Henry in Portugal set himself a goal to explore the West Coast of Africa. Prince Henry was looking for a possible sea route to India with valuable spices and merchant goods. In 1430, he appointed a college of knowledgeable people to study geography and collect information about far away places.

(224) The prince financed explorations of the West Coast of Africa and financed an expedition to discover a way around Africa to India. The college chose Vasco da Gama to lead the expedition. In July 1497, Vasco da Gama sailed from Lisbon. After many adventures, he reached the West Coast of India and returned to Lisbon with a big

load of pepper. The trip took two years. He had lost 75% of his men but he gave the Europeans a new vision of the world.

(225) The King of Portugal asked the Pope for a monopoly of the trade with Africa and India in return for doing missionary work in all of its bases. The king got this in two bulletins. The first bulletin in 1481 gave all new land south of the Canary Islands to Portugal. The second bulletin in 1493 awarded Portugal all new land west of the 38-west longitude meridian in the Atlantic Sea. The natives were converted to Roman Christianity wherever new land was colonized.

(226) Most intellectuals of the Renaissance had now accepted that the earth was round and felt that by sailing off to the west across the Atlantic one should be able to reach India or China. Christopher Columbus presented this idea to the royal couple, King Ferdinand and Queen Isabella of Spain. The idea was intriguing to them. They had watched with envy how their neighbor Portugal grew rich from the trades on the African West Coast.

(227) Financed by the Spanish royal couple, Columbus set sail on August 3, 1492 with three ships: two smaller caravels about 70 feet long, Niña and Pinta, and a larger commander ship, the Santa Maria. On October 10 at 2:00 a.m., after 30 days at sea, they sighted land: the Bahaman Island of San Salvador. After exploring the "West Indies" for six months, Columbus returned to Spain, much honored by the King and the Queen. He made a total of four trips, all the time believing that what he had discovered was an area of India.

(228) In 1505, another explorer, Amerigo Vespucci, felt that this was not India but a new continent. A German publisher of maps felt this was exciting news and named the new continent America on his new 1507 maps. The name stuck, despite taking some of the glory of the discovery from Columbus.

(229) The king of Portugal reacted to the news of Columbus' discovery by addressing the Pope and claiming that the Pope had given him the right to the Indian trade. The Pope, himself a Spaniard, suggested a compromise. A new treaty of 1494 gave to Spain the new land west of the 46 west longitudinal meridian and the land east of it to Portugal. This gave Portugal a claim to Brazil when it was

discovered in 1500. Brazil, therefore, speaks Portuguese and the rest of South America, Spanish.

(230) Magellan sailed for the first time around the world in 1519. In 1768, Captain James Cook discovered New Zealand and explored the West Coast of Australia with his ship Endeavor.

(231) The rulers of England and France noticed the success of the Spanish and Portuguese overseas trade. Which one of the four would dominate the sea-trade?

# Church Reformation, 1500-1600

(232) At the end of 1400, the Catholic Church stood at its zenith. It owned much of the farmland in Europe, at least a third. The church formed its own army to defend and police its property. It did not pay tax on what it owned. The working free farmer paid 10% in taxes to the church. The farmer paid about 30% of the tax in the form of work for the neighborhood prince. When the farmer died, his family paid the prince 50% in inheritance tax—a formula that seems very modern.

(233) A prince who would like to ascend to be king needed the blessing of the Pope. This provided an opportunity for the church to win influence. The church built enormous cathedrals all over Europe, including the largest cathedral ever, Saint Peter's Cathedral in Rome. The church sold positions of bishops to the highest bidder. Several epidemics of plague spread with devastating results. The disasters were blamed on sins committed by the people. The priests preached of the impending doomsday. Witches were burned, heretics tortured, and ascetics starved and beat themselves to be accepted into heaven. Many donated their worldly goods to the Catholic Church.

(234) A major and very large income for the Catholic Church was to sell indulgences (certificates of forgiveness for past and even future sins). Everybody everywhere was engaged in religion. **The Roman Church constituted the largest enterprise of the time, if not the largest enterprise ever in history.** It had its own constitution and its own (canon) law. The Pope was the director, the Curia was its

judicial court and fiscal department, and priests its bureaucrats. The cash coming from donations and collections of 10% from all farms, from income of all its own farmland, and the selling of indulgences, all required a large organization.

(235) The bank that handled the cash, the Medici Bank in Florence, became the largest bank in the world. It had loan offices in all major capitols, financing the major enterprises for that capital, which were usually wars. The church became preoccupied with all its worldly interests.

(236) The influence of the Pope crossed all borders because there were no national states, only realms—areas with tax obligations to a monarch or a prince. The English and the French royal realms had started to take national form but the German section of the Roman Empire still continued a strong bond with Rome. After several generations of inheritance divisions, Germany was divided into 200 princely or royal realms and 3000 independent city-states. Like in the Italian city-states, the movement of renaissance "humanism" had spread to Germany. Democracy was budding but the small size of the cities was a constant threat to their independence.

(237) Erasmus, a scholarly Dutch monk born in 1466, had made a New Latin translation of the Bible from the original Greek text. The Erasmus Bible turned out to be quite different from the previous St. Jerome Bible in use for the previous 900 years. Erasmus was not openly opposed to the church but questioned the practices of selling indulgences, fasting, celibacy, pilgrimage, confession, the burning of heretics, relic worship and prayers to saints. Erasmus corresponded by letters with many scholars and kings in Europe and became very influential.

(238) Martin Luther, born in 1483, came to play an important role in history. The 22-year-old Martin became an Augustinian monk. He was asked to teach ethical philosophy and theology at the University at Wittenberg and was selected to follow his superior by foot for an 800-mile-journey to Rome.

(239) Martin found lay people in Rome mocking the clergy, monks living in sin, the Pope out fighting with his army, and a mass production of indulgences for pilgrims. Martin was disturbed.

(240) Martin went home, studied Erasmus's Bible and re-examined himself, his religious belief, and his most pious conscience. He came to the conclusion that the church had no right to sell indulgences for money. The church's obligation was to spread God's word, not to sell forgiveness. The church could give forgiveness in God's name but God's forgiveness was unlimited for the one with faith and a change at heart.

(241) Martin Luther formulated his ideas in 95 theses. He posted them on the door to the church in Wittenberg October 31, 1517. Since Gutenberg in Germany had invented the printing press in the year 1400, printing was now common. Within a few months, the 95 theses were read all over Western Europe. This was a big step. A hundred years before Jan Hus, a Bohemian scholar, had been judged in a church council in Constancy to be burned at the stake for urging people to rely on the bible instead of the church's interpretation of the bible.

(242) Three years later Luther declared that because the church still was slow in reforming itself, the state could take over the leadership of the church. The "state" meant mostly the king of that country. The king taking over the authority from the Pope was indeed a revolution against the Pope and the Catholic Church. In a second publication the same year, Luther examined the seven sacraments of the church: Baptism, Confirmation, Communion, Marriage, Confession, Last Rights and the Vows of Priesthood. Luther found bases in the Bible for only two: Baptism and Communion. This was to attack the basic dogma of the Catholic Church. In another pamphlet, Luther established that the clergy was not more worth to God than a layman was, because "we are all equal to God."

(243) Pope Leo X countered by issuing a "bulla" (bulletin) condemning Luther and ordering his work burned. When the bulla arrived in Wittenberg, students rallied to Luther's support. The bulla and also the Canon Law for the church were burned. Erasmus in

Holland applauded Luther's courage. According to a church observer 9/10 of the local people were said to have supported him. Still, in a trial, Martin Luther was declared an outlaw. He had to go into hiding for a year. During this time, Luther translated the Erasmus' Latin Bible into native German. The first church service according to the Lutheran dogma and in native German that everybody could understand took place already in 1522, only five years after the posting of Luther's 95 theses.

(244) The Lutheran message spread rapidly all through Northern Europe and England. The Protestant movement began to create its own energy. Actually a new form of Sumerian statehood had been formed. Before the reformation movement, the Pope was a super national authority directing the combined mission of his and his anointed kings against mostly Muslims, Jews in Europe, and natives in newly detected lands. **Kings in the Protestant Lutheran states formed local Sumerian states independent from the Pope**.

(245) The Confederate states of Switzerland, all without kings, had a deep response. Ulrich Zwingli (1484-1531) and Jean Calvin (1509-1564) were both active in Switzerland. It is significant that the Pope chose and still takes his personal guard from this independent country and remembered in present day dress of the Vatican guard.

(246) Different kings found it personally advantageous to break with Rome. A newly elected king of Sweden, Gustav I Vasa, did not have any money. Gustav requested from the Ting that the Church should be responsible to him. The request was approved. The Roman archbishop left the country voluntarily and Gustav confiscated all church property for himself—some 300 farms. Supported by the state church, he ruled the whole country from then on as if it all was his. **The Sumerian type state had arrived in Sweden**.

(247) The second king taking advantage of Luther's publications was King Henry VIII in England. As is well known in history and not for the last time, the English king had problems with his wife. Henry wanted to be divorced from his wife Catherine of Aragon in Spain because she did not give him a son for his throne. The Pope would not allow the divorce. Henry responded by calling on the Parliament

in 1534. The Parliament declared that the king had supremacy over the church and also, in an act of dissolution, that he could confiscate all the church land. The move was nationally popular. Protestantism was further secured with the 45-year-long rein of Henry's second daughter, Elizabeth I. She had to defend England from invasion by the new Spanish Emperor, Philip II, who tried to invade England with his "invincible Armada." Philip lost both the battle in 1590 and also the Spanish dominance of the sea to England.

(248) The Netherlands, the home of Erasmus, became the third country to accept the Lutheran teachings. Philip II of the Spanish crown had through different bloodlines inherited to rule the Netherlands (Holland, Belgium, and Luxembourg). The Netherlands was located at the openings of three major rivers into the Atlantic. Cities located here were the largest seaports of Europe. Some 400-500 ships would leave from Antwerp and the other seaports every day. These towns were major trade centers, similar to the antique Athens and the renaissance cities Genoa and Venice. The Netherlands had until now been governed under an act called Estate-General, which kept them very independent from any influence of the Spanish Crown.

(249) Philip II started to tax Dutch commerce, but when merchants refused to pay, Philip responded by sending in troops. Two Protestant Counts, Egmond and William I of Orange (1579-84), led the resistance. Egmond was invited to a meeting to discuss a settlement. When he showed up, he was decapitated. Two hundred years later Goethe and Beethoven immortalized Egmond's legend.

(250) Philip with a larger army subdued the southern part of the Netherlands, Belgium and Luxembourg. These countries are still Catholic. Holland stood firm and after 80 years of war became the first Protestant Republic of the time. Amsterdam started a bank system based on credit, secured by bonds and taxes from its citizens similar to that of Genoa. Holland became a leading country of finance; its currency, the guilder, became an international currency. Holland withstood Spanish military pressure and undertook its own colonization despite its miniature size. Holland is still Protestant. As

in Renaissance Florence, art flourished in Holland with Rembrandt, Hals and other world-renowned artists. William III of Orange (1672-1702) was married to an English princess, the daughter of James II of England. **William III of Orange was elected as King William III of England. King William signed and thereby established people's power in the Parliament with some democracy in England. England does not have a formal constitution. The law, anchored in the will of the people through the jury system, has met the needs of the people.**

(251) Ignatius of Loyola (1491-1556), an army man turned monk, organized in 1534 a Catholic religious organization, the Society of Jesus. Ignatius was its "general." The Jesuits were not monks in the common meaning, living in poverty and serving the local community, but well-educated and mannered teachers. The Pope dispersed the Jesuits to become advisers to many rulers. They used their influence over kings to fight Muslims, Jews, and now also Protestants. In Paraguay, they formed their own statehood. Jesuits were advisers to the kings for both their national and their international policy. In the national policy, they encouraged the use of the Inquisition courts in pursuit of "infidels"; in international policy, they encouraged war against the "infidels."

(252) The Inquisition was in modern terms a religious prosecution of Muslims, Jews and Protestants. The suspected infidels were called into court and had to prove that they no longer believed what they used to believe. This was, of course, very difficult. In Spain, hundreds of Jews were executed, usually in the market places as a warning to the rest of the population; still more left behind all that they owned and fled the Christian country for a Muslim country. Muslim authorities allowed infidels, provided they paid extra protection tax. **In 2004 the Catholic Church published a review of the Inquisition and officially asked for forgiveness.**

(253) In France, King Henric II, a true Machiavellian, did not break openly with the Pope, but instead made a deal. Henric II could appoint his own bishops and collect the biggest portion of the church tax for himself. He, therefore, felt that he had no reason

to break with Rome. The Protestants in France were Calvinists but were called "Huguenots" (German: *Eidgenossen*) and as a minority had to fight for their rights in this Sumerian type country. Eight civil wars between Catholics and Huguenots followed. King Henric died and his Catholic widow, Catherine of Medici took over as regent for her young son. Catherine had Jesuits as advisers. In a conciliatory move to the Huguenots, Catherine agreed for her daughter to marry a Protestant Prince of Navarra on the day of St Bartholomew in 1572. All the Huguenot noblemen were in Paris for the occasion. While the church bells were ringing, the church doors were closed and all Huguenot guests killed. It was followed by a slaughter of Huguenots in the streets of Paris. Thousands of Huguenots were killed that day in Paris and still more in all of France. The Protestants were not granted legal recognition in France until 1685.

(254) The Lutheran reformation movement impressed the Roman Church itself. Pope Paul III and his follower Paul IV started commissions to make suggestions for internal improvements. Nepotism became outlawed, education and behavior, particularly clergy having concubines, was scrutinized. The church forbade the clergy from gaining any personal economic benefit from their work. Bishops were made responsible for the education of the clergy and its behavior.

(255) **The dogma of the church was reexamined at a church meeting in Trent in Northern Italy in 1545. The meeting lasted for 18 years. The meeting confirmed that the church had the exclusive right to interpret the Bible. The right for the church to sell indulgences was re-confirmed.**

(256) The Hapsburg family that ruled much of Europe at this time, Emperor Philip II in Spain and his cousin, Emperor Ferdinand II of Austria were both devoted Catholics; **actually there was a Sumerian type relationship between the Catholic rulers and the Catholic Church, both supporting each other.** The Roman Church had been enormously successful and was already close to 1300 years old. Knowledge and life were interwoven intimately with the message and

dogma of the Church. The Hapsburg family felt responsible to defend the Church against the new reformation movement.

(257)  Philip took up the fight with the Netherlands and England as mentioned above; Ferdinand took up the fight with the German and Scandinavian states. Ferdinand hired a very adventurous mercenary general Wallenstein to bring Czechoslovakian Protestants in line. Denmark came to their help but Wallenstein beat both the Czech and Danish armies and occupied the Danish peninsula. Ferdinand felt strong, made plans for his son to be named king of Rome and issued a decree asking all German kings and princes to return all church property to the Church. As a compromise, they were allowed to stay Lutheran but Calvinism was outlawed. Hardly any prince complied with the decree.

(258)  France, despite being Catholic, had nervously seen itself surrounded by the Hapsburg family land: Spain in the south, Netherlands in the north, and Germany in the east. Ruled by a Catholic Cardinal, France encouraged the Protestant Sweden to help the Protestant German princes and offered to finance part of the expedition against the Catholic emperor. This Machiavellian diplomacy was conducted in secrecy.

(259)  Denmark had already been subdued. Sweden might be the next target if the emperor succeeded in uniting Germany under the Roman Catholic crown. On the other hand, Sweden, if successful, saw a possibility to combine the Protestant princes of Northern Germany into a Protestant Federation.

(260)  The King, Gustav II Adolphus, Gustav Vasa's grandchild, had a meeting with the Assembly, which recommended that Sweden would be better off fighting a war on German soil. The army was mobilized and Gustav Adolphus landed in 1630 on the German coast with 14,000 troops, an all-national army.

(261)  The Emperor Ferdinand's army lost two convincing battles. He was now willing to settle and annul his edict of returning church property. The annulment was signed in Prague in early May 1635. King Gustav Adolphus had been killed in the second battle. Axel

Oxenstierna, the Prime Minister, took over as regent for the Gustav Adolph's four year-old daughter, Christina.

(262) Right after the peace agreement was signed on May 21, France came out in the open and declared war on the Emperor. Now the war took another turn. Instead of a war for religious freedom, it became a war for booty and land. It is estimated that Germany lost a third of its population in this fight between different Sumerian states for land and taxes.

(263) **Hugo Grotius, born in Holland, lived as adult in Paris. He saw brutality crimes without restraint in the war and wrote in 1625 "The Law of War and Peace," the first treaty of international law. The French Cardinal Richelieu expelled Grotius from France. Prime Minister Axel Oxenstierna appointed him as Swedish ambassador to France and sent him back to Paris. Later, Queen Christina gave him a Swedish life pension. The town of Hague raised a statue of him in his honor in 1886. The international court is now placed in Hague.**

(264) Eventually, the peaceful end of this "Thirty Year War" was accomplished in Westphalia 1648. When the son of Axel Oxenstierna hesitated to represent Sweden, his father told him: "Don't you know, my son, with which little wisdom the world is ruled?" I found it appropriate to quote him for the beginning of this manuscript.

(265) The German princes could determine the religions in their states but it had to be Catholic, Lutheran, or Calvinistic. The princes could keep their confiscated church land. France got land west of the Rhine, while Sweden received the German Baltic Coast.

(266) Other results of the peace agreement at Westphalia were: Protestantism became generally accepted; the Roman Church paid attention to its religious activity; England and Holland became the dominant powers at sea trade, France became the dominant political power on the European continent and Sweden became the dominant power around the Baltic Sea. The two Hapsburg Empires— the Spanish (with its capital in Madrid) and the Roman (Austria and Germany with the Emperor seat in Vienna.) were big but very incoherent, divided into many Royal and Prince states.

(267) Agriculture still continued as the basic livelihood for another 300 years. We stop this review of history and take an inventory of how history, so far, is standing up for the "Nine Pillars for History."

## The 500-1600s Versus the "Nine Pillars"

(268) **Survival:** The food supply was still very local and, therefore, dependent on how the harvest of a particular year turned out. Eventually, trade in grain increased so local problems could be somewhat avoided, but hunger was never far away.

(269) Western Europe seldom lacked fresh water for it has many fresh water rivers and lakes. In the time period described here, bacteria were not yet known. Although physically clean, water used for drinking and cooking could be infected and spread epidemic diseases like cholera and plague. The plague in 1348 killed 50% of the population in Europe. The "First Pillar" was still met to the best of the understanding of the time.

(270) **Shelter:** The king and his court never felt safe in their dwellings. A neighbor king could raid the kingdom at any time (mostly in the summertime). Kings and aristocrats felt the need to build bigger and bigger castles to defend their domains. The castles were, if possible, built on a high and easy defensible ground. The farmers would build their houses close by or inside a surrounding wall in order to protect their dwellings. This became the model for the medieval towns.

(271) War with a neighbor for land had been part of the agricultural society ever since early Sumerian times. Agriculture was the main industry and land was its prerequisite. The incentive principle was that a successful war controlled more land. More land brought in more taxes. More taxes made possible more soldiers and an opportunity for conquering more land.

(272) Most kingdoms had a very simple constitution: The king owned and decided most things. The king ruled by a holy decree and saw to it that his family inherited his title. The anointment of the king at the time of his crowning assured a blessed status. This had

evolved already in the Sumerian time. Most of the time, the power rested with the king but at times, if he was lazy or uninterested, power was delegated to a powerful royal court. The kings' daughters were married to other king's sons, thus securing the borders of their father's domain. Aristocrats would marry members of other aristocratic landowners. Common farmers owning land would see to that their daughters married sons of landowners. The church had an institutional ownership of land, but many bishops looked at the land, that they controlled, as theirs. The Catholic Church secured its land by having the bishops and priests live in celibacy. Ownership of land split society according to royal, aristocratic, church-owned, farmer-owned, and those who owned no land. If not a landowner, you had no voting rights and, in many countries, had no right to leave the estate where you were born, a so-called serfdom or bond service. The difference between a bond-service on a big farm and a slave was indeed small in most countries.

(273) Everybody paid taxes to the king except the church and the high aristocracy. Eventually, more and more land went into the hands of the church and the aristocracy. In about 1200, the Church owned 25% of the agricultural land in Spain, in England 20%, in Germany 30%, and in France and Denmark 50%. Taxes to the king were a constant threat to the dwelling for the small independent farmer and led to several uprisings by farmers in Scandinavia, Germany and even by the lords in England. In England, the lords finally required the new king to sign the Magna Carta before he was anointed. In Scandinavia, he had to give a verbal promise not to impose any taxes without the approval of the Ting. The ceremony was called hand proofing. The written document lasted longer than the handshake. Thus, the "Second Pillar" was not met for the people in general. Continuous wars made living for everybody insecure. Lack of home security because of high taxes caused many farmer uprisings.

(274) **Cleanliness:** There was a need to keep the dwellings clean but community support for doing so did not exist in most places. The old Roman water aqueducts were crumbling and the new towns were too poor and small to start such major undertakings. Sewer systems

existed only sporadically. Most garbage was disposed of in the streets and cleaned from the streets, at best, weekly. The sewage-filled streets provided excellent growing areas for rats with bacteria spreading diseases. The history of Rome's aqueducts was still alive and could have been a model for at least some cities. The "Third Pillar" was, therefore, not met to the best of the day's knowledge.

(275) **Art:** Much of the beautification was related to the church activity. With the increased trading and the emergence of the rich artisan and the trading middle-class, eventually a sectarian demand for artwork evolved. Demand for artistry in writing, painting, music, jewelry and entertainment became slowly more and more widespread. The "Fourth Pillar" was probably met according to economic ability, but art stayed mainly in the privileged homes. The great difference between the standard of living of the privileged and particularly that of the farm worker caused many farmer rebellions during the period.

(276) **Communication:** The church was a main meeting-point of the town and its surroundings. The king's orders to the people reached his subjects by being announced in the church. There were very few written news bulletins because very few people could read. In 1400, Gutenberg invented the printing press. This invention would eventually play an extremely important role for future communication. At first, the printing presses were mainly used to print the Bible in Latin. Soon, the Bible was translated into mother-languages. John Wycliff wrote the first English translation in 1380, Martin Luther wrote the German translation in 1522, and Olaus Petri led a team of translators for a Swedish publication of the Bible in 1526.

(277) The written language of the Bible led to the standardization of a mother-language. People learned to read. Communication started to grow from being very local—confined to towns and villages—to reach the size of nations with a common language. The reading public grew to include a more sectarian public besides the priesthood. The printing of the Bible and religious pamphlets grew to the printing of moral stories, entertaining stories (Georg or "Jörg" Wickram in Germany), history books, and some news stories. Most printing presses were owned or controlled by the king or the Church. News

was essentially censored because the origin of the news came only from the dictatorial king or church. The "Fifth Pillar" was not met. The Sumerian States of the time controlled the masses by controlling their education, knowledge, and news.

(278) **Community:** Community support was either through the local church or the town council. Individual support was otherwise limited and stayed mainly within the family. The family took care of its children, giving them the education they needed for making a living on the farm or in a trade. The emergence of the guilds was an assurance for staying profitable in business. Professions would often go from father to son. The family would care for their elders. The local village as a group cared for those with no family support through community poor houses. Monasteries helped to care for temporary emergencies, such as caring for the sick and providing a safe resting-place for the traveler. Defense was linked to the feudal system, was local and subject to repeated raids or war expeditions. The "Sixth Pillar" was probably met, but support outside the family was very humiliating. It was not a happy time for the under-privileged.

(279) **Religion:** The right to worship your own faith was restricted, particularly if it deviated from that of the church headed by the king. Often the territorial ambitions of the church coincided with the king's, leading to holy wars like the Christian Crusades, the Muslim Intifada against the Crusades, or wars between different Christian and Muslim denominations. The Catholic Church was the bond that had held much of the continental Europe of smaller states together. The Inquisition was its police enforcement. After the reformation the Church, both the Catholic and the Protestant Church supported their kings and were jealously intolerant of each other and also of other religions. Religious deviations were called heresy in any language. Heresy could lead to death, according to the Canon law of the Catholic countries and the Sharia law in Muslim countries. The "Seventh Pillar" was not met.

(280) History has shown over and over again that religious administrations become intolerant and are quick to start war when

their power is mixed with a state's political power in a Sumerian manner.

(281) **Medicine:** Medical care was generally accessible to most, but care was not very scientifically advanced before 1800. There was always some wise woman or man providing some kind of care. Monasteries and nunneries often built and ran hospitals. Bacteria were not known and epidemic diseases went through the populations at fire speed and killed millions before each epidemic ebbed out. Yet, the "Eighth Pillar" was met to the best ability of society.

(282) **Trade:** Trade became more and more important as agriculture grew and the technique for farming improved. Deep plowing started, as well as rotating crop farming. The farmers and their wives found it more practical to sell extra farm produce and buy what they earlier had made by hand at home. Farmers' markets became major business centers for a multitude of products.

(283) The range of a horse and buggy limited trade on land, but trade across the sea increased. Ships could take larger loads longer distances even if only sailing ships were available. The robber routes that the Vikings and the explorers had opened became trade routes. Medieval times improved the quality of life for many people despite mainly local trade and the many difficulties of sea trade.

(284) Trade people and clever artisans were in demand and slowly replaced some free farmers for influence. In major shipping cities around the Baltic, in Netherlands, England and Italy guilds were formed, became rich and independent, and asked for participation in city government, even challenging the old king/church aristocracy. The trade people built larger dwellings when their resources allowed and contributed to the defense of their cities. The "Ninth Pillar" was met to the ability of the time, but was hampered by tolls and taxes.

# China

(285) China's national history, like the early societies of Mesopotamia, Egypt, Greece, and Rome, was formed by its geography. The Pacific Ocean formed the national border to the east,

the Himalayan Mountains to the south, and large areas of deserts to the west. China was open on the north. Here the Chinese built its large wall to keep out invaders.

(286) China's history started some 4000 years ago and began similarly to other primitive agricultural societies in an agriculturally suitable river valley—the earliest, in the valley of the Yellow River in the North of China. Many small city-states ruled by a local king were first formed. Eventually most were subdued and dominated by one major king (emperor). Like in all the early societies, a generic king considered himself a God or earthly representative of the all-powerful Creator/God. Once the position as king was achieved, usually by war, his son inherited it.

(287) An Emperor, Son of Heaven, ruled the country with absolute power derived from his connection to the heaven. Food for the people depended on the weather. The Emperor was the one who would represent his people in an offering for rain or whatever the crop needed. Appeal for good weather was the most important work for the Emperor. If the harvest were not adequate, people would starve.

(288) A dynasty king buttressed by a religious support organization kept China in the usual Sumerian State form. Different family dynasties ruled China until 1912, when China became a republic.

(289) Before 1800, trade in China was mainly local. Worldwide trade started to reach China in early 1800. China did not have any professional experience in world trade. Europeans and Americans filled China's need. China felt cheated and started uprisings against foreigners. These were crushed. English and French troops looted Peking after one uprising in 1860 that led to even stricter control of China's international trade. Foreigners like England, Russia/Soviet Union, the U.S., France, Japan, Germany, Belgium, and Sweden were now competing for special trade contracts. Eventually the foreigners, under U.S. leadership, decided to make China an even playground for all of them. England continued to collect the customs.

(290) The country was essentially a power vacuum. A race between different powers for the occupation of different parts of China started. France declared its interest to be in Vietnam and the Mekong delta.

England received a 99-year lease for Hong Kong and free control of Burma. Japan was the most aggressive and actually invaded Korea and Manchuria. Japan's interest collided with Russian/Soviet Union interest in North China. This led to a war between Japan and Russia/Soviet Union in 1904. President Theodore Roosevelt negotiated peace 1905: Japan could keep Korea and part of South Manchuria, while Russia/Soviet Union kept part of North Manchuria.

(291) The Chinese people questioned whether the Emperor-system was outdated. A parliament transferred the government to a people's representative Assembly in 1912.

(292) The treaty of Versailles after WW I confirmed Japan's holdings of North China. This awoke a lot of nationalistic resentments. A young physician Sun Yat-sen, who had been part of the republican movement sought help from Soviet Russia/Soviet Union. The Soviet Union assigned Michael Borodin to help organize a nationalistic, communistic organization, Kuomintang, to free the country. Sun, glorified as a national hero, died in 1925. The Kuomintang movement continued, but eventually split up into one nationalistic branch led by Chiang Kai-shek and one international, communistic branch led by Mao Tse-tung.

(293) In 1937, Japan declared that China's mainland was their preserve and went on to occupy part of it. Japan occupied most of China during WW II. Japan attacked Pearl Harbor on December 7, 1941. After WW II, when the U.S. and its allies had defeated Japan, Japan had to give all occupied land back to the restored independent China.

(294) A civil war between the Chiang Kai-shek and the Mao Tse-tung forces re-started and led to victory for the Mao-communists. The nationalists established a government in exile on the Island of Formosa (Taiwan). Today, the Communist regime of China claims that Formosa belongs to continental China by its geography, while the U.S. is defending the right of the people of Taiwan for self-determination.

(295) The Communist government of China is based on a principle called "centralized democracy." The people's higher congress is elected

by and responsible to the lower-level congresses, the "democracy" part of the equation. Members of both congresses are elected for five-year terms. The high level congress elects the Central Committee, which in turn sets policy for all lower organs corresponding to the centralized part. The Central Committee members head the different Administrative Departments and meet semi-annually or when called upon. For the in-between-time, the Central Committee elects the Standing Committee of the Political Bureau. The Chairman of the Communist Party heads the Standing Committee together with several vice-chairpersons and a Secretary General. The principle of unity of power rather than separation of power governs the whole system. This is opposite to the system in the U.S., where power is balanced and checked between three branches—the executive, the legislative and the judicial.

(296) China's national higher-level congress has about 3000 members and may get together every one or two years. It does not have any working committees similar to those in the democratic congress. The national congress is presented a status report of the nation and puts its approval on what is presented. It approves the financial report and the budget and elects the chairman of the party for a four-year term.

(297) One representative from each 50,000 citizens composes the lower level congress in industrialized areas, but only one per 400,000 in farm areas. Minorities, armed forces and Chinese overseas have some allotted deputies. Everybody above age 18 can vote, provided they are not insane or deprived of the vote by law. This excludes voting rights for anybody who has officially expressed criticism with the system or has been branded a counter-revolutionary.

(298) The Communist Party controls the government by having all-important positions filled from within the party. All constitutional acts are submitted to the central committee before submitted for legislation. All media of mass communications as well as cultural and educational institutions have to stimulate mass support for the system as in a Sumerian type government. Jurisdictional debate is not allowed. Each village has a people's court, which is elected by the local

congress and has to report on any counter-revolutionary talk. The power of the people's court supersedes that of the local government and is enforced by a local militia and the local garrison of the army.

(299) China has during the last ten years gone through a slow evolution towards a freer government. Where it stands relative to a balance of administrative powers has to be left for the people of China themselves to analyze.

(300) China was estimated to have 1338 million people in 2012 with less than 56% in agriculture. The GNP was $6500 billion, second largest in the world next to the U.S., with the GNP/citizen estimated at $5,400. It is interesting to notice that the low, state controlled per capita income of a dogmatic, one party Communist country threatens the work for millions of workers in countries where salaries are negotiated by free labor unions. Defense costs were officially 2.1% and foreign debt 25% of GNP. China has in recent years recognized international contract agreements and has since then had a significant increase in international investments. China was awarded the Summer Olympic Games in 2008.

# Japan

(301) Japan's history has also been formed by its geography. It consists of four main islands, from south to north named Kyushu, Shikoku, Honshu and Hokkaido. The land area is about 90% of California or 80% of Sweden. The land is by geological terms very young with still active volcanoes and earthquakes. At least 7000 earthquakes are registered each year, some very devastating, as the ones in 1923, 1998 and 2011. The climate is temperate and rainfall dependable, making it a delightful area to live in. The islands are far out in the Pacific.

(302) The Pacific Ocean is a dangerous neighbor, for a typhoon hits approximately once a year. To reach the islands from the mainland was in early times a major and risky undertaking. This left the islands fairly isolated until about 1500 years ago. A horse-mounted warrior tribe from the mainland landed and took possession of the

islands at that time and became the dominant race and aristocracy of the islands. The first King or Emperor was Jimmu Tenno. He was, according to tradition, a grandson of the Sun Goddess, Amaterasu. The flag of Japan is a sun. This tradition pointed towards a Sumerian State form.

(303) The parental affection resulted politically in a devotion to keeping the Imperial Family in the center of the royal court but outside of power struggles. The Emperor family-line is uninterrupted as a figurehead from the very first emperor 1500 years ago until present time. The family still retains a sword, a jewel, and a mirror from the original Emperor. Different influential family dynasties similar to those of China executed political power. Like the rest of the world, families close to the court would fight for control of land and people. This lasted for 700 years. The first families fighting for power for a long time were Taira and Miramoto. Shoguns were leading armies of samurais, professional warriors.

(304) Two invasion attempts by the Chinese, in 1274 and 1281, led by Kublai Khan were unsuccessful. The first Europeans, the Portuguese, arrived in 1542. Many Catholic missionaries arrived, the first being Xavier, one of the five co-founders of the Jesuit Order. A Dutch sailing ship arrived with an Englishman, Will Adams. The shogun liked Will. Will told the shogun that the Jesuits were the fore-troops of real troops to invade the country. The shogun got suspicious and had the Catholics expelled or crucified. Finally, all Europeans were forbidden to enter the country.

(305) Self-imposed isolation lasted until 1853, when Captain Perry arrived with several naval ships from the U.S. and demanded access as part of the recent interest in Asian trade. When Japan became aware that the world outside had passed them by, it eagerly set out to catch up and in the 1930s it was ready to play politics on the world scene. This was described in detail in the China chapter.

(306) After WW II, Japan lost 52% of its pre-war land, 80% of its shipping, and 30% of its industrial capacity from two atomic bombs and many conventional bomb attacks. During the occupation by the U.S. military, Japan was given a Parliamentary Constitution similar

to the constitutional monarchies in Europe. The Emperor remained a figurehead. The Parliament consists of two chambers. The Upper House has 252 members elected for six years by a combination of personal and party elections. Half of its members are up for election every three years. The Lower House has 500 members, elected for four years, with 300 in personal elections and the rest in party elections. The Prime Minster is elected from the Lower House and selects his ministers to his Council of Ministers. None of them can be from the military. The system does not exclude women, but no woman has served in its Council of Ministers.

(307) The Liberal Democratic Party has had the majority for the past 50 post-war years. The long time in power of one party has led to a marked independence of state bureaucracy. Industry and state administration has also had a close relationship. Such a policy favored the forming of cartels in manufacturing, distribution, and employment. Big manufacturers and the state enterprises promised lifetime employment that led to inflation of prices to the detriment of consumers. Japan is still the third largest economy in the world. Japan had an estimated population in 2002 of 127 million with 2% in agriculture and fishing. In 2002, the GNP was estimated at $3550 billion and the GNP/citizen was $34,300. The defense cost was 1% and external debt $0.

(308) Japan became the third largest economy in the world in 1989. That year, the victorious Soviet Union of WW II self-collapsed. The second largest economy in the world in 1989 was the other loser in WW II, Germany. Germany was even more bombed out than Japan; all its cities were crumbled brick piles. England and the U.S. also gave Germany a democratic constitution. The economic recovery and the physical rebuilding of Japan and Germany since WW II is amazing and a convincing argument for the value of free democracy as the basic constitution for any country.

**For Further Reading:**

(309) *The Far East, A Modern History* by Nathaniel Peffer, University of Michigan Press, ISBN 58-62522.

# Early Americas

(310) Religion is generically a belief system based on knowledge. Religious philosophers, prophets or religious administrators have formulated different religions according to their best possible knowledge of the time and besides serving their own political agenda. Religious procedures can therefore take the most bizarre expressions.

(311) One of the most bizarre expressions in history is that of the Aztec religion. The Aztec community was a warrior culture living off slaves and tributes from surrounding vassal states similar to the Muslim customs and modern dogmatic states. Soldiers would be admitted to heaven if they died in battle for their "holy" purpose. Priests of the Aztecs taught that the success of its people in this pursuit was relative to the amount of human hearts and blood that was offered to the gods. One of their gods was the Sun. Each evening the Sun got tired and the Night took over. In order for the Sun to recover from fatigue and return each day, the Sun needed food of human hearts and blood. The Aztecs built the temples on top of tall pyramids in order to have the temples as close to the Sun as possible.

(312) In 1490, when the temple of Huitzilopochtli, the war god, was consecrated, 20,000 (possibly 80,000) slaves or prisoners were sacrificed in four days, a maximum of 17 seconds for each sacrifice. Each offer would yield about a gallon of blood. The event would thus provide the god with 20,000 hearts and 20,000 gallons (80 tons) of blood. As a religious ceremony this, if true, is as ridiculous as witch burning, but in the history of religions nothing matches this macabre mass killing.

(313) All through history, religious leaders, like those of Islam and Christianity, during their early military missionary expansion periods promised a life in heaven for the warriors who died for their

religious purpose. **This kind of missionary work by the sword has nothing to do with religion and can best be likened to turf wars of street gangs.**

(314) Every religion has to be judged according to the knowledge of the people at that particular time. The perception of most religions has changed as people's knowledge has improved.

(315) The Indian states in the Americas were all of the Sumerian type with a king ruling from an anointed position and supported by the religious administration. They all collapsed like a house of cards when the Spaniards arrived with guns.

(316) Bullets do not care if they hit high or low culture, important or unimportant persons. Machiavelli's point is still true: **Every successful country needs a strong defense, the "Sixth Pillar." History has shown that a society that has accumulated something desirable but appears defenseless will, sooner or later, be subject to invasion.** This happened to all the early Sumerian states in Mesopotamia. It happened to Egypt, Greece, Rome, Baghdad, Constantinople; it happened to the early states of Africa, India, China, and America, all throughout history. Culture is not enough; guns speak their own language and have their own agenda for dominance.

## France

(317) The Frenchman Charles Montesquieu went to England to study its constitution. His book, *L'Esprit des Lois* (*The Spirit of Laws*), was published in 1748. The publication became a historical event. He admired the English constitutional system and had become familiar with John Locke's philosophical writings. **Montesquieu drew the conclusion that power in government had to be met by some matching power; otherwise, as history shows, it would always be abused.**

(318) Both John Locke and Charles Montesquieu wrote their work on the basis of historical and theoretical analysis with only the People's Rights in mind. Neither of them had any political ambitions.

(319) When a political party in power writes a constitution, the party tends to change the constitution to perpetuate its own interest and eliminate or hurt the opposition. Any constitutional change proposed by the regime in power should be looked at with suspicion.

(320) **Forever true, like an axiom of politics, is the observation by the historian Lord Acton: "Power tends to corrupt, and absolute power corrupts absolutely."**

(321) **Montesquieu divided Power of a Regime into an Executive, a Legislative, and a Judicial branch and made these branches totally independent from each other.**

(322) England had restrained its royal power with its Magna Carta in 1215 and had its revolution of the people in 1688. The USA had its revolution in 1776 and France had its in 1789; an All Mighty God-Anointed King or somebody to whom he delegated power had ruled France until 1789. When the bottled-up people's movement finally started in France, it broke out with unrestrained power.

(323) In the beginning, people had ambitions to institute a Montesquieu constitution but were sidetracked by different demagogic leaders. In a very short time, France went through numerous different constitutional designs. They all clearly demonstrated that unchecked power leads to abuse. It is illustrated in the lively history of France's long and winding conversion into a democracy.

(324) King Louis XIV was a minor when the old King Louis XIII died in 1643. Louis XIII had never been interested in running the country and had delegated that work to two church cardinals, first Richelieu and later Mazarin. Mazarin died when the king was 24 years old. The church administrators asked the young king: "To whom shall we report to now?" "To me," answered Louis XIV. Louis instituted a parallel administrative organization that reported directly to him both for the army and the bureaucracy. Very soon Louis XIV had total control of the country.

(325) Louis controlled the taxes, decided their size and what to spend them on. With the money, he built the largest land army in Europe. Like any Sumerian type king, he attacked his neighbors and collected more booty and taxes. The king stayed in his big palace

outside Paris, Versailles, for much of his 72-year reign. The court supporting the king at his palace was enormous with some 500 persons preparing his meals. It was theater in everything: eating, getting up in the morning, or going to bed at night. The court stood around and admired him. The similarity to the courts of the Aztec kings was striking. In history, Louis XIV has also been called the Sun-King. Everybody flattered the king, nobody dared to criticize him, and to be one of the many mistresses to the king was to have honor, money and power. The ruler of this Sumerian type state was sublime.

(326) Voltaire, one of France's most admired writers, spent three years, 1726-1729, in England. There he had his first encounter with democratic freedom and free speech. **Voltaire had the French people smell some of the English freedom by writing: "Truth has not the name of a political party." "I do not agree with what you say, but I will defend to death your right to say it." These were cornerstone thoughts of democracy for which Voltaire was banned from France.** He settled just outside the border and fed the country challenging thoughts of democracy. Voltaire died in 1778. His body was brought back to Paris after the 1789 revolution and was placed in Parthenon, the resting place for France's heroes.

(327) France in the late 1700s had about 26 million farmers, merchants and artisans. They paid for the expenses of the court and the church with their taxes. Most of the court consisted of, besides the king and his family, 400,000 noblemen and their families. They all had big estates, free from taxation. The church owned a third of the cultivated land and was also free from taxes. The state budget had a deficit of about 100 million francs each year. The king tried various taxes He taxed salt and corn and made people more and more angry. Finally, the people refused to pay more taxes.

(328) The National Assembly had to be called and met for the first time in 125 years in May 1789. The king, Louis XVI, heard a lot of dissatisfaction and tried to disassemble it. On July 14, the public stormed the Paris prison, the Bastille. July 14 became France's

National Independence Day. In August, a new constitution was made into law. The first National Assembly had one Chamber.

(329) A preamble confirmed the natural and "imprescriptible" right of every citizen to liberty, equality, property, and security. The constitution abolished serfdom, monopolies, noble privileges, and dues to the church. The constitution created equal taxation and equal civil and military promotion (earlier reserved for the nobles), and made court representation free.

(330) The "Nine Pillars" had been neglected under the past Sumerian system. Constitutional changes had to be introduced to meet them. The liberty and security demands addressed free communication and freedom to organize for community support, the "Fifth and Sixth Pillars." The demand for equality rights addressed the need for community support with equal rights in courts and at the workplaces, the "Sixth Pillar." The demand for property rights secured the dwelling, the "Second Pillar," as did the abolishment of serfdom. The abolishment of monopolies met the demand for free trade, the "Ninth Pillar." The right to civil and military promotions, as well as free courts, met the demand for fair and equal community support, the "Sixth Pillar." Freedom from church taxes was an introduction to free religion, the "Seventh Pillar." Representatives controlling taxation was also a way of securing family life and limiting the king's power. Taxes are the citizens' earned money, donated to the state for the citizens' common need as established in a public referendum. **The tribal security of the cave had evolved into an economic as well as a legal security for the individual and his dwelling.**

(331) The King's veto power was limited and church property was nationalized. The Pope, defending his property, did not support the new constitution. Clergy was divided between those who supported the constitution and those who supported the Pope. In June of the following year, Axel Fersen, a Swedish nobleman, adventurer and old lover to the queen, now back in Paris after having served as an officer in Washington's army, helped the king, queen and their two children to escape. They were all caught and returned to Paris as prisoners.

(332) Louis XVI was freed in September, after he promised to follow an improved second constitution. The September Constitution divided the country into new administrative units: departments, districts, cantons, and communes. It also outlined the power for the king and his ministers and for the National Assembly. The king could not dissolve the Assembly, had no veto power, and could not declare war. Voting rights were limited to adult males who owned property—about 75% of the male population.

(333) Two politically competitive groups formed the new National Assembly: one right wing (Girodins) and one left wing (Jacobins). **The term "Right" in history writings from now on implies more individual responsibility; the term "Left" implies the individual leaving the responsibility for his or her welfare to the government.**

(334) The Rightists had the majority in the beginning. The country was restless and bankrupt. The king and the Rightists thought that a war might help to unite the country and also help the finances with some booty and taxes. Officially, the war would spread the freedom message of the revolution to the rest of Europe. Belgium, part of the militarily weak Austrian Empire, was attacked. The war did not go as expected. The French soldiers shot their own aristocratic officers and many soldiers and officers deserted.

(335) The disastrous Belgian (Austrian) War unleashed demonstrations by the Leftists in Paris. The king's palace was attacked in August 1792. Paris itself was organized into communes. The Paris communes selected an Executive Commune Committee that took over the power from the National Assembly. The leaders were Danton and Robespierre, both Leftists. The Commune executed 1200 Catholic priests, royalists, and aristocrats together with other prisoners, who happened to be in the prison at the time.

(336) Next on the Paris Commune's agenda was how to deal with Louis XVI. With a majority of one vote in the Assembly, he was guillotined on January 21, 1793; the queen was executed the following October. The two children went to prison to be turned into commoners by the prison guards.

(337) The Leftists arrested 29 leaders of the Rightists in June of the same year. The Leftist leaders wrote a new constitution; written by those in power, it inevitably led to dictatorship. Under the leadership of Danton and Robespierre, a "law of suspects" was started. This court was the sectarian correspondence to the Inquisition court. People were brought into court with both judges and jurors paid by the dictatorial regime and had to prove that they believed in the present political policy. This court had 11,500 people guillotined in ten months.

(338) Finally, Danton and Robespierre were themselves executed by their own party. Within the next two years, the constitution shifted back and forth three times between Rightists and Leftists, each time executing each other. Food shortage became critical with everybody fighting and no one attending the farms.

(339) The society was essentially lawless with no security and no respect for any of the "Nine Pillars": there was lack of food, insecure dwellings, lack of community support in the courts, and lack of freedom to communicate. Soldiers might walk into a home, arrest you and accuse you in a court that could not be trusted for a fair trial. No one dared to talk and express an opinion. Mass media was controlled. Anything you said to anybody could be held against you and lead to arrest. In courts, you were assumed guilty and had to prove your innocence instead of vice versa.

(340) In October 1795, a new constitution went into effect. It lasted from November 1795 to November 1799. The constitution had an Executive Branch of five Directors, an Assembly consisting of two chambers, a Financial Branch, and a Judicial Branch, each branch independent of each other. This constitution had some of the design for division of power.

(341) The Directory re-started the war with Belgium. This time it led to involvement by Austria and eventually England, Germany, Italy, Poland, Russia/Soviet Union, Spain, and Turkey. The war also reached the colonies of the different European countries. England blocked any trade with France and occupied many of France's colonies. In fact, the French Revolutionary War was a world war

with France facing the world just like Germany would do twice, 120 and 140 years later.

(342) The most successful French officer was Napoleon. After victories over Italian and Austrian armies, he started to dictate a peace agreement without consulting the Directors in Paris. Napoleon set up his headquarters in Milan. From there, he collected money to supply two armies and sent back art booty to Paris for the establishment of the Louvre National Museum. Napoleon was 28 years old at the time.

(343) In September 1797, there was another regime crisis between Leftists and Rightists in Paris. Napoleon sent back a list of Directors he would like to see in place. A coup accomplished a New Leftist dictatorship. About 1100 Rightists were shot and thousands sent to prison. Papers were confiscated. The Paris City Police took over the power. The Assembly was nullified.

(344) In November 1799, there was yet another regime crisis with a new constitution. Three Consuls replaced the five Directors: Sieyes, Ducos, and Napoleon, one of which was to be a figurehead or First Consul. Napoleon became the First Consul.

(345) In December 1799, Napoleon changed his work description from passive to active First Consul and became the dictator of France.

(346) After only ten years, the people had lost the control of their destiny. People-power was back to where it had started before 1789. All blood spilled on the way had been in vain. With a Sumerian type dictator in power and access to soldiers by conscript, more blood than ever would be spilled over the whole world.

(347) The executive power rested with the First Consul. He could, if he liked, consult with his second and third consuls. The dictatorship was based on universal suffrage. However, Napoleon himself selected the officials for the bigger cities and the central departments.

(348) Legislation started in Napoleon's council, was sent to the Assembly for a vote and became law in the Senate. This proved to be too slow a process for Napoleon. He soon went directly to the Senate and directed the political decisions as he used to give orders in the army—by decrees. The council consisted of 29 members. Napoleon listened to the committee and made his decision.

(349) The law in France was of the Roman Justinian type. This meant a central authority wrote it. It had not been updated since Louis XIV and many laws had been added by the revolution. Thus, Napoleon initiated a committee to write a total revision. This Napoleonic code became the model for many European countries that did not have the English Jury system.

(350) The police maintained strong power and used espionage to find out about any dissenting movements. The press was censured. Theaters and arts had to honor the regime to secure Napoleon's position. In the presence of the Pope, Napoleon crowned himself as emperor of France on December 2, 1800. Napoleon and the Pope disagreed regarding to whom the clergy should report and also who owned the church property in all conquered countries. Napoleon did not allow negotiation on this point. The Pope excommunicated Napoleon. Like Charles VIII of France had done in 1494, Napoleon ordered the Papal State occupied. This meant that the Pope and the Catholic Church were forced to follow Napoleon's agenda. The Sumerian State Form was back, complete and ready to go to war.

(351) Napoleon as dictator violated the "Nine Pillars" as much as the previous dictatorial kings and the Leftist and Rightist regimes. Security for dwellings was not improved despite the new laws because censured mass media and spies with an intrusive police power restricted the freedom of the society. Religion was placed under government control. The people's representation was a sham. Napoleon bypassed the people's Assembly and selected the highest bureaucrats himself. Papers and theaters were directed to glorify Napoleon. **In fact, Napoleon was the first modern leader to institute a modern mass media support. It was made possible by large paper presses and by the fact that more people could read.**

(352) In 1802 a peace agreement was signed with England in Amiens. France sold the Louisiana Territory to the USA. The sale of Louisiana gave Napoleon fresh money. He restarted the war the following spring. The only remaining major enemy in Europe was England, which blockaded the sea trade for France. Napoleon built a fleet and prepared to invade England. These plans were spoiled

when Admiral Nelson won the sea battle at Trafalgar. The land battles were more successful. Napoleon subdued Austria twice and married the emperor's daughter, Marie Louise. He became part of the 1700 years old Hapsburg dynasty when a son was born in 1811. The child, Napoleon II, was made King of Rome.

(353) Napoleon could now draw taxes and conscript soldiers from all of Western Europe except England, Russia/Soviet Union, and Sweden. England continued to block France from any cross-Atlantic trade. Napoleon countered by blocking England from any continental trade.

(354) The world, as Napoleon saw it, was all his except for England, Sweden, and Russia/Soviet Union. Napoleon made a deal with Russia/Soviet Union and Denmark to split Sweden between these states and France. Russia/Soviet Union would get Finland, Denmark southern Sweden, and France the Swedish provinces in northern Germany. Napoleon suddenly changed his alliance with Russia/Soviet Union and announced he would take the responsibility to free Poland and Europe from the barbarian invasion from the east. Poland had been divided between its neighbors three times in the past—the last time in 1795. Napoleon assembled a Grand Army of 600,000 men, one-third Frenchmen. The army entered Russia/Soviet Union the last week in June 1812 and reached Moscow in September. The town was burning and empty of food. The Czar Alexander refused to negotiate. Napoleon waited for five weeks, but had to return before the winter arrived. Winter came early and during the long march back, most of the Grand Army succumbed. Only 100,000 men made it back to France.

(355) The occupied areas of Germany and Austria became restless in the summer after Napoleon had lost his army in Russia/Soviet Union. Napoleon entered the Swedish provinces in Germany. This forced Sweden to join his enemies. A combined force of Russia/Soviet Union, Germany (Prussia), Austria, and Sweden met Napoleon at Leipzig in October 1813. A second Grand French army was totally defeated.

(356) After the battle, Sweden, at the encouragement of England, attacked Napoleon's allied Denmark and convinced Norway to join Sweden in a union. This was the last time a Swedish Army took part in any war. The union with Norway was peacefully dissolved in 1905.

(357) Napoleon abdicated in March 1814. He was exiled to the Mediterranean Island of Elba between his birthplace Corsica and Italy. He could consider Elba as his own country and was given 700 soldiers as a personal guard. Louis XVIII, a brother to Louis XVI, was crowned as a constitutional monarch of France in June.

(358) Napoleon returned to France from Elba in March 1815. He called for his old veterans and volunteers to join him to beat all "French enemies." Many Frenchmen joined him but Napoleon was again defeated at Waterloo by a combined English, German, and Dutch-Belgian army.

(359) Napoleon had to abdicate for the second time. He was now transported to the Island of St. Helena in the Atlantic, West of Angola, in South Africa. Napoleon died on May 5, 1821, only 51 years old. The cause of death was cancer of the stomach. Napoleon's son died from tuberculosis in Vienna. When Hitler occupied Vienna, he had the son's heart sent to Paris.

(360) **One wonders how it could happen that people of a people's revolution could, after only ten years, give up all independence and return to the old Sumerian type of government and also follow its leader to their own death**. At the beginning, no state was threatening France. Rather, it was the success of Napoleon as a general that got everybody exited. Each French soldier showed his physical dominance over his neighbors. Possibly it is a bewildering mass psychosis in the wake of a successful hero, similar to the hooligan expressions at some sporting events. Possibly soldiers looked forward to the three days of free robbing that soldiers were allowed after a victorious occupation. The "Nine Pillars" has no answer.

(361) In 1815, Louis XVIII came back from England as king of France for the second time. A new constitution was formulated, similar to the one in England: a two-chamber parliamentary system with a constitutional monarchy. After the Rightist regime got the

power, it blamed the Leftists for the revolution and the war, and killed its leaders. The constitution was changed again favoring the Rightists. Louis died in 1824. Charles X, Louis' brother, became king. Clergy took over all education and the Jesuits returned. Those who lost their property during the revolution were compensated with one billion francs. The press became strictly controlled. Only landowners could vote.

(362) An adulterated "Nine Pillars" with limited personal freedom and manipulated mass media backed by a state-regulated religion had returned the Sumerian state.

(363) Still another revolution started on July 26, 1830. Charles X abdicated in favor of a family member Louis Phillipe. A new constitution was again written. The king and the schools became separated from the church. Press censorship was abolished. However, in 1834 the right to meet in associations was restricted and press censorship was reinstated. Another revolution, a "Second Republic," started in 1848 and a new constitution was written.

(364) Again, the press became restricted. **Note how the press always is restricted when leaders have their own agenda, and not the people's interest in mind.** As noted before, constitutional changes initiated by leaders in power should always be looked at with suspicion and not be instituted easily.

(365) The "Second Republic" returned to the 1789 constitution. It had one Chamber. A relative to Napoleon I, Louis Napoleon, was in the running for the presidency. For popular appeal he referred to his relationship and namesake Napoleon I. With modern press propaganda he made his uncle Napoleon into a national hero. The state brought Napoleon I back in 1840 and built him an impressive gravesite in Paris, at the Chapel of the Invalides. To see the grave, one has to bow one's head because the sarcophagus stands below the public balconies.

(366) Louis Napoleon III made a successful coup on December 2, 1851, the 51st anniversary of the crowning of Napoleon as emperor. Napoleon III made himself the emperor. The return to "Empire" began with a new constitution. Press became restricted. General

elections were to be held only every six years and were performed with lots of gerrymandering (redrawing of voting areas) to favor certain interests. The Lower House was in session only for three months of the year and was not allowed to choose its chairperson. It could not publish its debates. Opponents went into exile or did not dare to speak.

(367) The "Fifth, Sixth, and Seventh Pillars" were again restricted with manipulated press and limitation of personal freedom.

(368) On July 19, 1870, the Emperor would not accept a German prince as king of Spain. France feeling surrounded by German interests was the official reason. Consequently, France declared war on Prussia, the largest of the many member-states of Germany. Prussia defeated France in a quick war in August. The Emperor and Empress, as usually, fled to England. France gave up Alsace and Lorraine. Germany, led by Prussia, was for the first time declared one political unit, the nation of Germany.

(369) A "Third Republic" of France was formed in a revolution in 1870. As usual, the Pope and the State fought over education. In 1880, all primary education became free, secular, and compulsory. Jesuits were banned from public education.

(370) France wrote a new constitution in 1875. It had two chambers with equal legislative power, but monetary decisions had to originate in the Lower House. A President was elected for seven years by a joint session of the two Houses. In the next 70 years, until 1940, France had 14 presidents and 99 regimes. Ministers were collectively responsible to the Lower House. The Council of Ministers became weak because it consisted of combinations of interests in the Lower House. If the Ministry lost a confidence vote, it had to be replaced. There was no division of power between the executive and legislative branches. The president was elected from the parties in the legislative body and not directly from the people, not separating the legislative from the executive branch.

(371) In early 1900, international powers in Europe were divided into two balanced power camps: Germany, Austria-Hungary, and

Italy in one, and England, France, and Russia/Soviet Union in the other.

(372) A Serbian Nationalist shot the heir apparent of Austria during his visit to Serbia in June 1914. Thus, Austria-Hungary, a Sumerian State with a dynasty ruler supported by its church, declared war on Bosnia. This led Russia/Soviet Union, another Sumerian State, to mobilize, which led Germany, still another Sumerian State, to declare war on Russia/Soviet Union and France. Germany invaded Belgium the next day. This led England, in a defensive move, to enter the war on France's side. Ships from the USA were torpedoed all the time. The public in the USA was stirred and the USA entered the war in 1917 on the English, French, and Russian/Soviet Union side. Russia/Soviet Union collapsed in 1917 before the war was over and became involved in a civil war with its communist revolution. Germany gave up when its troops on the western front were dying like flies from the 1918 flu and its allies Austria-Hungary, Bulgaria and Turkey were defeated. Peace was signed on November 11, 1918. Alsace and Lorraine were returned to France.

(373) Labor organizations in France started to have influence in politics from 1879. Trade unions were legalized in 1884. The General Confederation of Labour (French: Confédération Générale du Travail or CGT) was formed in 1895 and became the national representation of organized labor. The CGT was in 1919 split with one section, the Confédération Générale du Travail Unitaire (CGTU), associated with the International Communist Organization under Soviet sponsorship. In 1937, a communist revolutionary coup was detected and its leaders arrested.

(374) Social legislation marked the time up to WW II all over Europe. In France, the new laws led to old age pension, unemployment insurance, 40-hour work weeks, graded income tax, nationalization of defense industries, recognition of negotiated labor contracts, and union representatives in factories to work with management.

(375) The social improvements addressed and met several of the "Nine Pillars." The assurance of income despite unemployment met the need for secure food and dwelling in hard times. The 40-hour

working week and secure income allowed for quality family time and extra money to beautify life and dwellings. The freedom to assemble and form unions was an expression of personal freedom and community support. **The security of the cave life had evolved into a national social support program for the individual and his family.**

(376) The French National Bank was set under political control. France left the gold standard and started to print paper money, which led to inflation in the thirties. The multitude of regimes in France during this time made France rather ineffective in foreign politics. Hitler in Germany used the occasion to test his expansion policy and could do so rather unchecked.

(377) On September 1, 1939, Germany invaded Poland. England and France declared war on Germany the same day according to a reciprocal defense act. Russia/Soviet Union joined Germany at the end of the three-week war and helped itself to the spoils of Poland. (It was actually the fourth time Russia/Soviet Union took part in a division of Poland. The previous divisions were in 1772, 1793 and 1795 while Poland had an uncompromising veto in its constitution.)

(378) On May 10, 1940, Germany invaded France by passing through and occupying Holland, Belgium, and Luxembourg. France was conquered in a three-week blitz war and armistice was signed on June 22 in the same railway carriage that Germany had signed its defeat in 1918. Alsace and Lorraine were returned to Germany. Northwestern France was occupied and the rest assigned to a puppet regime placed in Vichy with retired war hero from WW I, General Petain, as president. Petain maintained the constitution of 1875.

(379) Allied troops invaded France under leadership of General Eisenhower on June 6, 1944, D-Day. By August, English and American troops stood outside Paris. General Eisenhower had seen about 50,000 young American men killed in the battle on the way to Paris. On August 24, before the allied troops who had climbed the cliffs of Normandy were scheduled to enter Paris, De Gaulle, a self-declared leader of a provisional government, drove to Paris and received the jubilation of the people for himself.

(380) The Vichy government was declared not having ever represented France. General Petain was exiled to an island in the Atlantic. With De Gaulle as president, the Third Republic had continued uninterrupted. De Gaulle reinitiated the old Napoleon tradition of an anti-Anglican policy and propaganda.

(381) The American and English soldiers who died on French ground in the liberation of France had still not died in vain. Democracy was saved for most of Western Europe and most of Europe was and is not smitten by any affinity to Napoleon.

(382) A "Fourth Republic" was established in October 1946 and a new constitution accepted. **Women gained voting rights.** The ministry was still subject to dismissal if not formed on a singular majority in the Lower House. Fifteen different parties constituted the Lower House. Since the communists were the most disciplined party, much of the time was spent trying to keep them out of power. The communists were financed by and took many of their instructions from Commintern in Moscow, the organization started by Lenin in 1919 to spread Soviet communism internationally. **Ho Chi Minh from Vietnam and Pol Pot from Cambodia were schooled in Paris in the French Communist Party.** Supported by Commintern, they went home and launched the communist revolution of their home countries. Another communist leader in Paris was a previous member of the Nazi Vichy regime, Francois Mitterrand. Now a communist, Mitterrand was against the Marshall Plan and anything American. English expressions or influences were censored as during the Napoleon time; a neo-Napoleon movement was started.

(383) The Marshall Plan saved the European post-war economy and helped the rest of Europe and even the USA to recover from the war effort.

(384) France had 25 different governments from September 1944 to 1958.

(385) After WW II, Colonial areas wanted to become independent from European dominance. France tried to keep its dominance in Vietnam and Algiers with military force. The 25 different governments of post-war France were incapable of keeping a logical line in its

policy. De Gaulle was called on to formulate a new constitution. He met with the many party leaders, except with the communists, to help him.

(386) A new constitution for the "Fifth Republic" was approved in 1958. De Gaulle became president. The Constitution had a Senate and a Lower House. A "separation of powers" was to be accomplished with "law making" at the Lower House and "rule making" at the ministry level. The Ministry was responsible to the Lower House, thereby retaining people's power. A higher percent majority for dismissal assured the stay of the Ministry. The executive and legislative branches were not separated. The president could simply dissolve the Lower House. The neo-Napoleonic attitude continued. Anything American was discredited in the state supported mass media. De Gaulle went to the French speaking Quebec and encouraged its independence from the rest of Canada. England was excluded from the EU movement. De Gaulle was largely perceived as arrogant and authoritarian even in France. Demonstrations against him broke out in May 1968. Algiers became free. The USA inherited the problem in Vietnam. De Gaulle lost a referendum and retired the next year.

(387) A new kind of press reporting evolved in Paris shortly after WW II as very excellently described by a Swedish journalist stationed in Paris at the time, Knut Ståhlberg. He called it "opinion-journalism." The classical journalism would report events and save opinions for the publisher's commentary articles. Now the journalists themselves would express opinions on what was reported. Reporting became itself opinion forming. (Knut Ståhlberg: *Storklockan in Paris*. Norstedts Förlag, Stockholm, 1995 ISBN 91-1-949282-0).

(388) **Journalists belonging to a particular political party became market makers for specific political ideas.** The parties in power quickly took notice. News to be reported and commented on was selected, so that the parties' own policy, both its national and its international, always was supported. **In some countries like in Sweden, with state supported TV stations, 70% or more of the journalists belong to a given party.**

(389) **The most effective political propaganda machine in history, the state controlled TV channel, was established.**

(390) The French State has monopoly over the radio and TV stations through the Office de Radiodiffusion-Télévision Française (ORTF). The control was originally done in two ways: first by hiring journalists who supported the regime; second by designing the TV frequency so only French receivers with 819-line resolution would receive the signal. This system could not be used for color. Eventually France selected the German PAL system with 625 lines. Radio could not be controlled as effectively. Independent stations opened up just outside the border of France and fed France ideas of democracy just like Voltaire had done. The dominance of state television over people's thoughts and news was and still is prominent in France, as well in the rest of Europe with state supported television stations.

(391) De Gaulle was followed by Pompidou in 1969 and in 1974.

(392) Iran's Islamic revolution was launched from France in 1979.

(393) Francois Mitterrand was elected president in 1981. Not many can match Mitterrand's political career. During the German occupation, he joined the Nazi administration in Vichy. After the war, he was a leader of the Communist Party. The Communist Party took its instructions from Moscow through the Commintern. He blocked any American or English policy effort. When De Gaulle tried to change the constitution so the regime would not change every couple of months, Mitterrand opposed him. He obviously tried to maintain the disorder and thereby advance the very disciplined communists. To get sympathy during the election campaign, he arranged for his car to be shot at while he was hiding in the bushes. The phony ambush was discovered, but Mitterrand still managed to come back to public life. The Socialist Party did not have a nationally known leader. Mitterrand was nationally known, even if mostly for scandals. When he was asked to join the Socialist Party, Mitterrand continued his anti-American propaganda, now as a socialist.

(394) Mitterrand sensed what people hoped for because of the high unemployment. He promised nationalization of all big companies in the next presidential election. He won. As president, he praised de

Gaulle's new constitution that had made the presidency strong. He dissolved the Lower House, won majority also there, and nationalized the big industries.

(395) The purpose of the nationalization of industries was to secure employment. The state business had until then mostly been limited to general services, like mail service and railways. Such employment by the state was perceived as secure because the state had both monopoly and the purse. The thought was that the same security could be extended to large market industries. **The state doing market business led to corruption, inflation, and more unemployment, and did so in all countries that followed the French example.**

(396) The right flank was back in the next election. Jacques Chirac was elected premier minister between 1986-1988, lost his run for presidency in 1988 to Mitterrand, but came back in 1997 and was reelected president in 2002, a position he held until May 2007. Nicolas Sarkozy was elected the nation's new president and according to the official exit poll France was heading for a right-wing revolution.

(397) The French people tested a new form of constitution in 2002, proposed by the party in power. In that election, they elected both the president and the total legislature at the same time, both for five years. The hope is that simultaneous election of the president and all representatives will make the presidency strong and "effective." The changes will certainly pull the executive and the legislative power together, but without much check on each other. The Frenchman Montesquieu, as noted above, warned of such a system already in 1748.

(398) **One may wonder how the world would have looked if France had taken Montesquieu's wisdom to heart at that time, before the French Revolution and before Napoleon. The future will show if this last constitutional change will be final in the political laboratory called France.**

(399) **The changes in the constitution of France will have implications for all of Europe because France is a major part of EU. The other major state within EU is Germany. Neither state has much merit in the history of democracy, but each generation has the**

opportunity for its own history. Talk of a European Constitution is starting at the time this manuscript is written. The big challenge will be if France will *"frenchise"* all the other 24 EU nations or a balance will be allowed.

(400) France was one of six originators of the European Community (EC). The others were Holland, Belgium, Luxembourg, Germany, and Italy. France is also one of the founding members of the European Economic and Monetary Union (EMU). The population of France in 2002 was 65 million, with 1.7% working within farming. The GNP was estimated at U.S. $2,751 billion and GNP/citizen to U.S. $43,000. Defense cost 2.3%, national debt 87% of GNP.

**For Further Reading:**

(401) *France, A Modern History* by Albert Guerard. The University of Michigan Press ISBN 58-62523.

# Russia/Soviet Union

(402) The Russian/Soviet Union history is again a product of its geography. Seven-eighths of the land is as close to the North Pole as Canada. It consists of an enormous plain, stretching from the Baltic to the Pacific but split in two halves by the Urals, a chain of low mountains stretching from north to south, at the most 6000 feet (2000 meters) high and not really hindering movement across the plain. The climate sets the rule of living on the plain. Perma-frost dominates the farthest north with very limited vegetation. South of the perma-frost dominates the arctic tundra. Mostly pine and birch forests cover the land south of the tundra. A belt of fine agricultural land stretches across the land south of the forests. In the southeast, the plain turns into semiarid land with grass. Eventually, this arid land turns into a desert close to China.

(403) The plain is cut into parts by slow moving, large rivers emptying into the Arctic Sea in the north, into the Black Sea and the Caspian Sea in the south, into the Baltic Sea in the west, and into the

Pacific Ocean in the east. Many of these rivers interconnect either naturally or by canals, providing for far-reaching barge shipping in summertime.

(404) Many different tribes roamed this enormous plain reaching across the Asia-European landmass, more than double the size of the USA. Most of them were hunters and the more advanced animal herders with very little interest for borders. Mediterranean influences via the Black Sea divided the agricultural society into a southern and a western part.

(405) The Scandinavian Vikings discovered that it was possible to travel by boat from the Baltic along the Dnieper River to the Black Sea and along the Volga River to the Caspian Sea. The first route led to Constantinople and a second to Baghdad; both cities were rich and of interest for adventurers. The route along the Dnieper was so convenient that the Vikings set up permanent trading centers in the 800s.

(406) A Viking named Rurik founded Novgorod in 862 and is considered the father of Russia/Soviet Union's first dynasty. Kiev along Dnieper eventually grew into Russia/Soviet Union's first major city. The early princes of Kiev were all of Scandinavian descent and had Scandinavian names like Karl or Ole(g). Oleg brought Novgorod and Kiev together under one dynasty.

(407) Kiev, Moscow, Novgorod and other local cities formed a loosely federated first state. Much of the country population lived in area tribes rather than in city-states. Political boundaries on the large Russian/Soviet Union plain were fluid and depended largely on the aggressiveness of the fiefs. Before the year 1000, Oleg and his followers attacked Constantinople six times. Oleg's descendants enlarged the realm until it geographically was second only to the Roman Empire.

(408) Vladimir became the first christened leader in 986. He had all his citizens christened by decree and built the first stone church in Kiev in 996. Vladimir, like Charlemagne, set aside one-tenth of state income for the church. At first, the Patriarch in Constantinople appointed the leaders of the church. The rituals of the church were

that of the Byzantine Church, creating a beautiful atmosphere with choral chanting. Most families had icons at home. Writing was learned from two monks, Cyril and Methodius. Cyril developed the Cyrillic alphabet, which is the basis for the present Russian/Soviet Union alphabet.

(409) A fief or prince had a council of advisors called *Duma*. In time, the Duma developed into nobility called *boyars*. The prince required a service from the boyars. The service tended to become inherited. The city assembly, the Verche, represented the average free man. For the Verche to make a decision required unanimous agreement. This made decision making very difficult. The Verche elected many of its princes until 1400. Most princes were elected from the dominant families. Different cities of the federation in the Kiev State were independent but a common background slowly grew into a sense of nationality. The external threat of invasion occurring in 1200 strengthened this feeling of nationalism.

(410) Many herd-raising Mongolian tribes lived in the area around the Lake Baikal north of Mongolia. These tribes herded horses. In 1206, one of the Mongolian leaders, Genghis Khan, gathered the tribes and with a cavalry of 100,000 invaded and subdued all of China. The Cavalry became the new modern unstoppable weapon.

(411) Strengthened also by Chinese early technology, Genghis Khan decided to conquer the world and almost did. His son, Kublai Khan, created dominance over a larger area than any conqueror in history has ever done. Eventually, the Mongolian Empire included all of China, where they started the Yuan Dynasty, plus Asian and European Russia/Soviet Union, Tibet, Syria, Mesopotamia, Turkey, and parts of Persia. They defeated the Poles and Hungarians and reached the Adriatic Sea across from Rome. The Mongolian Empire set up headquarters for its European Theater in Saray City, 200 miles north of present Volgorad (in USSR Stalingrad) along the Volga River.

(412) The military and the economic principles of the Mongolian Empire were very simple. The Khan only kept a cavalry, which traveled very fast for the time. A modern German strategist would call it blitzkrieg. Both the men on their horses, the horse by its weight,

were weapons. No heavy weapons were yet invented. The cavalry needed no supply lines because they advanced along agricultural areas that provided food and water for both people and horses. Once an area was conquered, they would count how many people survived their attack and ask for as much tax as they thought they could get while still allowing the farmer to survive to produce more. In front of them lay open the whole Euro-Asian plain. The Khan would set up a larger army with the taxes coming in from a conquered area, conquer more land, collect more taxes, build a still larger army, and so on. The Khanate was just a big army supported by taxes from conquered agriculture. Local religions were never a concern.

(413) The Khanate was unique in that it did not do any agricultural work itself, only doing what a farmer might call "taking the cream off the top." The Khan would determine that so much tax should be delivered to them. The Russian/Soviet Union princes had to see that it was done. No one was asked why or for what the taxes were to be used. There was no people representation or possibility for people to assemble and assure their own future.

(414) The Khan had three population counts preformed in Russia/ Soviet Union. The Russian/Soviet Union princes came to Saray and were given a certificate to collect taxes for the Khan. To have such a certificate was popular among the princes because not only could the prince collect tax for the Khan, he could also pocket some money for himself. The princes who were successful would be given a larger area to collect taxes from. One of the best tax collectors was the prince of Moscow. The Moscow prince put more and more area under his influence.

(415) The major Khanate fell apart into smaller independent and quarreling Khanates. Eventually, the Khanates got weaker. Finally, when the prince of Moscow, Ivan III, refused to pay the Khan his portion of the taxes, war broke out. The Khan lost the war at the end of 1400s.

(416) The 38-year-long reign in Moscow of Ivan III began. Ivan put the neighbor city, Novgorod, directly under his rule by dissolving its Verche and Duma. Boyars disloyal to Ivan were sent to people-empty

Siberia, starting a practice later followed by all other rulers of Russia/ Soviet Union.

(417)  Under his rule (1503-33), Ivan III set as his goal the unification of all Russian/Soviet Union-speaking areas. He turned his attention to the old Kiev. His predecessor had already moved the major Patriarch from Kiev to Moscow. To have the head of the Russian/Soviet Union Church reside in Moscow gave Moscow special prestige.

(418)  In 1472, Ivan married a niece of Constantine XI, the last Byzantine Emperor. Constantine XI had died when the Turks stormed Constantinople in 1453. Ivan took the title of Czar, meaning emperor. He claimed that he was the defender and head of the Byzantine Church, Russia/Soviet Union its empire, Moscow its capital, the third Rome. The Sumerian State format of a dynasty king supported by the religious leadership lived on. The family crest of his wife with a two-headed eagle reflected his connection to the Byzantine Emperor. Ivan further attempted to aggrandize himself and traced his bloodline back to the Viking Rurik and through him further to the Roman Emperor Augustus. The two-headed eagle remained the crest for Russia/Soviet Union until the 1917 revolution and is back as the crest for the post-communist Russia/Soviet Union.

(419)  Ivan's 17-year-old grandson became Czar Ivan IV in 1547. He was married the same year to a boyar's daughter named Anastasia Romanoff. In history, Ivan is named "The Terrible" because of his sadistic and paranoid attitudes. Ivan did not trust the Duma and instituted several side colleges to advise him: the "Chosen Council," the "Zemsky Sobor" or "The Assembly of the Land," and the "Oprichniks," a secret police.

(420)  While Anastasia was alive, she had a calming effect on her husband's emotional turmoil, but she died young in 1560, when Ivan was only thirty. At her death Ivan's paranoia culminated. He took sacks of gold with him and walled himself up in the city Alexandrov, outside Moscow. In Alexandrov, he established a kind of monastery with him as the abbot and the group he trusted most, the Oprichniks, as monks. Ivan now called himself Prince of Moscow and appointed another person as Czar of Russia/Soviet Union.

(421) Under Ivan's orders, the Oprichniks stormed the country on black horses, in black clothing and with a dog's head (to bite the enemies of Ivan), and a broom (to sweep away treason) on the saddle. They killed boyars and any others of whom Ivan was afraid of, and confiscated their property. Ivan himself confiscated half of the old cultivated land in the country. Ivan's ultimate motive was to get control of the farmland and control people living on that land. This action gave him financial independence from boyars. Ivan was in complete autocratic power when, after eight years of paranoid terror for thousands, was through.

(422) Sweden and Poland hindered Russian/Soviet Union extension to the west, but land south, east and north were very thinly populated, of diffuse ownership and could easily be claimed. Remnants of the old Khanates gave some resistance to Ivan's forces, but without any natural defenses they were all swallowed up. By 1647, Russia/Soviet Union had claimed all east land all the way to the Pacific Coast north of China. The country had almost tripled in size when Ivan died, at 54 years old, in 1584.

(423) After Ivan IV followed three decades of confusion at the Moscow court with many contenders to the throne. Eventually, descendants of the Romanoff family would rule Russia/Soviet Union for 300 years until the 1917 communist revolution. The first Romanoff Czar, Michael, was elected by the Duma, but future czars were all inherited and ruled as total autocrats. The increase of power of the throne and its court decreased the power of the farmer. Alas, the farmer became a slave, sold as property together with other properties. To secure a Russia/Soviet Union farmer's life, many farmers signed up for a monastery. This left them outside army conscription and any worries for food and roof over their heads. The oldest monastery just north of Moscow, Holy Trinity, had 100,000 monk-workers.

(424) The czar who introduced Russia/Soviet Union into the western world was Peter I. He was only 24 when he took the office of Czar in 1696. In the spring of the following year, Peter took a group of court officers with him to study western technology and warfare.

Together they visited Germany, Holland, and England for a year. Peter brought back with him many artisans and other experts.

(425) Peter declared that advancement at the court should be on merit and not just inherited. This was a first small step towards community support in that all had equal right for advancement within an occupation. Peter saw it from his point of view; he needed an effective, new administration to support himself.

(426) With his new naval knowledge, he attacked the Turks that had blocked off the Black Sea as their private sea. He was driven back but took it as a lesson, built a second fleet and tried it again, this time with success. The victory did not make much difference to the Sultan, but it was noticed in Europe that Russia/Soviet Union now had an effective ruler.

(427) The old king of Sweden had died and was followed by his son, Charles XII, who at only 15 years old had inherited his Sumeric position. The neighbors saw a possibility for added land and taxes. Together they had a population ten times that of Sweden. Denmark, Poland, and Russia/Soviet Union agreed to attack together. Very young, below thirty, and ambitious kings, all with Sumericly held dictatorial powers, led each country; three of them were cousins. Charles XII, the king of Sweden, was 17 when the "Nordic War" broke out in 1700.

(428) Poland at this time was in a strange situation. It had a constitution with a so-called "Librium veto" that required unanimous agreement between all representatives to agree on a proposal or to override a veto. The Parliament could hardly agree on anything. Somebody always had his own agenda, often supported by neighboring states. Eventually, this would lead to the division of Poland between its neighbors and enslavement of its farmers, a good lesson on the importance of a right constitution.

(429) In the beginning the war went well for Charles. He subdued both Denmark and Poland and won a promising, but not decisive victory over Russia/Soviet Union. With an army of 40,000 men, Charles invaded the huge plain of Russia/Soviet Union in July 1707. He was again successful in the beginning, but Peter was burning

the cities ahead of the Swedes and attacking supply lines to make it difficult to refurbish food for soldiers and horses. The winter closed in fast and became the worst on record in Europe. When summer returned, Charles had only 14,000 very tired men with very limited ammunition. The final battle took place July 30, 1708 near the town of Poltava. On the second day of fighting, the army was promised a safe retreat back to Sweden. The fighting stopped, promises were forgotten, and now as prisoners the Swedes were marched to Moscow and led through the town like the Romans used to do with their booty. Most of the prisoners were offered to locals as "helpers" in the rebuilding of Russia/Soviet Union. Charles escaped to Turkey.

(430) The battle at Poltava became of decisive importance in history. Russia/Soviet Union's modern history began. In the peace agreements, Russia/Soviet Union and Prussia took over much of the Swedish provinces around the Baltic. From now on, all political decisions in Europe always included both Russia/Soviet Union and Prussia (future Germany).

(431) Peter started the modernization of Russia/Soviet Union. Peter introduced tax on anything people had to trade or, in other words, a sales tax. Instead of household tax, he introduced individual tax that Peter called "soul tax." He had found people huddled together in the households to avoid individual tax. Peter took a census of the people and registered every man in the army. He built factories at the government's expense and started to mine the Ural Mountains. Peter requested the men to shave and the women to take part in social life. He set up standards for house building, started schools and universities, sent Russian/Soviet Union students abroad to learn, started the first newspaper. Peter reformed the Russian/Soviet Union calendar so it conformed to the European version. Peter had seen a model for his country and used his despotic power to change the old model to the new. Many of the changes improved the living standards for the people. However, the constitution was not changed. Peter died in February 1725. The dynamics for continued improvement was never implemented. Eventually, Russia/Soviet Union would again fall behind in living standards and freedom for its people.

(432) **Emperor Nicholas II (1894-1917) felt he was "God chosen" to defend an anointed autocracy or God's will on earth.** He continued discrimination against anything foreign. Nicholas heard a lot of complaints when he finally had a meeting with the Parliament (Duma). Instead of doing something about the complaints, he dissolved the Duma. Nicholas resigned in February 1917 in the midst of WW I. Bolsheviks took over power in November.

(433) Lenin arrived to St Petersburg in the spring of 1917. He called for a farmers' and workers' revolution. Nicholas and his family were shot in the night of July 17, 1918 in a house cellar in Jekaterinburg, Siberia. Lenin formed the Soviet Union and issued the first two decrees of the Soviet Government.

(434) The first decree divided, without compensation, all large farms into small landholdings. The second decree made peace with Germany with no demand for land or war compensation. Freedom was offered for all occupied lands, Finland, Ukraine, and the Baltic States Estonia, Latvia, and Lithuania.

(435) Civil war broke out between the communists and the "royalists" in 1918. The Russian/Soviet Union Civil War lasted for two years. The Red Army invaded Ukraine. Landholdings in the east and against Turkey were extended.

(436) The first result of the communist revolution was starvation. Twenty-two million adults and children had to be fed by international relief, half of it from the USA. Eventually, the party accepted a more flexible New Economic Program (NEP).

(437) Lenin took over as dictator at the Party Congress No. X. All "factionalism" became forbidden and only Communism was allowed. The churches were closed, news and assembly controlled. This compromised the right for free communication, free assembly and free religion—the "Fifth, Sixth and Seventh Pillars"—right from the beginning. Dwellings and food supply being dependent on the state bureaucracy for distribution jeopardized the "First and Second Pillars."

(438) Lenin started Commintern in 1919. The title of Commintern changed names several times, but the goal remained the same.

Commintern was to be the missionary of communism to spread the communist revolution to the rest of the world. Communist parties in different countries could seek financial and intellectual support from the Commintern. Meetings of communist parties from different countries would be held in Moscow to discuss their progress. The Russian/Soviet Union Communist Party leadership was the host and even the Russian/Soviet Union Party would turn to Commintern for directions.

(439) In every country where Commintern Party took over power, the "Fifth, Sixth and Seventh Pillars" were violated and the security of decent dwellings and food supply jeopardized.

(440) Towards the end of his life, Lenin got Alzheimer's disease. He was shot and severely injured in August 1918, had two strokes, and died in January 1924.

(441) Joseph Stalin became the leading personality in the Soviet Union. He secured his position by having old members of the party killed or exiled to Siberia. Some fled to the west. Stalin became the chairman of the Communist Party and saw to it that only loyal friends stayed in the party leadership. Every communist became a spy on his fellow neighbor and could report to the secret police, the Checa. A tyranny based on the "Law of Suspects" was started just like in the beginning of the French revolution. Teachers would ask the children what their parents were discussing. Everybody had to think and talk the party. Those who questioned the system were sent to one of several thousand work camps along the Trans-Siberian railroad. (The Nobel Prize winner, Alexander Solzhenitsyn, has described this from his own experience. Since the fall of the Soviet regime the BBC has made excellent TV documentaries with interviews of the prison guards.) **In history, Hitler's Jewish extermination camps are the only matches in size to Stalin's Siberian deportation programs. Both the Soviet and the Nazi programs involved millions of enslaved people. How this genocide eventually would affect the gene pool of this part of the earth can only be speculated. The scale of the immense human suffering cannot be formulated in words. The Soviet Union and Hitler's Germany were Sumerian States in modern clothing, a**

**dictatorship wrapped in a political dogma instead of in a religious dogma.**

(442) Stalin, permanent in total power, had to address foreign politics. Russia/Soviet Union joined the League of Nations (the precursor to United Nations) in 1934, the same year that Germany left the League. Russia/Soviet Union made an official commitment not to involve in any subversive activities in its neighbor countries Poland, Finland, Estonia, Latvia, and Lithuania. The promise lasted until 1939.

(443) In 1939 Stalin and Hitler signed a non-aggression act. What this meant was that they would leave each other in peace while they attacked their neighbors in the usual Sumerian way.

(444) Germany invaded Poland on September 1, 1939. England, according to a common defense pact with Poland, responded by declaring war on Germany the next day. Russia/Soviet Union invaded Poland on September 16. Germany was to add western Poland to its realm, while Russia/Soviet Union added Poland's eastern part. Russia/Soviet Union occupied at the same time the three Baltic States, Estonia, Latvia and Lithuania and invaded Finland. Only Finland, although small, was possibly able to resist such an occupation. Finland resisted Russian/Soviet Union troops in a winter-war and was drawn against its will into WW II on the German side when Germany later invaded Russia/Soviet Union in 1941.

(445) The German invasion was stopped at Stalingrad and the nucleus of the German Eastern Army destroyed. The Soviet Army retook lost land, forcing the German army back all the way to west of Berlin. Hitler killed himself in his bunker in Berlin. One of his officers had to sign a non-negotiable surrender for Germany. In the peace agreement, the USSR incorporated into the Soviet Union East Poland, the Baltic coast from Poland up to Finland including the three Baltic States, part of East Finland, Bess Arabia, Bukovina, Transkarpatia, and the Pacific islands Kurilerna and Sakhalin.

(446) Stalin also placed puppet communistic regimes in all occupied neighboring states in East Europe, including Poland, East Germany, Czechoslovakia, Austria, Rumania, Hungary, and Bulgaria.

The Commintern expanded Soviet influence inter-nationally by supporting communist parties in other countries. At home, in newly acquired land and in all vassal states, a "law of suspects" was introduced. Any possible resistance was eliminated by a rule of terror and transfer to the Siberian slave camps of any suspect individual.

(447) Stalin died in 1953. Nikita Khrushchev followed Stalin as the leader of the Soviet Communist Party. He publicized Stalin's terrorist regime for the home public. When Nikita tried to limit the service time for the politically elected his colleagues fired him in 1964.

(448) The "law of suspects" was re-introduced by Khrushchev's follower, Leonid Brezhnev. At home and in all Vassal states, only one candidate could be voted on—the one decided on by the Communist Party and approved by Leonid. Soviet tanks made sure that Soviet influence was not challenged in any of the vassal states. An uprising in Hungary was suppressed in 1956; Czechoslovakia was invaded in 1968. Brezhnev died 1982 and was followed by old party members. The old inefficiencies in administration continued until people were short of food.

(449) Since the time of Peter I, Russian/Soviet Union politics up to the communist revolution had three ambitions:

1. To expand Russian/Soviet Union landholding on the Euro-Asian continent;
2. To maintain Royal dictatorship in a Sumerian type of Government; and
3. To control farm labor serfdom.

(450) The results of this policy led to the communist revolution in Russia/Soviet Union and the beginning of the Soviet Union.

(451) After the communist revolution, the Soviet Union had three ambitions:

1. To expand Soviet landholding on the Euro-Asian continent;
2. To maintain Communist dictatorship in a Sumerian type of government; and

3. To control farm and industrial labor worldwide.

(452) The results of this policy led to the fall of the Soviet Union and disaster for many of its vassal states simply because the "Nine Pillars" would never be met under a Sumerian type dictatorial constitution.

(453) **One just cannot lock up the opinions of millions of people in one dogma.**

(454) **Communism has an interesting history, very much deserving our review.**

(455) Modern communism started with Karl Marx, who did not have or ever earned any money. A personal friend and son of a manufacturer in England, Friedrich Engels, sponsored him. Marx grew up in Germany. He studied history and philosophy in Bonn and Berlin. He earned a doctorate in Jena in 1841. He started a paper expressing politically radical ideas and had to leave Germany. After some time in Paris, he moved to Brussels and later to England where he lived most of his adult life and eventually died. While in England, he published his most important works, *Das Kapital* and *The Communist Manifesto*. These became the theoretical basis for international communism.

(456) *The Manifesto* was published in 1848, at a very critical time in human history. The industrial era had just started. Industrialization of farms forced million of farm workers to the cities, looking for work in the factories. Salaries both on the farm and in the factory fell below living standards. This condition was unique in history.

(457) As a philosopher of history, Karl Marx watched the worker abuse and sought an explanation in his studies of history. He felt it was all rooted in the class conscious society: the class of king, aristocracy, church, entrepreneurs, all with capital, on one side and the class of workers striving for social equality on the other. Marx meant that history had shown a continuous struggle between these two classes and that workers were being exploited. An employee working for long hours and for low wages was indeed an exploitation of labor. The prevailing belief systems of religion and philosophy

still supported the present society. Marx called on workers to unite, and, in a revolution, replace the old belief system by a Worker Dictatorship. Convinced of victory, because there are always more individuals as workers than work creators, Marxism spread to workers in most industrialized countries, forming a dogmatic, left wing labor unions in its wake. In democratic countries, labor unions negotiated better working conditions for its workers. In Russia/Soviet Union, the communist revolution replaced the old dogma with its own dogma of a Communistic Dictatorship and formed the USSR. Nikita Khrushchev, who threatened the USA with nuclear war during the 1963 Cuban Missile Crisis, visited the UN plenum session in New York, removed his shoes and hammered the desk with a promise that the grandchildren of the representative from the USA would live under communism. Stalin's daughter and Khrushchev's son are now proud citizens of the USA.

(458) **The Soviet Union collapsed by itself in 1989. A dictatorial regime collapsing by itself, without internal or external military challenge, is very unusual in history, if it ever has happened before. It left millions of its citizens in poverty and starvation. Why?**

## How did a Soviet Communist Regime Measure up to the "Nine Pillars"?

(459) **Survival:** No personal ownership is allowed in a communist country. All private enterprise is confiscated. With ownership disappeared entrepreneurship. Private property could not be placed as security for a loan. No venture capital was available. Why would you risk something, if you or your children could not own anything? Those assigned to work on the farm and their friends always had food and shelter, but there was very little incentive to produce food and shelter for others.

(460) To tell a co-worker that he is not needed is the most difficult task for any boss. On the farm, in factories and in the administration inefficient jobs were created particularly for party members and their

families. A subconscious agreement was made to keep the status quo. The state paid and picked up the consequences.

(461) In the Soviet Union, there was no competitive market telling factories which products and how much of those products were needed. Factory orders came from a central planning office: produce so much, so fast, and at such a price. Bureaucrats had a difficult time to make realistic estimates of all the variables, resulting in enormous inefficiencies. Factories provided work, but not a profit. Factories not earning capital according to profit could not grow according to the demand. The inefficiency of the farms and the disharmony between factory production and demand created a lack of money for food. The problem could be hidden for a while by printing money and with vassal states selling food to low prices under imposed contracts, but eventually the economy would collapse. The need for food became urgent. A human cannot live without food for more than a few weeks; hunger is strong after only a day or two.

(462) The Soviet State was at the same time the producer, the distributor, and the consumer. The individual existed for the state not the state for the individual. The individual or his environment had no representation in the regime. The party dogma was the only version of reality and ideas presented to the leadership, but the dogma originated from the leadership. To complain on quality or safety was to attack the Soviet system, the State itself, and that was non-patriotic and could lead to a ticket to Siberia.

(463) The Soviet State built nuclear reactors, but they were of poor quality and with poor safety regulations. Since the Soviet Union fell, the rest of the world has had to help and pay for the clean up of all the dumping of nuclear and other waste that the communist regime left behind. The nuclear meltdown of the Chernobyl plant caused major radioactive contamination all the way to Lapland in the north of Sweden.

(464) The Communist bureaucrats kept the nuclear meltdown secret from the Soviet people. U.S. surveillance detected and reported the meltdown immediately. Swedish scientists made public the nuclear fallout in the north of Sweden. The Soviet population in the

surroundings of the fallout suffered many genetic changes, resulting in radiation deaths, deformities, and cancers.

(465) In summary, the Soviet regime left its people short of food and energy, with contaminated water and air.

(466) **Shelter/Cleanliness:** The Soviet government nationalized and mechanized the farms. This caused enormous movement of people from farm to cities, similar to what occurred when tractors were introduced in the West. The Soviet State built large apartment buildings in the cities, trying to keep up with the demand for housing, but building materials were in short supply. Bureaucrats had to assign just so many square feet per person. Several families using the same apartment reduced the personal living space to a bed with a curtain around it and with common kitchen and bathroom facilities. This made it difficult to personalize his or her small living space, particularly as all earned the same assigned salary. The whole income went to making a living with very little left over to personalize the life or beautify the surroundings. Alcohol was the only thing cheap and the only release from a dull reality.

(467) The crowded living conditions made it difficult to maintain a clean environment. Waste management became strained. Materials for the buildings were often in short supply in the centrally, ineffectively planned economy. Buildings became difficult to maintain. Five story buildings did not have elevators, or, if they had, the elevators were soon out of order with no one responsible or able to fix them. In short, the "First, Second, Third and Fourth Pillars" were all violated.

(468) **Art/Communication:** Communication in the Soviet Union was controlled. Press and television were state owned, as was all printed material. News and commentaries to news were slanted to promote the regime and the system. All art was state supported, but was also obliged to promote the political philosophy of communism. Deviating attitudes were persecuted. Nobody dared to express any critique, either in a small or in large groups, because somebody might be a spy for the government. Criticizing the government could be a ticket to Siberia. The "Fifth Pillar" was totally annihilated.

(469) **Community:** Community support was good only if one was part of the Communist Party. Labor unions were not allowed. Jewish people and other non-Russian/Soviet Union minorities were discriminated against for employment and schooling. The Communist Party controlled the courts. To be called into court was to be alone against the Soviet State. The "Sixth Pillar" was violated.

(470) **Religion:** Religion, according to Karl Marx, was a residual from the class society and incompatible with communism. Religion or religious holidays were not officially recognized in the Soviet Union. The Orthodox Church was forbidden, most priests were unemployed, and its churches were often used as storage facilities or stables, but still, a few families celebrated in secrecy. The "Seventh Pillar" was officially declared unnecessary. The political dogma replaced the religious dogma in the support of a dictatorial leadership. The Sumerian State still lived on, now in the modern cloak of mass media and police control.

(471) **Medicine:** Medical access was generally available. Everybody had access, but the care was often of poor quality because of limited finances and inefficiencies. Doctors were not allowed to visit the West and therefore unable to keep up with the progress made there. Abortions were free and were used as birth control. When President Yeltsin after the Soviet fall needed cardiac surgery, he called on doctors from the USA to treat him. The "Eighth Pillar" was provided for, but compared to what was available in the rest of the world. its standards were low. The people eventually became aware of this fact.

(472) **Trade:** Personal happiness was always secondary to the common good in the communist regime. This was true except for the trusted highest political officers. The classed agricultural society before the Soviet Union was replaced by a classed political society of the Soviet Union. The elite Soviets, the nomenclature, could always pursue happiness by special privileges. They were allowed to shop in special shops and allowed to travel. What is described here applied to the Soviet Union, but as that system was a model, it more or less applied to many other communist countries. The "Ninth Pillar" was restricted within a bureaucratic framework.

(473) In short, the Soviet regime violated all the "Nine Pillars" for any humanity to survive. The regime did not serve its people; it served itself just as the ancient Rome regimes had done and that is why both eventually collapsed.

(474) Michael Gorbachev took over the post as Secretary General of the Communist Party in 1985. He admitted the deficiencies of the system. A new internal policy started.

Gorbachev changed three areas:

1. Glasnost, freedom of speech, openness;
2. Perestroika, a change of the economy; and
3. Democratization of Russia/Soviet Union.

(475) President Reagan on his visit to Berlin in the spring of 1987 said: "President Gorbachev, take down this wall." The Berlin wall fell in November 1989. The Soviet Union had to withdraw its troops from East Germany, Hungary, Czechoslovakia, and Poland. In 1990, the Soviet Constitution was changed to allow other political parties, but it still favored the communists, who had been in power for 70 years.

(476) The old communist leaders tried to re-establish their power in a coup in August 1991, placing Gorbachev under house arrest. Boris Yeltsin called on the army and squelched the coup. After being elected president of Russia/Soviet Union, the largest Member State of the USSR, Yeltsin used his power to forbid the Communist Party in Russia/Soviet Union. The Baltic States and Georgia declared themselves free states. Yeltsin was the first head of state to recognize a free Estonia, my wife's homeland.

(477) The Member states of the USSR—Russia/Soviet Union, Ukraine and Belarus—met in Minsk and declared the USSR dissolved. Gorbachev resigned. A new "Federation of Independent States," OSS, was formed in December 1991 with Yeltsin as president. Eleven of the original fifteen member states were included. The remaining old communists in the Parliament (Duma) continued to block any reforms. The lack of food and other necessities started an inflation that reached 2500% in one year. Yeltsin as president called on his

right to dissolve the Parliament and asked for new general elections in September 1993. The old communists called this a coup, declared Yeltsin fired and themselves as the rightful leaders. They blocked the parliament building and tried to take control of the state television station. President Yeltsin called on the army and had them all expelled from the government building.

(478) For the first time ever in its history, free elections in Russia/ Soviet Union took place in December 1993. The election was also a referendum for a new constitution. The president became powerful at the cost of the Parliament. As usual in a young democracy, there were many parties that could collectively be divided into four groups: liberal democrats, center parties, residual communists and nationalists.

(479) None of the party groups had a majority and President Yeltsin managed to introduce reforms. State property was to be privatized by issuing stocks to workers in the factories and other state institutions. Without any laws on the books for citizen's rights and property rights, the Mafia and corruption gained control. In the privatization that took place, cronies from the old regime helped each other to take over the state property. Taxes were not collected. Those whose livelihood came from the state—the army, state employees and those on pensions—were left without salaries. The public transportation and distribution systems broke down, resulting in a stoppage of trade. Both native and foreign trade could only take place by bartering. The currency, the ruble, could not be trusted because of the high inflationary pressure the communists had left behind.

(480) President Yeltsin had poor health at times. The parliament tried in 1999 to declare Yeltsin unfit for presidency but the 301 votes majority could not be mustered. Yeltsin declared he would retire before his term was over and selected Vladimir Putin as his candidate for president in the fall 1999. Putin was elected as president in the June 2000 election and is now president. Putin's background in public work was as Director for the secret police under communism.

(481) The Russian/Soviet Union Constitution from 1993 calls for a President, an Upper House (Federation Council) and a Lower

House (Duma), a Constitutional Court, Judicial Appeals Court, an Arbitrator Court for labor disputes, and a Director of the Federal Bank. Everybody is elected for four years. A State Security Council after the USA model was added the following year. The Upper House is composed of two delegates; one the governor, from 89 larger cities and regions. The Lower House is composed of 450 delegates, half of them from proportional parties in election districts, half from one-man districts. The Upper House elects higher bureaucrats and the president. The Lower House makes laws. The president can issue special decrees as temporal laws. Some of the regions, particularly the national regions, declared independence from the central government. Putin has hindered this. A movement for total independence in Tjetjenia was stopped by force simply by leveling its Capital with the ground by massive bombing and warfare.

(482) President Putin has made several basic changes in the constitution. The governor of a region automatically being a representative to the upper house was changed to a representative for the governor. President Putin divided the country into seven super regions with directors reporting directly to him. The directors are responsible to see that federal law and decrees are followed in their region. Television and many papers were nationalized in 2001. With President Putin administratively controlling the whole nation plus all its newsmedia Russia/Soviet Union now looks pretty much like any past historic Sumerian nation. My wife found it remarkable that Russia/Soviet Union under President Putin's leadership deployed many army exercises along the borders of the three small and defensless Baltic States.

(483) Russia/Soviet Union has 141 million people with 7% farmers in 2002. The GNP was estimated to $1480 billion and the GNP/citizen $19,500. The Defense cost was 4% and the foreign debt was 9.6% of GNP.

*Gunnar Sevelius MD*

**For Further Reading:**

(484) *Russia/Soviet Union and Soviet Union* by Warren Bartlett Walsh, ISBN 58-10123.

# Germany

(485) Much of German history has already been told. We learned how the Frank king Charlemagne carved out the part of the Roman Empire, which comprised Western Europe. Charlemagne's three grandchildren each inherited one part: France for Charles, Germany for Louis, and Italy for Lothar. Their children in turn had their inheritance rights to land. Germany and Italy were divided up into many princedoms and kingdoms. Germany consisted of some 400 member-states.

(486) Prussia took over the Swedish holdings on the Baltic Coast of Germany after Sweden had lost its Nordic War with Russia/Soviet Union in 1708. Prussia together with Austria became the dominating member states in Germany. After Napoleon had stirred up the European map in 1806, the "Roman Emperor" title for the ruler of Austria was meaningless and the Roman Empire in history ceased to exist.

(487) In 1866, Prussia degraded Austria to a second place among the German member states after a quick seven-week war. All the states north of the river Main were included in the Prussian realm and four years later they all had a common constitution. Prussia became the nation of Germany after the short, successful war with France 1870. King William I declared himself Emperor of Germany.

(488) The second emperor of this young state was a very boisterous and demagogic ruler, Emperor William II. He stirred up a lot of emotions with his talk of Germany's right to take part in world politics, specifically colonial politics, important at the time. When the prince of Austria was shot, emotions took over in Europe and WW I broke out in 1914.

(489) Russia/Soviet Union settled with Germany after large losses of life in the war and the 1917 communist revolution. The armies on the Western Front stalled. Germany started a trade blockade against England with a general submarine war on the Atlantic. This aroused the USA to enter a war in Europe for the first time. The USA entered the war in 1917 and made the difference. When Germany lost the war 1918, the Emperor fled to Holland where he died forgotten.

(490) Germany became a democratic regime under a "Weimar" Constitution. Germany was obliged to pay $132 billion in golden mark as war indemnity. With no gold backing up the German mark, the printed German currency became worthless. One dollar was worth four billion printed marks in 1923. Clumsy bartering became the only way to trade or exist.

(491) In 1924, an American economist Charles Dawes set up a program by which Germany was given 800 million gold marks as a loan. Germany would repay it slowly, year by year. The paper mark could be exchanged at the rate of 1 trillion to 1 new mark. With the help of this new money, trading resumed. In new negotiations in 1930, indemnity payments were fixed at 121 billion marks in 59 payments.

(492) Hitler's National Socialist Party made a political appeal by refusing to pay the indemnity. The party became very popular and the largest party. The Communist Party was the third largest.

(493) After the collapse of the New York Stock Market in October 1929, unemployment became very high. There were about six million unemployed in Germany in 1932. In an election in January 1932, Hitler's party had 3 of 11 seats in the cabinet. He called for a new general election already in February. His party started intimidating the opposition candidates, even burning the Parliament building, a fire that Hitler blamed on the communists. Hitler got a majority in both the assembly and the ruling cabinet.

(494) Like his hero Napoleon, Hitler asked for an "enabling act." The enabling act meant he would have permission to issue decrees directly for implementation and bypassing the Assembly. He got a yes-vote for this, actually after having all communists arrested or

excluded. Hitler became the dictator of the "Third Reich." The first Reich had been the Roman, the second that of Emperor William I. Since Hitler could not reasonably be called emperor, he was called Fuehrer and Reichskanzler.

(495) Hitler appointed Joseph Goebbels as minister of "enlightenment" and propaganda. On June 24, 1933, the National Socialist Party was declared the only party legally permitted. Hitler purged his own party on June 30, 1934. Members not trusted were killed without trial. On August 2, the old general and president Hindenburg died. The president's office was combined with that of the chancellor. On August 19, this was confirmed with a general public vote. Eighty-three percent of the 43 million voted yes. Hitler's position was now legalized.

(496) Hitler's chief of police, Himmler, with his elite SS-troops, took over the civil control of the country. Goebbels started a propaganda campaign attacking Jewish people. Press, schools, universities, theaters and the arts, all had to preach the dogma of the Nazi Party. People of Jewish descent were arrested, put in slave camps or killed, and their property confiscated. The money from this activity was used for remilitarization.

(497) The violation of the "Second, Fifth and Sixth" of the "Nine Pillars" was started. Dwellings could never be safe. The individual, unless he belonged to the party, could not feel safe in his home. The Jewish people were persecuted in their homes and their businesses. Communications in the form of radio and press, and community support in the form of schooling and courts, were under strict government control, always supporting and enhancing government policy and its leaders. No other political parties were allowed. **The Sumerian State had returned in its modern clothing: one dictator supported by a political dogma. Anything or anybody deviating from the leader's political dogma was persecuted. Religion was left alone. In return, the Pope stayed quiet.**

(498) Hitler's next official goal was to unite all German people into a large, all German-speaking Germany. (Hitler, born Austrian, called Germany without Austria the Little Germany). He succeeded with

this without much opposition from England, France, or the USA. In March 1938, Hitler occupied Austria and a year later Czechoslovakia.

(499) Czechoslovakia at that time was an ally of England. There was still no real opposition from England. Hitler was now convinced no one in the west would interfere with his plans. In August, he made a secret pact with the Soviet Union to divide Eastern Europe between them. This was a Machiavellian move of power politics. Fascists hated communists and communists hated fascists because they were both after total, undivided power. What Hitler and Stalin had in common was a desire for booty and taxes from conquered small neighboring countries. The stage was set for WW II.

(500) On September 1, 1939, Germany invaded Poland. England and France declared war on Germany. The Soviet Union joined Germany in the last week of the war. Poland was split between Germany and Russia/Soviet Union after 35 days of war.

(501) The hoarding of Jews in all the new land took now on gigantic proportions. An industrialized extermination of Jews took place. Eventually six million Jews were killed in the many concentration camps. The greatest atrocity and genocide in all of human history happened in our modern, Christian time and in an otherwise civilized country.

(502) The experience of Hitler's Germany demonstrates that with an offer of employment one can make most people do any kind of work, even industrialize the killing of people.

(503) In this short review of world history, it seems there are three reasons for atrocities:

1. The booty/taxes/land reason;
2. The religious dogmatic idea reason; and
3. The political dogmatic idea reason.

(504) **The booty atrocity has a selfish individual goal. The religious atrocity has a selfish goal of a specific religious organization. The political atrocity has a selfish goal of a specific political organization. Certainly, none can be justified on any basis of individual democratic rights. A democratic organization must**

allow for different personal, religious convictions and different political solutions to be submitted for public scrutiny. Any forced oppressions or restrictions will lead to a skewed purpose of the government or, and very often, to war. This review of history points to the fact that all homeland atrocities and many of the wars have originated under a Sumerian type of government where a certain dogma is forced on to people.

(505) A democratic society gives the power to the people. Therefore, it is important for the people to be educated with freely communicated knowledge—knowledge also open for critique. Teaching of world history is fundamental for any society or the society will repeat its mistakes from generation to generation. History is like a movie of humanity: you cannot judge the show by starting in the middle. To understand the whole "Show of History" you have to follow it from its first frame. Our history is there to be learned from so we can build our present needs for our needs in the future. The "Nine Pillars" will hopefully give some guidance.

(506) In the Finnish-Soviet Winter War of 1939, Finland succumbed, but with big losses for the USSR. Finland's success gave Hitler the idea that the USSR might be an easy catch at the right time.

(507) In May 1940, Hitler's army invaded in rapid sequence Holland, Belgium, France, in April Denmark and Norway. Hitler used a long proven success formula for war strategy: (speed) x (mass). Napoleon had used it with great success. Genghis Khan had used it before with even greater success. In the middle of June, France asked for an armistice. While in Paris, Hitler went to his hero's grave and paid Napoleon his respects. Hitler arranged for the heart of Napoleon's son to be moved from Vienna to Paris.

(508) Hitler's fascist ally, the dictator Mussolini of Italy, felt he should take part in this easy game and had Italy attack both Greece and North Africa, antique Roman vassal areas. Mussolini's dragon was a paper dragon. Germany had to come to Italy's help and occupied all of the Balkan countries and North Africa.

(509) June 21, 1941, Hitler invaded Russia/Soviet Union. Hitler hoped to have control of Russia/Soviet Union in about six to eight

weeks. There would be no need for winter equipment. Finland had in the winter of 1938 shown how ill-prepared the Russian/Soviet Union army was. The invasion was successful in the beginning. The huge front stretching from Finland to the Black Sea advanced easily.

(510) Japan wanted also to be part of the axis' success. They bombed Pearl Harbor in December 7, 1941, resulting in the USA joining both the European and Asian wars. The USA entered the European war for a second time and for the second time the USA came to play a decisive role for peace between the Sumerian type of governments in Europe.

(511) **In Europe, "claim to land" is often based on "our sons died for this ground." American mothers have now in two world wars left their sons in the European soil, a soil that most of them have never seen and certainly never claimed. Each time USA troops have come to Europe, it has been because democracy has been threatened. Democracy has been saved for Western Europe each time. I am originally a European, who has never lost any of my family in a war. Although families in the USA are not asking for it, I hope I speak for many European families when I say, I am humbly thankful for the sacrifice the American mothers have made, having lost their sons in European wars.**

(512) After the war, Germany was divided up into four occupational zones: one each for the USA, England, Russia/Soviet Union, and France. France was invited to participate in the occupation only after some argument. France had really not taken a greater part in the war than any other of the occupied countries. Berlin and Vienna were also divided up into separate occupational city zones. Both Berlin and Vienna were located inside the Russian/Soviet Union occupational land zone. The Americans suggested combining the three western occupational land zones into one. This was done first with the English and later with the French authorities. Germany now had two occupational zones: one Eastern controlled by Russia/Soviet Union and one Western controlled by the Allied forces. All native Germans east of Oder or outside any of the occupational zones were transferred into the two East or West occupational zones (12 million

Germans were transferred). Hitler had asked for all Germans to live within Germany. Now they were.

(513) **The two occupational zones are good examples of the difference between the democratic way, allowing for the "Nine Pillars" to be free, and the dogmatic communistic way, trying to control them. Both zones started from the same base, with cities in ruins.**

## East Germany

(514) General Zhukov became the head of the Russian/Soviet Union Military Administration of all the occupied countries in East Europe. Eastern Germany was divided into two parts: land east of Oder was simply added to the USSR vassal state, Poland. Only the area west of Oder, between Oder and Elbe, was made into an eastern occupational zone.

(515) All bank accounts were immediately blocked except for a maximum withdrawal of 300 marks. All private banks were closed. All firms, organizations, and private individuals were ordered to hand over all gold, silver, currency, foreign banknotes, deeds and other valuables. Factories were dismantled and railway cars and tracks if double were shipped to Russia/Soviet Union. Press and radio were censored. All farms larger than 247 acres (100 ha) were confiscated without compensation and organized into community farms. All political parties were forbidden except socialist parties. These were gradually combined into one party, the Communist Party. This single party elected representatives from seven administrative districts of the country. The president was elected from a joint session between two chambers. All mass media were under the control of the Communist Party. Few people were allowed to travel outside the country. Labor unions were not allowed. In 1952, a special armed police was established and checked all antigovernment activity. Supplied with heavy weapons and tanks, the police crushed an uprising in 1953.

(516) The USSR declared East Germany independent in 1954. Since East Germany did not need to pay any more war indemnity to USSR, they would enter into the Warsaw Treaty Organization and contribute to the defense of the eastern block. All weapons were, of course, bought from the USSR at a non-negotiated, non-competitive price.

(517) As in the USSR, just about all the "Nine Pillars" were violated in East Germany. Access to medical help was free but of substandard quality.

(518) The lack of freedom in the country made most of the people who did not directly benefit from the system want to escape to the West. In August 1961, East Germany built a wall to lock in its entire population. History has many examples of walls to keep enemies out, but a wall to keep its citizens in is absurd and a unique event in world history. After the wall was erected, it made East Germany into a prison. Between 1949 and 1961, it is estimated that 2.5 million people fled from East to West Germany. Many were shot when they tried to escape to the West.

(519) The wall between East and West Germany came down in November 1989. The poor living standard in East Germany and all the oppression was revealed to the world.

## West Germany

(520) West Germany was given a free democratic government with free mass media. Political parties and labor unions were free to organize. Free trade was encouraged. The West German zone was divided up into 11 bonded states. A military commission supervised the democratization during the early years. In 1949 West Germany was given the name Federal Republic of Germany with its capital in Bonn. The supervision became civil—the Allied High Commission.

(521) The civil supervision lasted until May 1955, when West Germany was declared independent, entered the North Atlantic Treaty Organization (NATO), and began to establish its own armed forces

(522) The U.S. offered a Marshall Plan to rehabilitate the German economy. The Marshall Plan was U.S. monetary aid to Germany similar to the Dawes Plan after WW I. The Marshall Plan led to a rapid rebuilding of both the cities and the factory base. Russia/Soviet Union tried to block any more rehabilitation by blocking any trade between the East and the West. This was particularly critical for West Berlin, which was located in East Germany. The USA responded with an airlift to supply every need of 2.5 million West Berliners. The airlift went on for almost a year in 1948. More than 2.3 million tons of goods had to be airlifted before Russia/Soviet Union gave up on the blockade.

(523) After the end of the war, a Frenchman, Jean Monnet, promoted the idea of a unified Europe for its democratic nations. Both the military and the civil supervision of Germany had organized a common supervision of the steel production in the Ruhr area. West Germany's first chancellor, Conrad Adenauer, and France's president, Charles De Gaulle, were both open to the thought. In 1951, Belgium, France, Italy, Luxembourg, Holland and West Germany signed a treaty establishing the European Coal and Steel Community. There would be no trade or work barriers for steel and coal among these six nations. In 1968, they eliminated tariffs between themselves. This led to economic growth and a better living standard for these six nations. The European Community (EC) was born. It was to be followed by the forming of the European Union (EU). In 1970, the EU started to regulate the exchange rate of their currency leading towards a common currency, the Euro, in 2002. The European Monetary Community (EMU) was born.

(524) Other countries were invited to join the EU and EMU. It requires two steps to join. Step one is free trade and free movement of labor and capital. Step two is to join the European Monetary Community (EMU). EMU requires members to have a stable currency with limited inflation. More European nations have been admitted to EU than to EMU.

(525) The Berlin Wall came down on November 9, 1989. East Germans voted in free elections for the first time in March 1990.

The Allied Forces recognized a unified Germany on September 12 of the same year. The two Germanies joined their legal and social systems and became one state on October 3, 1990. Germany joined the EU at the same time.

(526) The unified Germany is a multi-party democracy. Germany was a major economic power of the world already before the unification. Germans are keenly aware of the suffering the country has caused in the past and is doing much to remedy that. The united Germany no doubt will be an important part in our future.

(527) The unified Germany had in 2011 a population of 83 million with 3% living off farming. The GNP was $3,000 billion and the GNP/citizen $44,111. The cost of defense was 1.38% of the GNP. Foreign debt was 81% of GNP.

**For Further Reading:**

(528) *Germany, A Modern History* by Marshall Dill, Jr. The University of Michigan Press ISBN 60-13891.

(529) *Hitler—A Study in Tyranny* by Allan Bullock. Harper & Brothers, New York ISBN 0061311235.

# England

(530) England differs from other European countries in that it is an island, triangular in shape. The tip of the triangle is Scotland. The base surrounds London with the areas of Wessex (west), Sussex (south), Essex (east), and Kent and West Wales as two protruding peninsulas on each end. Above this base from the west to the east are the areas of Wales, Mercia and East Anglia (West Anglia was on the other side of the Channel from where the Anglicans came). North of this band is the North Umbria and above this Scotland. North Umbria is large and is divided into Bernicia in the north and Deria in the south.

(531) **England has only been conquered twice in its history. The cultures of the two conquerors have formed the history of England.**

(532) The Romans were the first to conquer England. They controlled its southern part. The Roman Emperor Hadrian built a wall across England to defend his Roman property. Parts of the wall are still present. The Roman missionary monk Augustine christened England in 700. The southern half of England became a vassal state to Rome.

(533) Vikings were the second conquerors of England. The Vikings did not just raid but actually colonized England. The leader would later become a local king. The Vikings introduced the first coins to accomplish taxes and trade. Each settler, a free man, coerl (Swedish: *karl*) had an area, higid (Swedish: *hemman*) large enough for a family to live from. The Vikings divided the country into provinces with local administrations similar to that in Scandinavia. The alderman (Swedish: *ålderman*) governed the provinces. Rules for both the society and the individual were formulated in the provinces. The rules for society became the basis for the local administration; the rules for the individual became a jury of peers. This was how the Viking society worked. Free men met at the "Ting": a court for settling disputes and an arena to discuss and decide on common goals. Everybody stood up and had his voice heard; the majority or the side that was voiced loudest got its will. There were no written records. A handshake was the signature. The decisions had to be followed, because memory was good. Later, England, similar to the continent, went through its own feudal period. At this time England became a kingdom where the king looked at his country as his own property while the Pope in Rome ruled the clergy across all national realms. The feudal England went through the usual family intrigues of the different royal houses and after the Reformation also its religious conflicts. Fortunately for England, some of its early kings were not impressive. The Parliament took over the administrative power early compared to what happened on the continent.

(534) **Political leaders rooted in the people of different trades took the helm of England through the Parliament, freed England from the Pope, and made England the first industrialized and the**

**first globally trading country. In this sense, England became the heir of ancient Greece with dominance over sea and trade.**

(535) England's democracy may be rooted in its Scandinavian or Greek/Roman heritage, or may be simply rooted in the fundamental tribal need of the "Nine Pillars." England's dynamic history of both constitutional government and of common law has made England a model for many modern democratic countries, including the United States. One may follow how the English nation is slowly formed, first ruled by the king and his council, and how each task in the council becomes a specialized ministry. **The dictatorial power of the king was in 1215 restricted by the human rights document, the Magna Carta. The representation of the people is slowly formulated into the two-house Parliament. The Parliament takes over the control of the ministry. Finally, the Parliament introduces the modern social support system of the country. England was the first industrialized country in the world; thus, it was the first country that had to solve the many social conflicts that followed industrialization.**

(536) King Sven I, king of Denmark, conquered England in 1015. Knut (1016-1035), his son, added Norway to his large domain. A clever administrator, Knut organized local administrations and initiated the most elaborate law that so far had appeared in England, the Dane law. Knut also introduced taxes to be used for civil defense, the Dane geld.

(537) At the death of Knut's grandson, the local ruler invited a member from the Old Danish dynasty living in Normandy to come to England. Edward the Confessor was asked, came and ruled from 1042-1066. Edward had no son. He wished for another Normandy prince to follow him. A year before he died, Edward invited Duke William of Normandy to come to England. Local kings did not approve of William and crowned King Harold II of Kent in January in the abbey church in Westminster that Edward had just built. In October, Duke William invaded England. He defeated Harold at Hastings, in 1066, and had his own coronation in December also in the Westminster Abbey.

(538) William I (1066-87) took over a well-developed country. An administration and a tax system were already in place. Currency was regulated by weight of coins. William introduced feudalism and demanded that all knights give him an oath of support. Landowners held their land holding as pay for duties to the king. The king's administration came from the aristocracy. William owned land on both sides of the Channel. **Wars between Sumeric kings in England and Sumeric rulers in France lasted off and on for the next 900 years.**

## The Birth of Human Rights
## The Magna Carta Versus the "Nine Pillars"

(539) A constant problem for the feudal kings of Europe was who, the king or the Pope, selected the bishops. The Pope insisted it was his right to determine. The priests talked directly to the people and had, therefore, a great influence on people's opinions. The Pope wanted to have priests, who would take the church's side in conflicts between the king and the Pope. For the same reason, it was important for the king to have a clergy, who supported him.

(540) A pitiable king and intrigue maker, John (1199-1216), a brother to King Richard I (Lionheart), challenged the Pope. John did not want to see the Pope's candidate, Stephen Langton, as new Archbishop in Canterbury. John's poor reputation and a strong Pope at the time, Innocent III, led to the Pope ordering a stop to all church services in England and the excommunication of John. John gave in. The Pope demanded that all of England and Ireland should be under his control for church matters and that John had to pay the Pope an annual fee. John increased taxes to meet the extra fee. The extra taxes led to unrest among those who had to pay. **The archbishop, Stephen Langton, whom the Pope and John had argued about, wrote the first Bill of Rights, the Magna Carta, in 1215. John refused to sign it and died the next year. John's son, Henry III (1216-72) had to sign the Magna Carta before he would be accepted as king.**

(541) The Magna Carta was a contract between the king on one side and the aristocracy, the clergy and the citizens on the other. Coincidentally, the Magna Carta happens also to have nine clauses. Some of the nine clauses of Magna Carta overlap with the "Nine Pillars." However, the Magna Carta addresses a specific time and specific circumstances in history.

(542) **Clause I states that the church should be free from the King's influence, covering the "Seventh Pillar," separating religion from central government.**

(543) Clause II contains statements on feudal laws with regulations of inheritance. The danger was no longer from roving tribes and dangerous animals. A despotic king imposing arbitrary rules and unreasonable taxes was now the threat to family security. Laws to secure the individual from arbitrary rulings of the king were needed. This was still in accordance with the **"Second Pillar," a secure dwelling.**

(544) Clause III states that free men could not be required to do more service than they owed or be imprisoned without lawful judgment of peers. All were assured freedom to assemble and express an opinion without risking retributions. The third clause is in accordance with **the "Second, Fifth and Sixth Pillars," the need for security and privacy of the home and freedom to communicate and assemble.**

(545) Clause IV regulates weights used in trade. The clause regulated rules for tradesmen, **addressing the "Ninth Pillar" of trade.**

(546) Clause V states that fines should not be arbitrary but in accordance with the degree of the offence and the judgment should be done in a court. The fifth clause again addressed the security of the individual, making certain he/she was not subject to arbitrary rules **but assured of fair community support, the "Sixth Pillar."**

(547) Clause VI outlines rules for the behavior of royal officials and those of local governments. No officials could take private property without immediate payment. The clause forbids arbitrary rules or

threatening a free individual or his family in his home, meeting the needs of the "Second Pillar."

(548) Clause VII has rules regarding the care of the royal forest and hunting rights.

(549) Clause VIII contains solutions to specific problems caused by the king.

(550) Clause IX contains rules for the maintenance of the charter by 25 members of the aristocracy. Disputes should be settled by a majority vote. The king should not do anything to revoke the charter. **It was the base for the permanence of the "Sixth Pillar," freedom to assemble and work as a group, the very foundation for the forming of a Parliament.**

(551) Five of the "Nine Pillars"—the second, fifth, sixth, seventh, and ninth—can be considered to overlap with the nine clauses of the Magna Carta. The physiological needs of food, water and fresh air, the need for cleanliness, art and medical access were not covered. Society really did not yet have much to offer in improving any of these needs. The needs for human rights and the control of arbitrary rules by the king were more pressing.

(552) The Magna Carta was posted in all courts so it was to be known to everybody, similar to the written rights of citizens in ancient Athens and Rome. **Making the Magna Carta public and posted all over England has been praised as a major event for the advancement of Human Rights.**

(553) The Magna Carta had one weakness: The aristocracy alone supervised its implementations without any checks. The nobility was able to favor themselves at the cost of the general public. One member of the Parliament, John of Gaunt, Duke of Lancaster, used his position to enrich himself to such a degree it was said that the Duke owned a third of England.

(554) **The selfish enrichment of a minister in charge of the money purse demonstrates that not only the king's power has to be controlled and checked; the power of anybody who has access to the public money has to be controlled.**

(555) Henry VIII (1509-47) broke with the Pope and turned England into a Protestant country. The decision was a popular one with long lasting consequences. The income from church property stayed within the country. The omission of the confessions in the Protestant Church changed the whole cultural attitude. The Catholic Church and its priests were no longer in the center of each individual's life; the individual self, his work and service to society became the center. The society and the Church would fight over who would control the individual. This fight would preoccupy the English life for the next centuries.

(556) Elizabeth I (1558-1603), Henry's second daughter, had seen the results of her Catholic sister's, Mary I (the "Bloody"), uncompromising policy relative to church matters. Elizabeth's policy was that of moderation. She chose William Cecil to head her private council. He turned out to be one of England's best ministers. Protestant émigrés dared to return. The queen encouraged manufacturing and international trade. Trade with Antwerp, Hamburg, West Africa, and West Indies increased. Trade monopolies were given for coal, copper, brass, salt, and glass. Quality of manufacturing was improved by establishing apprenticeships. **The Royal Stock Exchange was started.** Justices of peace checked on prices and salaries.

(557) Yet, the battle between Catholicism and Protestantism continued. We have already told about how Philip II lost his "Invincible Armada" to Elizabeth II and how England's rule of the sea began.

(558) Elizabeth died in 1603. Her will stipulated that Mary Stuart's son, James I of Scotland, who had remained Protestant, would follow her. By combining the two crowns, the English Island would become inviolable from the sea. The allied countries of England and Scotland are politically referred to as Great Britain. For the sake of simplicity in this short review, we will continue to refer to Great Britain as England.

(559) James I (1603-25) and his son, Charles I (1625-49), started a French style pompous court. The king asked for more taxes. The Parliament required at least audits.

(560) The Parliament declared that meetings of the Parliament had to be called at least every three years and could not be dissolved. The Parliament had to approve all the king's ministers. The Parliament should decide on any reformation act of the church in consultation with the Church. The Parliament also demanded control of the armed forces.

(561) Charles rejected the new legislation. Civil war broke out. Oliver Cromwell led the troops for the Parliament. The king fled to Scotland after a couple of skirmishes, returned from Scotland with an army, but was defeated and executed January 30, 1649.

(562) **The new Parliament established it should be rooted in its people with rights for everyone (with property) to vote and with religious freedom (except that Catholicism was segregated against by many) and equality before the law.**

(563) Without a king, the Parliament was now in sole power. The leader of the Parliament was the religious puritan Oliver Cromwell. The royal property was confiscated and arbitrarily distributed. Religious and Puritan standards of citizen's daily life were imposed. As the army had the real power, military officers replaced many members in the Parliament. Cromwell had the country divided into districts ruled by generals and their militia, all enforcing a religious Puritan lifestyle.

(564) **Cromwell was, in fact, a one party dictator, supported by the army and church in the old Sumerian way.** The ruling council had membership for life. A House of Lords and a House of Commons was created only to modify the impression of dictatorship in England.

(565) Cromwell died in 1658. After Cromwell, the nation was tired of his military rule, in history called a "tyranny of saints." Cromwell's dictatorship became so hated he was dug up from the grave and hanged post mortem on the anniversary of the hanging of Charles I. Still unwilling to compromise, many Puritans left for North America and wrote their own history in the New England area of North America. The Parliament worked out a deal with the Dutch to take over New York and to connect the colonies in the North with those in the South.

(566) Charles II (1660-85), the son of Charles I, was jubilantly welcomed back to London. Charles II's daughter had married the Protestant General William III of Orange. Despite this, Charles made secret plans with Louis XIV of France to restore Catholicism in England. He joined France in the war against the Protestant Dutch led by his son-in-law William III of Orange. France paid Charles a lifetime pension. In that way, he did not need to ask the Parliament for money. Charles II dedicated his Catholic Brother, James II (1685-88), to follow him as king.

(567) The third Earl of Shaftesbury, Anthony Ashley Cooper (1671-1713) led the Parliament. He had the constitutional philosopher John Locke as councilor and physician. John Locke was a philosopher who posited the theories of people representation and government power. His ideas about government "Two Treatises on Civil Government" and "Letters on Toleration" were eventually published around 1690. **John Locke concluded that the power of the king was based on a contract between the king and the people**. The people must be represented in the Parliament. Rights cannot be inherited. Through the close friendship between John Locke and the third Earl of Shaftesbury, the Parliament passed in 1669 laws based on John Locke's theories.

(568) The leaders of the Parliament approached William III of Orange, the husband of James II's daughter, Mary. William and Mary accepted as co-regents (William III ruled 1689-1702 and Mary II 1689-94) and promised to follow the new laws.

(569) **The army supported William III in England's non-bloody people's revolution in 1689. King James fled to France.**

(570) **England became now the first monarchy in history totally based on the will of the people. The Parliament became the law-making institution and the one that determined taxes. The king was the head of the church (a Sumerian residual) and the army, but the king had to have the Parliament's approval to declare war.**

(571) The king would be given an annual budget and his expenses would be audited through a bank, the Bank of England (founded in 1694). Annual budgets made yearly meetings of the Parliament necessary.

(572) The Parliament made judgeships irrevocable except at the request of both houses and disqualified anybody in the House of Commons to profit from the Crown. Possibilities for conflict of interest were slowly closed and arbitrary decisions restrained. To meet all the needs of the "Nine Pillars" is a slow and difficult process. Almost 500 years had passed since the Magna Carta controversy.

(573) England's greatest parliamentarian, William Pitt the Elder, Earl of Chatham, was at the helm of the regime in England during the reign of George III. William Pitt saw a future for England in trade and manufacturing. He was here addressing the ninth of the "Nine Pillars." **Trade and manufacturing served humanity. Owning land and taxing the farmer just served the king and his children to keep fancy courts in big castles. A new period was slowly emerging.**

(574) George III (1760-1820) was the grandson of George II. His father had died early. He was only 22 years old when he was crowned and was to be king for one of the longest times in English history. He inherited his grandfather's war with France and a need for money. **Different schemes for imposing and collecting taxes was rationalized and tried. One proposal was that the different colonies in America ought to pay taxes to the homeland.** The colonies were not represented in the decision of their taxation. On July 4, 1776, the 13 colonies in America declared independence and war with England. England lost the war and the USA was granted independence in 1783.

(575) The leader in England was now William Pitt, Junior. He led England through the Napoleon wars, but continued to support the industry and trade as his father had done. After James Watt invented the stationary steam machine, it was no longer important for factories to have access to a waterfall for power. All industries grew but particularly those of iron and cloth.

(576) England's politics of trade and manufacturing was now well ahead of the rest of the European kingdoms, preoccupied with the ancient self-serving war/land/tax politics. As politics in England was set by the Parliament, the king played a smaller and smaller role.

(577)  A new period in history with a different prerequisite, a self-propelled machine, was also emerging.

(578)  Victoria (1837-1901), George III's granddaughter, was happily married to Albert and had nine children during her long reign. She was 22 years old when she became Queen. Her happy family life became a model for Victorian England.

(579)  **The time was politically characterized by the social consequences of the mechanization of agriculture, factories with a large labor force, the expansion of the transportation system for the larger markets, a press with a large readership, and Charles Darwin's publication in 1859 of** *The Origin of Species.* **Darwin's publication about the evolution of the species challenged the Bible's story of the Creation and provoked much private and public discussion. Religion as the "Seventh Pillar" of society still survived. The need for religion, the "Seventh Pillar," was deeper and more general than science could explain. Religious freedom was confirmed and extended to the Roman Catholics. The Pope opened several bishop seats. Lowering the demand for owning property in order to be able to vote doubled the voting public.**

(580)  **The American Civil War from 1861-1865, the unification of Italy in 1861, and the ascendancy of Prussia to become the kingdom of Germany in 1870 also influenced the time in Europe.**

## The Birth of the Labor Movement

(581)  The first 30 years of Victoria's regime was characterized by the policy of the third Viscount, Henry John Temple, 3rd Viscount Palmerston (1784-1865). He tried to keep England from getting involved in conflicts. Benjamin Disraeli, Earl of Beaconsfield (1804-1881), became the prominent Tory or "right" wing leader after Palmerstone. An equally strong speaker, William Ewart Gladstone (1809-1898) was leader of the "left" party, the Whigs.

(582)  **The sharp disputes between these two political leaders were the beginning of the two-party system. Their strong influence on politics left the royal house only as a registrar of the votes.**

**Besides being a national symbol of independent continuity, this is the political role of the English monarchy today.**

(583) The different mechanical inventions during this time caused social upheaval. The social changes had to be met with an accommodating legislature. The secret ballot was introduced in 1872. Grade school was made compulsory with local school boards. Trade unions were allowed to picket. A public health act was created.

(584) Voting rights were extended to all males in 1884, tripling the electorate. This gave rise to a separate labor movement and the formation of a third party, the Labor Party (1900), which took many of its members from the Whigs. The 63 years of Victoria's reign saw the old agriculture populations move into the cities at the same time as the total population doubled. **England solved the social turmoil caused by the industrial revolution with negotiated peaceful reforms despite Karl Marx's choice to make England his homeland.** There is nothing in the world one cannot negotiate. If one party does not allow negotiation, it is likely that party has a secret or secondary agenda like in the frequent breakdowns of the negotiations between Israel and Palestine.

## The Birth of a Social Support System

(585) Edward VII (1901-1911) saw labor unions introduce compulsory membership fees. **The greatest insecurity for a laborer was his income during unemployment, sickness, and old age.** In 1914, the coal miners worked out an eight-hour workday and old age pension. The liberal party of the old Whigs, but now called "liberals," felt that the House of Lords, with many members from the country aristocracy, were continuously blocking many of their social reforms. They introduced legislation so the House of Lords only had suspensive veto in such legislation. This was an enormous change in the way the constitution worked. The constitutional change would pass if it went through three separate voting sessions; it was accepted in 1911. That same year the Saturday as a half workday went into effect, as well as national health and unemployment insurance. Union membership

increased from 2.5 to 4 million and the unions got their own press in 1911. **Women received their voting rights in 1926.**

(586) On the continent, Germany's demagogue emperor was boosting its new navy and demanding German participation in colony politics. Tension grew and alliances were formed—Germany and Austria against England, France, and Russia/Soviet Union. The crown prince of the Sumerian type government in Austria was shot in Sarajevo in July 28, 1914. WW I broke out. USA's participation ended the war and Germany lost. Russia/Soviet Union had its revolution. The Russian/Soviet Union vassal states on the Baltic and Turkish on the Balkan became independent. Germany's African and Asian colonies were split between England and France.

(587) The post-war homefront was dominated by putting five million returning solders to work, paying off the war loan to the USA, and economically helping Germany and Russia/Soviet Union back on their feet. A letter from the Soviet Commintern to the British Communist Party to violently overthrow the British government became public. The revolutionary plans left Russia/Soviet Union out of any further help from the west.

(588) Constitutional questions with the colonies became more and more pressing. The 1931 statute established that the **"Dominions are autonomous communities within the British empire, equal in status, in no way subordinate to one other in their domestic or external affairs though united by a common allegiance to the crown, and freely associated as members of the British Commonwealth of Nations."** Slowly, this attitude of communication and negotiations worked itself through the old colonies. Some went their own way; others stayed within the Commonwealth for trade.

(589) The master demagogue Adolf Hitler dominated the thirties and started a new type of Sumerian government: a dictatorial leadership built on a political dogma, enforced by secret police and control of mass media. Hitler's Sumerian type aggressive moves towards Germany's neighbor nations led to WW II. The USA entered the WW II and made again the difference. Germany again lost the war.

(590) England had by itself carried much of the cost of the western front in WW II because Germany had rapidly occupied much of Western Europe. The immediate postwar period was dominated by loan negotiations with the USA. A pressing issue was also the buildup of a social support system. Big industries were placed under state ownership in order to solve many social problems, particularly unemployment. The success of the program was limited. There has now been a movement back to private industries.

(591) **The "Second and Sixth Pillars" for security for the family in the form of a "cave" and group support had gradually evolved into that of a national social security system for the individual and his family. The "Fifth Pillar" for free communication evolved into free mass media. The need for community support, the "Sixth Pillar" had grown into an independent court system, free representation in court and laws controlled by peers in a jury system, free organization of labor unions, and voting rights for everybody.** The degree of socializing services was waxing back and forth and had to find its equilibrium some time in the future. England had no written constitution. **Tradition had replaced it. Since the publication of the Magna Carta in 1215 and through its jury system the whole law book was based on the will of its people.**

(592) England has been a member of EU since 1973, but not of EMU. England is an original member of NATO.

(593) England has only three political parties: the Labor, Liberal, and Conservative parties. The population of England was 59.8 million in 2011 with 2% in farming. The GNP was estimated at $1520 billion and the GNP/citizen at $38,811. The defense cost was 2.32% of GNP. Numbers for external debt were not available.

**For Further Reading:**

(594) *Great Britain to 1688, A Modern History* by Maurice Ashley. The University of Michigan Press ISBN 61-8033.

(595) *Great Britain Since 1688, A Modern History* by K.B. Smellier ISBN 62-12161.

(596) *A Free Nation Deep in Debt, the Financial Roots of Democracy* by James Macdonald, ISBN 0-374-17143-2.

## European Union/EU

(597) In order to understand present day Europe, one has to understand how Western Europe is organized in what is called the European Union. How the EU will affect the "Nine Pillars" is not yet known. Right now there are movements for and against the EU. The union is supposed to ease free movements of people, products, and capital. Such movements improve trade the "Ninth Pillar" and support such a policy. But any change creates a counter movement. (For the history of the European Union, the reader is referred to the post war Germany.)

(598) The EU consists of 27 states since May 1, 2004. Alphabetically they are: Austria, Belgian, Bulgaria, Cyprus, Czech Republic, Denmark, Germany, Greece, England, Estonia, Finland, France, Holland, Hungary, Ireland, Italy, Latvia, Lithuania, Luxembourg, Malta, Poland, Portugal, Romania, Slovakia, Slovenia, Spain, and Sweden. It is administered by 1) EU Commission, 2) EU Parliament, and 3) EU Council of European Union. The membership of Bulgaria and Rumania is in progress. Their full membership requires judicial reforms and control of corruption of organized crime. Turkey has applied for membership but the application is presently resting.

(599) Seventeen European countries are not members: Albania, Andorra, Belarus, Bosnia-Herzegovina, Croatia, Macedonia, Iceland, Liechtenstein, Moldova, Monaco, Norway, Russia, San Marino, Serbia and Montenegro, Switzerland, Ukraine, and Vatican City.

(600) **The EU Commission** is the driving force and consists of a Chairman and one representative from each state. The 26 governments together elect the Chairman of the Commission. The Chairman-elect elect the 26 Members of the Commission in consultation with the different governments and which political area that needs to be covered. The Chairman, eight vice chairmen and 18 regular commissioners are all elected for five years. The Commission is

supported by professionals in a) the Economic and Social Committee, b) the EU Judicial Court, and c) Permanent Regional Committees from each country. All work is under the financial scrutiny of d) an auditing committee. Their seat is in Brussels, Belgium, but it has also an office in Luxemburg and representative offices in each country. The chairman and all commissioners act in the interest of the Union and not in the interest of individual states.

(601) **The EU Parliament** consists of 754 members elected by direct election from each country. Mandates are divided according to populations but, as in the presidential elections in the USA, small population states have compensating votes.

(602) The member states represent some 500 million people with more than 100 different political parties but members have still organized themselves into seven political blocks. The parties in the Parliament sit so they are organized from the left, meaning with central social planning, and to the right, meaning decentralized, local control and entrepreneurial freedom as also expriencd in the American Democratic and Republican Parties. The Parliament, jointly with the Council, discusses and approves European laws and budget for the Commission. The Pariament has the power to dismiss the EU Commission or any of its members. The Parliament does not have a regular meeting place, but moves between Strasbourg in France for larger meetings and Brussels for smaller.

(603) **The Council of EU**, or for short the Council, is the only decision-making institution and has 2500 secreterial members divided up into six departments. The Council balances the intersts of the states with that of EU. It meets weekly in Brussels or Luxembourg. It consists of one member from each state, which one, depends on which question is to be decided on. If a question of economic nature is on the agenda, the finance ministers attend; if an educational question is on the agenda, the educational minister of each country attend, and so on. Specific questions delegated to the Council are those of security and international matter that concern the whole EU. The Council can sign for international agreements. The voting power in the Council is proportional to the population of each state

with some modification to accommodate smaller states: Decisions are made with 72.3% majority for most questions making decisions conservative. Admissions to EU have to be unanimous. Each member may require verification that the vote represents 62% of the total EU population. **A General Secretarate** with its departments supports the Council. The chairman of the council **rotates** among original member states every six months.

(604) The EU is not a United Nation and not a Federated United State like USA, but seems to be a way to implement and standardize access to work and capital all through Europe, not giving up too much of the nationality of each state. Laws and programs are mainly those that have been proven effective, or not effective, between states in the USA. They are one by one initiated by the Commission, discussed in the Parliament and decided on in the Council. The system is an effective way to spread democracy through all the different EU nations and cleaning out different monopolies and cartels. Nothing originates directly from, or is decided on, by the people and this may need to be addressed some time in the future. The democracy rests on that each state, large or small, has equal say in the Commission's ongoing standardization process. When the Council addresses foreign policy and this does not agree with that of the major member states, EU may break apart into national states, as it did for the second Iraq war.

(605) The past French president Giscard d'Estaing has been working on a constitution for EU. It was accepted in 2004 but has to be ratified by the different states. EU will be a Union based on a treaty between the members states. The Union will have a common foreign policy when this new constitution is accepted. One of the commissioners will be designated to be responsible for foreign policy. (http://europa.eu.int/futurum)

(606) The European Union is comprised of member countries with varying levels of industrialization, socialization, unionization, monetary politics, medical, health, and safety regulations. The different regulations needed to be coordinated so as to allow for a

free movement of people, capital, and products, thereby securing a peaceful European landscape, which is the ultimate goal for the EU.

(607) **The European Council of Ministers**, not to be confused with the EU Council of Ministers, is a quarterly meeting of Prime and Foreign Ministers from each state. They meet in the country of the chairperson of the EU Council. The European Council discusses general directions of politics. It does not make any decisions but can make strong recommendations because of the political weight of its members.

(608) **The EU Judicial court** consists of 27 justices, one from each country. It interprets the different rules. The EU Justices rule in disagreements among states, organizations, and individuals regarding EU questions. There is one lower level and one for appeals. An ombudsman from each country helps individual citizens to appeal to the EU Judicial court.

(609) The immediate and so far most important effect of the EU has been the dismantling of duties and local monopolies or cartels common in the different small countries. This will eventually lead to cheaper prices and better control of inflation for consumers in Europe. In Sweden prices of building material, clothing and food have been held back since joining EU.

(610) Most of the old Soviet vassal states are applying for admission to the EU. Some states have now met safety, economic, and hygiene standards. Salaries are a problem. Before a state can be admitted into the European Economic Community, the EMU, and be allowed to use the common currency, the Euro, the state has to show that it can control inflation and not to be caught in the trap of the "Tragedy of the Commons." (See Part IX.) Denmark, England and Sweden have not joined EMU despite being part of EU.

(611) EU has 5% farmers. GNP/citizen in Sweden's is close to the average within EU, but it varies from 35% (Latvia) to Luxemburg which has a GNP that is 180% of Sweden. Luxemburg is the seat of the EU Judicial Court. Greece is close to going bankrupt. The five-fold spread in GNP between Latvia and Luxemburg points to a majority issue with the EU.

# United States of America/USA

(612) While the geography of the countries of the Euro-Asian continent formed its inhabitants, the people of immigrants formed the countries of the new continent. The American continent had its indigenous population. The most populous and most advanced cultures, the Aztecs and the Incas have been described. In North America, the population went through the usual evolution from hunters to agriculture, but many resumed a nomadic hunting life after the introduction of the horse by the Spaniards.

(613) The immigration to North America came mainly from Western Europe from the countries that dominated the sea in 1600—the French, English, Dutch and on a lesser scale the Swedes. They all charted trading companies and encouraged settlements in North America. The French in Canada with Quebec as the center, the Dutch in New York, the Swedes in Delaware with Wilmington as the center, and the English all along the rest of the Atlantic coast from Maine to Georgia. The Dutch took over the tiny Swedish settlement in a skirmish and the total Dutch settlement was turned over to the English without a shot in 1664.

(614) The different emigration policies of the remaining two powers, France and England, formed the future settlers' composition of the country. France had Jesuit advisers and limited emigration jealously to French Catholics. The English encouraged people of any nationality and any religious denomination to immigrate. The Atlantic Coast was in 1733 organized under different charters into 13 colonies: Massachusetts, New Hampshire, Rhode Island, Connecticut, New York, New Jersey, Pennsylvania, Delaware, Maryland, Virginia, North Carolina, South Carolina, and Georgia.

(615) The chartered trading companies worked by assigning an area of land to a group of landed immigrants, who would select a leader and form a council to legislate common laws or affairs. The council designated a portion of the land to common land and divided the rest between the settlers for a low price. The council would form

an Upper House when the settlement became larger. Two representatives from each town would form a House of Commons.

(616) People in the north tended to live in towns and travel to their smaller farms. Those in the south tended to live primarily on larger farms, in Manors, more isolated from each other. Where the religious Puritans settled, the minister was likely to be the leader of the council. William Penn, a Quaker, formed a future model for an American state. He promoted his chartered land by pamphlets as a land of green garden cities, cheap land to farm, and just freedom. Philadelphia became the second largest English city. When the colonies grew more populous, a statute of the royal crown, issued by the council of the king, replaced their charter. The royal council sent an English Governor to look out for royal interests. This became an early subject of conflict.

(617) In 1700, the population in the colonies had grown to about 250,000 and was now growing even more rapidly. The time was characterized by the centralization of administration directly from England and its effect on the economies of the colonies and also by the competition with the French for the colonization of the rest of the continent. The French immigrants were fewer in number and therefore engaged the Indians to help them. They explored and fortified the area from Quebec down throughout the Ohio valley all the way to New Orleans. The "Seven Years' War" between France, Russia and Austria on one side and England and Prussia on the other had already started in Europe and was now extended to the colonies. Quebec fell in 1759. Peace was signed in Paris in 1763. England was given the right to all land east of the Mississippi River.

(618) The Seven Years' War in Europe ended with the Paris Treaty, but the conflict between the colonies and their homeland intensified. England sent troops freed from its European wars to the colonies and insisted the colonies pay for them. The royal council also made a law to collect duty on trade in the American Colonies. The colonies had asked for neither troops nor duties. The purpose of the duty was taxation and, still worse, taxation without representation. The troops were there to enforce the new laws. A few patriots in the garb of

Indians with war painted faces climbed a ship with tea and dumped 342 chests of tea into the harbor. The English governor insisted that the damage be paid for and the villains brought to court or for the council of the state to pay for the tea.

(619) For the first time, the councils of the different colonies met in a Continental Congress in Philadelphia in 1774. The Continental Congress answered for all colonies that the council of Boston should not be held responsible. All 13 colonies supported Boston and the state of Massachusetts on this question, referring to the rights of humanity. **The rights of the British citizen had been talked about before; now for the first time the question was the fundamental rights of man. George III, the king, insisted on his rights as sovereign. The English Parliament gave its support to the king with both military and economic measures.**

(620) A second Continental Congress met on July 2, 1776 and on July 4th declared independence. The formulation of the Declaration of Independence made it one of humanity's most beautifully written documents. It lists many of the abuses used by bigger states over smaller and the dictatorial central powers over its people. The declaration very humbly describes why it takes these extreme steps for freedom.

(621) The declaration was originally written in one long paragraph. I will divide it into single statements and refer to the "Nine Pillars" that it notes are violated by the king. If a claim is that of an imposing law, it is taken as a violation of communication and community support. If a claim is a military threat, it is taken as a violation of a safe dwelling. If a claim is restricting commerce, it is taken as a violation of trade, the "Ninth Pillar." These comments are within a parenthesis with a "P" followed by a number to which pillar the "P" refers.

# The Declaration of Independence
## In Congress, July 4, 1776
## The Unanimous Declaration of the Thirteen
## United States of America

(622) *When in the course of human events it becomes necessary for one people to dissolve the political bands which have connected them with another, and to assume among the powers of the earth, the separate and equal station to which the Laws of Nature and of Nature's God entitle them, a decent respect to the opinions of mankind requires that they should declare the causes which impel them to the separation.*

(623) *We hold these truths to be self-evident, that all men are created equal, that they are endowed by their Creator with certain unalienable Rights, that among these are Life, Liberty and the pursuit of Happiness (p 1-9). That to secure these rights, Government are instituted among Men, deriving their just powers from the consent of the governed, That whenever any Form of Government becomes destructive of these ends, it is the Right of the People to alter or to abolish it, and to institute new Government, laying its foundation on such principles and organizing its powers in such form, as to them shall seem most likely to effect their Safety and Happiness.*

(624) *Prudence, indeed, will dictate that Governments long established should not be changed for light and transient courses; and accordingly to all experience has shown, that mankind are more disposed to suffer, while evils are sufferable, then to right themselves by abolishing the forms to which they are accustomed. But when a long train of abuses and usurpation, pursuing invariably the same Object evinces a design to reduce them under absolute Despotism, it is their right, it is their duty, to throw off such Government, and to provide new Guards for their future security. -- Such has been the patience sufferance of these colonies: and such is now the pillar, which constrains them to alter their former Systems of Government. The history of the present King of Great Britain is a history of repeated injuries and usurpation, all having in direct object the establishment of*

*absolute Tyranny over the States. To prove this, let Facts be submitted to a candid world.*

(625) *He has refused his Assent to Laws, the most wholesome and necessary for the public good.* **(p 5,6)**

(626) *He has forbidden his Governors to pass Laws of immediate and pressing importance, unless suspended in their operation till his Assent should be obtained; and when so suspended he has utterly neglected to attend to them.* **(p 5,6)**

(627) *He has refused to pass other Laws for the accommodation of large districts of people, unless those people would relinquish the right of Representation in the Legislature, a right inestimable to them and formidable to tyrants only.* **(p 5,6)**

(628) *He has called together legislative bodies at places unusual, uncomfortable, and distant from the depository of their public Records, for the sole purpose of fatiguing them into compliance with his measures.* **(p 5,6)**

(629) *He has dissolved Representative Houses repeatedly, for opposing with manly firmness his invasions on the rights of the people.* **(p 5,6)**

(630) *He has refused for a long time, after such dissolution to cause other to be elected; whereby the Legislative Powers, incapable of Annihilation, have returned to the People at large for their exercise; the State remaining in the mean time exposed to all the dangers of invasion from without, and convulsions within.* **(p 2)**

(631) *He has endeavored to prevent the population of these States; for that purpose obstructing the Laws of Naturalization of Foreigners; refusing to pass others to encourage their migration hither, and raising the conditions of new Appropriations of Lands.* **(p 5,6)**

(632) *He has obstructed the Administration of Justice, by refusing his Ascent to Laws for establishing Judiciary Powers.* **(p 6)**

(633) *He has made Judges dependent on his Will alone, for the tenure of their offices, and the amount and payment of their salaries.* **(p 6)**

(634) *He has erected a multitude of New Offices, and sent hither swarms of Officers to harass our people, and eat out their substance.* **(p 2,6)**

(635) *He has kept among us in times of peace, Standing Armies without the Consent of our legislature.* **(p 2,6)**

(636) *He has affected to render the Military independent of and superior to the Civil Power.* **(p 2,6)**

(637) *He has combined with others to subject us to a jurisdiction foreign to our constitution, and unacknowledged by our laws; giving his Ascent to their Acts of pretended Legislation:* **(p 6)**

(638) *For quartering large bodies of armed troops among us:* **(p 6)**

(639) *For protecting them, by a mock Trial, from punishment for any murders which they should commit on the Inhabitants of these States:* **(p 6)**

(640) *For cutting off our Trade with all parts of the world:* **(p 9)**

(641) *For imposing Taxes on without our Consent:* **(p 6)**

(642) *For depriving us in many cases, of the benefit of Trial by Jury:* **(p 6)**

(643) *For transporting us beyond Seas to be tried for pretended offences:* **(p 6)**

(644) *For abolishing the free System of English Laws in a neighboring Province, establishing therein an Arbitrary government, and enlarging its Boundaries so as to render it at once and example and fit instrument for introducing the same absolute rule into these Colonies:* **(p 2)**

(645) *For taking away our Charters, abolishing our most valuable Laws and altering fundamentally the Forms of our Governments:* **(p 5,6)**

(646) *For suspending our own Legislature, and declaring themselves invested with Power to legislate for us in all cases whatsoever.* **(p 5,6)**

(647) *He has abdicated Government here, by declaring us out his Protection and waging War against us.* **(p 2,5,6)**

(648) *He has plundered our seas, ravaged our Coast, burnt our towns, and destroyed the life of our people.* **(p 2,5,6,9)**

(649) *He is at this time transporting large armies of foreign mercenaries to complete the work of death, desolation and tyranny*

*already begun with circumstances of Cruelty & Perfidy scarcely paralleled in the most barbarous ages, and totally unworthy the Head of a civilized nation. (p 2,5,6,9)*

(650) *He has constrained our fellow Citizens, taken Captive on the high Seas to bear Arms against their country, to become the executioners of their friends and Brethren, or to fall themselves by their Hands. (p 2,5,6,9)*

(651) *He excited domestic insurrections amongst us, and endeavor red to bring on the inhabitants of our frontiers, the merciless Indian Savages, whose known rule of war fair, is an undistinguished destruction of all ages, sexes and conditions. (p 2,5,6,9)*

(652) *In every stage of these Oppressions We have Petitioned for Redress in the most humble terms: Our repeated Petitions have been answered only by repeated injury. A Prince, whose character is thus marked by every act, which may define a Tyrant, is unfit to be the ruler of a free people. (p 5)*

(653) *Nor have We been wanting in attention to our British Brethren. We have warned them from time to time of attempts by their legislature to extend an unwarrantable jurisdiction over us. We have reminded them of the circumstances of our emigration and settlement here. We have appealed to their native justice and magnanimity, and we have conjured them by the ties of our common kindred to disavow these usurpations, which would inevitably interrupt our connections and correspondence. They too have been deaf to the voice of justice and consanguinity. We must, therefore, acquiesce in the pillar, which denounces our Separation, and hold them, as we hold the rest of mankind, Enemies in War, in Peace Friends. (p 6)*

(654) *We, therefore, the Representative of United States of America, in General Congress, Assembled, appealing to the Supreme Judge of the world for the rectitude of our intentions, do, in the Name, and by Authority of the good People of these Colonies, solemnly publish and declare, That these United Colonies are, and of Right ought to be Free and Independent States: that they are Absolved from all Allegiance to the British Crown, and that all political connection between them and the State of Great Britain, is and ought to be totally dissolved; and*

*that as Free and Independent States, they have full Power to levy War, conclude Peace, contract Alliances, establish Commerce, and to do all other Acts and Things which Independent States may of right do. And for the support of this Declaration, a firm reliance on the protection of Divine Providence, we mutually pledge to each other our Lives, our Fortunes and our sacred Honor.*

(655) John Hancock and representatives from each of the thirteen states signed the declaration.

(656) The bonds with England were broken because the king violated several of the "Nine Pillars."

(657) England interfered in the colonies' trade. Soldiers appeared not at the request of the people for their security, but were threatening people's security. Judges, by being partial, threatened a fair community support. Laws were imposed without representation, which was a breakdown in communication and could lead to a lack of community support. The bond with England was not based on an administration for and by the people and started to have signs of a military submission.

(658) **The American Revolutionary War started in 1775 and ended with the treaty in Paris 1783.**

(659) The U.S. received the land between the Appalachian Mountains and the Ohio valley from England. English loyalists fled to Canada; some went back to England or to its possessions in the Caribbean.

(660) The Continental Congress had acted as a national government until this time. How should the newly born nation be administered?

(661) George Washington, the general who had led the war effort for the colonies, was broadly respected but did not want to be a king. A first constitution was drawn up as the Articles of Confederation, where each state was an independent unit. It became necessary to have a central office to handle foreign and interstate affairs. Constitutional conventions were held in every state, negotiations were worked out, and eventually one constitution was ratified by all states in 1788. **The first state to ratify the federal constitution was the previous Swedish colony, Delaware.**

(662) The Constitution of the United States starts with a now very famous preamble, which is worth repeating:

(663) *"We the People of the United States, in Order to form a more perfect Union, establish Justice, insure Tranquility, provide for the common defense, promote the general Welfare, and secure the Blessings of Liberty to ourselves and our Posterity, do ordain and establish this CONSTITUTION for United States of America."*

(664) **The U.S. derived much of its constitution from English law, but expanded the system with Montesquieu's concept of checks and balances within the three branches of government: the executive branch (the Presidency with its Federal administration), the legislative branch (the law making arm, that is the two Houses of Senate and Congress), and the judicial branch (the law enforcing arm, that is all the Federal Courts). Both the President and the members of the law-making houses are appointed directly from the people independent from each other, each having their own mandate for the election period.**

(665) The serious presidential candidates come from primary elections in different member states in which their personal and political appeal is tested. The strongest candidates submit themselves for election at the national party convention. The one elected by the national convention gets the full party support. He or she has to challenge the opponent in the final, national election of the president.

(666) The populous vote for presidency in each state first elects electors who then elect the President. The President, the executive, stays for his mandated period of four years, independent of which party has majority in the Houses.

(667) The President appoints Federal Judges for life but they have to be approved by both houses.

(668) **History since the English "honorable revolution" 1689 and the American Revolution 1776 has proven the strength of democratic government versus the totalitarian governments for modern states.**

(669) The original USA Constitution contained 15 Articles. Each Article was divided into sections to establish in detail how the federation should be administered.

(670) No one knew with certainty how the new constitution would work. Provisions for more amendments were therefore included. The Founding Fathers made it purposely hard to amend the constitution. In order to ratify an amendment, a two-third majority in both the Senate and the House of Representatives was required and also ratification by three-fourths of the different state's legislatures. **The first amendment added to the Federal Constitution in 1787 assured free speech and forbid a national church**.

(671) The new champion country of liberty ironically permitted slavery, largely because the economy of the country was 90% dependent on agriculture. The competing European agricultural economy did not depend on slaves, but was based on farm workers that through different laws were practically slaves. The continuous price pressure on this the oldest of all industries had created this condition. It had started already when Egyptian grain flooded Roman Italy.

(672) The attitude towards slavery varied among the states. The southern states, which depended on slaves for the workings of the big farms, were in favor of keeping slaves; the northern states, with smaller family farms and the beginnings of industrialization, were against it. **Delaware, the old Swedish colony, was the first state to outlaw slaves already in 1776**; other northern states followed. In the south, with its big majority of black population, much was at stake, both economically and politically.

(673) The continent was divided among three nations. USA in the east reached to the Ohio valley. France claimed the land between the Ohio and Mississippi and Spain the rest of the west. **The original charters for the first colonies went from coast to coast, which was known as "Manifest Destiny."** The virgin western land to the Ohio River was surveyed, divided into sections (1 section = 1 sq. mi. = 640 ac. = 320 hectares), with 36 sections making up a township. One section was reserved for schools. The price for one section was $1/ac. A square area between Maryland and Virginia was established for

a capital. The second president, Madison, was the first president to reside in the White House. Roads were needed to knit the country together, but there was no money in the government. Private enterprise built turnpikes to be used for a fee.

(674) The Western Reserve contained four million acres. When a territory had 5000 free adult males, it could send a non-voting representative to the National Congress. When the population had grown to 60,000, it could draw up a state constitution and enter the Union. Each state would have its own Bill of Rights promising freedom of worship, jury trials, and protection of "habeas corpus," or reasonable and due process of the law. A Federal Supreme Court would supervise the enactment of the Federal Constitution and other interstate activities

(675) Currency was a problem. In the beginning, the different states issued paper money but without a proper basis for the currency it depreciated rapidly. **Alexander Hamilton started a national bank**. Paper money was represented in value by gold held in security for the printed currency by the national bank. These measures made the USA ready to trade internationally. That international trade took off and the pursuit of happiness through trade (the Ninth Pillar) was not hindered. However, the limited gold in the world compared to the value of property and production eventually made gold impractical as a security. **(The gold standard had to be partly omitted. A standard based on trade and productivity has been inter-nationally accepted.)**

(676) Daniel Webster published his first dictionary and standardized the written language.

(677) Presidential elections occur every four years. Two senators from each state are elected for six years; one third of the Senate is up for election every two years. The two Senators are up for election at different times. The legislators are elected for only two years and are therefore an interim check on the president's mandate. The base for all the elections is the total population over 18 years old, modified by electors in the presidential elections. Each state has a different, but a set number of electors to balance the big populous states versus

the small states. If the electoral vote is even, the vote goes to the House of Representatives. Such an outcome required 36 ballots before Jefferson, the third President, could be confirmed in 1800. The flaws were remedied in the next election in 1804. These remedies held in the close election of 2000. Claimed flaws in the voting machines in the 2000 election are now being addressed. **Even such a simple thing as elections takes time and major invest-ments to standardize in a democracy.**

(678) **Since Napoleon was short of funds for his wars in Europe, he offered the French province of Louisiana to the USA for $15 million. The Louisiana Purchase was accomplished in 1803. Florida was bought from Napoleon's vassal state, Spain for $5 million in 1819. Alaska was bought from Russia in 1867 for $7.2 million. The USA extending its territory by a peaceful purchase is, as far as I know, unique in history.** President Jefferson in 1804 gave Lewis and Clark a commission to explore the new territory in the west.

(679) The Napoleon Wars marked the years in the beginning of 1800. The USA declared neutrality. Both England and France blocked each other's trade in order to try to subdue each other by starvation. The English aggressively violated American ships. Eventually, the USA declared war against England in the War of 1812. The war with England ended by itself by Napoleon's defeat at Waterloo, but the USA had been allied with the losing side. A border between the USA and Canada was established along the 49th parallel, as part of the settlement with victorious England. Oregon and Washington states were formed through negotiations between England and the USA.

(680) Two overriding issues characterized the following 50 years. First was the physical expansion and settling of the west. Second was maintaining the balance between the slave states and non-slave states. The Missouri territory gave birth to five new states: Louisiana in 1812, Indiana in 1816, Mississippi in 1817, Illinois in 1818, and Alabama in 1819. This kept the slave/non-slave states ratio at 12/12. Florida became a state in the Union in 1845.

(681) Mexico declared its independence from Spain in 1821. Claims from the royal Hapsburg family and Napoleon had complicated its

independence war. President James Monroe, in his annual address to the Congress on December 2, 1823, declared that the USA would accept the present colonies in America but would not tolerate any new or any transfer of colonies between European countries. This has in history been called the "**Monroe Doctrine.**"

(682) After Mexico had declared its independence from Spain, a land speculator, Stephen Austin, received a large land grant to settle 300 families from Colorado in Texas. Soon, there were 30,000 American settlers versus 3500 Mexicans. The Mexican president, Santa Anna decided to reinforce his military control. This was taken as a challenge. A Texas army under Sam Houston defeated the Mexican Army. A constitution was drawn up; Texas declared its independence in 1836 with an application to the Union. President Jackson wanted to maintain peace with Mexico and did not accept the application. Texas was accepted into the Union in 1856, after the Texas President Sam Houston pretended to flirt with England. England and the USA claimed the Oregon Territory in a partnership. A new treaty was negotiated; the territory was turned over to the USA in 1859 and eventually split into two states—Oregon and Washington.

(683) California was settled by large Mexican land grants. California was flooded with prospectors after John Sutter had discovered gold in 1848 in his water-driven mill. They soon outnumbered the Mexicans. California drew up a constitution and applied to the Union in 1849 without any skirmish with Mexico.

(684) The slave controversy dominated politics for the next 20 years. For the South, it was a question of economic survival. For the people in the North, it was a moral issue. The European 30-year war in 1600 had started on a moral basis of religious freedom, but turned into a land/tax grab issue. **A war based solely on moral grounds had never happened before in history.** Would people risk their life for a moral cause that really did not affect life in the North? Here slavery was already outlawed. Abraham Lincoln, the Republican Party candidate, had won the election on the promise that he would insist that the South accept a Federal Constitution with equal rights for all. When the Republicans now faced the possibility of war, they

hesitated. Different attempts to negotiate were tried. South Carolina in a state convention decided to secede from the Union and prepared for war. Other southern states followed within weeks. In February 1861, a Constitution affirming slavery was written and a Confederate States of America formed with the Capital in Richmond, Virginia. Jefferson Davis was elected President. The Confederate State sent two envoys to England to ask for its support, but the envoys were not even recognized. The USA Congress met in July without its southern representatives and authorized loans for 500,000 volunteer soldiers.

(685) The North had one of the USA's best presidents, poor generals, and great industry and railway transport system. The South had a poor president, a great general in Robert E. Lee, a poor industry and poor railway system. Much of the South's success would depend on a navy for transport on the rivers and across the Atlantic. The ironclad ships and the first submarine put the South at an advantage in the beginning.

(686) Two engineers played some role in turning the navy battle into a success for the North. John Dahlgren invented the soda bottle cannon, named so from its heavy base and narrow front. It turned out to be a very effective cannon for the ships. John Erikson, a Swedish immigrant and, the inventor of the propeller, placed two of Dahlgren's guns on a turret just above the waterline on his steel covered Monitor and challenged successfully the ironclad Merrimack. Without a navy, the South's defeat was just a matter of time. (The battle is regularly celebrated and reenacted on a lake in Philipstad, Sweden, the birthplace of John Ericson)

(687) The decisive land battle stood at Gettysburg, Pennsylvania, on July 3-5, 1863. Three thousand Northerners and 4000 Southerners lay dead on the battlefield, all together with 50,000 wounded, every one of them American. President Lincoln came to the site and gave a short speech that has become a pillar stone in the history of the struggle for human rights:

(688) *"Four score and seven years ago our fathers brought forth upon this continent a new nation, conceived in Liberty, and dedicated to the proposition that all men are created equal.*

(689) *Now we are engaged in a great civil war, testing whether that nation or any nation so conceived and so dedicated can long endure. We are met on a battlefield of that war. We are met to dedicate a portion of it as the final resting-place of those who here gave their lives that that nation might live. It is all together fitting and proper that we should do this.*

(690) *But in a larger sense we cannot dedicate – we can not consecrate – we cannot hallow this ground. The brave men living and dead who struggled here have consecrated it far above our poor power to add or detract. The world will little note nor long remember what we say here, but it can never forget what they did here. It is for us, the living, rather to be dedicated here to the unfinished work that they have thus so far nobly carried on. It is rather for us to be here dedicated to the great task remaining before us – that from these honored dead we take increased devotion to that cause for which they here gave the last measure of devotion:*

(691) *that we here highly resolve that the dead shall not have died in vain*

(692) *that the nation shall, under God, have a new birth of freedom*

(693) *and that governments of the people, by the people, and for the people, shall not perish from the earth."*

(694) General Lee surrendered on April 9, 1865. Five days later, John Wilkes Booth, a southerner, shot President Lincoln at Ford Theater. Vice President Johnson became President.

(695) President Andrew Johnson tried to follow Lincoln's policy of moderation towards the South, but the Republicans totally in power in the Congress declared the defeated South as a territory ruled by army garrisons. The 13th Amendment liberated the slaves. Slaves were given lands from the big manors. A 14th Amendment made sure the 13th could never be changed in the future and that everybody born in the USA had full citizenship rights independent of color of skin, race, national origin, and so on. The Republican Party insisted on a still stronger civil rights law in a 15th Amendment prohibiting any denial of voting due to color to complement the 13th Amendment. When

Johnson tried to veto it, Congress tried to impeach him. President Johnson stayed in office with one vote's margin.

(696) The reconstruction of the South had to start. Amnesty was given to everybody who would give an oath of allegiance to the Federal Constitution and loyalty to the Proclamation of Emancipation of the slaves. The southern states were again admitted to the Union. Georgia, the last state, accepted the 15th Amendment in 1870.

(697) The post-war years were occupied with the assimilation of the former slaves into the general population. Even if the law and the concept were morally correct, people had to learn to accept each other. As past slaves, African-Americans had not been schooled. Farming is what most knew and most of them ended up as tenant farmers.

(698) The South instituted a society in which the black and the white populations lived in separate areas, east and west part of town, had separate schools and separate travel accommodations. This pattern of segregation spread to include the entire country, the North and the South, including the army in WW I. They were asked to defend a nation in which they played a different role. All armed forces became fully integrated with equal opportunity for all in 1949. The WW II General, Dwight D. Eisenhower became President in 1952. He had seen the importance of fair integration of the army. The Supreme Court ordered in 1954 all schools to be racially integrated and required that children be bussed between schools to make sure that all public schools had pupils of all races. President Kennedy required all home loans to meet integration standards. This made it possible for anybody to buy a home and move into neighborhoods according to what they could afford. All factories having federal contracts had to have a working force that was proportional to the race of the surrounding population and to prove that they did not discriminate in their employment, promotion or pay schedule. Travel accommodations like hotels, trains and restaurants were forbidden to use discrimination for its customers. The discrimination laws were enforced. The demand for integration became a national movement. Women and minorities, based on national origin, race and handicap,

demanded equality with equal opportunity to be accepted and, if possible, be accommodated into both the workforce and the public life.

(699) Minority rights were accomplished through the courts on the basis of the Constitution with equal rights for all.

(700) Immigration to the USA throughout its history has been open. Anyone from any country has been welcome. Since the Old World was still essentially a farming world, producing food for the population, not much in the way of other industries contributed to the public's prosperity. In the early 1800s, weather and crop diseases caused famine in northern Europe, Ireland, and England, causing millions to flee to the USA. When the tractor was invented in early 1900, millions of farm workers all over the world lost their work. Those millions also fled to the USA. The western farmland and the eastern factories in the USA assimilated and gave a living to the largest voluntary people movement in history. The social upheaval that followed such an enormous people movement was solved within the framework of the U.S. Constitution.

(701) The large factories led to large workforces and large cities, the largest in the world, all within a few decades. Demand for housing, schools, water, food, police, fire control, sanitation, sewage, hospitals, and transportation all had to be met. Federal and state agencies were set in place to set sanitary standards and given power to enforce them. The huge scale of the investments in these enterprises had never been experienced in history. Big monopolistic trusts or cartels were formed. As in all unchecked situations, they used the great demand to personal advantage. Laws forbidding monopolies were introduced to control the abuse. The legal process to meet the needs of people is a continuous process. All of these changes took time, money, and political struggles to realize and are still going on. New loopholes for abuse are still discovered and checked. **Illegal bookkeeping by dishonest auditors of the supplier of energy to the State of California, the Enron Corporation, demonstrates that any access to public money may be abused and has to be checked.**

(702) A social support system was developed. Pension for elderly, handicapped, and unemployed was introduced in the thirties by President Franklin D. Roosevelt and is continuously corrected for inflationary living costs.

(703) Trade Unions were formed to negotiate salaries and improve working conditions. Laws established minimum wages, working time, and sanitary conditions in the factories and on the farms. The new laws did not come without political fight, but the changes were confirmed within the framework of the Constitution.

(704) The USA took part in both WW I and WW II and played the deciding role in both without any land seizure. For the USA, they were moral wars in order to save democracies.

(705) A competitive "cold" war followed WW II. The Soviet Union started to be more and more dependent on its vassal states for basic needs, particularly food. People were fleeing East Germany by the thousands. Even the wall could not keep people inside the communist block. East Germany, Poland, and Hungary all revolted and had to be kept down by Soviet tanks.

(706) Based on his personal experiences with Soviet Russia/ Soviet Union President Truman made a dogmatic commitment to try to block any communist military expansion anywhere around the word. The United Nations, mainly with USA troops, stopped the communist North Korean aggression supported by the Soviet Union and Communist China. The USA lost 30,000 soldiers in Korea. The USA also assisted France to stop communist aggression in Vietnam. France surrendered and the USA became the sole defender of South Vietnam, but was driven out of Vietnam after 50,000 casualties. A United Nations partnership stopped the military dictatorship of Iraq to take over Kuwait. The communist Serb's invasion and genocide of its neighbors was checked by NATO troops, but again mainly by the USA military. The Serb communist leaders wre imprisoned at the International Court in Hague, accused of violations of human rights.

(707) **All these military expeditions were moral police expeditions to defend the concept of democracy, not an action for national defense. In the long run such expeditions can only be done**

**with international support and a professional army, not with an army based on a general draft.**

(708) The population of the USA in 2012 was estimated at 310 million with 2% in agriculture. The modern GNP was estimated to be $14,700 trillion, with the modern GNP/citizen at $48,000. Cost of defense was 4.06% of modern GNP. Debt was estimated at 10% of modern GNP.

**For Further Reading:**

(709) *The United States to 1865* by Michael Kraus. The University of Michigan Press, ISBN 59-62502.

(710) *The United States Since 1865* by Foster Rhea Dulles. The University of Michigan Press, ISBN 59-6250.

# Part III

# The Industrial Period
## from 1826 to the Present:
## The Motor Driven Food Distribution Time

(711) The break between agricultural and industrial time went very fast compared to how previous periods emerged. A specific event may be assigned to the start of the industrial revolution. The key-event was when George Stephenson started his steam-locomotive on rails built between Liverpool and Manchester in the year 1826. People took notice of what possibilities the railway had to offer for the transport of people, goods, and specifically food products, the main industry of the time.

(712) Before the century was over, railways spanned a transport network across England, Western Europe, and North America. Distances over land that would need weeks or months to cover with horse and buggy could be covered in days with railroads. A human being was now empowered to bring himself and his goods over much greater distances. The circle for contacts went from horse and buggy horizon to global. World trade was already taking place by sailing ships, but compared with what now was possible with steam ships, it was just rudimentary. The steam engine was a unique invention. It was power that propelled itself just like a horse. The locomotive was appropriately called an iron horse. Actually, the pressure in the steam engine was measured in units of horsepower. The generic self-propelled engine transporting a large amount of food over long distances became the basis on which the industrial period with large cities was built.

(713) Food was produced not just for the family as during the tarp time or just for the local market as during cart time, but for the family meal of the global market.

(714) The steam engine was a popular mechanical breakthrough. Technical tinkering became the pastime of many men and every little boy, as even I can remember. The result was a flood of applications for patents of new mechanical inventions.

(715) In 1890, the combustion engine and the automobile saw the market. That year Carl Benz and Gottlieb Daimler, two early pioneers in car building, joined forces and started the first successful car manufacturing plant. The car was called Mercedes-Benz. MB has become the world's oldest continuously operating car manufacturer, with factories built in several other countries. After Henry Ford started the assembly line, a country's definition as an industrial nation became synonymous with having a car factory. The automobile like the locomotive was self-propelled. The automobile led to the building of a network of roads bringing people and goods closer together, even door to door.

(716) The cousin to the gasoline engine, the diesel engine, revolutionized farming. The diesel tractor replaced the horse and

numerous farm workers. More of the farmer's land could be assigned to commercial farming when the farmer did not need to feed horse or worker. Owning a tractor and other farm machinery required such a large capital investment that many smaller farms went out of business. Larger farms with fewer workers resulted in the greatest people movement in history. Before the farms were mechanized 95% of the population made their living from work in agriculture. After mechanization 95% of the people had to make their living in towns in service or in factories. Millions of farm workers moved to town or immigrated to young countries. This movement of farm workers is now going on in developing countries. Wherever it takes place, if it is happening too fast, it is causing major strain on social support systems. Ideally, it ought to happen parallel with the growth of local industries.

(717) Another combustion engine was the propeller engine of an airplane. The airplane made its debut in December 1903, when the Wright brothers, Orville and Wilbur, flew their little plane at Kill Devil Hill in North Carolina. The airplane enabled a new speed to transport. The jet engine later doubled that speed. People, goods, and fresh farm products can now be transported rapidly over long distances.

(718) The last step in self-propelled engines is the rocket engine. This made it possible to place communication satellites around the earth in space. Satellites allow us to have instant communication on a global scale. With rockets, other planets and solar systems can also be explored for a better understanding of our own universe.

(719) Energy to fuel these different engines is for the industrial society as fundamental as food for humans. All the engines mentioned above use some fuel that is burned for propulsion. A different kind of engine is the electrical. It, of course, uses electricity as fuel and has to stay tethered with its energy source by an electrical cable. It can be used locally or to run on rails but not to run anywhere else, not until practical batteries are developed.

(720) The technical know-how for the design of an electrical engine is similar to that of designing an electrical generator. Electricity from

generators is transferred to homes and factories for all kinds of needs for electricity. Water, wind, sun, natural gas, waste, or atomic power, each one at different costs, can drive generators. Now also a photocell can generate electricity.

(721) Other important inventions that bring people together are those in communications. Just in the last 100 years we have seen the birth of the large printing press, the telegraph, telephone, radio, television, and the personal computer with the Internet.

(722) All these technical inventions require a large engineering staff for support. Numerous engineering schools were founded at universities or as freestanding schools close to major industrial centers.

(723) Research spread to other disciplines of academia. Great strides were made in medicine. Bacteria and viruses were identified. Vaccines and antibiotics were developed for specific infections. In a sterile environment, surgery and delivery of babies had much-improved prognoses and also opened the field of organ transplantation. Many hormones were identified chemically so metabolic diseases like diabetes and thyroid diseases could be treated specifically. Through gene technology, we now see possibilities to treat many major diseases specifically instead of just symptomatically.

(724) The goal for this building process is for most people a family meal eaten in a safe, personalized home with access to a family support system and free moving global communication. This all can only be accomplished by a free global exchange of services.

## Industrial Time Versus the "Nine Pillars"

(725) This assessment of the "Nine Pillars" in industrialized countries would cover all the democratic countries covered in this book and others not mentioned.

(726) **Food:** The earth's population has grown exponentially during the industrial time. In the year 1800, the population of the earth was only 0.5 billion, while today it is more than 6 billion—12 times more. The rapid growth together with the movement of the

farm worker to the city has put a strain on both food supply and food distribution. Despite this development, most industrial countries have enough food for their own populations and even export food. Some countries have natural resources, which can be exchanged for food. Other countries, like Japan, have successfully started industries, producing products or services that can be exchanged for food and shelter.

(727) We saw in our review of history the family farm grow from a self-sustaining household to a local, national, and finally a global food producing farm industry. The improved agricultural productivity together with better transportation, international banking, international law, and currencies exchanges made it possible to reach the global market.

(728) The food shortage in some countries is due to political abuse and is unique to those areas. Some of the developing countries have similar problems. Local political problems and laws have to be resolved before such countries can enter into international trade.

(729) **Water:** The lack of fresh water in many areas of industrial countries is critical. Fresh water is needed for people, farms, and industries. This need creates a conflict around big cities in warm and dry areas. The overwhelming majority in the electorate of the city usually wins and has on occasion turned good farmland into desert. The subject of fresh water brings up the subject of land use: farmlands vs. city and non-farmland.

(730) **The size of the cities has been allowed to expand unchecked. Actually, mayors of big cities have been proud of the growth of their city during their political reign. The H/G time found by experience that a certain size of the band was most efficient for hunting and gathering within a given area. The same limitatations probably holds true for modern cities—a most efficient size for support and production.** There is a need for a national policy on city size and city location. What city families usually look for, besides work, is affordable housing with childcare, good schools, and recreational areas. These wishes do not need to collide with farm areas. Just the opposite is true. Such areas are not far from lakes, dams, seashores,

and mountains, areas usually unsuitable for farming. Now, the demand for such areas has instead created a market for a second home. It could equally well be for a main home, if work and support systems become available to those areas.

(731) **Air:** Air quality is adulterated by the exhaust from the many cars in slow commutes and many factory outlets, all due to the mega-size of the cities. In some cities, people have been forced to stay indoors because of poor air quality. Most sensitive are children due to their high metabolism and people with limited lung and heart capacity. It will take a major effort and investment to meet the problem of waste unless the trend towards mega-cities is not changed.

(732) **Energy:** Ninety-five percent (95%) of the people in industrial countries now live in cities and have to provide a service to humanity, which they can exchange for food and shelter. Many of the cities are mega-metropolises of several millions inhabitants. They have to be supplied with food, fresh water, and clean air, as well as energy to produce and transport their services or service products all over the globe. Many different kinds of energy resources have to be used: petroleum, natural gas, wood and waste, water, wind, sun, and nuclear. Some energy is used directly, while others are converted to electricity. New resources, like hydrogen, and nuclear fusion are being explored. These different energy resources are necessary for the survival of the industrial society, which rests on one basic, indisputable fact: **Food for the survival of 98% of individuals is produced by and gives work to less than 5% of the population.**

(733) Factories in the past had to be located close to a source for energy. This is how the first big industrial cities were built. The old industrial centers have continued to attract new industries because of the availability of a workforce, the entrepreneurial spirit, or banking resources. These ingredients created the mega-sized cities with millions of inhabitants. The cities have continued to grow, covering larger and larger areas of land with tremendous commutes to and from work for their inhabitants. A worker who puts in eight hours for the workday may need four hours to commute to and from work. A person needs eight hours for sleep. With 12 hours required for work and commute

that leaves only four hours for family life. **This is a family life of worse quality than the original cave life.** Public transportation may save costs and emissions, but not the more important factor for people: their private time. This concentration of industries in large metropolis is no longer necessary. A factory can be placed anywhere because energy can be easily produced or transported anywhere. Steps are needed to address these problems more fundamentally.

(734) **Safe Dwelling:** Trade unions in free democratic countries have negotiated salaries that allow many workers to choose between living in a single family home or an apartment. The dwellings have been getting safer since codes for buildings have been improved. Safeguards against disasters and inferior materials are being established. Technical improvements in heating, cooling, insulation from light, temp and sound, and security against crime are a continuous process. Different parts of the world are at different stages of this progress, depending on their needs and resources. The many laws regulating dwellings both for physical and financial security demonstrate the pertinence of this "Second Pillar."

(735) The continuous and rapid growth of large cities puts a pressure on the cost of city land. This eventually is reflected in an inflationary pressure on the price of the manufactured products, a bad by-product of the mega-city, not often mentioned. Increased production costs often lead to the transfer of the manufacturing to some other country with a cheaper product-producing environment, which has both good and bad consequences. **As we live in a global society, it is of value when work opportunities and therewith buying-power can be spread to less industrial countries.**

(736) **Cleanliness:** The development of large cities requires sophisticated supply lines for food, water, and energy, but also a support system to take care of both solid and gaseous waste. The pillar for cleanliness becomes so much more important when perhaps 100,000 people can be affected by one single mistake in the mass distribution system. The demand for good hygiene requires large investments to meet this pillar in modern cities.

(737) Cities are striving to build according to a sanitary code so dwellings can be kept clean. The technical know-how is available, but the system can be strained in areas where population growth is too fast. Not all towns in the world have sanitary codes. The pillar to re-circulate waste is important and part of the pillar for cleanliness. Waste handling and re-circulation of waste has by itself become a big industry in large cities. Different countries are at different stages of this development. These improvements are a continuous process. The pillar is recognized. A technical evolution to meet this requirement is taking place; the "Third Pillar" is obvious.

(738) **Art:** When families move into their dwellings, they will always start to beautify and personalize their home. This basic need has intensified trade for home products in direct proportion to the increase in population and people's income. Public art and entertainment is also an expression of the beautification of life. Life without art would be rather worthless. The need for art may not seem necessary to survive, but it is as eternal as human civilization and therefore a basic "Fourth Pillar" for a happy, healthy, and prosperous life.

(739) **Freedom to Communicate:** The ability to reach each other has improved immensely during the industrial time. People as buyers and sellers of goods are brought together by all the new communication and transportation inventions. The full impact of the global Internet is not yet obvious, but will be immense. Information for trade, knowledge, and family ties has become a true global phenomenon. The increase in work generated from this global economy is essential and will help further the growth and better the living standard of the earth's population. The historical, spontaneous fall of dogmatic societies with controlled communications dem-onstrate the futility in controlling communication. Communication grows in step with education. Education is always seeking the truth, a fundamental need for any society and a proof for the "Fifth Pillar."

(740) **Freedom to Form Support Groups:** The ability to assemble and the right to free speech have formed political parties and labor unions. These in turn have led to the establishment of laws to assure citizens a social support system for childcare, education, general

health and elderly care, unemployment, and the handicapped in a work environment and public places. It would be difficult to think of a society in which no one would be allowed to assemble and formulate common goals. Both secular and religious dogmatic states have tried to control the right to free assembly, but have all in a short while disappeared, leaving bloody blots on the pages of history. The history and success of democratic states is proof for this **"Sixth Pillar."**

(741) **Freedom to Choose a Religion:** Religion used to be connected to the central government when a king and/or a church organization were a part of the political government. Most industrialized countries separate church and government in their constitution and allow their citizens to worship according to a free choice of faith. **The permanence of religion in history proves it is a pillar of humanity; the variance of religions all through history proves religious freedom is basic.**

(742) **Access to Best Medical Care:** Access to a doctor and medicine is available to most people in industrialized countries, but limited in the non-industrialized, because of a limited com-munication system and economy. Even in the industrialized countries, medical access to care can be limited, but most have some kind of a medical safety net. By far, most individuals have a very low need for medical care, but a few individuals have a great need. It is impossible to predict who will need medical care and when. Because most people are healthy most of the time but, except for teens, worry about health, this is an ideal and profitable set up for a group insurance program. Many nations have nationalized medical care. The medical care is then paid by state taxes.

(743) When bills are paid from an uncontrollable state treasury, inflation in medical costs tends to accelerate faster than that of the general economy, where it is checked by market competition. Unchecked inflation in medical costs under state management may require that a growing portion of the state economy be devoted to medical care, because medical care in general is perceived as, and sometimes is, an uncompromising need. This could lead to the exclusion of other possible public needs.

(744) **The unpredictability but still low need for medical care for most individuals makes group medical insurance a very profitable undertaking. Nationalized medical care is simply another way to increase the state's income and state employment.** Nationalized or privatized medical care is available in all industrialized countries.

(745) Most medical conditions are due to life habits like the use of drugs, alcohol, smoking, lack of exercise, and poor eating habits. Public education about harmful lifestyles is in the interest of both the nation and the individual. Preventive industrial safety and hygiene programs are also part of medical needs. The need to have access to a trusted healer is as old as the first birth, first broken leg and first fever; it is a fundamental "Eighth Pillar." See also my health education books: *"Add Years to Your Life and Life to Your Years."*

(746) Epidemic crowd diseases entered human society at the dawn of agricultural time in what is now Iraq. Epidemics have killed 95% of farming societies several times over. Much of the next 6000 years have been spent on medical efforts to control crowd epidemics. Edward Jenner in his work with smallpox discovered a vaccination in 1798. Louis Pasteur, Robert Koch, and others in the late 1800s identified specific bacteria causing crowd diseases. By applying specific vaccinations against each crowd disease, humanity had finally a tool to control and, in regard to smallpox through vaccination, even to wipe out its existence in the whole world.

(747) It is a world tragedy of horrendous proportions and an ironic coincidence of history that under the sponsorship of a dogmatic Sumerian type government some of its scientists were sponsored to help manufacture and use the bacteria of crowd diseases or their toxins as weapons for mass destruction. **This was done in Iraq, the very birthplace of the 10,000-year-long evolution of human society. Indeed, it is important that we all learn our history from its first frame if we are going to make any progress on human rights and world peace.**

(748) **Free Trade:** Trade has gone through a rapid change for the last fifty years. The production and the distribution of products have

been helped by the introduction of computers and communication over the Internet.

(749) The industrial society rests on people's pursuit for happiness through trade. Producing a product that can be sold to others for their pleasure or need means work and a decent living for both the industrial and the farm population. Happiness is not to be found in just material things, but free trade does mean a higher standard and a more secure living for all people involved. **In the cave life, trade within the family band provided a slight time saving and a daily work convenience. This small convenience put society on its road to the present modern industrial society.**

(750) In the descriptions of countries, I have noted the percentages of their total population that are now living off food production. The rest of the population, sometimes 98%, trades its work for food and shelter. **The growth of humanity through freely negotiated trade has become an absolute "Ninth Pillar."**

# Part IV

## Governments of the World

## Introduction to Types of Governments

(751) There are many different kinds of governments in the world. Most governments may be characterized under either of two groups: Sumerian or Democratic. Most nations are easily recognized as to which group they belong.

(752) A Sumerian type government is based on the central control of knowledge and news for the people. The more land and people the Sumerian government controls, the mightier it is. The Sumerian government came to power in four ways: hereditary, military, religious or political.

(753) A Democratic type government is based on free work and free trade. The more work and trade, the mightier it is. It is independent of land. The rebuilding and economic recovery of the former Sumerian but since WW II democratic Japan and Germany, and at the same time, the spontaneous collapse of the Sumerian Soviet Union, is proof of this statement. Different democratic nations voluntarily coming together and forming a common trade market within a democratic EU is another proof of this statement. There are two types of democratic states, each different in making its decision: democracy based on multiple parties that may be skewed through local wheeling and dealings and democracy based on few parties where each party is responsible to the whole nation.

## Hereditary Sumerian Type Government

(754) **A Sumerian type kingdom of government is a leftover from the antique world. A king and his family or nobility dominates the country and is usually supported by religious or otherwise education controlled lifestyles, news, or knowledge.** This would mean a paternal chief or king, looking out for his flock. The king has all the power and sets the tone of the country. He transfers his power to his son or to somebody in his immediate family, or trusted member of his court.

(755) This kind of government was usually limited to small primitive tribes and is in modern time limited to countries where the king happens to own a major natural resource from which he can finance some of the "Nine Pillars" for his citizens.

(756) Many of the sheikdoms are modeled here. The citizens have access to food, clean and secure dwellings, good medical care, and good income with money left over for the pursuit of happiness. The population is usually small and homogeneous with much religious support. What such a government does not allow is a questioning of the status quo. Minorities can be discriminated against. It all depends on the king's attitude. The longevity of such a government depends on how long the king's income will last, how long the majority feel the status quo is what is best for the majority, and how the king sees his part in the international community and how the international community perceive the ruler.

## Military Sumerian Type Government

(757) A military constitution is usually instituted after a so-called military coup. Military leaders meet and decide how they want to rule a country after taking over the power by military force. **Any population can be held under submission through the threat of death.** The military government meets only a few of the "Nine Pillars." A dwelling may be clean and there may be enough food and income to support a family. This depends on the economic conditions

before the coup. The homes are not safe from government soldiers breaking in. Any neighbor can be a spy for the government. It may be dangerous to speak to others and certainly to assemble and to question the government. Press and TV news are strictly censored. Medical and religious support may be continued unchanged, but it often deteriorates from the strict control. Internal and external political reasons may or may not restrict trade. Trade depends on the leader's attitude to neighbors and his acceptance by the international community. Communist Cuba may stand as example of this kind of government.

## Religious Sumerian Type Government

(758) **Government based on one religious faith tends to discriminate against other beliefs. Such government is by the nature of faith absolutely convinced its own faith is the savior for everybody. The leaders use all their control of government to zealously spread their belief inside and outside their country, making the whole country into a missionary enterprise. Such a government meets very few of the "Nine Pillars."**

(759) Food and dwellings may be safe, but the individual needs are secondary to that of the country's religious mission. **Any sacrifice, including life by its citizens is holy and deserves a place in heaven.** Medicine is not hindered, but may be hampered by political and economic controls in trade. Communication is limited by press and news censorship. Community support is strong, providing one belongs to the official faith, but minority faiths may be discriminated against. **Social rules and art are judged according to religious norms. Iran may stand as an example. Iran has locked its constitution into the 800th medieval time frame with its Imam demanding the whole population to live according to Pope-like church dogma from that time. Shiites and Sunnis have been in wars with each other now for 1500 years just like the Roman Catholics and the Greek Orthodox Christians were for almost the same time. Only in modern time have the Christians made sense and admitted they had "forgotten"**

the Golden Rule for selfish power grab. Actually this historical fact proves that laws based on the Golden Rule is superior to any laws based on the Sharia tradition.

## Political Sumerian Type Government

(760) **Examples of past political Sumerian governments are the Communist Soviet Union, Serbia and the National Socialist Party of Germany. Together, they have masterminded the greatest atrocities in human history. They did this by controlling mass media and having a civil and secret police force that essentially allowed no individual freedom. The rest of the population was controlled with threats of terror enforced through large slave-camps. A modern example is North Korea, trying to empose the Soviet Union model of communism on to the North Korean people.**

(761) Often political Sumerian states have made its citizens so dependent on the state that their entire livelihood depends on the central government, its one party political support system, and administration. It is interesting to notice that as soon as one Sumerian regime fails, streets are filled with demagogues, playing on people's longing for security. The demagogues are still not offering security, but usually only a new twist of a Sumerian regime. **This has now gone on for 10,000 years and caused 10,000 years of war and suffering.**

(762) Ten thousand years is a short timespan within the 200 thousand years of human social history. Most of our history has been under the democratic rule of the "Nine Pillars of History" during the H/G prehistoric time. Actually, the first and only world conquest was done under democacy during this time. By pointing out and defining the "Nine Pillars," it is my hope that modern democracies can set their goals without being sidetracked by modern political or religious demagogues. It is imperative that world history becomes part of a citizen's education.

(763) While I was working on this manuscript the attack on the World Trade Center and the Pentagon occurred.

(764) The attack on September 11, 2001 demonstrates some specific problems originating from some one-party states, namely their unofficial involvement in or housing of terror organizations. If the terror organizations have both a comfortable home and access to large amount of money, they become a state within a state, a masked Mafia organization operating under the state's unofficial approval. They can exercise acts of war, while the official political state itself ideclares itself not responsible. **Both the organization itself and its support system have to be held responsible. The United Nations needs to recognize the problem and act decisively, as such deeds threatens the free democratic world. The previous League of Nation's lack of assertiveness led to its own demise and WW II.**

**For Further Reading:**

(765) *The Near East, A Modern History* by William Yale: The University of Michigan Press, ISBN 58-62524.

## Democratic Government Based on Multiple Parties (Sweden)

(766) Sweden is described as an example of a mature, multiple-party nation. Most states in Western Europe represent a democratic system based on multiple parties. Most of the countries have, like Sweden, four to seven different political parties, but some, specifically those just a few years past communist dictatorship, have twenty or more political parties. Most of the small parties represent narrow personal interests. In the mature democracies, the interests of smaller groups are presented to the larger national party's congresses and are included in their platform. The party platform is thereafter presented to the general population for scrutiny and vote.

(767) Some Western European governments, like England and the Scandinavian countries, are Constitutional Monarchies. The King has no political power; the presence of royalty is by tradition and for national PR-identification. For the last 20 years, many EU states

have been immigrant countries with 10-20%, many of them political refugees from Sumerian states. The refugees appreciate the political freedom but don't change their religion. This has made the otherwise very homogeneous countries subject for some political unrest. People wonder what to think of new mosques coming up among them and hear about Muslims involved with terror acts. Can a Muslim really accept the personal independence that is basic for a Scandinavian tradition?

(768) Political representatives are elected by general elections. Sweden used to have Europe's oldest constitution. It was first written in 1809, the second oldest in the world after the U.S. Constitution. A commission to review the constitution was appointed in 1954 and delivered its report in 1963. Since 1974, the Swedish Parliament changed from a two-chamber to a one-chamber system in order to enhance its own left wing assertiveness.

(769) The Prime Minister chooses his Cabinet of Ministers. Each minister heads a department of the government. Any member of the Cabinet can be dismissed by a no confidence vote. The ministers are chosen so the Prime Minister has a majority base in the Parliament. This makes the Executive Branch to have the same base as the Legislative Branch without a division of power. The system is called *parliamentary democracy*. The opposing parties will express their critical check of the Executive in the parliamentary chamber. The prime minister will listen to critique, but will always win with help from his majority base. If the prime minister loses a vote, the vote can go to a confidence vote for his whole Cabinet and can lead to new elections. This is a different system from that in the USA.

(770) A parliamentary system has some other checks and balances. An independent constitutional court is a first control, provided the Cabinet did not use an unchecked political buddy system in its appointments. The economic market, a second check, would respond by deflating the national currency, if the Cabinet pillaged the treasury for special interests. A third control of the Cabinet can be the mass media, provided it is independent from the political system. A fourth check can be a competing party, but this requires a party in close

balance against the party that dominates. Backroom wheeling and dealing takes over if the opposition is split between many parties. **The treasury may then be up for auction just like in the ancient Rome.**

(771) An important political difference between the USA and Sweden is that in the USA the constitution with assurance of freedom and human rights was written before any other laws and prevails above any new political winds. The Supreme Court in the USA makes continuous law reviews in order not to limit individual freedom and human rights. Since the adoption of the new constitution in 1974, Sweden's High Court has had few law reviews. **Sweden's Court is of the opinion that the "majority" is "right." The constitution is therefore continuously being changed in order to fit the agenda of the majority party.** (*Judicial Review and the Rule of Law: Comparing the United States and Sweden* by Nils Stjernquist, editors: Donald W. Jackson and C. Neal Tate, ISBN 0-313-28615-9)

(772) Looking back through history, majorities have ruled and still rule all Sumeric states. **A majority by itself is no guarantee of freedom, human rights, and democracy. This was proven in the USSR and Nazi-Germany. Instead, it has been the reason for large wars and atrocities. Still true is Voltaire's saying: *"The truth has not the name of a political party."***

(773) Judges in Sweden are not totally independent. Judges can be removed without having committed a crime according to the Instrument of Government 11:5. Judges therefore avoid politically delicate questions. Constitutional questions in Sweden can now be referred to the High Court of the European Union but this has so far never happened.

(774) **It is an interesting footnote to history in general that the Commission on Constitution in Sweden could not agree on defining "freedom" when the new constitution was to be accepted in 1974. This happened in a nation, possibly the only one in the world, whose heartland had always been free and whose farmers have never been in bond service since tribal time. Freedom is like good health: you don't appreciate it until you've lost it.** After several Commissions on Rights and Freedoms the Parliament decided in

1994 to accept the European Union's definition on Human Rights and Freedoms.

(775) Sweden is considered an advanced model for a socialistic, democratic country, the "Swedish Model." How does Sweden meet the need of the "Nine Pillars" for its citizens?

(776) **Survival: Food, Water, Energy, Air and Sex:** Sex is discussed separately in Part V, Section D. There is no lack of food in Sweden. Over-consumption is the problem rather than lack of food, just as much as in the USA. Food is of high quality and free from contamination. Sweden is located around the 60$^{th}$ meridian and therefore has no shortage of fresh water. It has over 100,000 fresh water lakes. Waterpower complimented by atomic power stands for local energy demands. The population and the cities are too small to have much influence on the air. Still, Swedes are trying to outdo all other countries with environmental concerns, mostly as a political merit. The king gives out a yearly water prize for the best clean water projects in the world. This is a young prize and, not yet as established as the Nobel Prize, which is 100 years old.

(777) **Safe Dwelling, Cleanliness and Art:** Most people in Sweden live in apartments with a very limited, but in most cases adequate space. County or state corporations together with trade unions often control the amount of apartments being built. The county corporations have not kept pace with the demand since WW II and this situation has created an immense black market for apartments in high growth areas, such as in Stockholm, while over-building is prevalent in low growth areas, such as in the smaller towns in the countryside. A smaller percentage than in the USA live in single-family homes. Many families still have a second home in the country. All living spaces are secure and built according to building codes with excellent sanitary controls. People beautify their dwellings according to personal priorities and financial resources.

(778) **Free Communication:** Communication in Sweden is technically on par with the very best in the world. People can communicate and assemble freely. This is established in a Freedom of the Press Act from 1949.

(779) Can the party in power, even in a democratic country, build a public opinion to its liking by controlling mass media? The way mass media are politically organized in Sweden requires a detailed examination in order to be understood.

(780) The "Swedish Broadcasting Commission" insures compliance with a "Radio Law." The Broadcasting Commission evaluates radio and TV programs in terms of their "factual accuracy and objectivity." The Cabinet through its Department of Culture appoints the board of the Broadcasting Commission.

(781) The government supports most radio and two of the three ground television stations. Radio, Educational Radio, and Swedish Television are owned by a non-commercial, state controlled organization entitled "Förvaltningsstiftelsen for Sveriges Television AB, Sveriges Radio AB and Sveriges Undervisningsradio AB." (Undervisningsradio = Educational Radio, Sveriges = Sweden's, AB = Corporation.). I will here simply call it the "Main Media Corporation" or "MMC." **MMC owns the three media corporations: Radio, Educational Radio, and Television Corporations**. This is established in the Parliament's written instructions from December 22, 1999. I have taken all the following information from these instructions.

(782) The Cabinet appoints the chairman and five members on the MMC's eleven members Board, making sure it has political majority. The names on the board do not have their political affiliation publicized behind their appointments.

(783) The Department of Culture (the Cabinet) appoints directly the Chairman of Board plus one other member for the boards of each of the TV and Radio and Educational Radio Corporation. MMC's Board appoints the other five members on their seven men Board, again making sure the Cabinet has political control of all electronic mass media.

(784) Cultural events like theater belong also to mass media programs. The Cabinet appoints all three members of the political directorship of the Department of Culture. This department provides 97% of the economic need for the 70 public museums and theaters

and much of the press support. Almost all schools are state supported, included one journalist school.

(785) **The Cabinet in Sweden controls television, radio, art, culture, press, and schools. Historically such situations have been typical for Sumerian types of governments.** Can possibly a political mandate be prolonged by mass media control? Sweden has at present seven official parties. Despite this, one party has for over 70 years ruled Sweden. It could easily be argued that this is due to the Cabinet's control of the different mass media. Seventy percent of journalists in the electronic mass media belong to the socialist party. A given stable of commentators for news reports or highlighted events may create opinions of the news.

(786) Many countries in Europe have state-supported television and radio as their main news channel. People need to know how their mass media are controlled politically. For homeland politics, there is some check from opposing parties. For foreign policy, there are no such checks. A certain foreign policy can even be promoted with intimidating street demonstrations supported by the whole state machinery. Hitler, who had to fight the communists, declared early that whoever controls the streets, controls the government. The streets were at that time the platform for mass political movements. This platform has now moved to the TV picture.

(787) When countries in Eastern Europe broke free from the Soviet Union, the main battle was over the control of the television station, nowadays the most influential and immediate mass news media. Politically independent mass media is an absolute pillar in a modern democratic society. Mass media should give the citizen of a democratic country the continued two-sided knowledge he/she needs in order to stay an informed voter.

(788) Political dogmas, like religious dogmas, are knowledge-dependent belief systems, which must be of freely informed choice. **Democracy expressed in a freely informed vote is an eternal human right established already in the tribal society.**

(789) **Freedom to Form Group Support:** Swedish laws forbid racial hate groups, but otherwise there are no restrictions to form support groups.

(790) Community social support in Western Europe is by the central government and the local county. **Sweden under socialist rule has promised security from cradle to grave and has essentially delivered, making almost everybody economically dependent on state policy. Local and federal taxes pay much of the cost.**

(791) **The cost of the government in Sweden has swallowed 55-70% of the GNP in the last two decades** [*Hur Mycket Politik Tål Ekonomin?* by Assar Lindbeck (English: How Much Politics Can the Economy Endure?) ISBN 91-34-50817-1]. **A similar security for the individual in Sweden is in Switzerland accomplished with only 30% of its GNP (oral communication from Professor Lindbeck).** It appears that the same party in power for a long time leads to a rusty machinery using lots of "oil." **Any donation program, state or otherwise, needs examination for how much money is used by the administration.**

(792) Inflation greater than 3% is not acceptable within the EMU. Sweden in the nineties had salary inflation of 7%. This means Swedes doubled their salary in ten years according to the "70-rule" ($7 \div 7$) and with that also their nonproductive pensions. With money distributed freely through the population, prices increased correspondingly. Housing, food, transportation, consumer goods, and state services like mail and telephone services have remained more expensive than in the USA. This is particularly true if one compares Sweden to areas that are similar in climate, similar in population density, or with similar "people pressure" growth. The currency itself had to be re-evaluated and placed on the international market as "floating" or valued according to its demand. The currency decreased 50% in value in 2001. Artificial valuations of work tend to lead to rampant inflation like in antique Rome.

(793) Unique and valuable institutions for community support are the Departments of Ombudsmen representing specific checks on the society, one each for legal affairs, for free competition, for ethnic

discrimination, for equal opportunities, for the rights of children, and for evaluating sexual discrimination, provided the ombudsmen have power.

(794) Like Sweden, most Western European States have only 2-4% farmers with the technical and service industry providing work for 96-98% of the population. The interest of the non-farm worker has a large political base and is in Sweden organized in a national office, covering all trade unions and state employees. Trade unions weigh heavily in the political arena and are working very intimately with political parties of their choice.

(795) Union negotiators are well informed and labor conflicts are unusual. Still many industries have, as in the USA, moved to a less expensive labor environment, have been taken over by foreign corporations, or exist on government support.

(796) Referring back to tribal time, it seems that any enterprise really is a tribal turf. **Both management and workers have to realize that they have to make a living off the same turf. The real boss is the customer.**

(797) **Freedom to Choose Religion:** Sweden had a state supported Lutheran State religion until 2000. Now the church is separated from the state. Discrimination against the faith of minorities is unlawful. Worship of any religion is free in all EU countries.

(798) **Access to Medical Help:** Medical care is financed by the local government and is of good quality, accessible to all for a minimal fee. Access to non-acute surgery is however at times limited by long waiting periods, up to several years, even for cancers. Politicians are now talking of a point system for access to care.

(799) **Free Trade:** Sweden has the highest taxes in the world but has recently removed the second tax of inheritance; this position requires a comment as it affects trade. Sweden has taxes not only on income, capital, and tax on all traded products but also tax on all work, a so-called Value Added Tax (VAT) of 24%. The 24% VAT can be a larger tax than the income tax for many people. Even regular food is taxed although at a slightly lower rate. The VAT-tax has led to two price settings, one official, paid with VAT and one

underground, bartered, and not paid. The VAT favors private trade men over salaried employees and hits percentage wise low-income people harder than high-income people.

(800) A modern industrial society consists of basically two parts: one that produces products and services for the consumers and one that provides the support system for the producers. The producers may pay for the support system by the required tax or, as an alternative, negotiate and buy the coverage from a private insurance provider.

(801) The producer paying for his own support system shops around for the best, adjusts to his needs and, through the applied competition on the support system, keeps the administrators of the support system eager to provide the best possible service.

(802) The producer works for the market. He/she is always challenged, works long hours, never has a safe employment, and may even lose his or her investment. **A farmer may lose his enterprise from both market and weather.** The producer needs cash to participate in the always-fluctuating market and hopefully its growth.

(803) A state bureaucrat being close to the tax purse does not fear the market and is not afraid of losing his job. More money may eventually land in the hands of the non-producing support system. **Senator Cato saw a similar problem in the antique Rome: "Simple thieves lie in prison and in stocks; public thieves walk abroad in gold and silk." Democracy, as all governments, has always to be watched so it does not turn into "cleptocracy"** (from *Guns, Germs and Steel* by Jared Diamond, 1997, ISBN 0-393-31755-2). Cleptocracy in government is best controlled by legal immunity for squealers and a totally independent mass media.

(804) Sweden's support system is paid by state taxes and administered by many bureaucrats. The non-producing people of state and county employees have to be in balance with the producing people of industry. Sweden has at present met most of the "Nine Pillars" except possibly the ancient tribal right expressed in independent media for communication of news and knowledge. This success cannot be argued. Private versus public administration of the support system are two alternatives that have to be weighed

regarding which one gives the best service for the least cost relative to other public needs. Every democratic system can always be improved. That is democracy. **A wise old farmer used to say: "There is more than one way to skin a cat."**

(805) The population in Sweden in 2011 was 8.8 million with 2% in agriculture. The GNP was $459 billion or a GNP/capita of $41,000. Defense cost was 1.2% of the GNP. The national debt in 2003 was 37% of GNP.

**For Further Reading:**

(806) *Democracy the Swedish Way. Report from the Democratic Audit of Sweden 1999* by Olof Petersson et al. ISBN 91-7150-761-2.

(807) *Capitalism and Freedom* by Nobel Laureate in Economy Milton Friedman, 1962, ISBN 0-226-26400-9.

## Democratic Government Based on Few Parties (USA)

(808) The Constitution of the United States of America is our model for a few-party system. Although other parties are allowed, they have played a minor role in the country's history. The Constitution was written in the year 1787 and ratified in 1789. Nothing like it existed at the time.

(809) **Referring to what he perceived as early tribe life, John Locke in 1690 in England stated, (paraphrasing):** *"before any formal country existed, an individual had a basic right and freedom over his person and his property. In lack of laws such 'state of Nature' becomes unsafe. People therefore in a free agreement formed a 'state by Law' without giving up on their freedom."* **John Locke also summarized:** *that right and freedom is expressed in a majority decision in a lawmaking representation. The people are the only ones that can decide about taxes because it is their money. An executive, approved by the people, may represent the country to foreigners but all are subject to the law of the people. The law,*

*established by the people, is the ultimate power. Power cannot be inherited.* These writings were quite revolutionary in the time of Charles II and James II and led also to the English people's revolution in 1688-89. John Locke's collected work was published in 1714, but some important work came out around 1690.

(810) **Charles Montesquieu, a historian from France, visited England at this time. He was impressed with how the political system worked. Montesquieu studied history and developed a theory:** *that all power had to be balanced by another power, otherwise power would be abused. He therefore proposed a constitutional system with three powers, an executive branch and a law-making branch, anchored in the people by general elections and a law-enforcing branch.* **The USA Constitution was designed on the basis of the theories of John Locke and Charles Montesquieu.**

(811) **The U.S. Constitution now has 25 amendments. The Constitution establishes the relation between 50 individual states with 280 million people and their Federal Government. No country nationalizes each year so many new citizens from all over the world as does the USA. A very strong feeling of American nationalism exists despite this young, multinational, multicultural origin of its population.**

(812) **The 214-year-old USA Constitution is now the oldest in the world except for possibly the Ting in Iceland.**

(813) **A specific and important role of the Federal High Court is to ensure that laws, made by the legislature, comply with the aim of the Constitution; that is, they do not limit personal rights or favor one division of the government or one section of the population.**

(814) A proposal for a new law may come from anybody by talking to his or her senator or congressman. If the representative sponsors the proposal, it becomes a Bill. The Bill is debated in working committees of both the Senate and Congress. The working committees may ask for information from lobbyists, that is, from representatives of the different commercial organizations affected by the proposals. The main effort here is the creation of work opportunities, but still assuring competition in commerce. Competing commercial interests

usually balance each other, if not, one can turn to the courts and have the court examine if a monopoly exists. Lobbying by different interest groups keeps legislators in touch with the real world and is present in all democratic countries. It is important that the interest of one group is not at the cost of another and that the right of a citizen, as an individual and as a consumer, is not jeopardized. Both houses must approve the Bill. The approved Bill is sent to the President for his signature to become law. The President may veto the Bill. The President's veto may be overridden by a two-thirds majority vote in both houses.

(815) Annual budget proposals have the same legislative process, but are originated by the Presidency. Each individual state has the same system. The elected Governor of state with his state staff acts as the State Executive.

(816) The President represents the nation internationally. The President signs treaties, but the Senate must also ratify each treaty. The President appoints his Cabinet of Ministers, and assigns each to lead one of the various Federal Departments. The President also appoints heads for various Federal Agencies, as well as judges for the Federal Court System. The Senate must approve all these candidates. This is a check on the Presidency.

(817) **With only two parties fighting for power, political competition never sleeps.** While one party is in power, the other party is like a hawk looking for any mistakes or any abuse of power. Any personal or political sidestep or government waste is made into a "scandal" in the independent mass media. Scandals also sell papers! Visiting foreigners seeing this "madness" may get the impression that nothing works in the USA. As a citizen, I say: "*Good, keep on checking each other. You both work for me and are paid by me.*" Democracy can always be improved. Elected officials serve on all levels of government—federal, state and local. Elected officials only serve for a limited time. Only judges have a lifetime appointments. **The local issues are presented with pro and con arguments with information of the fiscal impact on the citizen's taxes at each election time.**

(818) **Above everything and everybody stands the Constitution**. The nation's Supreme Court can be appealed to by anybody having his or her rights limited by something in the system. A classical case is the mother, who felt her son should not have to attend school prayer each morning at a public school. The case went to the Supreme Court. It was concluded that public schools were paid for by the public with different religious faiths, and should therefore not favor one particular faith. This one family changed a tradition in the whole nation. A minority that feels segregated, can in this way, always be heard in court.

## How Does the USA System Measure Up to the "Nine Pillars of History"?

(819) **Survival: Food, Water, Energy, Air and Sex:** Sex is discussed in Part V, Section D and Energy in Part V, Section E.

(820) Food in the USA is in abundance. A third of the food produced is exported to feed the rest of the world.

(821) Both food and water are held to the government's set standards. The standards are enforced by dedicated government agencies—the Environmental Protection Agency (EPA) and the Food and Drug Administration (FDA). Environmental impact reports have to be approved for all housing and industrial developments.

(822) Only fresh water can be used for drinking and food production. The Army Corps of Engineers and the Bureau of Reclamation control surface water together with special local water control districts, such as the Central Valley Irrigation Agency in California. Surface water is collected in big dams and distributed through canals to meet the need of water for human, agriculture, and industrial consumption. Local irrigation districts control local surface waters. Municipal supply of water is done by utility districts run by either the municipality itself or through a private contractor. Local health departments control rural areas with private wells. Local health ordinances will govern, through statute, the amount of contamination of private wells.

(823) Clean air can be a problem in mega-metropolitan, multi-million-size towns. The many cars and big industries expel pollutants that have to be controlled. The combustion residues can become a health hazard to citizens. EPA has the primary jurisdiction over air standards. Local air pollution control districts implement and enforce federal standard mandates. Technical problems are immense and require very large investments, but are still gradually being solved. Pollution in metropolitan areas is indeed decreasing.

(824) FDA and the Department of Agriculture together with local health departments control the cleanliness and suitability of food production and its distribution.

(825) **Safe Dwelling:** Family houses in the USA are larger than in most countries. A greater percentage of people live in their own houses than in any country ever in history. Sanitary laws and building codes are in place in all communities. City inspectors enforce the codes as houses are being built. Property right is based on the English property right laws. Trespassing laws are part of the judicial structure and enforced through the civil court. Federal property is limited to criminal laws in Federal court. A recent downturn in the economy has placed some unemployed people in temporary housing. Many drug addicts value their drug higher than housing and have also had to be sheltered in temporary housing.

(826) **Cleanliness:** All the above listed agencies, enforcing community cleanliness witness to the pertinence of this pillar. A very large industry supplies cleaning products to home and industry.

(827) **Art:** People are proud of their living space, particularly if they own it, and try to beautify according to their personal priorities and finances. The demand for art through all of humanity proves its pillar importance.

(828) **Freedom to Communicate:** The United States has been a leader in implementing new inventions for communication. The big paper presses, the telegraph, telephone, television, and the Internet are all intimately connected with modern American life. Freedom of expression is established in Article I of the Constitution: *"Congress shall make no law respecting an establishment of religion, or prohibiting*

*the free exercise thereof: or abridging the freedom of speech, or the press, or the right of the people peaceably to assemble, and to petition the Government for a redress of grievances."*

(829) **Mass media, regular press, radio, and TV do not have any government support.** They function on advertising and/or subscriptions. All of these forms of mass media are very independent. They compete for a large reader circle rather than promoting a specific political opinion. **One national radio and one national TV channel are partly supported by the Federal Government (7%) and partly by citizen donations. This channel always has two commentators representing the two political parties.**

(830) **Freedom to Form Support Groups:** The right to assemble is established in a clause of the First Article of the Constitution as noted above. Under this right, labor unions can be established and negotiate salaries for their members. Unions may not always be necessary but, by being present in many major factories, they set a negotiated floor for all labor salaries. The Congress establishes a minimum wage in work not organized under union contract. Many workers prefer to work without labor contract and trust his or her personal relation with their employer.

(831) Unemployment is paid from taxes in a state insurance program. Unemployment pay is not a given percent of previous salary, but a minimal pay. Unions help their members in times of unemployment and work conflicts. Many people pay for unemployment insurance themselves.

(832) Primary state schools are paid for by state or federal funds and include a free school lunch. Private enterprises compete for primary schooling contracts and seem to win acceptance in recent years. Childcare is paid for by the parents or occasionally by the work place. College or university has to be paid for by the student or his parents. For those without economic support, there are federal loans available, but the student has to maintain a "B" average. Gifted students have special scholarships available. Special considerations in admissions are reserved for minorities. Some students support their higher education by working.

(833)  The Federal Government pays for a general pension at age 65. Most people work until 62 and take a lower pension, while some, like me, worked until 70 for a higher pension, all depending on health, interest and personal finances.

(834)  According to SIPRI (Stockholm International Peace Research Institute Yearbook 2011 with reports from 2010) the cost of defense was 4.7% of GNP. With this defense budget, the USA has created the most modern and most effective voluntary army in the world. The US Army has been the main force in executing several police actions approved by the UN against Sumerian rogue nations.

(835)  **The loss of life in each war has gone from units of 100,000 in WW II, to units of 10,000 in the Korean and Vietnam Wars, and to units of 100 in the two Gulf wars and now with drones to singular numbers, all in an effort to spare civilian collateral causalities in war**

(836)  **Since the September 11, 2001 attack, individuals with warped religious dogmatism are trying to attack people with terror in USA in units of 1000, each one a civilian, just doing his or her civil job! Religious dogmatism can certainly make up righteous reasons in anything that fits a warped brain.**

(837)  **Freedom to Choose Religion:** Freedom to worship according to personal conviction is established in Article I of the Constitution. The churches often bring their members together for group support.

(838)  **Access to Medical Help:** Many large companies pay the medical insurance for their workers and their families. Medical insurance during employment years is otherwise voluntary and therefore not general. In this case, most workers pay for self-insurance. Most are able to do this from their salaries but some choose not to. Member States have in the past supplied a tax-supported safety net for medical care in the case a patient totally lacks funding. The medical profession tried to never turn anybody away for medical care. Since 2010 this is no longer true.

(839)  A federal medical insurance program covers only in part the medical need of the elderly. Most federal and state payments were rapidly eaten up by inflation, an inflation limited to the medical

field. Both pensions and medical costs have had to be supplemented with private insurance. An employer sometimes pays for this supplemental insurance. The State or federal governments pay in full for the insurance needs of their employees. Can state and federal government continue to do this under pressure from the increasing medical cost?

(840) The Kaiser Family Foundation estimated in 2004 that it would cost the Federal Government $125 billion to cover all the uninsured. Sweden has a state supported medical system, but with 50% debt. The USA could certainly afford $125 billion to pay for the uninsured, but with the Federal Government paying, it would probably not stop at this. Inflation for medical care, could threaten the whole system. The quality of medical care in the USA is among the best in the world. By far, most progress in medical care originates from the USA. Assured of access to the best possible medical help goes a long way to meet the needs of the "Eighth Pillar," but concern for paying for it can be a threat.

(841) Paragraph 840 was written in 2004. The cost of access to medical care for the last ten years has since deteriorated to critical levels. Inflation limited to health care cost within U.S. has risen to past 16% of the GNP per year. The circumstances are so unique for the U.S. system that it has required a specific review addressing the complicated situation in the U.S. I reported on this dissertation also elsewhere and will quote it here.

## Specific Medical Cost Issues

(842) Dr. Jeffrey M. Lobosky, a board certified neurosurgeon with a long professional experience, points out that for the last some 20 years doctors avoid to work in the emergency room and within the fields of orthopedics, neurosurgery, vascular surgery and OB-GYN because the malpractice insurance fee in these fields today is $200,000 to $250,000 per year or greater than the cost of living for the doctor. (*It's Enough to Make You Sick,* Rowman & Littlefield Publ. Inc. 2012. ISBN 978-14422-1462-0.)

(843) The economical fissure in the medical access system stretches between patients who have adequate medical insurance and those who do not. Some years back this was not a major problem; doctors and hospitals just swallowed the cost. As the cost has kept on increasing this unpaid cost of access became more and more difficult to accommodate.

(844) The Federal and the State governments split the cost for uninsured patients but the bill that is eventually paid still just covers only 20% of what insured customers pay.

(845) When hospitals and doctors complained the Congress responded with a law, the Emergency Medical Treatment and Labor Act (EMTALA), that requires that all patients that seek help in the emergency room have to be treated, whether they have the means to pay or not. The law is enforced with a $50,000 fine. Besides the $50,000 fine a malpractice shadow is hanging over the whole scene. No doctor with any self-preservation would enter such an unfair battlefield.

(846) Behind of his/her doctor medical license stands the four facetted economical interest zone: a hospital service with unionized workers, the pharmaceutical manufacturer for supplying medications that are patented for 16 years, an insurance company mitigating the doctor fee through a group insurance bill with an army of bill-processing people and, finally, a malpractice insurance company mitigating the risk of every medical procedure supported by an army of malpractice lawyers soliciting any reason to sue the medical support system. Malpractice lawyers won't even charge a fee for the opportunity to sue a doctor, hospital or a pharmaceutical manu-facturer knowing that just about all claims are settled outside of court with the major portion of the settlement going into the lawyers' pockets.

(847) The participating cost-demands are all part of the unlimited Eighth Historical Pillar need and assured to be paid in the shadow of the doctor's medical license; the doctor is really just a pawn.

(848) A malpractice insurance company does not have much incentive to control its abusive access because the medical need is a

pillar need (the Eighth) and will always in some way be compensated. The cost of malpractice forces many young doctors to sign up and limit their work to hospital salary employment, where the hospital helps to pay the malpractice costs. This practice pressures young doctors to seek employment in only for-profit run hospital chains with only for-profit incentives. Such hospital incentives make the hospital a manufacturing plant that places cost control before a personal patient care.

(849) The malpractice game destroys the doctor/patient relationship. Already the father of medicine, Hippocrates, warned against talking bad about colleagues. The public is really not an informed judge of medical interventions. Hippocrates had newly licensed doctors promise not to talk bad about each other. But, of course, lawyers never made such a promise and live off controversy. The "law making" part of government has more lawyers than doctors, making sure that patients' rights cannot be compromised—and the malpractice game in the U.S. continues.

(850) In June 12, 2012, the Government Accounting Office (GAO) reports that the medical malpractice adds less than 2-5% to the total medical bill. However the total medical bill is between $2-3 trillion and therefore still adds substantially to the cost. The main problem is that it adds very substantially to the bill insuring the doctors and hospitals, which has also other consequences like the choice for young doctors' work or choice of specialty.

(851) Medical care should be as good as possible, but to challenge **any** risk and to charge **any** cost as judged according to a **layman's** jury-judgment could be abusive. In 2008, U.S. doctors and hospitals paid $11 billion to insure themselves from malpractice claims. *(The Economist Jan.16, 2010.)* **The litigious attitude within the medical pay zone is indeed out of control**.

(852) Adult working people in the U.S. pay for their own medical insurance from their salary, but as it is voluntary, people may choose not to. This is true and common for many young people, who think that nothing will happen to them, and is particularly common for drug addicts who certainly will have health problems, but who don't

care. People without insurance are a burden for the state Medicaid system (still more than half federally funded).

(853) If the final years of one's life end up to be a family member with a handicapped stroke or a Alzheimer's syndrome, the cost for years of total nursing care will ruin the finances of most families in the U.S. The cost for long-term medical care in the U.S. causes elderly their most anxiety. Regular medical insurance has left out the cost of long-term insurance (longer than 90 days) in their regular medical care contracts because cost of end-of-life care tends be so high. The family may step in but few can ill afford the major cost and efforts this demands. Families give up their equities in their homes to accommodate a generation change with some dignity but many times not even this will cover the cost.

(854) I have two unique perspectives.

1. First, I grew up in Sweden and have worked as a licensed physician in both Sweden and the U.S. I have worked both as a clinical physician and a medical scientist. I have also worked as a medical director for a major U.S. corporation. As a medical director, I had an insight into the insurance side of the medical business. Together my past experiences have given me a unique knowledge of the workings of medical cost in both U.S. and Sweden.

2. Second, in retirement, I have studied political history as revealed through nine sides of anthropology and have written a book, *The Nine Pillars of History*, where access to medical care is Historical Pillar need number eight.

(855) Access to medical care is a Historical Pillar need for any society. The Nine Pillars of History share three characteristics:

1. They are eternal; the Nine Historical Pillars were all together present from the start of human society 200,000 years ago and are still critical parts of society;

2. They are interdependent because they are all present at the same time; and

3. The cost for society of any of them cannot be controlled except by competition.

(856) All nations in history have had as a goal a system for its citizens that would meet people's need for security according to the Nine Pillars of History, but none has so far defined all of them and recognized their influences over society. **The Nine Historical Pillar need has to be sustainable from one generation to the next in order for any society to survive. This is fundamental to the Nine Pillars of History concept.**

(857) The necessary competition within each Historical Pillar need has to be recognized. It is this type of competition that is denied when considering cost of medical access. With a four-faceted economical interest zone within medical cost it is still very unlikely competition can control the cost in a foreseeable future. An economical market always fails to control costs due to a monopoly power. Professionals within medicine, law, indemnity and pharmacy all earn their living in the shadow of the physician's medical license. History has shown that any monopoly-power will destroy a society, be it dogmatic religious or dogmatic political. A medical need, a life or death situation, has to be perceived as a situation with a monopolized need. Medical access should therefore be looked upon as a threat to society just like any threat to any of the Nine Historical Pillars.

(858) What about the public sector? The U.S. and Sweden, or actually all of Western Europe, stand at a crossroads. Access to medical support is a Historical Pillar need. **The basic question is: should the common tax base finance a Historical Pillar need that cannot be controlled without competition?** The cost will take from other needs financed from the common tax fund and will eventually affect the cost of all production and therefore jeopardize production-workers' access to their own Nine Pillar needs. **This question still has to be answered with an unequivocal yes.** Only a person with insight in history can answer this question with conviction. **Yes, because we need to preserve dignity in generation transitions. The U.S. has done more for preserving democracy than any other nation. In my opinion the American citizens have earned and deserve this dignity.**

(859) To provide for the birth of a child is now too expensive for a young couple without insurance that to even plan for for a child and to provide for an Alzheimer-sick grandmother would bankrupt any couple in the U.S. **Health insurance has to be mitigated across generations and has to be mandated so the total population together carries the responsibility. This is what binds a nation together just as the responsibility for defense. Citizens form a community across generations, a community that generations can be proud to belong to, and even die for, a community with <u>dignity</u>.**

(860) The family impact for long-term medical care in Sweden is mitigated through contribution from the local tax. The senior care in Sweden is housed in local, especially dedicated, well cared for, medical housing with 24/7 nursing care. This allows citizens to leave his/her time in this life with a dignity, a dignity to be followed and working for in the new generation.

(861) According to the Census Bureau's 2011 report, the U.S. has 50 million uninsured, mostly working citizens. The U.S. Congress has mandated to include the medical coverage for all 50 million of non-insured people.

(862) All health workers are a selected, intelligent and exceptionally trained group and of society recognized for their knowledge and integrity. In order to win the public's trust the team has gone through extensive training, has specific licenses and has generally recognized documentation to practice informed and rationally controlled practice of medicine and also to educate the public about consequences of damaging life habits. The medical team is thereby allowed to charge a fee for its service. Hopefully competition limits the medical cost to a reasonably value within a certain national area. Inflation within the medical field still tends to be high because of unlimited competition and the patient's eagerness to pursue the best possible care.

(863) In my publication *The Nine Pillars of History* I compared and analyzed the cost of access to medical care in Sweden and the U.S. In order to limit the length of this correspondence I will here limit myself to the description of the U.S. system. The medical care in the U.S. is mostly on par with the medical standard in Sweden or most

OECD (Organisation for Economic Co-operation and Development) countries. OECD countries essentially mean Western Europe. The standard of living for medical providers is also about the same. The GNP/citizen corrected for Purchasing Power Parity (PPP) ranks Sweden in 2010 as number 8 and the U.S. as number 14.

(864) The medical efficacy based on medical evidence such as the survival of a newborn and of its mother and the longevity of the general population are both spot-wise worse in the U.S. than in Sweden. Despite worse results in the U.S., the cost corrected for PPP of both countries, the cost of access to medical care in the U.S. is 50% greater than that in Sweden (17% vs. 9%). Sweden is the only Western industrialized country that actually recently decreased its medical cost. Sweden has 20% immigration and accommodated this addition of citizenships by introducing competition in medical care. Japan is a second country that also had a decrease in its medical cost, but this is probably due to a specific shrinking within its large aging population. Sweden decreased its medical care cost only with 0.7% in 2011, but still, it was a decrease.

(865) As money is the cause of all evil, we might take a closer look into how money for access to medical care is utilized in each country and do this from a holistic view or how people in both countries lives.

(866) Doctors in Sweden have a lot more free time for their families and a lot more security for their employment and family. Most Swedish doctors have a salary contract with a regulated 8-hour workday, special compensation for holiday and night work, a regulated 6 weeks vacation, a one-year parent holiday (split with wife). For their children, the doctors have free childcare, food and transport all through high school. The doctor has had study support for his/ her higher education, medical and pharmaceutical coverage from childhood all through retirement including for long-term sickness; i.e., Alzheimer's, and including paid cost for burial. The local and federal tax base supports a "from cradle to grave" social support system. Sweden has for the last couple of voting periods had a right wing political coalition government. The shift from left to right is mainly driven by the imposing cost of medical care. During the

present right wing leadership independent doctor services have been allowed to open medical clinics in competition with government, provided quality care is maintained.

(867) In the U.S. doctors have to pay for their seven-year medical school, have a minimal salary during their one-year internship and three-year residency working up to 60 hours a week with no consideration for holidays. Doctors who are through with their residency and finally ready to start their practice do not dare to work in some areas of medicine that have high exposure to malpractice claims. The litigious atmosphere in the medical field in U.S. has essentially broken down the access to medicine. The whole system is, if not totally broken down, at least fractured along economical fissures.

(868) In Sweden the malpractice claims go first to a medical board of uninvolved, generally recognized competent colleagues. This professional board makes a judgment of the involved parties before the problem is addressed in a court. Most conflicts are resolved at this level without any cost. With most complaints settled before court it would take a very serious claim for a lawyer to pursue a further claim.

(869) Another explanation to the difference in medical cost in Sweden vs. the U.S. is that the government in Sweden is in control of its large national market. The buying power of a state has more negotiating strength than individual doctors and hospitals. Also in Canada, the cost of medicine is cheaper than in the U.S. The government can, at times, be a smarter buyer of medicine and medical equipment than one that has to look out for different privileged connections.

(870) Paying for health care in the U.S. is a labyrinth system of individual, group, state and federal resources. Two separate armies of people execute bills—one army that writes the bills and one that pays for the bills. Individuals or a myriad of more or less comprehensive group plans plus state-run "Medicaid" or federal run "Medicare" pays for the bills. Such billing system adds 30-35% to the medical bill while the one-payer Medicare bill adds only 3-5%.

(871) The cost of medical insurance was a part of the U.S. car company's financial difficulties. The same problem is now facing federal and state employees. The public will not pay for an unlimited cost of state and federal employees' medical costs and retirement. The public request a negotiated cost control, not a free for all give away from those sitting close to the tax paid state and federal money-purse. A buyer from the common tax purse really doesn't have much incentive for cost control.

(872) Final long-term care at old age in the U.S. requires special insurance. Private retirement communities attached to long-term adult medical care has been a solution for a few lucky ones to meet the cost of the end of life medical cost with dignity. The private investment for this type of insurance is accomplished by selling their equity in their family home. The attached medical care unit is still paid for from federal Medicare plus private insurance.

(873) Both in Sweden and in the U.S. retired people try to stay in their home as long as they physically can. Both Medicare and Medicaid give some help to pay for home care. (Google Medicare or Medicaid for information about home care.) In Sweden all home care is supported through the local tax base with intimate knowledge of the individual needs.

(874) Pharmacies in U.S. are usually independent services. They may have contracts with hospitals, be small independent pharmacies, or very large corporate chains. Patients pay for the cost of filling a 30 or 90-day prescription. Pharmacies charge $10-$15 or more for filling each prescription. Some chains arbitrarily determined that they couldn't be responsible for a prescription beyond 30 days—even for chronic conditions. For any longer prescription they refer to mail delivered medication. Why? What is the rational reason except for more frequent fees?

(875) Many of the people in the U.S. without medical coverage are foreigners. If people are working legally and paying tax they should be able to have access to medical care as all legally working people. Everybody in the U.S. does have access according to the so named *Obama-care*. The basic question is—who pays for access,

specifically if the patient is unable to pay by choosing not to partake in the common effort?

(876) An open and informed discussion within a democratic system has to decide which way can be considered most fair for most people without jeopardizing anybody's right to their own Nine-Pillars-of-History-needs even with dignity at the end of life. The eventually chosen way has to be a two-way street for a society to survive.

(877) **The purpose of tribal life** was to be able to raise a family for the tribe's survival. **The purpose of modern social life** is to raise a family, educate the children to be of service to our modern society and for our self to contribute our service so we leave this life with a dignified memory left for our modern society to maintain and live by. The quality of life achieved in a modern society should therefore be sustainable.

(878) In order to accomplish these goals for the richest country in history we have to analyze the problem in a very rational way.

(879) Our modern civilized society has implemented old age pensions, minimum salaries, and health and unemployment insurances as expressions for this effort towards our common social goal. The cost of these social services has for most modern countries landed on the common tax base.

(880) The term "Commons" with capital "C" and ending in "s" stands for an economical problem affecting what I call "what many own, nobody owns" or is responsible for. **The Common tax base is a "Commons."** To have the cost of access to old age pensions and the other social services mentioned is after a while taken for granted. **Should cost of acsess to medicine be placed on a "Commons" may have serious consequences in the long run for any nation because, as a pillar need, medical cost cannot be controlled.**

(881) Medical care often covers life-maintaining and life-threatening situations that make a patient totally dependent on the medical support system - in a way- a monopoly situation. The Nine Pillars of History pointed out that monopoly will lead to social destruction, be it from political or religious monopoly. Here I must

again recognize that the social need for medical care is a unique situation that may lead to social destruction. **Medical care has to be placed on the side of defense as a common necessity but should still be controlled through competition just like defense cost.**

## Fundamental Medical Cost Issue

(882) After having described the total problem in general terms, we might now be ready to address it more specifically.

(883) Given is that in 2010 the cost of access to medical care in U.S. is rising to an unsustainable 16% of Gross National Product (GNP) and still rising 2-3% per year; and soon, double that in other industrialized countries. In Sweden medical cost in 2010 was 9% of GNP when corrected for local Purchasing Power Parity (PPP). Even at 9% medical cost in Sweden was crowding out other social obligations. Such percentage increase is unsustainable for any organizations that subscribe to underwrite it. (Klugman, Blinder). To face the problem we have the following choices:

1. **Take a Passive Role**
   **a. Wait for crisis to culminate; kick the can down the road.**

   (884) President Bill Clinton tried to introduce a medical care bill in 1993. I worked at Lockheed at the time. A local branch of Kaiser Permanente had provided Lockheed employees with access to medical health care for many years. Kaiser Permanente is an organized HMO, Health Maintenance Organization. President Clinton tried through a mandate to impose a plan similar to the Kaiser plan to cover medical coverage for all citizens. Pressure from insurance companies and smaller employers blocked a general plan. Lockheed still picked up on the idea and offered for other, not yet organized medical groups, to get together and compete with a Kaiser-like plan (HMO). This held back medical cost for some time while the

surrounding offices matched the Kaiser plan. This was ten years ago. Now even Lockheed is requiring its new employees to help pay for medical cost. Now, in 2016, no employees have medical coverage.

(885) According to the Wikipedia Henry J. Kaiser and a Physician Sidney Garfield founded Kaiser Permanente medical group in 1945. The Permanente group operates in nine states and the DC, has 8.9 million members served by 14,600 physicians, or one per 600 patients. In its recently reported year, the non-profit Kaiser Foundation Health Plan and Kaiser Foundation Hospital entities reported a combined $1.6 billion in net income on $47.9 billion in operating revenues or 4.3%. Each independent Permanente Medical Group operates as separate for-profit partnership or Professional Corporation in its individual territory, and while none publicly report their financial results, each is primarily funded by reimbursements from respective regional Kaiser Foundation Health Plan entity.

(886) HMO-organization has helped to have access to medical care while having access to work. Still, the cost within the HMO keeps on going up. Many employers opt out for plans for new employees or ask employees to help to pay for the increased cost. The situation raises the need to renegotiate new contracts like for state employees in Wisconsin. Many employees have now lost their job and with that also lost their access to medical care and eventually access to any Nine Pillar need.

(887) The Federal government plans to add 50 million new citizens to the same size medical provider base. This certainly accelerates the whole problem. Who will or even can pay?

## 2. Take an Active Role

(888) England made physicians into public salary employees after the Swedish model. France, like the Kaiser Health Plan, has made all doctors independent contractors but here medical cost is even higher than in Sweden ($3,470 for Sweden and $3,696 for France). All OECD countries have a medical cost at around 9% of GNP. In a Federal report released June 2012 on cost/PPP corrected GNP the medical cost will climb to 20% of GNP in 2020. This report is according to Kaiser health care news and a Bloomberg financial report 2011.

(889) The Nobel Laureate Milton Friedman addressed the cost problem for access to medicine already in the 1970s. His solution was to open more medical schools and graduate more physicians. Also Dr. Lobosky is asking for "lots of more doctors and doctor extenders." This would help but would not address all facets of the medical four-facetted economic interest pyramid.

(890) The graduation of more physicians' extenders would help. With physician extenders is meant physician's assistants, nurse practitioners and nurses specialized for specific medical treatment like pregnancy, delivery, tuberculosis, diabetes and so on. Kaiser Hospital has made efficient use of physician extenders. But small independent medical offices are not apt to hire medical extenders. Besides, most of us enjoy the personal care that individual offices provide. Medical care is indeed a very personal need filled only through a personal, confidential relationship.

(891) Most medical situations are however not that complicated that eleven or more years of training is

necessary. A triage referral system would certainly help, specifically for emergency admissions.

1. Single payer would lower administration cost from 35 to 3-5%
2. I propose to measure efficacy according to the following recipe.
3. Most medical situations are so common the treatment team has worked out routines to meet the need. The profession has numbered all procedures and generates its cost accordingly. This information is computerized and therefore offers a unique opportunity to check the medical efficacy of any procedure, any medication. Using a computerized program I proved medical efficacy for health education at Lockheed. (See my publication: *Add Years to Your Life, and Life to Your Years Part I.*)
4. A computerized test program does need not to be for a whole country. It can be limited to a geographical area recognized for excellent medical care and good computerized medical records. El Camino hospital in Mountain View, California, with its surrounding individual and group practices may together comprise such a sample. The El Camino hospital is a not-for-profit hospital recognized for its superb care. The surrounding patient and doctor populations are typical for a well-planned community. This information can be used as a measuring stick to compare against for-profit medical enterprises.
5. Start a medical review board for every medical county as a first instance for patient complaint.
6. Require a legal tort program for any state receiving Federal assistance.
7. A review of medical malpractice policies.
8. A review of pharmaceutical prescription policies.

(892) **Free Trade:** Production in manufacturing has been automated and made work less physically demanding, but also caused the loss of many jobs. The Internet has enlarged the sellers' market and even focused promotion and thereby brought producers close to consumers. All together transfer time and shelf and storage time has diminished and made less costly. Jobs have been lost and the job markets have become international so production is transferred to where labor costs are lower. The investments have benefited those who are able to make use of the many new inventions and eventually new customers. The inventions can be expensive to implement and have driven many small operators out of business, just like the tractor did in the beginning of industrial time.

(893) New jobs have also been produced in designing, producing and serving these new inventions or work they have created. Changes like these happen every time a major invention enters production or distribution and goes on continuously on every production floor and within all distribution industries. The movement has created fewer but larger factories, fewer but larger distribution chains, and fewer but larger service industries. Lawmakers have to be aware of the risk for monopolies or cartels. The number of major publishing houses has recently decreased from hundreds to less than ten in the USA. A concentration of mass media is by itself a risk for free speech. Here lawmakers have to be particularly diligent so that free speech is not threatened.

(894) The pursuit of happiness is established in the commerce clause of the First Article of the Constitution. Free trade is assured within the Federation. Free trade internationally is subject to negotiations with other countries and is done under the auspices of the work of the World Trade Organization (WTO). The USA is a major trade partner for many countries.

(895) Trade gives everyone an opportunity to pursue individual happiness and fills our Nine Historical Pillar Need by being of service to our fellow man.

# Conclusion

(896) There are two genetically inherited needs in all living animals: the need to propagate and the need for the species to survive. In tribal time the specie need grew into a social need for the tribe to survive based on The Golden Rule:

(897) Jewish: *You shall love your neighbor as yourself.* Leviticus

(898) Christian: *You shall love your neighbor as yourself.* Mathew

(899) The "Nine Pillars" have evolved from these two basic physiological pillar-need of the individual and have become necessary for a modern free, happy, healthy, and prosperous society.

(900) My premise in the beginning of the manuscript was that the "Nine Pillars of History" could be traced to its beginning 200,000 years ago, that all the hardships brought upon people through history have been due to restrictions of some of the "Nine Pillars," and that all progress in history has been due to improved access to the "Nine Pillars of History." The "Nine Pillars" are not associated with a social revolution or any border war. Actually borders are hindrances. Ideally, states should be only administrative entities of the "Nine Pillars," like each state within the United States.

(901) The "Nine Pillars" points out that 10,000 years of war have been due to a flaw in the system of government, a Sumerian, dogmatic type government.

(902) **The "Nine Pillars" are costly and time consuming to implement. Each pillar do not need to be started all at the same time and do not need the same sophistication everywhere. Recognizing them allows countries to set goals or at least make implementation plans. Some countries need international support to get started. Serving each other in open and reasonable trade, thus creating work—work that can be exchanged for food, housing and the support system necessary for the security of a family life— is the ultimate goal for us all.**

(903) The three great steps in the evolution of humanity have been the introduction of the three most important means of food transportation: the handheld tarp, the animal drawn cart and the

engine driven transport. Each step represents the expansion of the distribution of food. The tarp allowed for food to be distributed within the family or the band during the H/G period. The animal drawn cart allowed for food to be transported to the local farm market of local cities. Engine driven transport has made it possible for food to be sold to a global market. Within a stone-age band, an individual's service to his own family in exchange for the cooked family meal and security has grown to the individual's service to a global family in exchange for his/her food and security.

(904) **In the beginning of the manuscript, it was postulated that the "Nine Pillars" from the H/G period were eternal needs. The modern "Nine Pillars of History" are indeed essentially the same as those establish during the H/G period despite that 200,000 years separate them. We may therefore conclude The "Nine Pillars of History" are:**

(905) 1. **Survival (food, water, air, energy and sex);**

(906) 2. **Shelter,** a well-implemented building code and a home free from government intrusions with laws securing the property from terrorists and marauders;

(907) 3. **Cleanliness,** with hygiene in food and living environment;

(908) 4. **Art,** in living space and time to enjoy it;

(909) 5. **Communication;**

(910) 6. **Community,** for common goals;

(911) 7. **Religion,** according to one's own conviction;

(912) 8. **Acess to Medicine;**

(913) 9. **Trade** of what we produce for our own "Nine Pillar" needs.

# Reference

*The Struggle for Democracy.* Edward S. Greenberg, Benjamin I. Page. 1999. ISBN: 0-321-07039-9.

# Future

(914) **The world population has become a global family. We, on the Earth, live off a few finite commodities because any other livable planet is more than a lifetime away. The finite commodities are: land with fresh water and clean air with energy for production and transport of food and industrial output that is of service to humanity and can be traded freely for our own "Nine Pillars of History."**

(915) **The fulfillment of the "Nine Pillars" in a democratic society assures a better world to live in. That is the promise that 200,000 years of history holds in sight.**

# Further Recommended Reading

(916) Michigan University series *History of the Modern Man* and Time Life popular history books: *The Life History of United States, Great Ages of Man, A History of the World's Culture* together with the Time's *Atlas of the World's History*.

(917) I read the American Heritage *History of the Presidency* and with admiration Will Durant's *The Story of Civilization* and *The Story of Philosophy*.

(918) I studied *The Theories of History* by Patrick Gardiner and similar publications, comparing the idea of this publication to other attempts to explain history.

(919) My *Encyclopedia Britannica* was always a handy resource. The CIA publication *World Fact Book 2002* and publications by the *Utrikes Politiska Institut* were also helpful in providing me with the statistical facts about each country. (This Swedish institute publishes in Swedish, non-party political information about different countries. (www.ui.se)

# Part V

## Analysis of the Golden Rule of Love and the Pillar Needs of History

*To Hilli,*
*Because the greatest is Love*

*—Corinthians I, 13:13*

# Preface

(920) In the preceding text, *The Nine Pillars of History: All as a Guide for Peace*, I filtered out nine needs that have been fundamental to humanity for the past 200,000 years. If the needs of the "Nine" are not met the situation apparently tends to lead to war.

(921) Each of the historical pillars has been part of humanity since the beginning of human society and each by themselves must serve the other eight. Access to medicine, for instance, must, with its knowledge of hygiene, serve the intake of food, water and secure the cleanliness of the home and so on. More of this will be analyzed later.

(922) One historical pillar, the "Seventh Pillar," **free choice of religion**, is more difficult to analyze relative to the other eight. Religion is historically a fundamental concept as old as humanity but also a metaphysical concept. Religion has offered different formats for each religion and has not been permanent through history. All the other eighth pillar-needs are eternal, are interdependent and have not change in their perception of their need. (If I am hungry, I need food; if I am sick, I need medicine and may need to communicate about it, and may need a support system to help me and so on.)

(923) Each world religion has had and still has a wide impact on humanity. It is therefore necessary to analyze each of the five world religions relative to each of the eight other historical pillars. Each world religion claims it lives by the Golden Rule of Love. This claim will therefore be examined at the same time.

(924) This is not to be construed as judging the mythology that surrounds all religions. It is simply an examination of how the resulting culture, socially and anthropologically meets the common denominators of the Nine Historical Pillars and the Golden Rule.

# Acknowledgment

(925) I want to extend my profound thanks to the many academic experts in different fields who reviewed the manuscript. Professor of Theological Anthropology, Anne Christine Hornborg, at Lund's University in Sweden reviewed and analyzed my early Swedish manuscript of Veda/Brahma/Hinduism, Buddhism, Judaism and Islam. Professor Emeritus of Theology at Lund University and a leading Protestant minister within the Swedish

Lutheran Church, Lars Österlin, reviewed Christianity and pointed out its cultural value. Many early references are in Swedish, but I have added corresponding reference literature in English.

(926) I have also had experts of religious studies in the United States review the manuscript and advise me of additional resources that touch on the subject. Robert W. Clark, Ph.D., Research Fellow, Tibetan Studies Institute Initiative, Stanford University has, through his thorough and wide experience in studies of different religions, has been particularly helpful in formatting and criticizing the entire manuscript.

(927) Professor Emeritus Van Harvey, Department of Religious Studies, Stanford University, suggested the English references on Christianity. Jim Fox, Associate Professor at the Department of Anthropological Science with special interest in Philology and who also happened to be familiar with the Scandinavian Languages, reviewed my referrals to Swedish words. Professor John Rick from the same faculty gave valuable criticism for my Part I and has again been a valuable advisor.

(928) Old friends, Joe Reagan, Ph.D. and Chief Scientist at Lockheed Martin and Wesley Alles, Ph.D. and Director of Stanford Health Education and now also design consultant to the YMCA for its health screening, provided editing corrections.

(929) My colleague Adrian Flacoll endorsed my choice of numbering the paragraphs, an advice I readily accepted in order to offer specific discussions.

(930) I have also attended lectures about Buddhism by Professor Robert Thurman from Columbia University, New York and attended lectures about Zen Buddhism by Professor Tim Barrett, Cambridge, Connecticut and by Venerable Jian Hu, Ph.D., Abbot, Chung Tai Zen Center in Sunnyvale, California as well as Professor Stanley Insler, Yale University, Connecticut speaking on the subject of Zoroastrianism.

(931) Although I have had many people review and criticize the manuscript (and they all have helped me with references), I alone am responsible for the evaluation relative to the Nine Historical Pillars and the Golden Rule.

(932) "Free choice of religion" is number seven of the Nine Historical Pillars. The need for a generic religion has existed ever since *Homo sapiens* began to think and form concepts that could be communicated. It felt natural to me not to question if religion was a

necessary pillar but to ask: do all of the major world religions meet the needs of the other eight historical pillars and specifically do they meet the true tribal Golden Rule of Love as they all claim? Together, we will try to answer these questions.

(933) Most religions have a dual format: a focused material object for prayer in our world that represents the god in the transcendental world and also a moral message for the society. We will limit this study to addressing these concepts for five selected major religions. We show them as examples of the technique to analyze a dogmatic idea objectively with common denominators, in this case, the Nine Pillars of History and the Golden Rule.

(934) This will not be an exhaustive study of the faith of each religion. The prior section of this book made a similar analysis of 200,000 years of world political history in some 30,000 words. I am again working very economically with words. I am here analyzing five religions with less than half of that number of words. The key has been that we can make a very short and objective analysis using common denominators. I have since learned, that the technique of few words was introduced to anthropology in the early 1900s by Bronislaw Malinowski, Professor Malinowski, saw "culture as a vast instrumental apparatus, the function of which was to satisfy human needs, both primary and derived." This conclusion is also ours. Our analysis is therefore limited to the most fundamental, anthropologic influence each religion has had and still has on its society as judged by the needs of the common denominators, the Nine Historical Pillars and the Golden Rule.

(935) Religions are based on very old metaphysical concepts and have been subjects for different interpretations such as Veda/Brahma/ Hinduism, Hanayana or Mahayana Buddhism, Biblical, Rabbinical and Reformed Judaism, Roman, Greek or Protestant Christianity, Sunni or Shiite Islam.

(936) The five world religions have successfully filled the human religious needs for a long time; the oldest, Veda/Brahma/Hinduism, for more than 4000 years and the youngest, Islam, for 1500 years, but all are very young compared to the 200,000-year-long history

of human society. The single term, Veda/Brahma/Hinduism, is in this text used for the religions grown out of Vedaism and the Indian culture. Historically, Buddhism grew out of "Veda/Brahma/Hinduism" and Christendom and Islam out of Rabbinical Judaism. I will only point to customs that each religion has started in order to distinguish itself from the other but will also refer to common customs, which will result in some repetitions of statements. That some customs overlap is totally naturally; this does not mean they necessarily copied each other but that they all work with a common human concept.

(937) Any effort to analyze the effect of religion on society is a difficult task. Many feelings and dogmatic opinions will be touched. The religious experience, the faith of each religion, is not being discussed. This would be too personal and an impossible task.

## A. Religion

(938) Religion is a metaphysical concept, which cannot be perceived by our five natural senses: smell, taste, touch, vision and hearing. This is different from a physical concept of nature, which can be experienced with our senses or with sophisticated instruments as the extension of our senses. The knowledge about nature has grown relatively straightforwardly with each discovery. Several scientists, independent from each other, have confirmed or denied such discoveries.

(939) The knowledge about nature stood still during the hunting and gathering (H/G) period because life was only from hand to mouth. Life during the agricultural period was from year to year. Agriculture could expand with the extra help from animals and people. The expansion possibility led to new inventions. The knowledge about nature, its physics, chemistry and other sciences grew parallel with the 10,000-year-long expansion of the agriculture era.

(940) During the industrial period knowledge about nature has grown to include Earth's physical laws, those of the stars and those of atoms and even for physical laws common for all three worlds. It

is totally natural that we all want to know how the world was created and how it works.

(941) On the other hand, the understanding of the metaphysical world has not been along a straight path. The evolution of the spiritual world throughout history has been complicated with many different interpretations that cannot independently be confirmed, but are no less real to the human experience.

(942) Philosophers in metaphysics seek answers to such eternal questions as: Who created life and what is the purpose of life? What is right, what is wrong?

(943) At all times our intelligence has had a need to develop theories to seek logical continuity between concepts. This is why scientists have sought relationships between the different physical worlds and why the religious philosophers have spun links between gods' metaphysical world and that of our own observations. During all of history Shamans, medicine men, Brahmins, monks, priests, ministers, mullahs, imams, rabbis, philosophers, or as we amateurs have had our own interpretations of the metaphysical, the spiritual, world. Our explanation depends on our knowledge available at our given time. The more our concepts reflect people's actual experience, the easier and broader they are accepted.

(944) Professor Immanuel Kant was a philosopher who thought through the problems of the metaphysical world in the most thorough way. He lived all his life in Konigsberg, later Kaliningrad, between the years 1724 and 1802. Professor Kant taught philosophy and logic at the local university.

(945) In his book *Critik der reinen Vernuft* (English: Critique of the Common Sense), Kant concluded that religion, in its generic form, is a metaphysical concept that can never be proven by laws of nature. Religion has to be based on dogmatic terms. Professor Kant used the word "transcendental" to describe "God." God, according to Kant, is a generic concept that transcends the physical and the metaphysical world. Kant did not analyze specific religions but the reasoning was based on generic concepts and would be true for any religion. Kant came to the conclusion that any religion has to rest on the moral

experience of a whole society and that any god's purpose would be to meet the moral need of society, a concept that ultimately rests on the tribal perception of the eternal Golden Rule.

(946) Our life within a religion will live on forever in the memory we leave behind to our society. Brahmin authors, Buddha, Moses, Jesus, and Mohammed all have eternal life in the moral memory they left behind to their societies.

(947) *The Nine Pillars of History* gives an answer to one of the eternal questions: What is the meaning of life? The simplest answer to this question is: **To survive**. Life started, when the first DNA-organelle invaded a one-cell body and initiated cell division. The DNA-organelle has since been stimulated to build more and more complicated plants and animals, all adjusted to survive within their surroundings. At the top of this evolution is the speaking, concept-forming and in social group-living human, the *Homo sapiens.*

(948) The first humans formed family clans for a better chance to survive the 190,000-year-long Hunting and Gathering (H/G) period. The H/G-clans wandered out from Africa, conquered and successfully inhabited the whole world. The Nine Pillars of History were derived and defined from this time. They became the social need and the moral norm for the best chance to survive for all following members of the Homo sapiens. The needs of the "Nine" continued during the following 10,000-year-long agricultural period but were now added to the perceived needs of the metaphysical gods, who controlled the outcome of the food production. The outcome of a harvest was fundamental for survival during this second historical period; a period filled with huge buildings housing a place for prayers to fill, among other needs, the need for a successful harvest.

(949) We have to go far back in history to analyze religious concepts, much further back than archeology allows us to go. Language is the tool to express religious concepts. Religious concepts started soon after we learned to speak. Language therefore offers a way to reach beyond archeological evidences and into the earliest time of tribal living.

(950)  I will now refer to Swedish several times because I happen to know it as my mother language. I feel it is somewhat serendipitous that I can do this because, at least for me, it contributed to a better understanding of our present subject, religion.

(951)  Swedish is an old Indo-European language, part of the Scandinavian, Anglo-Saxon and the Germanic language group, or one of many that has evolved on the Euro-Asian platform. Historically, Sweden has been remote, isolated, and uniquely always politically independent. Some original linguistic concepts and expressions from the earliest time have survived rather unspoiled in Swedish. I will use them as an example of how early people reasoned. Parallel concepts exist in many other languages not familiar to me.

(952)  Breathing, the activity to move air in and out of the body, is one of the very first signs of life when a child is born and the last sign of life, in our last sigh. *"To breathe"* in Swedish translate to *"att andas."* The Swedish word "andas" is derived from the substantive "ande," which in English would translate into the substantive *"spirit."* A "spiritual life" would in Swedish be *"ande liv."* The English word *"breath"* would in Swedish be *"ande dräkt"* or the "the "dress" of the "spirit," a "dress" that could be perceived but not seen (in Spanish: *anima*). The breath moving in and out of the body identifies a person's spirit. The spirit was already perceived as different from the body and introduced a dual concept. The body is left behind to the profane world when the spirit has left it. I postulate that spiritual life was originally born from observing the breath.

(953)  The sun was an all-dominating resource for energy, part of the "First Pillar." The yearly renewal of life in nature became a spiritual concept. The sun sending its life-giving rays to the earth could be observed. That the sun had great influence on nature was obvious to all. The spiritual concept was extended to the sun, an all-creator sun-spirit. Only one spiritual creator was worshipped during the Hunting and Gathering (H/G) period. This early creator had no human image and did not take part in the daily life of humans. **The early humans had no heaven or hell concept.**

(954) The sun and the moon moved and were eternal. Parts of nature also moved and were eternal; air moved in the wind, water ran in the rivers and rain moved with the clouds. Animals moved and plants grew. Animals and plants multiplied and died just like humans. Life or "spirits" permeated everything. Eternal spirits became gods, who lived in a world of gods, the metaphysical world. Greek has the word "*pneuma*," Hebrew "*ruah*" and Hindu/Sanskrit "*atham,*" are all words expressing wind and spirit. Pneumatology is the learning about spirits while the pneumo part of the word stands for many words that have to do with air, such as pneumonia for inflammation of the lung or pneumatic tire for an air inflated tire. This analogy illustrates how basic concepts continue within different concepts in all languages.

(955) Fluctuations of nature influenced the outcome of the harvest during the agricultural period. The fluctuations became specific spirits or gods. The spirits were given names, human forms, appealed to, offered, and prayed to. After a successful harvest the gods were celebrated with yearly festivals.

(956) Some early tribes invented ways to bring out the spirits of certain plants. These spirits took over the behavior of the individual. These products became spirituous brews or smokes.

(957) Tribal life learned early that dirt and what was excreted from the body or what was close to remains of death, were harmful. Women during "menstrual excretion" were "unclean." The "excreted newborns" were not accepted within society before they had been cleansed and had been "baptized" with water. All of this knowledge became rules of daily cleanliness or religious, ritualized taboos.

(958) In the agricultural period the work on the farm was repeated and exposed to the same challenges every year. Offerings and prayers were set into systems. Specialists (Brahmins, monks, rabbis, priests, clergymen, mullahs, imams) with "extra effective" rituals within special ritual buildings or homes of gods (temples, topas, synagogues, churches and mosques) had personal, exclusive communications with the gods. Gods, who were already personified, formed families with a Father God, Mother God and even with extended families. The

mythology was woven together to mirror earthly family life in order to be easier identified with or remembered. Each god had control over his or her special field of family or group activity.

(959) During the H/G period there was no personal ownership of the food production, the area for hunting and gathering. A general ownership did not work for a farm or city society where everything depended on the work effort of the individual. In the agricultural community personal ownership became a necessary part of morals and a basis for additional social laws.

(960) The history of the English word "conscience" is interesting in this discussion. The word "conscience" is composed of the old Latin words "con" (common) and "science" from the Latin word "scientia" (knowledge). "Conscience" in other words defines a metaphysical concept, the "common knowledge," the inner voice, which tells you what is right according to the experiences of the society. Swedish has a similar word, "*samvete.*" "Samvete" literally stands for "sam" (common) and "vetande" (knowledge).

(961) There is no difference between how the brain of the first humans worked and that of modern humans. The same way as I think and try to form concepts as logically as possible from the knowledge I have; in the same way the first humans thought and pondered over concepts from the knowledge they had. The earliest humans were similarly spoken to by an inner voice when thinking. They used and we still use the same word-concepts when they were pondering or when talking. If the talk is in a different language the brain makes the translation automatically provided we had learned the other language. I may think in either Swedish or English when I ponder to write right here. That is why my sentence building sometimes is a little different from yours, but I hope I will come through with my message anyway.

(962) Many people think of the conscience-thought-pondering process as if their God is talking to them. This can also be understood as a moral thought-feed-back from laws and traditions of society. Such thoughts require a definition of morality. What is moral in Stockholm may not be moral somewhere else.

(963) The voice of the conscience in this society is not recognized as the voice of your own but is the base for the dual concept of body and soul. The soul has the moral superiority and the authority over the body. **The moral authority of the group-soul gives religious morality enormous power over the actions of the individual body. Through history a church building becomes a symbol, a totem of the group-religion. In modern Iraq the Sunnis and the Shiites still destroy each other's mosques in order to hurt each other's group-soul. This dogmatic killing of each other's body and soul has gone on for 1500 years. It is all due to brainwashing in cultures empty of the Golden Rule. Wake Up People! Reach for democracy while you still can!**

(964) It is interesting to note that Emile Durkheim, through extensive ethnological studies of the old religions of Australia, comes to a similar connection between conscience and society, the individual soul being part of the collective soul of the tribe. Dr. Durkheim attempts to define religion: *"A religion is a unified system of beliefs and practices relative to sacred things, that is to say, things set apart and forbidden – beliefs and practices which unite into one single moral community called a church, all those who adhere to them."*

(965) **The need for survival, the security of the individual and his family is the driving force for the psychological need for the moral rules of the whole society. No one can kill, steal from, lie to, and sexually attack his neighbor without punishment. If not punished for amoral deeds, the society will break apart and no one will feel safe. These are rules by which the humanity populated the entire world during the 190,000 years of tribal life.**

(966) Dr. Sigmund Freud in his life-long work of psychoanalysis postulated that the human need for religion is based on a "childhood neurosis for humanity." We all have to grow from a dependent child to mature adult and leave behind the individual childhood neurosis for security. According to Freud this is why most religions are patriarchal with a strong father-god as the original creator. Professor Freud further explains the need for religion as a child's wishful thinking, an illusion, as we all have to face the hostile challenges of social life,

fate from natural events and the ultimate end of earthly life. Most people stay in this childhood illusion. Education based on science removes some of the illusions and leads to what Freud call "education to reality." Buddha called the same thing "enlightenment to reality."

(967) Ever since the beginning of agricultural Sumeric time have royal or central powers formulated rules for society. Royal laws are therefore usually angled to the advantage of the central power. Individual human rights in such societies have historically always come in second, both despite and thanks to religion. The Golden Rule set the moral rule in tribal time. The Golden Rule still lived on and was eventually revived when democratic thoughts evolved through a jury system based on commoners' experiences.

(968) The most general moral social rule in history and which also has been more or less specifically accepted by all five world-religions, is the Golden Rule: Love your neighbor as yourself. "Love your neighbor as yourself" is a pleading request. Nobody can be forced to love your neighbor as yourself. The rule has therefore needed a reward system.

(969) I now have to make an excursion from our theme about the world religions and visit the generally accepted oldest and still active religion, Zoroastrianism. Zoroastrianism has influenced all world religions. Accordingly, it demands a short description before we continue.

(970) Under the Persian king, Cyrus I, Zoroastrianism was the state religion. King Cyrus conquered the world powers of his time, Egypt, Syria and Mesopotamia. Babylon was ravaged in 539 BC. The Jews who had been enslaved in Babylon for 70 years were allowed to return home to Jerusalem.

(971) The Arabs conquered Persia (Iran) in their jihad missionary expansion in 651 AD. Iran became a center for Shiite Islam after Islam split into Shiite and Sunni fractions. Any trace of Zoroastrianism was driven out. All Zoroastrian priests were killed and their temples destroyed. Survivors hid in some mountain caves. Small colonies of families fled to Bombay, India, and formed the community of Parses. They worked with trade and could thereby survive on the side

of the Indian agriculture. They secluded themselves as a caste and melted into the regular social caste environment up to the present day. There are only some 100,000 members in the world. Outside of India there are small clusters of Zoroastrian communities in the USA and in other democratic countries with assured free religion. I met one taxi-driving family in Stockholm and many at Stanford University during lectures about their religion. Today Zoroastrianism is no longer sectarian but an open, non-discriminating communion.

(972) The Indo-European tribe, Aryans, invaded both Iran and India some 4000 years ago. They lived at a time relatively close to the old hunting and gathering time that had many spirits in nature but only one creator. Agriculture in the area had been present for 3000 years. They now had to accept the many gods of agricultural time, the gods who gave you a harvest.

(973) This old hunter/warrior religion had a reform prophet, Zarathustra. He is believed to have lived in old Persia, some say at the time of Moses (Insler). Many say he lived in the century preceding Buddha.

(974) Zarathustra was a physician/poet/philosopher seeking an answer to the meaning of life. He wrote some 200 poems of which 17 have survived. His thoughts have been saved in a book called, *Gathas of Zarathustra*. "Gatha" was the mother language for Zarathustra. (Could this language be related to Goth? I don't know.) Zarathustra wanted to be the healer of the world. He wished to do this by giving the world the "Truth" and healing it from what he called, "Disease" or "Evil." In order to sustain the order and stability that he observed in nature, he divided his humanity into units of home, districts and countries. In each unit he demanded respect for the father, the elders and the authorities. The One God, Ahura (Lord) Mazda, was both the Creator and a friend of humans in their fight against "Evil" or "Disease." "Truth" was to accept the law of community and to bring prosperity to all people in this and another world. Zarathustra's definition of "Truth" could be written in the constitution of any modern country.

(975) A benevolent Lord Mazda had created the world and the humans and given humans the freedom to live either for Truth or for Evil. For every Truth there is an Evil; there is no middle ground. Humans are free to choose but have to take the consequence of their choice. **Education helps people to make the right choice**.

(976) Lord Mazda's final goal was the purification of his creation. He accomplished this by supporting people with good thoughts and deeds and by punishing people with bad thoughts and deeds. People who choose Truth will come to Paradise; those who choose Evil thoughts (Disease) will go to Hell. **This is the first time in human history one benevolent but soul-judging God offered a life after this, either in a Paradise or in a Hell. This was a voluntary reward system**.

(977) **Rabbinical Judaism, Christendom and Islam actually copied Zoroastrianism. All three used the reward principle and had a similar reward.** Faithful members of Judaism, Christendom and Islam are all promised a life after death in a gardenlike Paradise where nobody gets sick or old. Unfaithful will have to stay in a dark and hot hell.

(978) "Paradise" is indeed, a Persian word and means a framed, fenced-in garden. Old Persian carpets with framed flower and animal motives are symbols of Paradise; sitting on a beautiful Persian carpet is to sit in Paradise (Professor Insler).

(979) Veda/Brahma/Hinduism and Buddhism use the reward principle for the faithful and offer a better earthly life next time around in its soul transmigration system; besides, Buddhism offers different levels of hell and heaven.

(980) The belief in a reward of a life after death has been important in the history of religions. Life after death is still a metaphysical concept. It cannot be proven one way or the other. It therefore requires tolerance for different interpretations. The purport of the Golden Rule is to form an attitude of tolerance towards your fellow man. The Golden Rule and the Nine Pillars of History are the norm for the democratic society of the 190,000-year-long Hunting and

Gathering period. **The Golden Rule forms the fundamental rule for a society governed by its citizens.**

(981) The Parliament of the World's Religions is trying to find common ground for the different world religions. The Parliament met last time in 1993 in Chicago and was attended by 6500 religious leaders. It has published a proposed "Declaration of a Global Ethic," which essentially is an elaboration based on the Golden Rule. (See Hans Kung).

(982) In order to assure that religion is not abused for taxing uneducated, naive people but really serve humanity, each of the five world religions will be evaluated from how they each meet the human needs of the Nine Pillars of History and the Golden Rule: love your neighbor as yourself.

(983) **The purpose with this manuscript is to create a better understanding for democracy with the ultimate goal of peace between different cultures.**

# References

(984) For further studies of H/G period consult the Internet with key words: Paleolithic archeology, human evolution, and modern human origin.

**For Further Reading:**

(985) *Guns, Germs and Steel: The Fates of Human Societies* by Jared Diamond, W.W. Norton & Company, ISBN 0-393-31755-2.

(986) *The Dawn of Human Culture* by Richard Klein, 2002, Nevraumont Publ, ISBN 0-471-25252-2.

(987) *Mapping Human History, Discovering the Past through Our Genes* by Steve Olsen, Houghton Mifflin Publ. Company, ISBN 0-618-09157-2.

(988) *Hunting and Gathering Period: The !Kung San, Men, Women, and Work in a Foraging Society* by Richard Borshay Lee, Cambridge University Press, 1979, ISBN 0 29561 0.

*(989)* *Hunters and Gatherers Today,* by Steve Olsen published 1972 by Holt, Rinehart and Winston, Inc., ISBN: 0-03-076865-9.

*(990)* *Dawn of Man, the Story of Human Evolution* by Robin McKie, published in 2000 by Dorling Kindersley Inc. ISBN 0-7894-6262-1. Originally the book was to accompany the BBC television program in 2000 *The Ape-man,* televised in the U.S. as *The Dawn of Man* by TLC, The Learning Channel, in the same year. The book by Robin McKie gave me the original inspiration for *The Nine Pillars of History.*

*(991)* *Tro Vetande Mystik: Svensk Religionsfilosofi 1900-1999 En Anthology.* Johan Modee (red.), 2000, ISBN 91-7139-484-2.

*(992)* *Anthropological Approaches to the Study of Religion,* Michael Banton, red. (1966) London: Tavistock Publ. Inget ISBN 0422725102.

*(993)* *Ojibwa Ontology, Behavior and World View,* 1960, A.I. Hallowell.

*(994)* *Culture in History: Essays in Honor of Paul Radin,* New York, Columbia University Press, Card Number: 59-13776.

*(995)* *Nature and Society, Anthropological Perspectives,* 1996, Philippe Descola & Gísli Pálsson, Ed. Rutledge Publ. ISBN 0-415-13215-0.

*(996)* *Stone Age Economy,* Marshall Sahlin, 1972, Tavistock Publ., ISBN 0-422-74530-5.

*(997)* *Ecologies of the Heart, Emotion, Belief and the Environment* av E.N. Anderson, 1996, Oxford Press, ISBN 0-19-509010-1.

*(998)* *Purity and Danger, An Analysis of Concepts of Pollution and Taboo* av Mary Douglas. Publ by Routledge and Kegan Paul, 1966 ISBN 0-7100-1299-3.

*(999)* *Declaration of the Religions for a Global Ethic,* Hans Kung.

*(1000)* *The Elementary Forms of Religious Life* by Emile Durkheim, 1915, Free Press, no ISBN.

*(1001)* *The Sociology of Religion* by Max Weber, 1922, Beacon Press, no ISBN.

*(1002)* *The Origin of Languages* by Merritt Ruhlen, 1994, John Wiley and Sons, ISBN 0-471-15963-8.

*(1003)* *The Gathas of Zarathustra,* 1999, Mapin Publ Co, ISBN 1-890206-09-1.

(1004) *The Future of an Illusion* by Sigmund Freud, Translated by Peter Gay, 1961, W.W.Norton & Comp. LTD. ISBN 0-393-000831-2.

(1005) *A Handbook of Living Religions.* Ed. by John Hinnells (Penguin, 1991) ISBN 0140135995.

(1006) *World Faiths.* S.A. Nigosian (St. Martin's, 1994) ISBN 0312 08414-5.

(1007) *The Sacred Chain.* Norman F. Cantor (Harpers, 1995) ISBN 006092652-X.

## Veda/Brahma/Hinduism

(1008) The homeland of Veda/Brahma/Hinduism is India. Its history is close to the history of India and its geography.

(1009) India is a relatively isolated peninsula protruding southward from the Euro-Asiatic continent. The enormous Himalaya Mountains isolate it to the north, the Arabian Sea to the west and the Bengal Sea to the east. Today there is a railroad crossing the Khyber Pass into Pakistan, but all these natural hinders were difficult to overcome in old times. The peninsula is only seven times the area of California yet is inhabited by more than a billion people.

(1010) Although much progress has been made in the modern democratic India more than 50% of the population in India was illiterate only 70 years ago. Going back just a little further in time both Asia and Europe had very few people able to read and have a scientific understanding of the world. This is important to remember when describing religions. A religion reflects thousands of years of efforts to communicate with very large populations, unable to read but still, having a fundamental need for security and a moral purpose for life.

(1011) The first inhabitants of the Indian peninsula lived along the coast but a later group, Dravidians, an agricultural people, inhabited the river valleys of Indus in the West and Ganges in the East.

(1012) A group of Aryan warriors invaded the Indus River Valley about 3500 years ago. The Aryans came from somewhere north on the Euro-Asiatic plate and climbed the Khyber Pass into Pakistan, part of India at that time. The Aryans took over the ownership of the land and expelled the Dravidians or used them as slaves.

(1013) The Aryans at first were a religious warrior people similar to the Aztecs in Mexico. The priests transmitted the good luck from the gods, first for conquest, but after the Aryans had become farmers, also for a good harvest. India, like Europe, split into hundreds of small states fighting for control of land, people and taxes. At times, the land was united under one strong warrior.

(1014) India has been the origin of many great religions, actually world religions, but we will only touch on Veda/Brahma/Hinduism and Buddhism.

(1015) Veda/Brahma/Hinduism dominated India's very early and late religious history. Rulers who demanded either Buddhism or Islam dominated the in-between-time. Buddhism, which is pacifistic and whose followers cannot kill according to its dogma, became a fiasco for the freedom of India. As Zoroastrianism had been annihilated in Persia shortly before, Buddhism disappeared almost totally from India after the Islamic conquest. This took place during the latter half of our first millennium and the first part of the second (700-1500). Sumeric kings, supported by Veda/Brahma/Hinduism, Buddhism or Islam, have governed India during its four or five thousand years of history until modern time. India has been a free state since 1950. India is now the world's largest social democracy and has free choice of religion in its constitution. This followed a relative short transition period in the early 1900s, during which time England had strong influence on how India was governed. Nepal is the only state in the world that still has Veda/Brahma/Hinduism as its state religion.

(1016) India consists of 85% Hindus, 11% Muslims and the rest are other religions. Muslims from the previous Muslim-dominated India have separated themselves from the ancient geographical India and formed three independent states: Pakistan, Afghanistan and Bangladesh. **Afghanistan with less than $500/capita GNP and Bangladesh with less than that are two of the world's poorest and least educated countries. Afghanistan is trying to hang on to no-education, particularly in regard to the education for women. In**

**this regard, Pakistan is waiving where to stand but is happy to take any American handout.**

(1017)  Veda/Brahma/Hinduism is the oldest of the five world religions and therefore has a close connection to the religions of the original H/G period. Veda/Brahma/Hinduism, like the "H/G religion" has not had a dominating prophet, no Buddha, Moses, Jesus or Mohammed and no Pope or special, all-embracing, standardizing organization. This fact makes it unique among the five world religions. Four thousand years of freedom offers unique learning experiences for both society and religion.

(1018)  The Dravidians, living in the warm climate of India, retained their dark skin they had from their past in warm Africa. The Aryan clans during thousands of years of living in the north had adapted to the cooler climate in the North with lighter skin. The color of the skin became a mark between a ruling people and its slaves. A caste system was born. Veda/Brahma/Hinduism is not only a religion but also a social system built from a caste plan. Strict caste formalities rule both social and family life and continue to this day.

(1019)  The Aryan society consisted originally of three social groups: priests, warriors and shepherds. **From now on I will often use the word "priest" generically for a person hired to work for a religious community and assigned to teach and promote its religion.** The Aryan shepherds became dirt farmers when they had conquered the land. The conquered Dravidians became the workers of the farms and stayed in the beginning outside the caste system. Eventually, after hundreds of years, the Dravidians were accepted within the religious community but as a fourth caste, the Sudra. Other castes have been accepted in modern time, now, with at least 2000-3000 different castes being added. Members of the old castes never accept new members.

(1020)  The caste system was probably an expression for the sixth historical pillar, assurance for group support; that is to say, castes kept its members together by supporting each other within the society.

(1021)  The priests, the Brahmins, received their information from the gods. They determined the rules. The system was similar to the guild system in Europe during the Middle Age and somewhat akin to modern labor unions in the industrial time. The caste system is religiously regulated, is much more enforced and often marked with physical margins between castes. There are at times observed that not even a shadow of a member can fall on a member of another caste. The caste system is supported by parents' concern for the family's best chance for survival, both in the choice of a partner for their children and the children's choice of occupation.

(1022) The Aryans call themselves "the ones who are born twice," once at the actual, biological birth and the second time at the spiritual birth. This event in other religions would be called confirmation or bar mitzvah for Jewish boys. The spiritual birth takes place after studies of the Veda books under the tutorship of a Brahmin priest. At the second birth, the "confirmation," the candidate receives a rope across the left shoulder as a visible sign of being an accepted member of the group. The Brahmins always wear the rope as a sign of their dignity. Other Aryans wear the rope only at special occasions.

(1023) The Brahmins put their stamp on the whole social community. The tradition of defining different periods of people's lives started during the Brahmin period. An Aryan child, always a boy, had to be schooled by a Brahmin, live with and serve the Brahmin in order to receive the right Vedic knowledge and also to learn many of the Vedic songs by heart.

(1024) **The system developed by Brahmins has been copied by the other four younger world religions in establishing religious schools.** The value of a religious school is its education in social ethics. **The danger in religious schooling can be dogmatic intolerance towards other religions, an elitistic attitude towards fellow man. This became an abuse in early Christianity and Islam and still is in radicalized, dogmatic Islam.**

(1025) **The Brahmins designed the cult ceremonies.** In order to be of service to the community they suggested offerings to certain gods, each specializing in its field, such as to the ones controlling rain, fertility or health. A Brahmin starts his prayer session by calling for holy attention by ringing a bell and pours his offering over a holy fire. The smoke of the offer rises up to the god with the message. This was a very pragmatic message for simple people and is now a tradition.

(1026) **The ancient Aryans, like the Egyptians, believed that life after death continued but was better than present earthly life.** When the dead had been cremated their physical parts returned in the smoke to the gods from whence they had come:

**The meat to the God of Earth**
**The blood to the God of Water**
**The speech to the God of Fire**
**The breath to the God of Wind**
**The hearing to the God of Direction**
**The vision to the God of Sun**
**The thinking to the God of Moon**

(1027) What was left of the dead, the Karma, was formed together into a new personality, **a first description of transmigration.**

(1028) Another description of transmigration is the "five-fire format." According to this, the human had been created by a "five-fire-offer." A dead person after cremation rises with the smoke and via the Night enters the Cosmic World. Here he or she will stay until all the merits of the good deeds have been accounted for. The rest of the dead, the Karma, has to return to earth via a similar road. It falls down as rain, is taken up by plants and eaten by certain people. The parts from good people will land in good mothers' wombs; the parts of evil people would enter evil mothers' wombs or the wombs of dogs or pigs. The theory has become so accepted that it is never discussed and again lives on from the tradition.

(1029) Veda/Brahma/Hinduism rests on ancient epos, written with thousands of verses. The earliest eposes are called the Vedic books. The Veda texts are four in number: Rig, Sama, Yahur and Atharva Veda. The Brahmins learned the eposes by heart and transferred them in this way from generation to generation from about -1500 to about -600 when they were written down. During the following 1000 years new generations of Brahmins added several new eposes with their own thoughts and religious texts.

(1030) The written language was Sanskrit, an early Indo-European language. Panini (from 400 B.C.), working within Sanskrit, wrote the world's first grammar. Together, the texts constitute the greatest religious tradition in the world. As with the Bible and the Quran, and what is common in all religions, many of them are considered as godly manifestations. Most people today do not understand Sanskrit but the sound of the words as scanted by the Brahmins in mantras or prayers are believed to bring power. Similarly, without people understanding the meaning, Latin text was scanted or chanted in the medieval Christianity and the sound of the words was thought to bring power.

(1031) Despite all disasters that can happen to agriculture, one could see an eternal world order in one thousand years of tradition. People were thankful that the sun rose every day, that the farm gave its harvest and that the good and positive in society was honored and the evil punished.

(1032) The importance of the gods diminished. The gurus (teachers) themselves started to ponder about the creation of the earth and preach their own interpretations. This was the time, about -500 (B.C), when Buddhism and other sects separated themselves from Veda/Brahma/ Hinduism.

(1033) Gods had to get in line and follow what was called the rite-power. The power of rites was recognized in the Vedic hymns. First one god and then another had the overall power during the past centuries. The gods were dethroned and became inactive. The possibilities opened for the concept of monotheism. Philosophers sought the meaning of transmigration. Gurus (teachers) sought bliss and happiness in the world of gods. The knowledge to reach this was a spiritual liberation from earthly desires and doubts. The ideal was a continuous calm and rest, a cosmic, blessed god's world, a Nirvana. The cosmic God, Brahma, replaced the earlier great God, Prajapati.

(1034) Despite Brahma's overall power it is a passive god-concept. Brahma is pictured with four heads, one for each cardinal direction.

Brahma sees and hears everything. Brahma is the one with, or the same as the infinite world soul, the Athman.

(1035) Differences in the names of gods were due to varying language traditions; differences in appearances of gods were due to different myths with unique artistic interpretations. The style of architecture of the temples depended on what building materials were available.

(1036) Veda/Brahma/Hinduism, as the oldest religion, started the first tradition of holy places. These are spread all over the country. Pilgrimage between all the places has kept and still keeps India united despite all of the many gods.

(1037) Nature religions are full of spirits. In India it is possible to identify yourself with 3.2 million different gods. Out of this multiplicity has crystallized a more theoretical foundation for a few people, a close-to-god concept.

(1038) The name for the cosmic god, Brahma, was the same or similar to the name of the priest, Brahmin or Brahman, with only the accent as difference. The similarity accentuated the close connection of the priest to the cosmic God, Brahma. The cosmic god is an old concept and has had many names. In this text "Brahma" is recognized as the main God, the Creator of all gods. Brahma is mentioned first in the Rig-Veda.

(1039) Brahma is often referred to as the Atman. Brahma has the syllable "br" which still live on in the English word "breath or "breathing. "*Atman*" is also an interesting word. It has an Indo-European origin and has the same spiritual heritage as the earlier described Swedish word "*anden,*" for "breath." In German the corresponding word is "*atmen.*" The Atman became the very soul and essence of life, a bridge between the material and the spiritual, between the physical and the metaphysical world, between life and the "World soul," a synonym for the Creator.

(1040) Death, according to Veda/Brahma/Hinduism, can be experienced in the quietness of a dreamless sleep. The "desire" or human's "Karma," the residual after all good-deed-credits have been used up in the other world, awakes and drives the body to go on in a re-birth. Only the holiest individuals, free from desires, do not need to be reborn. They will reach everlasting peace, the Nirvana, and become eternal parts of the world soul. The earthly life in Veda/Brahma/Hinduism, and also in Buddhism, is experienced as a struggling existence. Brahma's world is also described as more physical, a paradise, where nobody becomes old, the men are served by beautiful nymphs and get all their desires filled. (This description is most likely written by men for men.) A religiously faithful man is awarded a paradisiacal life after death.

(1041) All these descriptions are authors' ways to describe something metaphysical with a more pragmatic value setting. Concepts were separated into two groups: either living with a consciousness or concepts of dead material, without ability to think. The gods changed from representing material concepts such as the sun, moon and the wind and instead began to stand for social concepts in the community of humans. In advanced forms Brahma appears, at times, as a personal God, at times as an impersonal absolute.

(1042) Humans seeking blessing ought to perform spiritual exercises, like yoga, and make him/herself free from material influences in order to reach his/her inner spiritual nucleus, the "World Soul."

(1043) This spiritual desire for peace of mind is supported by a bewildering number of rituals connecting human life to nature and to the cosmos. The year is divided into moon-months; both the year and the month are divided into one part with increasing light and good fortunes and one part with decreasing brightness and bad fortunes. The sun's fortune-bringing ability changes with the equinoxes; the moon's influence changes at the time of the full moon. Position of the planets is also important for making decisions. Numerous calendars with astrological interpretations are printed and are part of everyone's daily life. Astrology, which began in the old Sumeric culture, at least some 7000 years ago, has survived as a metaphysical concept in many cultures. It may either be part of religion or be employed as an independent, cosmic "adviser."

(1044) The close connection of Hinduism to nature is expressed in its mythology. Prominent mountains and rivers are holy and part of the "life" of major gods. The mighty River Ganges' importance in Veda/Brahma/Hinduism is well known all over the world. Millions of pilgrims come at certain times of the year for a soul-cleansing bath. On the 24th of February 2001, a most holy day, 20 million were assembled in one place, the largest gathering of people ever recorded in the world. The economical outfall of all this pilgrimage has created competition between different holy places. All world religions since Veda/Brahma/Hinduism have accepted, or have not discouraged pilgrimage as a religious ritual. Pilgrimage is indeed a strong expression of community, the "Sixth Historical Pillar." The other four religions have all copied this tradition.

(1045) Veda/Brahma/Hinduism marks 16 life-rituals; many of them are common with those of all religions such as the baptizing, the confirmation of religious membership, the celebration of the end of studies, marriage, the end to professional activity and the final expression of paying respect at death. Besides these rituals Hindus may have rituals for placing of the semen for the purpose of conceiving a child, praying for a boy, prepare a woman for delivery and a delivery ritual often at the woman's original birthplace, the first time a baby is brought outside the home, the first time eating solid food, has a first hair cut, has ears pierced and when a boy receives a Brahman's holy rope across his left shoulder and starts his studies of the Veda books. The rituals concentrate on the education of the boy because the boy is the one who has to care for the family in the Indian agricultural society. The girl, when sexually mature or according to law after age sixteen, is joining the boy's family when married. Marriage is often arranged by the parents when the children are small, all to assure continued well-being of the two joined families through the parents' old age. The girl's family assures the bride's well being by providing her with her own rich dowry that remains her own. Some of these traditions in modern time have been complemented by federal or state support systems. A Hindu who takes part in the rituals and participates in their maintenance becomes a moral member of society, its common moral character and purpose. He accepts the tradition. At the same time the tradition becomes legitimized.

(1046) Vishnu became one of the most popular gods. Seventy percent of present day 700 million Hindus consider themselves belonging to Vishnuism. Vishnuism is the part of Veda/Brahma/Hinduism, which has been most successful in spreading internationally. The god Vishnu is identified with the sun but he can also step down to the earth and take the forms of different humans, "avatars." At least ten different avatars are recognized. Many of the avatars have much mythology in common with later religions. One Vishnu avatar is the man, Manu. Manu was warned about a great flood to come and told to build a large ark to save only the good part of the world. Still another popular avatar is that of Krishna who tells of a blessed life through the love of people. Another avatar of Vishnu is that of Buddha who hereby is included within Veda/Brahma/Hinduism. Many Vishnu faithful men paint a V on the forehead to officially declare their religious communion.

(1047) The most important Vishnu text is the Bhagavad-Gita authored about two hundred years before or after the beginning of the Christian calendar. It is part of the even larger epos, the Mahabharata. The Mahabharata brings forth a personal god, a personal relationship based on love and trust with the God Vishnu/Krishna. In this concept man's soul, the Atman, seeks connection with God. Man is forgiven and saved from Karmic consequences and rebirth through his belief and trust in Vishnu/Krishna. Vishnu, the Creator of the world, has come down to the earth as Krishna to save man by the teaching of love and forgiveness. The Mahabharata contains a Commandment of Love: "Man should not do to others what he doesn't want others to do to him." Yet, like the Bible, the Mahabharata is filled with accounts of man killing his brothers and sisters with the support of, and often under the command of, his deity. **A mature cultural attitude takes a long time to evolve when truth is not known.**

(1048) Mahatma Gandhi (1869-1948), one of the most well known Vishnu members, learned to feel and participate in the pain of others through his studies of Vishnu. Using pacifism and asceticism he successfully worked for India's independence in 1947. A Muslim murdered Gandhi the following year.

(1049) The second most popular god within Veda/Brahma/ Hinduism or with 28% members is Shiva, an earlier fire god. Shiva is the God of Death but at the same time the God of Fertility. Shiva conquers Death. The cult symbol for Shiva is a phallus surrounded by a vagina. He thereby assures the survival of the family. Devoted Shiva male-members paint three horizontal lines on their forehead to make public their identification with their god and communion.

(1050) Kama, the God of Love, has arrows as cult symbol. Kama was mentioned in the early Atharva-veda. Kama is described in the generally known book Kama Sutra. Kama Sutra is still a popular instruction manual for sex play.

(1051) Brahma, Vishnu or Shiva is considered masters of the heaven and the earth. Brahma, Vishnu and Shiva can also be considered as pantheism, a common three-folded unit, and an all-reaching power. The three-folded unit stands for the World soul, similarly to the Brahma. Besides these god-concepts there are countless numbers of local and family gods and also demons. These different beliefs do not disturb the faithful because a specific god concept cannot anyway be proven. Here Veda/Brahma/Hinduism is indeed true.

(1052) The purpose of isolating the soul from the material body was to come closer to a spiritual salvation or redemption. A person's individual account of good and evil deeds according the teachings, the Dharma, rests on personal responsibility in this life with Karmic recompense in the next. If this is considered as the manifestation by a Main God or by a personal Absolute is a personal choice. If the god is Brahma, Vishnu, Shiva or some other King of Gods or something Neutral is judged as unimportant.

(1053) The tolerance of Veda/Brahma/Hinduism meets the Golden Rule: *love your neighbor as yourself*, and is also covering the need of the "Second and the Seventh Historical Pillars" for home security and free choice of religion.

(1054) The conclusion one has to draw of the long and colorful family of gods in Veda/Brahma/Hinduism is that everybody has a need to have an intimate prayer relationship with a moral god-concept in support of his/her existence within a society. When the humans left the H/G period and the support system within the clan was replaced with individual ownership in the agricultural period, a new support system for individuals was needed. Group support was formed within castes based on social standings and professions. This was easily done within the stable society of the 10,000-year-long agricultural period but has partly collided with the group supports within modern industrial societies.

(1055) The God concept within Veda/Brahma/Hinduism and its need to meet the individual's security rests on moral and social traditions formulated in its rich religious literature, offer-ceremonies, a peaceful prayer and meditation.

## Veda/Brahma/Hinduism and the "Nine"

(1056) **Food, Water and Energy:** Veda/Brahma/Hinduism covers these needs by praying to different gods, mainly to those meeting the different needs of an agricultural society.

(1057) **Secure Home:** Veda/Brahma/Hinduism offers family security by social and moral, religious traditions: not to kill, steal, lie or feel envy or commit adultery.

(1058) **Clean Home:** Veda/Brahma/Hinduism is all about cleanliness both for body and soul.

(1059) **Art:** Love to gods is expressed both in richly decorated temples and decorated homes, often with home altars.

(1060) **Free Speech:** Veda/Brahma/Hinduism has religious schools, which can be dogmatic; in modern times Indian secular laws moderate the impact.

(1061) **Group Support:** Group support can be strong within castes and families but can also collide with modern democratic movements across caste lines. Group support is strengthened by paintings of the face, haircuts or other special tributes through the dress, the assemblies into large pilgrimages or community celebrations, special calendars or enactments of mythological stories. Such traditions have later been copied by other world religions.

(1062) **Freedom of Religion:** Veda/Brahma/Hinduism has historically demonstrated great tolerance towards other religions within India. Political conflicts may still occur where religion is part of the political system.

(1063) **Access to Medical Care:** The old Veda/Brahma/Hinduism offered assistance in healing by praying to different gods. Modern India has a medical and social support system.

(1064) **Free Trade:** Veda/Brahma/Hinduism sets great detailed rules for the old Calisaya (merchant) caste. Modern India is part of the World Trade Association.

## References

(1065) *Indians Religion*, Helmut von Galena, 1967, ISBN 9-44-0084-4.

(1066) *Hinduism, Historian, Tradition, Manifolds*, Knot A. Jacobsen, ISBN 91-27-09772-2.

(1067) *Religionernas Indien* av Rolf Grönblom, 1999, ISBN 91-88796-43-4.

(1068) *Bhagavad Gita. Som den er* av A.C: Bhaktivedanta Swami Prabhupada, ISBN 91-85580-42-2. Original title: *Bhagavad Gita, As It Is*, Los Angeles 1983.

## Buddhism

(1069) The historical Buddha was a man who lived about 2500 years ago in northern India. He was probably born in 448 B.C. and lived to be 80 years old. His given name was Prince Siddhartha Gautama. The story goes that his father did not want his son to experience the many problems of life and surrounded the castle property with a wall. The prince spent his first 29 years within the beautiful world that his father built. He married a beautiful princess and had a son who, as an adult, followed in his father's footsteps.

(1070) Gautama became curious about the world outside. He had his white horse saddled and rode out to discover the real world. He met a man sick with plague, a begging monk, an old man and saw a dead man, all for the first time. Gautama became conscious of reality. He regretted his sheltered, meaningless life and left his family and home.

(1071) Gautama sought the company of some ascetics in order to seek the meaning of life. After having almost taken his life by excessive self-torture he concluded that asceticism by itself did not offer an answer.

(1072) When Gautama was 35 years old he discovered what he called the "Golden Middle Road" and was from then on called the Buddha, the "Enlightened." The mythology of the enlightened Buddha was tempted three times by a demon named "Mara" before going out to preach and saving the world with the "Golden Middle Road." It is interesting that the prophets, Jesus 500 years later, and Mohammed 1000 years later, were also tempted by the Devil three times before they would start their missions. Gautama, now a practicing physician like Zarathustra, did not derive his wheel of law from a religious experience and did not see the human as a dual, body and soul, creation.

(1073) In his sutras, Buddha introduces a "five aggregate" concept, the Tulku. In the five aggregate's concept Buddha replaces the old Veda/Brahma/Hindu concept of the World Soul, Atman or the later western concept of body-soul with its deconstruction into five parts: 1) our physical form or body, 2) our feelings, 3) our sensory perceptions, 4) our thoughts and 5) our consciousness. At death only the body dies, the other four concepts live on in Tulku and will go on to rebirth in a new body.

(1074) When a person dies his four no-form-aggregates, the Tulku, leaves the body and enters Buddha realm, a Pure Land. The person's Tulku length of stay in Pure Land will be according to the person's Karma, the sum of good and bad deeds. When the time is up the person's Tulku will have to enter a new body and start its rebirth and life's struggle over again. Only those of complete enlightenment will avoid rebirth and will enter Nirvana for a final rest.

(1075) Buddha studied people's behavior. **He defined "good" and "bad" deeds and made simple rules for people to get along with each other. The definitions were not dogmatic but generic and had great appeal to a wide audience, the widest peaceful acceptance in human history.**

(1076) Swedish, as referred to earlier, is a very old and isolated language that happens to be my mother language. At the risk of appearing boring or partial, but really just because I happened to know the language, I have had several opportunities to refer to connections between Swedish words and old Indo-European words or word concepts.

(1077) I am tempted in this context to take notice of an old Swedish word and concept, "lagom," which in Swedish means: "not too much, not too little, but just right, nothing extreme, "a middle-of-the-road concept." "Lagom" consists of two words: "lag" which means "law" (as well as "team") and "om" which means "about" in the sense "what the law is about." In other words, within a generally accepted rule of the "society-team." The concept exists in many languages but a special word for the concept, insofar as I know, exists only in the Swedish or the Scandinavian dialects. Buddha experienced the "middle-road concept" as a law. **A "lagom-law" might save people from dogmatic fantasies and could be a useful concept for a larger world.**

(1078) I am also amazed that the devil in Sanskrit time was named "Mara." I would think the word "Mara" is connected to the Swedish word "mara," standing for a bad demon. Mara appears also in the English word "nightmare."

(1079) Buddha organized a monk communion and wrote 253 specific rules for his monks to follow: Among other things, Buddhist monks had to keep themselves and their living quarters clean, be polite, live in celibacy and live only from alms; rules copied or common with all later monk organizations of other religions. Few would succeed to reach Nirvana within Buddha's original strict rules. This form of Buddhism is therefore called the "small wagon",

Hinayana Buddhism. In a modified form of Buddhism, the "larger wagon", Mahayana Buddhism, anybody, (not only monks) following the teachings of the Dharma can reach Nirvana. In this larger wagon Buddha may be worshipped not only for ethics but also for other god concepts such as for a successful harvest. Max Weber in his classical analysis of the sociology of different religions points out that practical adoptions of local traditions and needs are common to all religions. During the agricultural time period all religions adapted to the agricultural year, all except Islam.

(1080) Veda/Brahma/Hinduism incorporated Buddhism with Buddha as one of Vishnu's human avatars. On the other hand, Buddhism became a reform movement for Veda/Brahma/Hinduism but kept some of its concepts like yoga.

(1081) Buddha considered himself a physician, not a god, and did not want to be portrayed as such. After Buddha's death, eight of India's kings built very characteristic buildings to house Buddha's relics, a so-called *stupa*. Stupas later became altars within Buddhist temples. To walk around the stupa counter clockwise so the heart is closest to the stupa became a tradition later copied in Islam.

(1082) Veda/Brahma/Hinduism at this time was taught in Sanskrit, the language that only the privileged could understand just like Latin of Europe in the Middleages. Buddhist moral rules were given in local language. More people could identify him- or herself with Buddhism.

(1083) **Buddha considered castes as unfair.** Castes were based on born rights and not based on person's Karma, the sum of good versus evil deeds. Everybody, even sudras, the lowest caste as well as the casteless "untouchable" could be part of Buddhism.

(1084) King Ashoka, historically India's greatest and most successful warrior king, lived in 300 B.C. period. He looked out over his large battlefield with thousands of dead and decided to never make war again. He accepted and lived by Buddha's teachings, made Buddhism the state religion and supported its mission. King Ashoka founded India's greatest universities. He announced social principles of human rights and publicized his rules on stone pillars in the cities. One of the stone pillars stands on a Buddha Wheel of Law. Modern

India has such a wheel in its flag. The tradition to document human rights in stone occurred in democratic Athens at about the same time.

(1085) The original Dharma offered moral rules for society but did not address agriculturally related concerns. Buddha's moral rules in India were complimented by Veda/Brahma/Hinduism's nature gods for agriculture. Even Buddha recognized many of these gods. For Buddha the gods received their godhood from personal effort, some temporarily and some permanently. They were all part of a common universe with no beginning and no end, the Samsara, until they transcended and attained the Buddha enlightenment. None of these gods would create worlds in the Hindu, Jewish/Christian/Muslim way.

(1086) The Original Buddha Dharma-teaching is of two types, the nominal Dharma (represented in the words), and the experimental Dharma (what is realized through practice and meditation). If you fail to realize the Dharma, you remain in the cycle of birth and death (Samsara).

(1087) It goes beyond the purpose of my project to analyze each form of Buddhism. Where Veda/Brahma/Hinduism did not exist, as in distant China, Buddhism expanded to an almighty god concept, which met the need for both food and a secure social life. In this way Buddhism adapted its message to the needs for each region to which it spread. Often lay people, who had read the Dharma text made the adaptation.

(1088) Buddha's closest friends wrote down his teachings after his death in the language of Sanskrit and, later, some in Pali. The collection is now Buddhism's holiest text, Tripitaka, The Three Baskets, or three volumes of teachings (sutras), rules (Vinayas) and explanatory analysis (sastras). Different teachers have had their texts added and canonized to the original text. Some Tripitaka texts now comprise more than 50 volumes. Thousands of authors have translated Buddha's most specific moral rules into different languages. In this text I am using words of my own in trying to express my interpretation of the different translations that I have read.

My interest is limited to the most fundamental and anthropological results of the Buddha teachings.

(1089)  In his first sermon Buddha set, what he called, the "wheels of law" in motion. It is interesting to notice that Buddha called his mission the "wheels of law" instead of a religious, sacral message from a god. This is different from how most religions experience their religious beginnings. The Hindus believe the early Brahmins mediated their Veda books from their gods; Moses and Jesus received their law directly from God and Mohammed via an angel from Allah. **Buddha saw his message simply as a law of society, a society ruled by law, a most modern concept.**

(1090)  Buddha received his original enlightning during four yoga or deep meditation sessions. It is interesting that in the first of these sessions Buddha made references to language analysis. He called his teachings "Dharma," from the Sanskrit syllable "dr" meaning holding together or to give security for a small society, clan or family. (A Swedish word "sam-hälle" stands for a small community where "sam" stands for "together" and "hälle" for "holding"). This was done 2-1/2 millenniums ago when only priests could read. Knowledge was limited to what the priests knew and the world was full of deities and demons. Buddha addressed human behavior in a most logical way making him one of the world's deepest thinkers. His logical analysis of society remind of Immanuel Kant's. Different translations use different words. The reader is encouraged to read different translations with their elaborations.

(1091)  Zarathustra, 500 years before Buddha, defined "Truth" as the acceptance of the law of the community with purpose to bring prosperity to the people of this world or another world through education. The Nine Pillars of History revealed that education, and thereby "Truth," can be twisted by dogmatism and is not an assurance for "Truth." Buddha expands and explains the concept of "Truth" with four "Noble Truths" and offers an eight-step path to reach "Reality," the ultimate "Enlightenment" and "Truth." Buddha's first Noble Truth states that life is constantly changing. A constant change does not have permanence and therefore life really does not exist as permanent but only in a flash of time. We can never be totally satisfied because our wishes change all the time. Besides we will get sick and die all within a flash of time.

(1092) Buddha conceived of a Universe with several expansions and contractions such as several "big bangs." He did so 2500 years before Steve Hubble had confirmed the Big Bang theory. Buddha came very close to present scientific knowledge just through meditation. The Big Bang occurred some 15 billion years ago. Buddha did not measure time in Big Bang periods but had a unit, Kalpa, at least equally big, to describe his flash of time concept. In this sense everything we humans can perceive with our senses is present only in a flash of time. **This is enlightening reality.**

(1093) Buddha's second Noble Truth describes how dissatisfaction is formed from 12 connected steps that all feed on each other. It starts with 1) Poor knowledge. Knowledge here is not lack of academic information but lack of the insight of reality, the ability to see the real world as it is, an insight that can only be gained from meditation according to Buddha. The absence of this knowledge leads to 2) impulsive body and speech reactions, 3) wrong awareness and 4) bad thoughts with bad body reactions as perceived by our different ways from 5) the six ways of sensor contacts: seeing, hearing, tasting, smelling, touching and thinking. 6) This awakens feelings and 7) desires from 8) locked in dogmatic attitudes with given 9) expectations starting all ready from 10) our birth all through 11) life and 12) death. Although nothing is permanent our constant desire for permanence, our attachment to people and things, still directs our life. This hunt for permanence creates permanent unhappiness. **This is enlightening reality.**

(1094) The third Noble Truth is that unhappiness can be healed by 1) stopping cravings for sensuous desire, 2) stopping the desire for permanence, 3) filling the lack in your knowledge, and 4) stopping a dogmatic attitude towards the world. **This is enlightening reality.**

(1095) **The true happiness is to have reached the state of Nirvana, the Pure-land or Buddha-land. Nirvana is found right here, right now. This is the enlightening reality of the fourth Noble Truth.**

**The Fourth Truth can be realized by accepting the eight spokes that hold together the wheel of law:**

1) The right attitude to recognize the four noble truths
2) The right intention or with an ethical purpose in life
3) The right speech or to tell the truth
4) The right action not to kill, use alcohol or be adulterous
5) The right livelihood or not to harm others or nature
6) The right effort or with only good thoughts in mind
7) The right awareness of the world as it is
8) The right meditation

(1096) The spokes of the wheel of law demand an ethical life essentially based on the Golden Rule but also give practical advice to achieve peace of mind with yoga and meditation. This is remarkable because meditation is a way of connecting a basic physiological function, breathing, with your brain activity thereby calming both; it is brain cleansing or thought focusing. Focusing of thoughts is an important part of religious ritual in most religions. Veda/Brahma/Hinduism uses yoga similarly to Buddhism. The focus in both religions is the individual. Buddha realized that different levels of education required different sophistication in meditation. A "tantric" form of Tibetan Buddhism uses pictures of deities with large eyes for eye contact with the one who meditates or prays and thereby helping to focus thoughts.

(1097) Many religions use totems on which to focus. Christianity uses pictures of holy persons, saints. Christianity has altars turned in one direction, towards East, where the sun rises. The Christian assembly focuses its thoughts by everybody turning towards the altar for the common prayer.

(1098) Islam, like Judaism, forbids pictures. Judaism requires focused prayers in mornings and evenings. The Muslims pray five times a day, every 3 hours, and at each prayer time to focus their thoughts on Mecca. The prayer, the saying of mantras and yoga all serve similar psychological purpose, to focus thoughts.

(1099) **As already referred to, the mind has authority over the body. Focusing thoughts by meditation or prayer has very strong power and can even wipe out self-preserving instincts. This is the background to brain washing and is why some religious fanatics' feel compelled to commit suicide, kill fellow man and bomb fellow man's church or mosque, Wake up fellow man! You have today seen an enlightment.**

(1100) The Buddhist has many prayers: Shortened and freely translated the Buddha daily prayers are:

1) I take refuge in the Buddha.
2) I take refuge in the Dharma, Buddha's teachings.
3) I take refuge in the Shanghai, the enlightened followers of the Buddha.
4) I vow to attain Buddhahood for the sake of all beings.

(1101) The Buddhist has many vows but the five basic (*panda silo*) are:

1) I will not kill
2) I will not steal
3) I will not commit sexual misconduct
4) I will not lie
5) I will not use intoxicants

(1102) These general rules tell what Buddhism is all about. The prayers are related to Buddha's organization. **The five vows are necessary social rules from tribal time.** Monks use these rules as prayers in their daily routine. Buddhist children learn these prayers in grade school. (This reminds me: I had to learn Moses' Ten Commandments in grade school in Sweden.) Buddhist monks repeat these prayers as continuous mantras 108 times, with one extra prayer for each set of ten, "just in case." Later religions duplicated this tradition. Christianity and Islam repeat short prayers or holy epithets of God or Allah. Christian uses five sets of ten with an extra for each set "for just in case." Islam just demands Muslims to use sets of 11—11, 33 or 99. Rosaries, a string of pearls, help to keep count and keeps thoughts focused. The tradition is a way to demonstrate the participation in their religious community, the bond with their community

(1103) With prayer number 1 the Buddhist seeks security through the belief in Buddha and his rules.

(1104) With prayer number 2 the Buddhist learns to accept fate and live according to the Dharma. He is relieved from thoughts of envy and desires. Envy and desires are the cause of all unhappiness and suffering according to the path of the eight steps.

(1105) With prayer number 3 the Buddhist seeks security within the Buddhist communion, the historical "Sixth Pillar" for group support.

(1106) With prayer number 4 the Buddhist sets his goal.

(1107) Most old religions make social laws part of its religious dogma: Veda/Brahma/Hinduism, Buddhism, Judaism Christianity and Islam (with the Sharia) have all canonized holy laws for society. **When these collide with common law derived from the people, usually the common law is closer to the truth (Weber). This has been true in the United States and England for laws assuring individual rights with personal responsibility relative to the society.**

(1108) Buddha, a pacifist, could not accept that group security also includes military defense for the group. This neglect had great consequences for the Buddhist movement.

(1109) Mohammed, Islam's founder, started his sword mission, the "jihad," around 610 A.D., a thousand years after Buddha. Mohammed and his later caliphs justified military conquest as Islam's holy mission. Arabian hoarse riding warriors invaded India between the years 700 and 1400. Both Hindus and Buddhists believed in transmigration of souls through all living things and would therefore not kill. India was easily conquered but the Arabs were too few to convert all of India's population to Islam. **Mosques replaced the temples for Veda/ Brahma/Hinduism and Buddhism in their holiest places. The**

**greatest universities were destroyed in order to control at least India's higher education.**

(1110) Agriculture had to continue to produce food. Veda/Brahma/ Hinduism was therefore allowed to pray to their gods for good harvests but the Hindus had to pay an extra tax in order to keep their religion. Buddhism, mainly an ethical system, disappeared totally from all of India. However, Buddhism continued in countries far away from Muslim warriors, such as on the island of Sri Lanka and in areas high in the Himalayan Mountains, Far India, China, Korea and Japan. Here Buddhism became a God concept and Buddha was prayed to for both food and security.

(1111) Bhutan, Tibet and Nepal, themselves warrior countries high up in the mountains, were felt not to be worth the trouble of conquering. These countries continued their clan-like living but turned to Veda/Brahma/Hinduism or Buddhism in the 1400s. Politically dogmatic Communist China in recent times occupied Buddhist Tibet and is now infiltrating the last Hindu state, Nepal. Communist China is justifying its dogmatic army occupation by claiming that they are freeing these countries from past feudal lords.

## Buddhism and the "Nine"

(1112) **Food, Water and Air:** Buddhism outside India stands for both the needs of clean food and a clean soul. Buddhism provides strictly social rules or a moral belief system for the society.

(1113) **Secure Dwelling:** Buddhism addresses the family security within the "wheel of law." Buddha addressed the family life and neutralized the most common reason for unhappiness, the urge for sensual desire and envy. The law also forbids the use of drugs like alcohol, the killing of anything living, demands a chaste and honest life with honorable work.

(1114) **Cleanliness:** Buddha demands that his monks are polite, appear well cared for, usually live in life of celibacy without demands from society and keep their monasteries exemplarily clean.

(1115) **Art:** Art has been small-scaled compared to that of Sumerian connected religions. Beautiful temples were eventually built. The largest temple of the southern hemisphere is for Buddha.

(1116) **Communication:** Monks communicated in mother language, through exemplary living and in a common uniform: a big yellow or red hat and orange cloak.

(1117) **Community Support:** Community support was essential. Gautama established in the Buddhism's third prayer to look for security within the Buddhist's communion. Monks lived by alms and therefore in a submissive position to the society. The communion had no military defense. The consequence of this has been described and became decisive in the history of Buddhism to present day.

(1118) **Freedom of Religion:** Buddhism is tolerant as established in the Third Noble Truth by having an open attitude towards the world. Buddhism has, since King Asoka's time (274-232 B.C.), never bean spread by the sword. Its missionary work is accomplished through teaching and exemplary living. **Buddhism, at its peak before Islam's Indian jihad invasion, reached a greater portion of the earth's population than any world religion has ever reached.**

(1119) **Access to Medical Care:** Gautama saw himself as a practicing physician. He taught a vast and profound system of medical diagnosis and treatment that is used throughout Asia and elsewhere to this day. In its pure form, it survives only in Tibet and parts of Mongolia. However it is the basis of both Indian Ayurveda and Chinese acupuncture, as well as other holistic medical systems. In 1978 the Director for Tibetan Medical Institute in Dharamsala, Dr. Drolma demonstrated its use at "grand rounds" at the Stanford Medical Center and the University of California, San Francisco Medical Center. Dr. Robert Clark, who has helped with this manuscript, translated for Dr. Drolma. Dharamsala is the home of the Dalai Lama and the site of the Tibetan Government in Exile. Some Buddha communions have a special Buddha devoted to medicine.

(1120) **Free Trade:** Gautama concerned himself with trade in that such work should be honest and not be with weapons to kill or with destruction of nature.

# References

*(1121)* *The Words of My Perfect Teacher* by Patrul Rinpoche, 1998, Publ. Shambhala, ISBN 1-57062-412-7.

*(1122)* *Buddha talade och sade,* after old interpretations by G.F. Allen and other authors and translated to modern Swedish by Åke Ohlmarks, 1983, ISBN 91-37-08276-0.

*(1123)* *Buddhismen: religion, historia, liv* by Knut A. Jacobsen, 2002, Publ. Natur och Kultur, ISBN 91-27-09021-3.

*(1124)* *Indiens Religioner* by Helmuth von Glasenapp, 1967, ISBN 91-44-008441-4.

*(1125)* *Essential Tibetan Buddhism* by Robert A.F. Thurman, 1997, Castle Books, ISBN 0-785-80872-8.

*(1126)* *The Tibetan Book of the Dead* by Robert A.F. Thurman, 1998, Quality Paperback Book Club, ISBN 8-172-23580-1.

*(1127)* *A Concise History of Buddhism* by Andrew Skilton, 1994, Publ. by Barnes and Noble, ISBN 07607-4829-2.

*(1128)* *Buddhism Plain and Simple* by Walpola Rahula, 1959, Grove Press, ISBN 0-394-17827-0.

*(1129)* *Old Path White Cloud* by Thich Nhat Hanh, 1991, Parallax Press, ISBN 0-938077-26-0.

*(1130)* *Cosmos* by Carl Sagan, 1980, Random House Publ., ISBN 0-394-50294-9.

# Judaism

(1131) The history of Judaism may be divided into three periods. The first period is the biblical. During this period the Jews had come out from the Hunting and Gathering tradition, had become farmers and continued to believe in the old concept of one God, had no heaven or hell and wrote the Torah with the Mosaic laws. (Scholarly Jews think their religion started sometime 3500 years ago or about 1500 years before Christ). The land with its harvest gave them their reward. The second period, called rabbinical or orthodox, started during the first Diaspora in Babylonia. The Jews had lost their land and their temple. Inspired by the local religion a rabbi, the Second Isaiah, wrote the Talmud. "Rabbinical" Judaism offered a reward system based on a heaven and hell, which emulated Zoroastrianism. The rabbi was always male; women remained quiet and sat apart from the men in the synagogue. The third period of Judaism is the modern reformed form of Judaism. In this form the rabbi can be male or female and females sit with their families. The service in modern Judaism is very similar to that of contemporary Protestant Christianity with equal rights for men and women but may still keep some of the ancient family traditions.

(1132) The Torah became the origin for three world religions, Judaism, Christianity and Islam. The Torah is called the Old Testament in Christianity. The Old Testament starts with the First book of Moses, the Genesis, or the story about how God created everything. God created first the physical world, then the living world and ended with the creation of the human in his image, first a man and then a woman from the man's rib (Sumer had a similar creation story). God placed the first humans, Adam and Eve in the Garden of Eden. The pair could remain there provided they did not eat the fruit from the Tree of Knowledge. The snake tempted both Eve and Adam to seek knowledge by offering them an apple to eat. Both Adam and Eve had an urge to seek knowledge and did so. They now became aware of their bare existence, without challenges. In their enlightened eyes maybe Paradise was not so paradisiacal. God showed them out of Eden to care for their life by themselves.

(1133) The pair had three sons: Abel, a shepherd, Cain, a farmer/ priest (generic term) and later, Seth. Judging anthropologically, the first two sons represented each of the top professions during the early agricultural time. The time of the story must be when the usual specialties within agriculture had already been established.

(1134) The shepherd and the farmer became angry at each other. The farmer, Cain, killed Abel the shepherd, Quarrels regarding land use between shepherds and farmers are as old as agriculture and did not end before the invention of barbwire in the 1800s.

(1135) After his crime Cain began wandering and is thought to have established the first city, naming it after his son whom he also named king. That the king inherited his title was instituted in Sumer, the first agricultural country six or seven thousand years ago and has continued ever since in almost every country in the world.

(1136) One of the shepherd's descendants had three sons: one continued as a shepherd, the second became musician and the third a blacksmith. Now the old shepherd could enjoy all the latest support systems: religion, art and artisan.

(1137) The priest, the son of a shepherd worshipped one single creator. To be a shepherd is really to be a culturally advanced hunter. The One-God-Creator, according to a shepherd's mythology, may be an inheritance from the One-God-Creator of the hunters in the Hunting and Gathering Period. Anyway, this was different from the many nature gods the surrounding agricultural people worshipped. Society had come to the great question: could one put the trust in only one god or should one, at least to be sure of food, pray to the gods for each power of nature?

(1138) The Genesis story continues. God was disappointed with his creation. The world had become full of evil with sons of other gods and their offspring. (Genesis VI:1) Only one man, Noah, had demonstrated solidarity with his God. Noah was a shepherd, who again had three sons.

(1139) God warned Noah of his plan to wash the world clean of all its evil by simply drowning it in a great flood. God told Noah to build an ark for his family and for one pair from every kind of animal. God let it rain for forty days and nights and drowned every living creature. A better life for both animals and humans could begin. All the earth's population would thereafter be descendent from Noah's sons. The sons built the first town, Babylon, in the area of Mesopotamia.

(1140) Note: A flood story is remarkably common in religious mythology. In fact, authors Sellier and Balsinger have collected a similar story from 217 different cultures.

(1141) One of Noah's descendants in the eleventh generation was Abraham. Abraham emigrated from the city Ur in Mesopotamia and wandered into Israel around 1950 B.C. Abraham had two sons, Ishmael and Jacob. Each of them had twelve sons with different wives. Ishmael became the stem father for the Arabs, who lived east of the Dead Sea. Jacob, who lived west or south of the Dead Sea, became the stem-father for the Jews. According to this biblical story, the Arabs and the Jews are cousins or half-cousins. Both peoples lived a nomadic life as shepherds in the desert. Both their languages are indeed of a common Semitic origin.

(1142) Jews living northeast of Egypt across the base of the Sinai Peninsula had a dry spell with poor pasture for their animals. They had to seek help in Egypt. They were assigned to work in the delta of the Nile, in a part called Goshen. The Jews, now immigration workers, were segregated from the Egyptian population and eventually ended up as its slaves.

(1143) The Second Book of Moses, the Exodus, tells about Moses, an adopted pharaoh prince but secretly of Jewish heritage, and how he led the Jews out from Egypt. Moses had problems keeping the Jews within their shepherd religion. God told Moses to write down the Ten Commandments on two tablets of clay. They are listed in chapter 20 of the Book of Exodus. In modern terms they are:

1) You shall have no other god before me (the God of Hebrew).
2) You shall not make any picture of God.

3) You shall not abuse God's name.
4) You shall respect the Sabbath.
5) You shall honor your father and mother.
6) You shall not kill.
7) You shall not commit adultery.
8) You shall not steal.
9) You shall not bear false witness.
10) You shall not envy your neighbor.

(1144) The Jews remained in Egypt for 400-some years. Other tribes formed states or independent cities where the Jews formerly grazed their animals. The Jews were not welcomed back and had to live in the worst part of the Sinai desert for 40 years. The prophet Joshua led the Jews across the Jordan River into, what at this time was called the land of Canaan. Eventually, they organized and found permanent living in its southern part. Here they formed an independent country, Israel, with Jerusalem as its capital. The constitution was that of the old Sumer or the same as in all the surrounding countries. The country had an anointed king with inherited royal power, supported by its religious organization. The first anointed king was Saul in 1025 B.C. King Salomon, son of King David and king from 965 to 922 B.C. built the first temple in Jerusalem. Like in all Sumeric countries, family quarrels started. The country was divided into two parts in 922 B.C., Israel in the north and Judah in the south.

(1145) The country, whether united or divided, was small. It was soon dominated by the surrounding, larger, military states. In 771 B.C. an ancient state, Assyria, occupied the Israel part and enslaved its people. Nebuchadnezzar, another warrior, this time from Mesopotamia, conquered Assyria and while in the area added the Judea-part to his domain. Nebuchadnezzar destroyed Salomon's temple in year 576 B.C. He brought the Jews with him as slaves back to his capital of Babylon, the first Diaspora. A neighboring king from Persia, King Cyrus I conquered Babylon seventy years later. He allowed the Jews to return to Israel. The temple in Jerusalem was rebuilt and finished in 520 B.C.

(1146) The Greek King, Alexander the Great, conquered Persia in 334 B.C. Alexander died after his expedition to India. His empire was divided between four of his generals. Israel became a part of Egypt. A King from Syria, Antiochus IV, conquered Egypt, incorporated Israel and destroyed much of Jerusalem a second time. The Jews rebelled and became free for a few years but the Roman General Pompeii's took over Israel in 64 B.C. A people, the Parters, occupied the country for four years. Herod the Great drove out the Parters. The Romans appointed Herod to rule Israel until 4 B.C. in the year modern Christian researchers believe Jesus was born. Herod was a great builder. He rebuilt Jerusalem's walls and built the third temple in 37 B.C. The new temple is said to be even greater than Salomon's temple. This was the Jerusalem that Jesus knew.

(1147) Rome, after 500 years of democracy, had become Sumeric and expected their leader to be worshipped as a god. The Jews, with a 1000-year-long tradition of worshipping only one god, tried several uprisings against the Romans. The Roman General Titus occupied Jerusalem and destroyed their temple a third time in the year 70. Emperor Hadrianus occupied Jerusalem after a major rebellion in the year 134. He destroyed the city, leveled the temple with the ground and forbade the Jews to live in Israel, the second Diaspora. Jews were allowed to live only in selected cities within the Roman Empire and, later, only within walled parts of towns, popularly called ghettos.

(1148) Only part of the west wall of Jews' third temple still remains in Jerusalem. It is before this "Western Wall" that Jews now focus their prayers.

(1149) Constantine, the first Christian Roman Emperor, made Jerusalem into a Christian city for 300 years starting in 330. His mother Helena built several Christian churches and memorials in the city and in the country.

(1150) Christians persecuted the Jews during Medieval times. Jews fled to countries controlled by Islam. Here they could keep their religion if they paid the special tax as a "protected people," an Arabic term for all conquered people other than of Arabic origin.

(1151) Up to present time and now within the independent state of Israel Judaism has never been part of a state religion ever since its short independences in King Saul's time. For all this time Judaism has lived by its own power, without the support from any state organization. Judaism has lived without the support from a farmer "tenth"-tax, without being allowed to own land during most of agricultural time, Judaism has been discriminated against and has for long periods actively been persecuted.

(1152) A short parenthesis about Jerusalem: The second Caliph, Omar, conquered Jerusalem in 640 and made Damascus to his capital. Jerusalem became one of Islam's three most holy cities for the next 400 years. An early caliph built the Dome of the Rock Mosque on the spot of Salomon's Temple (688-91). Mainly French crusaders liberated the town and controlled it for slightly less than one hundred years. The successful Muslim warrior, Saladin, retook the town. The Turks conquered Arabia, became Muslims and kept control of Jerusalem from 1517 until 1917. During WW I the Turks were on the losing German side. The UN placed Israel and Jerusalem under British protectorate and called it Palestine from 1922 until 1948. Since 1948 the UN has recognized Israel as an independent state. Surrounding Muslim states began wars with Israel but lost. Israel occupied West Jerusalem in a 1949 and the East part in 1967 and is now claiming an undivided Jerusalem as its capital for a fourth time in its long history.

(1153) What does Judaism offer its members that have given them this strength in their faith?

## Judaism and the "Nine"

(1154) **Food to Survive and Safe Dwelling for the Family:** Judaism has one god but no picture of its god; God is a concept, God lives in the images transmitted by the message of the Old Testament. The throne in the temple that Herod Built in Jerusalem was physically empty, with no statue or picture.

(1155) Originally, God was one of many gods. God was still a better god than the other gods in the world. During the first Diaspora with the writings the Talmud by the Second Isaiah around 550 B.C. The Jewish god concept evolved into one single god concept.

(1156) Jews refer to the Torah and the Talmud and consider each of them to be living books, open for interpretation. Three thousand years of studying the words of the Torah has evolved into the moral law that has created the community of Judaism.

(1157) The communion between the individual and God is expressed in the Torah's first four Commandments: you shall not have any other gods before Me, no picture of Me, never abuse God's name, and respect His day of Sabbath. The personal prayer is a meditative connection with God. Some faithful Jews pray twice a day, morning and evening.

(1158) The communion rules are specified in the other six commandments: honor your father and your mother, do not kill, do not lie, steal or be envious of your neighbor. Their Golden Rule: love your neighbor as yourself (from the book of Leviticus) is the all-inclusive rule for the interrelationship of the Jewish society. Leviticus also lists the many detailed and specific social rules for the Jewish community. Christian and Muslim societies have partly copied these rules as they represented the common knowledge at the time.

(1159) The knowledge from the Torah is communicated through studies in the home and in the synagogue under the leadership of the rabbi. The understanding of the Old Testament is not locked in but is the subject for continued studies, often combined with actual historical studies.

(1160) The communion is the historical tradition from 3000 years of togetherness. The communion is reminded of its greatness during the time of King David, Saul's son, as well as of the time of slavery in Egypt and Babylon, the three destructions of their temple, the persecution during the time of early Roman heathendom and later by Christendom, the Nazi genocide in Germany and the UN creation of the modern Israel. The communion is reminded that their religion has survived all adversities and, really, has been the inspiration and model for the societies that have persecuted them.

(1161) The communion is also based on the experiences from when the Jews stopped being shepherds and became an agricultural people in Israel. The communion celebrates the yearly seasons, a successful harvest as a gift from God and gives thanks for the food that has not always been assured for Jews.

(1162) The security of the home is assured by the six social rules given in Commandments 5-10.

(1163) **Cleanliness:** Hygiene is also encouraged by social rules. Jews take off their shoes before entering their home and wash their hands before meals. They avoid certain foods, which were difficult to keep free from communicable diseases, such as trichinosis in flesh and intestinal infections from shellfish.

(1164) **Art:** Adornment has not dominated Jewish buildings. Attention has been a thing to avoid. Private art has been an expression for personal taste and resources.

(1165) **Communication:** Schooling the children in the Hebraic language for communication has been encouraged. With the Jews spread all over the Western World Hebrew became one of the first international languages for trade. One could trust people who were forbidden to lie or steal. Many Jews have been successful in international banking and trade. Schooling is either state supported or of four types: secular, Jewish, Arabic and Druze or private Torah-schools for ultra Orthodox Judaism.

(1166) **Community Support:** The communion was realized in actual deeds for the support of the poor in their society. The Jewish society in USA is one of the greatest donators to its distressed including those in Israel. In modern Israel 80% of the ultra orthodox Jews are employed by the state in religious studies.

(1167) **Freedom of Religion:** Judaism has not been in position to dominate other religions since ancient times. In the modern state of Israel a rabbi high court handles legal family matters.

(1168) **Access to Medicine:** Health care has always been important for the Jewish communion. The Jewish communion has more excellent doctors than any other community.

(1169) **Free Trade:** Trade has been an important part of Jewish life, as Jews have not been allowed to own land. Trade has been helped by strong moral code and by the Hebrew language reaching across national borders.

(1170) The United Nations recognized Israel as an independent state in 1948. Jews had experienced religious discrimination for 2000 years all over the world. Several million Jews returned home to Israel and created a most modern and democratic state. The UN supports the idea of the creation of an independent Palestinian state but not at the cost of the annihilation of Israel. This is what the conflict in the Middle East is all about.

# References

(1171) *Så här går det till, Judisk vardag och helg* av Harry Gersh, 1986. ISBN 91-85164-178. Title of the original: *When the Jews Celebrate.*

(1172) *Äventyr ur Bibeln*, Librarie Larousse, 1984, ISBN 91-7024-270-4.

(1173) *Namnet och Närvaron. Gudsnamn och Gudsbild i Böckernas Bok*, av Tryggve N.D. Mettinger, 1987 ISBN 91-7194-497-4.

(1174) *The Way*, Michael Berg, 2001, ISBN 0-471-22879-6.

(1175) *Walking the Bible* by Bruce Feiler, ISBN 0-380-80731-9 (pbk).

(1176) *Judaism*, edited by Arthur Herzberg, 1962 published by George Braziller, Inc; Library of Congress Card number 61-15498.

(1177) *Israel* av Kerstin Furubrant, 2003, published by Utrikespolitiska Institutet ISBN 91-7183-839-2.

(1178) *Ancient Judaism*, Max Weber (MacMillan, 1952).

(1179) *The Legends of the Jews*, Louis Ginzberg (Simon & Schuster, 1961).

# Christianity

(1180)  The Bible, the muniment or original reference text of three world religions, requires a historical review.

(1181)  The Old Testament (OT), the Christian name for the Torah, consists of 66 different texts: the five Books of Moses and other writings are the Jew's Holy Text. Christians added the New Testament to the Old Testament and call the two together their Holy Text, the Bible. Muslims refer to the Bible as a historical document, but not as a god inspired, canonized text. Mohammed asserted that some of the historical sites and stories of the Bible, particularly those about Abraham, took place around Mohammed's hometown in and around Mecca and eventually became the background for Mohammed's revelations. "Revelations," of course, are just claims, not historical facts.

(1182)  The interpretation of the text of the Bible has evolved during more than three thousand years and is still continuing. First, the Jewish community and, since the crucifixion of Jesus, also the Christians learned the stories by heart and transmitted them orally from generation to generation. In time the stories were written down and have been the subject for modern historical studies.

(1183)  The Old Testament constitutes 80% of the Bible. It was written in the West Semitic language, Hebrew, a language similar but not identical to the Hebrew spoken in present day Israel. The New Testament was written in Greek. Without the OT it is one of the smaller canonized texts of any large world religion. The central text, the one about Jesus, has to be repeated four times to make any substantial volume.

(1184)  The meaning of words will change over the passage of time. The interpretation of the original Bible text and the many following interpretations and translations have most likely maintained the primary meaning of its text but the exact original meaning has been, and still is, subject to continuing research.

(1185)  The original text of the OT was written with ink on scrolls of papyrus. The oldest still existing Hebrew fragments of the OT are from around the first century BC according to carbon dating. Seven scrolls were found in 1947 in caves close to Qumran by the Dead Sea.

(1186) The oldest Greek translation of the OT was written in the second century BC. The oldest, still saved copy of the whole Bible in Greek, Codex Sinaiticus, is from the 300s. It was held in the Monastery of Saint Catherine, built by the mother of Emperor Constantine at the base of Mount Sinai. After several visits to the monastery in the 19th Century a German professor of Biblical history succeeded in obtaining the Codex Sinaiticus. He had traveled there under the patronage of the Russian Czar, Alexander II, who later had it published in facsimile. The manuscript was placed in the Imperial Library in St. Petersburg. In 1933, the Soviet Union sold the codex to the British Museum for 100,000 pounds. The Codex Sinaiticus consists of 730 parchment pages from 360 goatskins. The words are written without spacing, making interpretation difficult.

(1187) The oldest Latin translation of the whole Christian Bible, the Vulgate Bible, was also written in the 300s. It has been the Catholic muniment, (original text), until the present. It has recently been replaced by a modern translation, called the "Jerusalem Bible."

(1188) **The Pope in Rome, Gregorious X, sent out an edict, declaring that his power was of God and could not be questioned by either royals or commoners in true Sumeric fashion.** The renaissance period in the 1500s questioned old traditions and had great interest in original material. The scholarly monk, Erasmus from Rotterdam, who lived much of his time in England, Italy and Switzerland, made a new translation of the NT into Latin.

(1189) **In 1517 Martin Luther translated Erasmus's NT into German and posted his 95 theses on the church door in Wittenberg, Germany.** Luther's German translation of the Bible was the beginning of translating the Bible into other local languages. A few years earlier, in 1500, Gutenburg had invented the printing press. The printing press helped spread new national Bible translations throughout Christendom and caused the Roman Catholic Church to begin to reform itself.

(1190) **In the 200-300s the tradition, that is to say the "spirit" of common understanding within the Christian communities, gradually organized itself into a "Holy Spirit" of togetherness. The faith in God, his son Jesus, and the Holy Spirit of the church**

**became the dogma for Christianity. The Christian Church created much of what has become Western culture. Social traditions evolved both within and around church activity. Every form of art became engaged in expressing both the mythology and the mission of Christianity. The church became the community center; its traditions and liturgy set social standards. Its ecclesiastical year combined itself with the agricultural year; its political policies merged with that of the regent.**

(1191) "Religion" had done this in all Sumeric countries for 10,000 years.

(1192) In Jesus' time, Aramaic was spoken, a language related to Hebrew. Hebrew is still spoken in some mountains of Lebanon. Jesus preached in Aramaic. His close disciples, Mathew, Marcus, Luke and John, or possibly friends of theirs, wrote the stories about Jesus in Greek. The Gospels were later translated into Latin. Greek and Latin were the languages, which reached outside local areas. The Christian message of the Golden Rule reached all the way to Rome.

(1193) In the Roman Empire there were many poor people. Rome was built on the backs of slaves from its early time. The only social security net was from family and possibly from friends. The language of the dominant part of the population was Latin or Greek. You could not participate in the official life in the Roman Empire if you did not know Latin and were not of Roman descent. The Christian movement grew but so did the Roman heathen resistance. Christians were killed in dramatic ways before the public in Rome's Coliseum; however, Christian courage was admired. The Christian movement grew faster, first among slaves and the suppressed, but in time, also among people in high positions.

(1194) The Emperor Constantine became impressed with the Christian virtues of honesty and modesty. He made Christianity the Roman state religion. He replaced the selfish, corrupt Roman administration with a Christian administration in a new capital, Constantinople. Constantinople was geographically more central and easier accessible than Rome. The emperor built the world's largest Christian Church, Hagia Sofia, close to his castle and appointed a high priest for the whole empire. Constantine was baptized just before he died in 337. Christianity became part of the central, royal power. **A Sumeric period of Christianity began. Christianity forgot its Golden Rule and suppressed all other religions and, typically, started also internal quarrels.** The high priest of Constantinople quarreled with the high priest of Rome about who stood "closest to God" and, thereby, who could collect the most taxes.

(1195) Constantinople and Rome emphasized their independence by each having their own way of communicating, Greek for Constantinople and Latin for Rome. Both church organizations emphasized their independence from of the Old Testament by discriminating against Jews, the originators of the text.

(1196) The mother of Emperor Constantine, Helen, was baptized before her son. She went to Jerusalem to find historical proof of Jesus' life. She found pieces of his cross and built several Byzantine Churches in the 300s. Persians destroyed these 300 years later. Arabs conquered Persia and Israel in 636, (Jerusalem in 630). French Christian Crusaders reconnected Israel with Christianity in 1099 and rebuilt many of the old Byzantine Christian Churches. One hundred years later the Arabs under leadership of Saladin re-conquered the area. This time the Arabs allowed the smaller churches in Israel to remain open.

(1197) In the early 600s Mohammed and his later caliphs started their holy sword mission for political control and taxing of their neighbors. **The Muslim jihad was very successful and eventually conquered the eastern half of the Roman Empire. Constantinople fell in 1453.**

(1198) To continue its independence Rome, the western part of the Roman Empire, had also to defend itself against the Muslim jihad. It had to accept the sword as a means for defense and religious mission. The Rome held its ground against the Muslim assault first at Pointer, France, and re-conquered Spain from Islam in the 1200s. Rome together with European royalty stopped the Muslim invasion at Vienna in the 1500s and re-captured some of the Balkan Peninsula. **Wars between Sumericly anointed kings, supported by** their religions, became yearly routines all through the medieval and the renaissance time. Everybody forgot or put aside the Golden Rule, the moral kernel, in all religions.

(1199) **Sweden serves as a good example of what happened in a Sumeric state at that time.** The newly elected king, Gustav I Vasa, adopted Luther's reformation in 1527. He confiscated much of the property of the Catholic Church in Sweden. His son determined that Luther's liturgy should be the state religion. His grandson, Gustav II Adolphus, entered the Thirty-Year War as the main defender of Protestantism. Sweden conquered the land around the Baltic Sea. In 1686 the parliament determined that only the Lutheran liturgy should be tolerated. To become Catholic would be penalized with death. War became the common day activity for the Sumeric Sweden.

(1200) **Sweden lost its Sumeric wars and received its first democratic constitution in 1809 and has not had any wars since. The Parliament determined that the king should "no one's conscience compel."** The priest, a state bureaucrat, still watched with stepfather's eyes all other religious movements. Six women in 1858 were expelled from the country for secretly becoming Catholics.

(1201) During all of the 1800s people had to attend church; the parish clerk tutored the psalms and the Lutheran catechism. The priests visited the families once a year and asked about their knowledge in catechism and could condemn people to be pilloried. The priests had intimate insight in every household. All marriages had to take place in the state church. Real freedom for choice of religion was introduced first in 1951 with free withdrawal from the state church, free forms of marriage and no requirement for teachers to belong to the state church. **The church was officially separated from the state in 2000.**

(1202) Public schools in Sweden are responsible for over 95% of education. Religion was removed from public school curriculum and with it Christian moral education. Such education of youth is now provided within of a family dradition attending the now independent Swedish Church and by independent religious organizations. **Sweden has become one of the most secularized countries. This**

**has happened to different degrees in many communities both in Europe and USA, where religious morals cannot be taught in schools supported by the general tax. It has also happened in countries where religious dogma has been replaced by political dogma.**

(1203) Christianity began when Jesus was born in Bethlehem. The prophets of the OT told for centuries about a Messiah, a mighty king, who would free the Jews from their oppressors. According to a tradition a star marked the place where Jesus was born. The Roman governor with local royal power heard a rumor that a Jewish king had been born. He decreed that all male children younger than two years of age and of Jewish descent would be killed. Jesus' family, the father, Joseph and mother Mary, fled to Egypt with their child Jesus.

(1204) The mythology surrounding religious missions always takes on its own life and becomes a theatrical tradition for telling the story of the mission. Millions of Christian school children have taken part in illustrating Jesus' birth in Bethlehem.

(1205) Jesus grew up in the town of Nazareth in Galilee. He might have been born in Bethlehem four or five years before year 1 and died possibly in 31. A monk in Rome named Dionysius Exiguus, who introduced our present calendar in the 600s, did not have as good information as modern researchers. The father of Jesus was a carpenter. Jesus therefore most likely was trained as a carpenter. He began his calling as a prophet at about age thirty. A friend and apocalyptic preacher, that is to say preaching redemption and of the coming of a new kingdom, John, baptized Jesus in the Jordan River.

(1206) The authors of the Gospels had a common agenda: to connect Jesus' life and mission with the Old Testament's promise of the coming of a godly savior, primarily for the Jews in order to give them a homeland, a kingdom, as in King David's time. The authors claimed Jesus was of David's clan.

(1207) More than 25 generations had passed from the time King David lived and Jesus' birth. There was a good chance to belong to somebody because 25 generations represents at least one million people. To really prove a family connection is a different matter. The authors of the gospels were not historians and would skip hundreds of years in order to tell a good story. The historical accuracy of the stories, mythological or historical, of both the Old and the New Testaments did not matter.

(1208) According to the gospels of Mathew and Luke a spirit came down in the form of a dove. A voice was heard naming Jesus as God's son. Jesus' mission lasted for less than three years. In the early time there were many versions of gospels. In the 300s four gospels were selected as the most accurate and were canonized or declared correct. The four holy gospels had already been named the "Gospels according to Matthews, Mark, Luke and John" around the year 150. The four gospels take up the first half of the New Testament (NT). The first three Gospels are similar and are called synoptic. These repeat similar episodes in somewhat different chronological order but all four describe Jesus' mission. The Gospel of Mark is thought to be the most original. The four gospels were written in the 90s. Many of the stories in the NT are described as if they happened just then and there, that the words came from Jesus exactly as told. This has always been authors' way to better catch readers' imagination.

(1209) The authors of the gospels had both a religious and political message in mind: they were again children of their time and place. They gave Jesus different titles like the "Anointed," a title for a god-connected Sumerian-type king. Such kings were still ruling all of the surrounding countries at the time. The Hebrew word for "anointed" is "Messiah," the Greek word is "Christ."

(1210) The Jews found it difficult to imagine that Jesus, this simple carpenter from Bethlehem, was the prophets' Messiah as mentioned in their Old Testament, and that he was coming to relieve the Jews from their oppression. Jesus' life, as described in the Gospels of the NT, is intended to prove that Jesus really was the prophets' Messiah as told in the Old Testament. The authors wished to prove this by emphasizing his miracles, such as the resurrection of a dead person and the restoring of the eyesight of a blind and other stories.

(1211) As a Christian, I have been taught that in his religious mission Jesus entered as the messenger between man and God. With his life and his death, Jesus, a living human being, exemplified God's message of love. Jesus promised to cleanse the humans from their sins by his own blood-offer on the cross. God resurrected his son from the dead on the third day. The son's faith in the power of his benevolent Father gave man hope for overcoming life's difficulties, particularly the one most difficult to meet, death.

(1212) Jesus lived an exemplary life by the Golden Rule: Love your neighbor as yourself and placed this rule above the Jewish law based on Leviticus. Jesus would break against the Sabbath, mingle with gentiles and called for repentance because redemption in a new Jewish kingdom was eminent.

(1213) Jesus was not quite clear where he stood relative to the Jewish and the Roman laws. Jesus broke against Jewish law with an attitude of disrespect for its details and its contemporary leaders. He challenged Roman law by the proclaiming the promise of a new Jewish kingdom. The Roman officials thought that he might lead yet another Jewish uprising. Only in the court did Jesus make the statement that "his kingdom was not of this world" but it was too late. He was judged to be a revolutionary both from Roman and Jewish standpoint and was crucified. His life was a minor, passing episode in the Jewish community. (All of this information is taken from the works of E.P. Sanders' book *The Historical Figure of Jesus.*)

(1214) The second half of the NT consists of a description of Paul's travel and elaborations on the Christian message in letters from Paul, James, Peter, John and Jude, James' brother. Paul, during his wide travels in the Roman Empire, developed a much wider horizon than Jesus had had. Paul extended his mission of love to non-Jews and accepted gentiles to his flock. He believed in the Ten Commandments but did not take some of the Jewish traditions listed in Leviticus, such as circumcision serious. The Jewish religion offered salvation only in deeds according to all laws of Moses. Here the two religions started to take slightly different paths. Paul's letters were written in the 30s. The Gospels were written 30-50 years later.

(1215) The Bible has many references to the Golden Rule. It is first referred to in the Third book of Moses called: Leviticus. The four gospels and the letters of Paul and James both refer to the Golden Rule several times. The wording here is from the New Jerusalem Bible, Reader's Edition, 1990, Double Day:

(1216) Lev. (19:18) Love your neighbor as yourself.

(1217) Math. (7:12) Headlined as "The Golden Rule": Always treat others, as you would like them to treat you.

(1218) Mark (12:31) You must love your neighbor as yourself. There is no greater commandment.

(1219) Luke (6:31) Treat others as you would like people to treat you.

(1220) John (16:12) Love one another.

(1221) Paul's Corinth (1: 13) Faith, hope and love, the three of them; and the greatest of them is love.

(1222) Paul's letter to Galatians (5:14) You must love your neighbor as yourself.

(1223) James, Jesus' brother and leader of the early church in Jerusalem is quoted in the Book of James:

(1224) (2:8) The supreme Law of scripture: you will love your neighbor as yourself.

(1225) John's first letter: To keep the commandments, especially that of Love.

(1226) (2:10) Anyone who loves his brother remains in light.

(1227) (3:10) Who ever does not live uprightly and does not love his brother is not from God.

(1228) (3:11) This is the message from the beginning, that you must love one another as He commanded us.

(1229) (3:23) His commandment is this, that we should believe in the name of his son Jesus Christ and that we should love one another, as He commanded us.

(1230) (4:7) My dear friends, let us love one another, since love is from God and everyone who loves is a child of God and knows God.

(1231) (4:21) Indeed this is the commandment we have received from Him, that whoever loves God must also love his brother.

(1232) In John's second letter, the law of love: It has given me great joy that the children of yours have been living the life of truth as the Father commanded us. And now I am asking you- dear lady, not as though I were writing you a new commandment, but only the one we have had from the beginning—that we should love one another. To love is to live according to His commandments: this is the commandment, which you have heard since the beginning, to live a life of love.

(1233) The fundamental message of the whole Bible and, specifically, the New Testament is simply the Golden Rule. The critical question is: to whom did Jesus and the apostles refer to when they asked you to love "your neighbor" or "one another?" E.P. Sanders and other scholars show that Jesus, a Jew, speaking only Aramaic, really limited his mission mainly to the countryside in Galilee and had mainly the Jewish public and future in mind. Also the apostles had a political Jewish kingdom in mind, when they talked about the "coming of a new kingdom."

(1234) Jews had always believed that God gave them a covenant and selected them for a certain ethical role, in other words, made them an elite. Both Christians and Jews, and before them Arians Hindus, and after them, Arabian Muslims, saw their faithful peers as a god-selected, elite group of people. **This is one of two greatest mistakes in the history of humanity. The misery that dogmatic religions have caused humanity can only be matched by the misery that later dogmatic political ideas have caused the human race. Dogmatism in both religion and politics has left a flood of blood for the past 10,000 years.**

(1235) Jesus, Paul and the apostles did not recognize that they, in preaching the Golden Rule, had touched on something that reached far beyond their peer groups. Historically, it may be compared to Columbus believing he was in India when really he touched on a very large, new continent.

(1236) The Golden Rule was not a written rule during the 190,000-year-long Hunting and Gathering time. It was the pillar social rule on which all the tribal societies were grounded. The societies were probably never without personal conflicts but were still peacefully growing thanks to this rule.

(1237) **We should not let the misery that religious or political dogma have caused humanity overshadow the fact that eventually they all must live up to the moral message of the Golden Rule. The Golden Rule, with its democratic respect and acceptance for individual rights, has and will always prevail. This moral rule reaches beyond Veda/Brahma/Hinduism, Buddhism, Judaism, Christianity, Islam and all other religions.**

(1238) **The Nine Historical Pillars together with the Golden Rule are the basic rules for a generic society, the fundament for all humanity. Any religion or government not living up to these rules is simply a scramble for power-grabbing and personal benefit. During the 10,000-year-long agricultural time literally thousands of different religions and Sumeric-like governments bear witness of this fact.**

## Christianity and the "Nine"

(1239) **Food, Water, Air, Energy and Secure Dwelling:** Christianity started to become a separate religion from Judaism because Jesus and Paul stressed the commandment of Love above the other laws of Leviticus. Paul, an international person, separated Christianity from Judaism and turned to reach all people, not just Jews. He de-emphasized many of the Jewish customs such as circumcision and many food restrictions. Paul thereby strengthened the Christian profile as a new religion.

(1240) The belief in God and Jesus as a symbol for the Golden Rule became two of the three dogmatic pillars of Christianity. The "Third Pillar," the Holy Spirit, became the symbol of its church organization and in the way the spirit worked within the communion. The strong emphasis of the Golden Rule gave the Christian community its group support, family comfort and security.

(1241) Christianity, at the beginning, was not connected to the happenings during the agricultural seasons. The example of Jesus' life was what was emphasized: his birth, death and resurrection and his message of love. In time, after about 300 years, the traditions of the seasonal experiences of the Goths and the Greeks were combined with those of Jesus' life. Jesus birth was combined with the Goths' midwinter offer at the return of the light period of the year; Jesus' resurrection was combined with the nature's rebirth in the spring; the fall was combined with the thanksgiving for food.

(1242) **Cleanliness:** Christianity did not introduce any new forms for cleanliness. Cleanliness was generally accepted as necessary. Sunday was generally a day to dress up in order to show respect just as Jews had done on their Saturday.

(1243) **Art:** Christianity used a lot of art to beautify their sermons and to communicate the messages of the New Testament of the Bible. The world's largest and most beautifully decorated church, Saint Peter's Church in Rome, was built in the 1500s together with thousands of other churches within Greek, Roman, and Protestant Christianity. Churches are all located centrally in the community and are usually it's tallest building.

(1244) The liturgy, the theatrical presentation of the Christian message and its mythology, is a part of the art in the Christian religion and is, as it is in all religions, a pleasant and inspirational cultural experience for all our senses.

(1245) The Orthodox Church liturgy emphasizes the holiness of the Bible as a book. A high point of the sermon is when the Bible is taken from the alter crypt and presented to the assembled communion.

(1246) The Catholic Church emphasizes the text, which is quoted while the assembly is standing. The text is later expanded on and explained to the communioty by the priest.

(1247) The Protestant Church presents the Christian religion in many different ways. Many do it in ways similar to that of the Catholic Church, others do it by having a member witnessing in front of the community. The degree of centralization of each church denomination determines the degree of standardization of a certain liturgy, the more freedom, the more variability. Some denominations allow the church professionals to get married; others do not. Some emphasize adult baptism, others do not; some stress natural birth control, others do not; some allow controlled abortion, others do not.

Some do not allow homosexual marriages, others do. Some do not allow members to seek medical professional help when sick, others do. Education of the Nine Pillars of History hopefully might lead to some common agreement.

(1248) **Communication:** Christian communication in Latin and Greek became the elite communication in the early period when it was combined with the king's Sumeric power and followed the king in all his wars. The late Pope John Paul II, the Polish pope, experienced dogmatic occupation during WW II. Thanks to him, the Catholic attitude towards war and other religions has changed. In 2000 the modern Catholic Church officially asked for forgiveness for its dogmatic attitude during its Sumeric period.

(1249) **Community Support:** Christianity developed great group support when it was persecuted during the Roman heathen time. When it was part of the central power it justified its position by caring for the poor, sick and for youth education. However, it also abused its central connection by discriminating against other religions. This might have been necessary at a time, when surrounding countries were Sumeric and spread their missions by sword. Discrimination from religion is indeed unlawful in modern, democratic countries. Religion has been a fundamental need for humanity ever since the Hunting and Gathering period. The moral rules derived from the Golden Rule in all religions are fundamental to the social community and will always prevail.

(1250) **Free Choice of Religion:** In modern times Christianity coexists with other religions in most democratic countries and is not part of the political leadership.

(1251) **Access to Medicine:** Modern Christianity has been supportive and has had a positive influence on medical care and research. Many hospitals are supported by Christian organizations. Many ministers and priests participate in medical care by giving psychological support. The preaching of faith with hope induces the production of endomorphins and helps healing processes.

(1252) **Free Trade:** Successful trade is based on respect and honesty.

# References

*(1253)* *The Holy Bible*, 1976, Giant Print Reference Edition, Thomas Nelson, Publ.

*(1254)* *Libris stora handbok till bibeln med förord* av David och Pat Alexander, 2001, ISBN 91-7195-393-0. English Original Title: The New Lion Handbook to the Bible.

*(1255)* Äventyr ur Bibeln, svensk översättning från svenska orginalet, Découvrir la Bible, 1984, ISBN 91-7024-270-4.

*(1256)* Trons vägar: om religion och livsfrågor av Per Beskow, 2003, ISBN 91-7118-914-9.

*(1257)* *Jesus and Judaism* by E.P. Sanders, 1985, Fortress Press, ISBN 0-8006-2061-5.

*(1258)* *Paul and Palestinian Judaism* by E.P. Sanders, 1977, Fortress Press, ISBN 0-8006-1899-8.

*(1259)* *The Historical Figure of Jesus* by E.P. Sanders, 1995, Penguin Press, ISBN 0-14-014499-4.

*(1260)* *The Anatomy of Hope* by Jerome Groopman, M.D., 2004, Random House Publ., ISBN 0-375-43332-5.

# Islam

*(1261)* Islamic history is evidence how small religious groups through bonding together within a Sumeric society can become a major world religion. The early clans lived mostly from sheep and camel herding in the warm and dry borderlands east of the fertile Iran, Iraq, Syria and Palestine. The various family clans lived in and practiced religion in tents that they transported as they followed the grazing patterns of their animal herds. The clans spoke similar Semitic languages.

*(1262)* Islam's history begins with an uneducated orphan boy born in the year 570 after the birth of Christ. The boy's uncle took care of him and gave him training to care for camel caravans. Caravan transport had become an important and profitable business with the increased trade between the East and West. A successful elderly

widow in Mecca hired the young man to care for her caravans. The widow married the young man on his 25<sup>th</sup> birthday and made him a leader of her caravans. The young man's name was Mohammed.

(1263) At age 40 Mohammed developed an interest in religion. A popular place of pilgrimage was the permanent, multi god temple in Mecca with the unique Ka'bah stone, a black meteorite. While traveling with his caravans he came in contact with the faithful of the other regional religions: the old Judaism, the new Christianity and the ancient religion of neighboring Persia, Zoroastrianism. Christianity had recently been written down as a reformed interpretation of Judaism. A Christian monk told Mohammed about the background to Judaism and Christianity.

(1264) Mohammed could not read but listened with interest to the tales in the Bible. The stories told about Abraham and Jews and how God selected the Jews as God's people through a "contract" and how the Jews could disobay the contract with serious consequences for the whole tribe.

(1265) As a mature man Mohammed withdrew to a cave in a mountain to think through what he had learned from Judaism, Christianity and Zoroastrianism. Mohammed had an idea, a "revelation." An angel, the Archangel Gabriel, told him to become Allah's selected messenger. Mohammed would require real **discipline and obedience** from his members in his reform movement. Mohammed had the revelation to tell the world: there is absolutely no other god than Allah (Allah in Arabic = God). To fail Allah is a death sin.

(1266) At the time it was common that a central power enforced a state religion. This was the Sumeric way of state leadership: government together with a church organization (generic term) held hands and supported each other economically and politically. Jesus had been killed when disobeying both religious and secular authority. Even today, Saudi Arabia has special guards to enforce Mosque attendance during Friday prayer.

(1267) Mohammed was 40 years old. In his remaining twenty years, Mohammed had 114 more revelations. The revelations were written down after Mohammed's death and were called Suras. The Suras were collected, became standardized and would eventually form the Quran. **Each Sura promises a life in Paradise for the faithful and a life in Hell for the unfaithful. The faithful must be subservient to Allah and must openly demonstrate his or her obedience.** "Islam" in Arabic means "obedience."

(1268) Mohammed took on the role as a reformer of Judaism, Christianity and the local multi-god, nature religions. It was not a very popular task. The local religious leaders, many who profited from the pilgrimage to the Ka'bah temple, were upset. Jews and Christians were skeptical. The Jews had already experienced a man of their own, who declared that he was the Bible-prophets' Messiah. The Christians had placed Jesus as God's son on the side of God together with a religious concept, the Holy Spirit of the Community.

(1269) Mohammed interpreted this new three-faceted God concept as if the Christians again were not faithful to God. In Mohammed's eyes the Christians had started just another primitive, multi-god heresy. Therefore Mohammed became convinced he needed to start a disciplined reform movement. Islam was born.

(1270) Mohammed recruited members within his family and his own tribe but not among the Mecca establishment. Most of them were economically dependent of the pilgrimage to the heretic Ka'bah temple. He had to leave Mecca and move to Medina, a town 60 miles north, in the year 622. [**Muslim leaders later determined that a Muslim calendar would start from this year. At about the same time the Christian Church began counting their calendar from the year Jesus was born. (Christian year = Islam year x 3/ 100 + 622). Every religion has its own way to reach into the life of everybody.**] **Mohammed at that time was 50 years old.**

(1271) Two farming clans in Medina had been arguing about which of them owned a particular piece of land. Mohammed was invited to come and act as an arbitrator. He was allowed to bring his followers. Mohammed and his small group arrived to Medina. He demonstrated his neutrality by raising his tent wherever his camel laid down to rest. Mohammed succeeded with his arbitration. The two local clans had to feed Mohammed and his followers during the arbitration time but this could not continue forever. Mohammed's religious organization needed money for its livelihood. Mohammed and his faithful turned to what they knew, the caravans and robbed them. The goal blessed the means; the first jihad began.

(1272) Legitimate caravans started from the now growing city of Mecca. Caravan robbery was a threat to Mecca's livelihood. A war between Mohammed's followers and the Mecca establishment broke out. Successes shifted but Mohammed was able to reach an agreement: he and his followers could visit Mecca for one year, provided they came without weapons. Young people could join his reform movement if their parents agreed.

(1273) Mohammed's movement grew. Before the year was over Mohammed had the Ka'bah temple cleared of pictures of heretic gods. Mohammed just claimed that the Bible's first man, Adam, originally built the Ka'bah temple and that Abraham, (the grandfather of both Jews and Arabs) had the Ka'bah temple repaired. The Ka'bah temple thereby would continue to be a place for pilgrimage but was now connected to Mohammed's religious reform movement. Income for the local people was now assured. The mythological stories were changed to include the references to the Old Testament. The geography was simply changed from Israel to Mecca specifically to the Ka'bah stone building. Mohammed simply claimed that the first man, Adam, had built the Ka'bah stone building and Abraham had repaired it. Who would question such stories when no one except the religious leadership could read and the only book available was the Quoran. The stories took root within the Islam Ummah community and were eventually canonized in the 900s.

(1274) Mohammed succeeded in uniting all the Arabs and became Islam's religious leader for the next ten years. Mohammed died at age of 60 in 632. He is buried under the mosque built where he first raised his tent in Medina. Mohammed's only survivor, his daughter Fatima, married the Prophet's cousin, Ali, but died soon after her father's death.

(1275) Many Bedouins felt their commitment had been with Mohammed as an individual. With his death the commitment was now over. Most of them left his reform movement. Mohammed's cousin and son-in-law, Ali, became the prophet's single and closest surviving relative. Sumeric traditions dominated this part of the world and would have great consequences for Islam.

(1276) The young Islamic community had no instructions for the change in leadership. Mohammed had been sickly in his last year. Abu Bakr, one of Mohammed's nine fathers-in-law, took over and led the prayer in Medina. The community selected Abu Bakr to "Caliph," translated as a "stand-in messenger." One person, the "Caliph," became both political and religious leader. **The Sumerian tradition lived on.** Abu Bakr started several war expeditions and succeeded to again join the Arabs but died after only two years. Omar, another of Mohammed's fathers-in-law, took over as Islam's Caliph.

(1277) The political situation around Arabia at the end of the 600s was the following: Constantinople was the capital of the mighty Roman Empire, now also Christian Empire. It reached all around the Mediterranean Sea. The Roman Empire was Sumerically governed but had two official languages both for its administrative and its religious messages. The Pope in Rome chose Latin; the Patriarch in Constantinople insisted on Greek. In the provinces very few people could read and hardly anyone understood who had the real power. To the north of Arabia, the Persian king ruled in the same Sumeric way with the support of its religion, Zoroastrianism. (The heart of ancient Persia corresponds geographically to about modern Iran). Here lived descendants from Aryans, not Arabs. The Romans and the Persians had for a long time been at war with each other over control of the area and had bled each other to exhaustion.

(1278) Dogmatic rulers also governed India, to the east of Arabia. The Indian religion was either Veda/Brahma/Hinduism or Buddhism, both with reincarnation as religious concepts and with pacifistic attitudes towards war.

(1279) Omar, the Caliph of Islam, was a forceful, Sumeric warrior. As leader for the united Arabic clans he began a religious jihad war against all of his neighbors. Omar used the speed and weight of the horse as his superior weapon. He quickly conquered Syria (635), Iraq (637), Israel (640), Egypt (642), and started the conquest of North Africa. He moved his capital to Damascus. Jerusalem had fallen already in 637 five years after Mohammed's death.

(1280) Mohammed personally never visited Jerusalem but claimed that he spiritually, in a revelation, visited the city. Angels had carried Mohammed on a temporary visit to heaven. Omar built the Rock Mosque on the spot from where Mohammed's heavenly visit had taken place. Omar had the faithful turn to Jerusalem in their prayers.

(1281) After just a few years a new political powerhouse had entered the world political arena. In the usual Sumeric way, a ruler supported by religion governed the new empire. As is common in all Sumerically governed countries central intrigues decide much of its politics. Omar was murdered after ten years of leadership.

(1282) Uthman, another claimed son-in-law to Prophet Mohammed, became the new Caliph. Uthman collected the notes of the prophet's revelations. These were Allah's words and would be kept as sacramental. No variations were allowed and have not been allowed ever since. All other copies were destroyed. Othman's Quran is saved in the old Constantinople, now named Istanbul. Othman was murdered after twelve years as Caliph.

(1283) Ali, the Prophet's cousin and other son-in-law became a next Caliph. The old leadership would not give up power. The "Nine Pillars of History" showed that war follows in the wake of all religious or political dogmatism. Ali started a civil war between ruling families, a Sumeric type war that has lasted until today, some 1500 years. The essentially uninterrupted jihad wars that followed were either for Islamic expansion or between different family fractions, in either case, for control of taxes. Lavish booty and pensions for generals and soldiers encouraged war participation.

(1284) There had been tension between Ali and Aisha, Abu Bakr's young daughter and Mohammed's favorite young wife. Rumors had it that Aisha had been unfaithful. This resulted in sura 24, verse 4, which condemns adultery and the spreading of rumors.

(1285) Groups of Muslims had insisted that leadership should come from the "People of the House." This would be in the traditional Sumeric way. Ali was number one among the "People of the House." Ali's party was called "Shia" and its members Shiites. Members of the other Muslim party are called Sunni and their leader did not need to be related to Mohammed's family.

(1286) A war between Shiite and Sunni families started. Ali had his capital moved to Kufa in Iraq. Ali was murdered after only five years as Caliph and became a saint within the Shiite form of Islam. His son, Hussain, was murdered in the city of Karbala in 680, an event called Ashura and commemorated yearly with self-flagellating marches within Shiite religion.

(1287) The Shiites are a small minority within Islam as a whole, but Shia-Islam is the state religion of Iran, Azerbaijan and Bahrain. Shiites in Iraq are numerically a majority but were discriminated against by the political leader (until recently) of the Baath party, the Sunni Sadam Hussain. Saudi Arabia's population is 10% Shiites and 90% Sunni. Most of the Shiites live in the northeastern section of Saudi Arabia where the largest oil deposits are found. This is of great concern for the Saudi Royals because the area is close to Shiite Iran and Shiite Southern Iraq. No Saudi Shiites are allowed to participate in the Saudi government.

(1288) Mohammed had at one time blessed his grandchildren by covering them with his mantle. At the same time he said the words in the Sura 33:33b: "God will remove the sin from you and cleanse you." Members of the Prophet's family are therefore called the "the Mantle People." The kings Hussain of Jordan and Hasan of Morocco are of the Mantle People.

(1289) The expanding jihad war mission continued. Via North Africa in the west it reached Spain in 711 and in the east it reached Sind in present Pakistan. The Arabs were always numerically a minority in the conquered countries. They had to find a system to rule all the conquered populations. They started a system that is called the "Omar's praxis." The inhabitants of the conquered countries were called "protected people." "Protected people" could not have higher positions in state administration, were not allowed to ride horses or mules, only donkeys, had to dress in special marked clothing and could not build houses taller than those belonging to Muslim's. Local religions were not allowed to build new churches, temples or synagogues, only to repair old ones. Even in modern times it stirred society when Christian Coptics tried to build a new church in Egypt.

(1290) Non-Muslims had to pay an extra Tax, the "Protection Tax." Those who had resisted occupation were killed or used as slaves. Slave descendants from the Indian army fled with their slave masters to Egypt after Baghdad's fall to the Huns 1258. In Egypt the slaves were released and have ever since lived on the roads in Western Europe as "Gypsies," a people "from Egypt" without a homeland. The slave tradition is still alive in some Muslim countries; newspapers print "absconder notices" which offer compensation for the capture of run-away slaves.

(1291) The jihad leaders would split the conquered property with the Islam community, keeping 80% for themselves and assuring pensions for the army. There were plenty of volunteers for the army both as leaders and soldiers. A similar jihad war mission, now internationally recognized as genocide, is presently taking place in some African nations.

(1292) Turks whose leaders were called Sultans and Huns, leaders known as Moguls and other horseriding herds people from north of the Oxus River, invaded the heart of Arab country, killed the leaders but adopted Islam and its "Omar praxis" as a successful formula for expansion. Muslim Moguls invaded India. Hindus in India have supposedly paid more taxes to the Muslim leaders than all the other people combined. The Muslim tax collectors would intimidate the Hindus by spitting down their throat if they neglected their tax obligations.

(1293) The large sums of taxes streaming into the Muslim capitals allowed for maintaining the world's largest standing armies and, later, also navies, assuring further expansions. The only serious threat could come from within. As in all Sumeric governments internal intrigues occurred and the empires collapsed. Western colonial powers filled the gap. Globalization of trade, global education and the global need for energy, the Historical "First Pillar," have brought these areas into new focus.

(1294) Going back to the Islamic Golden Age, 800-1600, the Omar praxis not only created the world's largest standing armies but also freed an intellectual elite able to collect the best of scientific knowledge from the lands Islam had conquered. Scripts from both the old Greek and Indian cultures were collected and copied in what was called the "Wisdom House" in Baghdad and in large universities in Cairo and Cordova, Spain. Arabic translations of ancient knowledge became the inspiration of the Renaissance movement in Europe.

(1295) As you may recall from the historical review in the "Nine Pillars of History," the Renaissance knowledge freed northern Europe from the theocratic dogmatism of the Roman Catholic Church and started the Protestant Movement. Protestantism led to scientifically based education. In England and the USA this led to democracy with free choice of religion and global trade.

(1296) Reactionary movements within Islam in Iran and Afghanistan have recently attempted to stop this evolution and locally enforcing a return to a theocratic government.

(1297) The strength of the Islam Empire is its disciplined religion, the "Seventh Pillar of History" and a common language for communication, the "Fifth Pillar of History"; the weakness is its lack of democratic election. The lack of a democratic constitution has led to 1500 years of war. War heroes are admired when wars are successful. Wars are just pain and insecurity when they are civil wars. Civil wars mean family insecurity, the "First, Second and Third Historical Pillars." It had taken 1000 years to build the Islam Empire; it took 500 years for it to fall apart. What actually happened?

(1298) The inhabitants in the conquered countries, which accepted Islam, became accepted citizens within Islam's spiritual society, the "Ummah."

(1299) The parts of the population connected with Islam through their faith in the Bible were called the "People of the Book." They received special, social rights. These rights were recognized within the Muslim state administration. Their religious leaders, bishops, patriarchs, and rabbis, were responsible for their communities. Thanks to these rights there are still non-Muslim shrines in Muslim countries. Muslims often point to this fact as a sign of their tolerance towards other religions because there are no Muslim shrines in re-conquered Christian Spain. This, however, is not the total truth.

(1300) During the hundreds of years that both Islam and Christianity were Sumerically ruled they competed and employed big armies and navies to try to dominate the other. Atrocities were common in both camps. Intolerance has been rather typical for theocratic, centrally connected dogmatic governments throughout history, bee it Christian or Muslim. Neither behavior is right. Based on the Golden Rule and the Nine Pillars of History there are no excuses for curbing individual rights. To give history and education a special color cannot hide this fundamental right.

(1301) Islam has a religious law, the Shari'ah, similar to that of early Judaism and Christianity. The Shari'ah law forbids defecting from Islam. Defecting in early Islam was punishable with death. This was also the case for defecting from early Christianity and typical for rules within all Sumeric Governments. Religious laws are based upon faith or divine revelations and applied to a community in order to maintain its religious faith.

(1302) Democratic societies have to serve multi-cultural communities with a multitude of different religions. Their common laws are derived from the community and are based upon social jurisprudence. Common laws have to be derived from society; they all have been so ever since we learned to form concepts to secure the survival of our 200,000 year-old human society.

(1303) Some religious rules come close to being rules of society, such as Moses' Ten Commandments. However Moses and his friends wrote the Ten Commandments with the different rules and taboos listed in the book of Leviticus four thousand years ago. These religious laws were written specifically for his Jewish society of the time. Mohammed and his friends continued many of these rules in the Hadith because they made sense at the time and many still make sense. The wisdom of our forefathers should never be underestimated but still, people's knowledge deepens with time and all societies change.

(1304) Common law evolved during tribal time and became common law under the jury system in England. Laws not based on society have to be judged as Sumerically influenced. Such laws have always had their own agenda for power over people, land or money and have historically, for 10,000 years, always ended with war. Religion is generically one of the Nine Pillars of History and will always be a part of our humanity. Laws of society must therefore protect religious freedom and cannot favor one religion.

(1305) The early infighting within Islam opened the fundamental question of how to select their leaders. Three families claimed Sumeric rights to leadership. The Sunni group wanted a good Muslim to be the leader, independent of family relationship with Mohammed. But who was a good Muslim without democratic voting?

(1306) The Shiites wanted somebody from Ali's family, the "Family House," to be leader but could also accept somebody from Mohammed's clan. An early Caliph, Abbas, was of Mohammed's clan. Caliph Abbas dethroned the Muslim clan of Omar, Omar who had made Damascus his capital. Caliph Abbas built his own capital, Baghdad, in 762. Baghdad became Islam's capital for the next 500 years. Djingis Khan's grandson, Hidalgo, attacked the city in 1258, robbed and destroyed the city and killed most of its inhabitants. The Ottomans, a Turkish family, filled the political void. The Ottomans accepted Islam and the Omar praxis for taxes.

(1307) The Turkish Ottomans conquered most of the Arab Empire and extended it with conquests of the Balkan Peninsula. Constantinople, as noted before, fell in 1453. The "Abbasid" Caliph, who fled to Egypt when the Mongols took Baghdad, "family-legitimized" the Turkish leader. Muslim leaders in Turkey were called Sultans instead of Caliphs. In India Muslim leaders were called Moguls. The power of both sultans and moguls corresponds to that of kings in feudal Europe.

(1308) The Caliph Othman would not allow any translation of the Quran. Children of the different Muslim areas have to learn Arabic in order to understand the Quran. Leaders were able to communicate with each other despite different local languages. The Arab language became a world language.

(1309) There have been discussions to combine, at least, all Arab countries under a common Caliphate. The idea has not taken root. Instead, what is discussed is leadership under the common Shari'ah Law. The basis for this is an interpretation of Sura 42: "Faithful, whose interests are being discussed, should divide between them, what has been allotted them." This sura is the foundation for democratic movements in the modern Islam. Summit talks to discuss common problems are held during Ramadan in Mecca, Saudi Arabia.

(1310) Islam consists of three dogmatic concepts: faith, duty and tradition.

(1311) A. Faith is expressed in a dogma: There are no gods but Allah and Mohammed is his prophet.

(1312) B. Duty is the religious duty to become Allah's servant. This must be demonstrated. Duty must be shown with devotion and respect in five separate actions:

1. Faith
2. Five daily prayers
3. Required alms
4. The fast
5. Pilgrimages to Mecca

(1313) C. Tradition, "Hadith," stand for the exemplified way of life, lived by Mohammed and the early Caliphs.

(1314) Tradition is more than the word "tradition" represents in western culture. It is a part of the religious dogma. In the Christian tradition it is closest represented by the concept of the "Holy Spirit." The Hadith is the liturgy, the rituals and a way of life connected with Muslim life. Twelve early Imams established the Hadith for the

Shiites. The final judgment for entering either Paradise or Hell is based on whether or not the Quran and the Hadith has been followed.

(1315) The Shari'ah law is a religious inspired law, just as Moses' law. The Hadith enforces the Sharia law, the dogmatic belief system for the "Ummah," the Muslim society. The close connection between tradition, law and society makes the concept very much like the Christian Spirit: the spirit permeates the whole society. Caliph Uthman canonized the Quran in the 600s. The Bible was canonized at about the same time. Canonized religions are typical for the Sumeric, theocratic leadership. **Both Christian and Muslim countries were now, and for some time to come, locked into the social values and the scientific knowledge known at that particular time in history. War between the two camps, initiated by their rival theocratic leaders, was assured until human rights values from Hunting and Gathering time slowly re-evolved as a modern democracy.**

## Islam and the Nine Pillars of History

(1316) **Food, Water and Energy:** (Air was not problematic at this time in history.) The first historical pillar has never been a prime concern for the Muslim leadership. Historically robbing the caravans was a common means of finding food and water. After becoming socially accepted in Mecca in the 600s they received pilgrimage donations. Since then the Islamic religion has received great political influence, first from taxmoney from "protected" occupied lands and in modern times through its control of some of the world's largest oilreserves that is, energy, the first pillar need.

(1317) The cost for a pillar need cannot be controlled but for competition. A lot of cash has resently been transferred into Arab lands. The cash transfer has resulted in a building boom and a feeling of religious superiority. This all, of course, has nothing to do with religion based on the Golden Rule; it is all due to a warrior attitude and a happenstance with the location of oil.

(1318) **Security for the Family Dwelling:** In the early times the Arab clan assured individual security. The clan lived in tents; the security was the family community. Allah is great but the family comes first is a popular saying in the Arab world. This attitude filled the individual security of the second historical pillar. That the family comes first is an expression for values rooted in the clan culture from the H/G time.

(1319) The family survival in agricultural time depended on whom their daughters were going to marry, what the dowry would be and in what way their old age would be secure. Parents and brothers assured that their sisters were saved for a special person. Many men still have difficulty in letting go of their responsibility for the future of the daughters in the family. This can lead to serious family conflicts. Such values have been softened in democratic countries where the state assures security for old age and the woman often provides for her own livelihood.

(1320) **Cleanliness:** Every man must bow and fall to the floor while praying in order to show his respect and obedience. Muslims must wash their hands, take off their shoes and be decently dressed when entering a Mosque. Every mosque has a place to wash. Women cannot enter while unclean from blood. These traditions are called "wudu" in Arabic. This compares with the old tradition of putting on Sunday clothes in many Christian communities. Such "wudu" traditions are important in the way different religions experience and look at each other. The cleaner the more respect for the religious tradition in the community, the superior feeling it gives its community members. During the first Millennium, the Muslims in general were cleaner and thereby felt superior to the Christians.

(1321) In the early times clean food was as important for Muslims as for Jews. Both religions had similar rules: animals should be slaughtered with the animal's head turned towards Mecca and its body bled empty of blood. Blood, meat from pigs and shellfish were considered taboo. These foods were most likely to carry disease, particularly in the warm climate of the Middle East. The traditions live on. That this food could be dangerous was obvious in early times. The bacterial cause was not known. Eating it was simply made taboo.

Such traditions are hardly rationally motivated any longer in modern countries with good hygienic control of their food supply.

(1322) The tenets of Islam, Judaism and Christianity are written by men for men and are essentially based on the same patriarchy. All the prophets are men and men wrote all the holy scripts. God, or Allah, is perceived as "Our Father." The man is created in the image of God, the woman from the man's rib. These myths started in old Sumer land and were copied as historical facts within Judaism, Christianity and Islam. Although all three religions are of very different age but **not from different knowledge-age**. They are all based on similar myths from the 10,000 year old Sumer agricultural period. At this time, blood was considered to be a carrier of disease for several, good reasons. Leprosy was a common disease and spread by body fluids. The woman was easily infected in connection with her monthly bleedings or bloody deliveries. The woman was therefore unclean for 40 days after delivery and could not visit the Mosque during her menstruation periods. Women had to sit separated from the men, quiet and with their head covered. This perception of womanhood has been common in all world religions and still lives on in some areas. The women's "uncleanliness" has in most religious communities resulted in that women never received an education or held a leading position in the community. **All these traditions are based on lack of medical knowledge or myths about women's biology. In modern times and with fact-founded knowledge such myths are totally without reason. They ought not to play any role in women's standing in our modern society.**

(1323) Muslims and Jews, both animal-hording clans from the desert, circumcise their boys and sometimes also their girls. To remove the foreskin in men can be hygienically motivated in a desert short of water. To keep the foreskin clean requires almost daily washing. To do the same in girls and even to remove the clitoris is a demand from a patriarchal, man-dominated community and has no hygienic basis. To remove the clitoris in women is the same as to remove the penis from the men.

(1324) **Art:** Modeled after Judaism, there are no pictures on the walls in a Mosque. The walls are often decorated calligraphically with beautifully formed words, many times with the 99 prayer epithets of Allah. If there is a drawing of the prophet of Mohammed in some old books then he is pictured without showing a face, all to show respect for Allah and his prophet; nobody could look like Mohammed.

(1325) The earliest mosques were built both for defense and for a place for prayer. They are built with very heavy walls. Later mosques can be architecturally very beautiful buildings. One of the most beautiful buildings in the world is the famous Taj Mahal in Agra, India. The architectural design of Muslim official buildings is an expression for the fourth historical pillar.

(1326) **Communication:** The Quran is sacramental to the faithful. According to the tradition the Quran contains word-by-word Mohammed's revelations. The message of the Quran is not that of Mohammed's but Allah's own message revealed through Mohammed. The words of the Quran cannot be questioned but its understanding has been open for theological studies during the past 1500 years. The Al-Azhar University in Cairo has been publishing the norms for the interpretation of the Quran, at least within Sunni Islam. Doctors of theology at Al-Azhar also act as a Superior Court of the Shari'ah law, as seen from the side of a religious "Ummah."

(1327) The midday prayer on Fridays corresponds to the Jewish Saturday and the Christian Sunday sermons. In the old times, when most people could not read, Christian priests (generic term) used the Sunday sermon to preach religious messages but also political messages, for or against the king. Worldwide, at least 50% of Muslims still cannot read, with a very low percentage of secondary education. The Friday sermon is therefore a time to listen to the prayer-leader's religious message and also to listen to his approval of present political stands. This gives the prayer-leader a special political standing in the Muslim community. Communications within Islamic dominated countries can become one-sided, limiting the fifth historical pillar for free communication.

(1328) Mosques are not only places to pray but also a place for lower grade schools, "madrasahs." Children, mostly boys, are taught Quran and basic Arabic language. This is often the only schooling for a large portion of the populations in many Muslim countries. This tradition would correspond to the church sponsored schools within early Christianity and the Vedic education of boys within Veda/Brahma/Hinduism. The larger mosques are often closely connected to large universities, some of the oldest in the world as they were taken over from Veda/Hinduism. These connections have, as has already been pointed out, made Arabic a world language and has helped Islam to become a world religion but has also fed religious dogmatism.

(1329) Professionals within Islam know the Quran by heart; many Muslims know at least big portions by rote. The "Quran" cannot formally be translated. The faithful, unfamiliar with Arabic, therefore must learn Arabic.

(1330) **Community Support:** The first duty for a Muslim is to confess his faith in Allah. The uniquely Muslim concept of God is that God (Allah) has to be an absolutely single, an only-one-god concept. To place anything at the side of Allah is a death sin. The Islam Community, the "Ummah" supports the Hadith, the "tradition" and vice versa. The Hadith is the spiritual, political and social bond between all Muslims in all countries. All are subject to Allah's will except man; man may be disobedient. The first couple, Adam and Eve showed this and so did man's history according to the Bible. Islam demands total obedience.

(1331) The daily prayer, the "salat," the second duty of Islam is an expression of community support. The salat must occur five times throughout the day, three times more than for the Jews. Both men and women perform the prayer with their face turned toward Mecca. To pray is to show respect for Allah and to demonstrate the brotherhood within the Ummah. The prayer is at the same time a protection from evil thoughts and temptations. One billion Muslims turning their heads towards Mecca in quiet prayer is, without doubt, and in a very demonstrative way, a clear sign of a great group support. Faithful

Muslims carry a Mecca compass in their pocket; some kneel on a leaning platform in order to compensate for the earth's curvature. The short time between morning, midday, sunset, evening and night prayer keeps all Muslims day and night focused on Allah. The prayer itself is partly ritual, helped by a string of pearls, a rosary, with 99, 33 or 11 pearls. Each pearl represents a selected epithet for Allah. It is repeated as for a Hindu or Buddhist mantra. Examples of epithets are: the Creator, the Savior, the Merciful, The King, The Holy, the Loyal, the Judge and so on.

(1332) Friday is the Muslim Holy Day and corresponds to the Christians' Sunday and the Jews' Sabbath. Each religion demonstrates their own identity by their own special holy day. They still all base their week on the seven-day week from Sumer time. The Friday prayer is always done in the Mosque with at least all men present. Attending females sit separated from men. In Saudi Arabia presence in the Mosque is obligatory and enforced by police on patrol.

(1333) To celebrate the "Ramadan Fast," is the fourth pillar of Islam. Ramadan is the ninth moon-month of the year. The Ramadan is not connected to the agricultural year. Ramadan follows the short moon cycle and therefore moves forward some each year with a complete circle each 33 years. The duties during Ramadan are not to have sex and to fast during daylight. The Ramadan celebration is a public expression of community support.

(1334) Hajj, the pilgrimage to the Ka'bah stone in Mecca, is Islam's fifth pillar and another expression of community support. Mohammed strongly urges all Muslims, at least once in their lifetime, to celebrate one Ramadan in Mecca to honor Mohammed's memory. Two million people from all over the world, everybody dressed in white, arrive to Mecca. They circle around the Ka'bah stone seven times counter clockwise so their hearts are turned towards the Ka'bah alter, the same way Hindus walk around their alters and Buddhists walk around their Topas.

(1335) The Bible prophet Abraham had a wife, Hagar. According to the Old Testament, she and her son Ishmael were turned away from Abraham's home to seek their living in the desert. Muslim pilgrims replay Hagar's story by running the 395 meters between two hills to find the well that saved her and her son's life. The graves of Hagar and Ishmael are placed close to the Ka'bah temple. As stated before and according to Mohammed, Adam originally built and Abraham repaired the Ka'bah temple. This myth makes the Ka'bah temple a unique focal point for all Muslims.

(1336) After the vist to the Kabah temple Pilgrims assemble on a large field for a common sermon. Later they walk along the path where Mohammed was tempted three times and throw stones at three stone pillars symbolizing the devil's three appearances for Mohammed just like the Mara did for Buddha and the devil did for Jesus. They visit Mohammed's grave in Medina and end their pilgrimage with a last visit to the Ka'bah temple.

(1337) The pilgrimage is an enormous communal experience for all Muslims. The pilgrimage is so popular that Saudi Arabia has to apportion how many pilgrims can attend from each country. Shiites are given comparatively fewer tickets. Communions give special respect to Pilgrims after their return to their homes. It can take a lifetime to save for the pilgrimage. The pilgrimage and the daily prayers are manifestations of a strong group support, the sixth historical pillar and the strong influence of religion in any community.

(1338) **Freedom of Religion:** A Mosque is a place for prostration, that is, where one can show one's respect and obedience for Allah by bending down on the floor in prayer. The Mosque is otherwise essentially built and works similar to a Christian Church. The minaret towers, from where the daily prayers are called are instead of the bell tower. The Mosque has a Mihrab, a niche, in the wall turned towards Mecca, which corresponds to the Christian abs, or sanctuary, turned toward the East greeting the sun. The prayer is led from a pulpit, the Minbar, to the right of the Mihrab. In Christian Churches the pulpit usually sits to the left of the abs. Islam considers members of other religions as gentiles just as Christians used to look at members of different religions during medieval time.

(1339) It is amazing to compare how each religion makes a Nish for itself, some based on the Golden Rule and some just based on its own dogma.

(1340) **Access to Medicine:** Al-Azhar University has taken a pragmatic stand to new medical discoveries and has thereby allowed modern medical access in most Islamic countries. Some Muslim countries have now very large incomes from oil and have thereby been able to give their citizens excellent medical support. Other Muslim countries are the poorest in the world and are limited to very primitive medical support.

(1341) **Free Trade:** Since the first jihad Islam's theocratic leaders have never needed to be concerned with negotiated trade or a successful harvest. Their livelihood was always secure from either the immense business involving pilgrimage or the taxing of "the protected people."

(1342) A secure income for the religious leaders is the Zakat, the 2.5% taxing of their own member's yearly income. "Zakat" is the fourth duty and a pillar of Islam. Zakat is the religious duty of self-taxing. The tax is donated on the 27th day of the Month of Ramadan. It is in remembrance of Mohammed's first revelation and the holiest day of the year. On that day Muslims give each other presents. Mohammed determined the size of the gift. He ordered a Muslim with four camels to give one goat to a poor member of the family and, if none in the family needed help, to a poor connected with his mosque. Modern economists have translated the Zakat gift to 2.5% of member's net-income for the year. Few Muslim countries have a working, public social support system. Only 2.5% to help poor explains the poverty in the world's Muslim countries.

(1343) The Quran defines very specifically who should receive Zakat: the poor, handicapped, those without work and parents, families of those in prison, travelers in need, if lawfully encumbered, Muslim missioners, Zakat workers and released slaves. Those, who give Zakat, should discreetly seek receivers. Zakat in Saudi Arabia has been regulated with a firm modern tax.

285

(1344) Trade in Muslim countries has in the past been limited to either oil or agricultural products, none based on a wider education of their populations. Education has been limited to boys only. Boys attend small madrasah type schools. Here the boys learn to read the Quran in Arabic. Girls are without any learning access. Lack of a wider higher education has limited broad-based entrepreneurship.

(1345) The mosque in Muslim countries is often used for political purposes. A political leader will be photographed while he prays; that is to say, he will expect to have the Islam community on his side politically. A sectarian leader cannot count on this kind of support. This makes it very difficult for a democratic type of government to have any influence in a Muslim country.

(1346) Some religious leaders within Islam issue what they call a "Fatwa." A Fatwa is a personally and religiously motivated deadly damnation of a specific person. In recent years, an Iranian Imam declared the author Salman Rushdie subject to a fatwa. Mr. Rushdie had to go into hiding in England for several years. A Fatwa dooms a person as an outlaw without any defense in a court of law. Fatwas have no place in a modern society founded on law. A Fatwa scares away any attempts for critique or reforms and does not meet the historical pillars for free communication (the fifth), free religion (the seventh) and free assembly (the sixth) and thereby again locks society into the time period of the 700s.

(1347) Some ridiculous mythological ideas can live on in such canonized, locked up societies. One such idea is that young men who die in the cause of religion go directly to Paradise and are served by 72 virgins. In modern democratic countries such places are called "houses of ill repute." The Vikings in Scandinavia had similar fantasies at about the same time (700-1000s). Mythological stories belong to the period of history in which they were created. Mythic stories that do not adjust to the education of the general population will appear ridiculous.

(1348) The Fatwa and the Jihad traditions indicate that at least some Muslims have their own interpretation of the Golden Rule or Islam's fortieth Hadith: "Not one of you is a believer until he loves for his brother what he loves for himself." A "brother" in this context could mean another Sunni but excluding a Shiite Muslim. Similar dogmatic beliefs have been common for many religions ever since Sumer time. This will lead to, and has always led to war. A "brother" in such context really stands for honest working people, serving each other and humanity in all its forms. This is the Golden Rule of all religions and any and all social life for 200,000 years.

(1349) **Religion has never been able to be part of the central power without abusing its power. This is the mistake that the Sumer society made because of its mythology some 7000 years ago. Such a tradition started wars between different mythological beliefs for the same time. The Golden Rule stands above all religions and can never be transgressed. This is founded on the human rights values from the 190,000-year-long H/G-time. This is also the truth democracies have established in their fundamental constitutions.**

(1350) Freedom House in New York has ranked political freedoms of all countries since 1974. Mr. Trofimov visited many Muslim countries as a reporter for the Wall Street Journal and reported his findings in his book "Faith at War." In 2004 it reported that more than 50% of those not free were Muslim.

(1351) Muslim countries can be democratic. A notable exception in 2004, according Yarislav Trofimov, was the African nation of Mali. Today in 2013 Mali is the latest country in Africa involved in civil war and Islamic Jihad.

(1352) In order to avoid mixing secular political values with religious values a group of American and European Muslims, having grown up and educated in democracies, met with Eastern Muslims in a effort to bridge the gap created by some lingering Sumeric traditions. The effort has been named the "Brussels model." The Brussel model seems to be successful in bridging the gap between East and West Muslims in some European and American communes.

(1353) Several dogmatic countries have recently come into large fortunes from their oil deposits. Hopefully, their Sumeric kind of leadership doesn't mix their financial fortune with that of a dogmatic, religious message.

(1354) All people of the world must still meet the need of the Nine Pillars of History and the Golden Rule. This has been true for 200,000 years. The tragic history of human rights versus dogmatic beliefs was described in details in the first parts of this publication.

(1355) Paul Lunde's 2002 fact book of 44 Muslim countries with facts accumulated from the year 2001 gives an objective picture of life within Islam. All 44 Muslim nations have censorship of news and education. Only those with income from oil have a GNP/capita income of more than $5000/year, 24 have less than $1000, eight $1000-2000, five $2000-5000/year. Brunei was the only country with a GNP/capita income of $26,286 comparable with the U.S. or Western Europe. "Infant mortality/1000 live births" is an indicator of access to quality medicine. It should, at most, be less than 10%. Only four Muslim countries meet this goal: Malaysia, Brunei, UAE and Bahrain. The same statistic for the United States is 6 per thousand and for Sweden it is less than 2.

(1356) In eleven of the 44 Muslim countries less than 50% of the population can read and in these countries only 50% of those who can read attend secondary schooling.

# References

(1357) *Koranens Budskap, svensk översättning* av Muhammed Knut Bernströms, 1998, ISBN 91-7118-8991.

(1358) *Familjeliv och levnadsmönster bland Mellanösterns muslimer* av Naser Khader, 1996, sponsrad av Nordiska Ministerrådet, ISBN 91-46-17167-3.

(1359) *Islam: Lära och livsmönster* av Jan Hjärpe, ISBN 91-1-923292-6.

(1360) *Islam.* PBS, 2002, in USA, a video program.

(1361) *Faith at War* by Yaroslav Trofimov, Henry Holt and Company LLC, 2005, ISBN -10: 0-8050-7754-4.

(1362) *The Heart of Islam* by Seyyed Hossein Nasr, 2002, Harper San Francisco, ISBN 0-06-009924-0.

(1363) *Islam, Faith, Culture, History* by Paul Lunde, 2002, DK Publ., ISBN 0-7894-8797-7.

(1364) *Al-Qur'an.* Trans. Ahmed Ali (Princeton, 1993), ISBN 069107499-2.

## Summary of the Seventh Pillar, Religion

(1365) Five world religions, their dogmas, traditions and ambitions have been described. The oldest, Hinduism, covers probably more than 4000 years; the youngest, Islam, 1500 years.

(1366) The question is: Do each of these five world religions fill the need for the nine historical pillars as derived from the 200,000 years of human social history? The answer is no. Some Christian and Islamic extremists still maintain dogmatic, religiously based laws from medieval times for common law.

(1367) The moral message of each religion is also examined. Does each of them meet the most fundamental and universal moral law for the human society, the Golden Rule? The answer is no. Some Christian and Islamic nations still maintain a dogmatic, religiously based Curia and Sharia law from medieval times for common law.

(1368) The experience has been that the concept "God" has varied within the different religions from a limitless number in Buddhism to more than a million god concepts in Veda/Brahma/Hinduism, and finally to one god concept in Judaism copied and made Sumeric during medieval time within Christianity and Islam. Some religious extremists still maintain Sumeric, dogmatic attitudes.

(1369) All god concepts are worshipped to satisfy people's ambitions and to fill their need for security when faced with life's challenges and death.

(1370) **The logical expectations of Sumeric, Islamic or Christian religion is 1500 years of war: for Islam itself even a kind of civil war between Sunni and Shiite Islam last time in the big war 1980-1988. The leaders of Islam are responsible. The religions themselves obviously lack original commitments to the Golden**

**Rule, a commitment lacking since medieval time when the Curia and Hadith were written and canonized.**

(1371) **Islam and Christianity are not alone in being responsible. A war between Sumeric countries in general is what has actually happened for ten thousand years.**

(1372) **We, all of us, indeed have what we all seek, an eternal life.**

(1373) First, we have an eternal life in the DNA memory that we have inherited and pass on to future generations. Second, we have an eternal life in the spiritual memory we leave behind to our family and to people we have touched in our life. Our memory is formed by our deeds and will be judged by a moral world based on the Golden Rule.

(1374) Buddha's concept "tulku" is a concept of the "left-behind-memory." Our left-behind-memory can and will indeed enter another body by the diffusion of ideas.

(1375) Veda/Brahma/Hinduism, the oldest world religion, has the god-concept Brahma, for the world soul and the creator of the world and its all other gods. Brahma is pictured with a head having four faces, one for each cardinal direction because Brahma can see and hear everything. A world soul can see and hear everything because we find it in ourselves, in our conscious hearts, where it speaks to us in all the world's languages and tell us the moral message of love: love your neighbor as yourself.

(1376) To listen to the voice of conscience for our deeds will give us a good life within our family, in our community and a dignified after-life. The moral voice of our heart is the voice that talked to Buddha and will also talk to you under meditation or through the voice of a moral world-soul whether it is called Brahma, YHVH, God, or Allah or given a million different names.

(1377) All religions have inspired values of beauty, which have enriched all cultures and individual lives. With art comes "culture." This is true for all religions, all through history. Religion creates family traditions, holidays, holy places, literature, music, sports and other art forms that surround us and might be called "our" culture. Religion in the form of culture meets the all circumscribed human value that art brings.

(1378) One important value in all religions is their moral message. Moral education does not need to be religious but should be emphasized early in life. The different mythological stories that have been woven into and around each religion's prophet or god-concept has really just been a way to communicate a moral message to a continuously renewed, often unable to read, very large youth population. Each year millions of young people have to learn to fit in with the societies of their parents. Hopefully all religions have the moral message of the Golden Rule as a base for the education of their youth.

(1379) The mythology of different religions has over time created variations in cultures. This is acceptable as long as each culture does not transgress against the Golden Rule for individual rights and the historical experience of the Nine Pillars. Most moral rules are universal. They go back to the 190,000-year-long Hunting and Gathering period and have proven their value throughout human history. These rules can be the basis for moral education of each yearly class of youngsters entering their societies. It can indeed be secular because it rests on the common social law of the land instead of on a specific religious message that will and always have led to war.

(1380) I am not a prophet, but if I could I would summarize what I have read so far as nine contracts with "My God" and "My Society:"

1. I pledge to defend and build My Society on the Nine Historical Pillars and the Golden Rule of Love.
2. I pledge to follow the laws set by my democratically elected government of My Society.

(1381) This also means:

3. I shall honor my father and mother.
4. I shall not envy my neighbor.
5. I shall not commit adultery.
6. I shall not steal.
7. I shall not bear false witness.

8. I shall not murder.
9. I shall not let my brain's perception of reality be influenced by neither mind-altering substances nor behaviors.

(1382) Dominance by different state religions was worldwide during the agricultural time until the end of 1600s when John Locke resurrected democratic thoughts from the tribal time. In developing countries some of today's political processes take place against this religious/historical background.

(1383) I hope that this review of the five world religions offers a wider perspective of the generic concept of "religion" and can promote tolerance between different religions.

# Reference

*World Scripture: A Comparative Anthology of Sacred Texts*, ISBN: 0-89226-129-3.

# B. Medicine

(1384) **Access to Medicine:** The eighth historical pillar of human needs has been part of humanity since its beginning, its first birth, its first fever, and its first broken leg. It seemed natural to ask: How has medical care met the other eight historical pillars?

(1385) **Food, Water:** In the history of religion we learned that the concern about what we eat and drink is important and has influenced our behavior. Modern medical knowledge has replaced many religious rules with scientific knowledge. Medical knowledge is fundamental to assure that the intake of food, water, air, energy and sex does not affect our health.

(1386) **Secure and Clean Home:** Medical knowledge continuously initiates environmental and hygiene codes in order to assure a clean intake and surrounding for our families.

(1387) **Art:** The benefit of art as part of medicine has only been studied lately. Beautiful art for the well being of the individual is finding more and more support by professionals. Children with severe diseases are given an encouraging surrounding. Elderly with difficult conditions are helped and their life prolonged by positive experiences.

(1388) **Communication:** Medicine as a profession has always surrounded itself with a wall of mysticism and foreign words. This was probably necessary in older times when medical knowledge was limited and the profession really did not have much to offer. In recent times scientific knowledge has progressed and modern medical treatment is founded on and confirmed by independent researchers.

(1389) Laymen's great interest for understanding how their bodies work has produced an entire medical information and education industry. I had possibly something to do with this. I started health education first at NASA in 1970 and continued at Lockheed until I retired in 1989. I have collected and updated what I wrote at that time. (See my publication: *Add Years to your Life and Life to Your Years, Parts I and II.*)

(1390) People want to know what a laboratory result means. Any laboratory report has four modalities: true and false positive and true and false negative. True positive means a test indicates a certain condition; false positive indicates the same condition but is wrong. The specificity of a test depends on how wide the normal range is. If this is expressed in a percentage of the mean the patient could more easily take part in the information and understand its impact. A test that is positive but its normal range is more than 40% of its mean is not very specific may need to be confirmed by other tests. This would be true all over the world, independent from laboratory procedures and laboratory units.

(1391) **Group Support:** Most progressive societies have some form of access to medical care. Many have organized either in voluntary insurance groups or taxpayer supported government programs or a mixture of the two. The cost of access to medicine has in the last twenty years increased at an alarming 9% rate, much faster than the general inflation rate and is not sustainable for most countries. In the U.S. the medical cost has increased at 16-17% rate almost double that in Western Europe and still with worse statistical healing rate. This prompted my colleagues, Professor Ed Ericson and Senior Fellow at Stanford University Wes Alles, Ph.D. and me to write a special report on medical cost control in Sweden and the USA. See page 357 for this report.

(1392) **Freedom of Religion:** Religion and medicine have often complemented each other. Faith is a strong medicine that gives hope and is important in a person's well being.

(1393) **Free Trade:** In order for medicine to grow and serve as many as possible it is necessary for physicians to exchange experiences freely. The restrictions imposed on doctors in the old USSR led to misery for much of Russian/Soviet Union population.

## Summary of the Eighth Pillar, Medicine

(1394) The eighth historical pillar is as old as humanity and must by itself also meet the other historical pillars.

(1395) Cost of access to medical care cannot be controlled but for competition. This fact requires special consideration of cost control for access to medical care.

## C. Analysis of the Remaining Historical Pillars

(1396) Having gone through the analysis of **religion** (the "Seventh Pillar") and **medicine** (the "Eighth pillar") versus the other historical pillars it was logical to ask: What about the other seven, the rest of the "Nine," do they also serve the other two?

(1397) The first historical pillar, the **survival** pillar (food, water, air energy and sex), is a given. None of the other pillars, or for that matter life itself, could exist without the "First Pillar." The "Ninth Pillar," the **trade** pillar, serves the same purpose. A successful family life depends on the exchange of services. This began by helping each other in the day-to-day chores in the caves and is also the fundament for the Golden Rule. In modern time, life is dependent on the global exchange of products and services.

(1398)   The second historical pillar, the **shelter** pillar, is also a rather given. Humanity could not survive if the family home was not secure. **Communication** for **community**support and defense, the "Fifth and Sixth Pillars" are necessary for a security of the home. Home security is also enhanced by good **cleanliness** within the dwelling, the "Third Pillar" need. Hygiene becomes more and more important the larger the community is. Nobody living in a modern city can question the importance of good hygiene.

(1399)   **Art**, the "Fourth Pillar," is interesting. After reading my first part of the Historical Pillars, Ernest Littauer, Ph.D. in Physics and an old friend of mine from Lockheed, pointed out that the need for art should really be renamed as a "need for aesthetical enjoyment." I agree with him. At one time I used the word "beauty." An editor suggested the word "art." Eventually, I settled for the word "art" because it is so simple. The connotation of "art" as a "historical pillar" can still be aesthetics.

(1400)   Art decorated the walls of the oldest caves and has also always been part of enhancing the personal look. Birds sing, dance, have decorative feathers and some even decorate their nests. All these routines are probably also in our genes. My strongest argument for including aesthetics as a historical pillar is that it has always been part of humanity; we have always wanted to improve and to beautify our life.

(1401)   We all have become small cogs of the big wheel called the "world society." We can no longer survive without exchanging our own small service for the large service each of our neighbors contributes. This need has become global. Our neighbor may live on the other side of the globe. We must all respect each other as neighbors.

# D. Sex

## The Male and Female Roles from Hunting and Gathering Time through Agricultural and Industrial Time

## Introduction

## Embryology, Anatomy and Physiology of the Human Sex Organ

(1402) Generic sex drive is much older than even our specie as *Homo sapiens*. The sex drive is certainly older than the nine historical pillars, which are dated from tribal time. All living creatures are sexually designed for their very best chance to survive within a given area for food and security.

(1403) The sex need really has its own life and has in many cultures its own separate word definition: our "sex life." Anatomically, it is to a large part separated from the functions of the rest of the body, the energy producing machinery of the body that let us move about. The sex organs have their own production glands (testicles and ovaries) and their own connections to the world outside the body. Our biological sex life for propagation matures about 12 years after the birth of a female and 14 years after the birth of a male and ends its life at around age 55 for a female. Psychologically our sex life may continue for some time for both sexes but eventually dies before our physiological death, provided we live long enough.

(1404) Our sex-need originates from the generic inheritance summed up in our X- and Y-chromosomes. The sex life may dominate the behavior of the specie while most active.

(1405) The embryological origin of the male and the female sex organ are the same and therefore both have the same nerve supply for stimulation. The larger and the smaller lips surrounding the vagina are in the male embryo sealed together to form the underside of the penis and the scrotum and are recognizable as a seam on the male organ.

(1406) In all of nature, including both male and female, seeds are produced with large number margins. Most seeds have no opportunity to fertilize and mature. During the life of a male his testicles excrete about 200 million sperm cells. The male sperm has one X or one Y chromosome imbedded in its head.

(1407) The ovaries produce about 50,000 eggs with only some 400 maturing into a menstruation or a pregnancy. The egg has only X chromosomes imbedded in its nucleus. The combination of an egg X and a male Y chromosome becomes a male XY; a combination XX becomes a female.

(1408) One egg matures and ovulates, in the middle between two menstrual periods. The egg is actively collected and transported through a muscular tube to the uterus, which implants the egg in its surface. If a sperm is present or will arrive in the uterus before next menstruation, the egg can be fertilized and lead to pregnancy. The human female can hardly produce more than one pregnancy per year and is really physically limited to how many total births she can carry.

(1409) Human society by itself can only accommodate a limited number of offsprings at the same time. Poor birth control in all but the last century led to population saturation and starvation in all of the old agricultural areas like in parts of Africa, Near and Far East, China, India and Western Europe. Western Europe suffered less than the other areas because of new land discovery in the 1500s providing the possibility to emigrate to the Americas, Australia and New Zealand.

(1410) The hormone testosterone is mainly formed in the testicles and excreted into the blood and thereby affects the whole male body. The testosterone gives the male physically and mentally his manliness.

(1411) The hormone estrogen is mainly excreted from the ovaries into the blood and gives the women her femininity, both physically and mentally.

(1412) Both male and female sex organs swell and enlarge when physically and mentally stimulated. Both sex organs have glands for production of mucus in order to ease copulation, the woman more so than the man.

(1413) Friction to the penis causes a local muscle spasm, the orgasm. The orgasm squeezes sperms through a muscular tube through the prostate and ejects them through the penis that delivers the sperm into the vagina. Friction to the clitoris causes spasm for the female uterus and causes sperms to be sucked into the uterus. In the uterus the sperm swims to meet the egg for its fruition.

(1414) Most animals cannot release an orgasm by self-stimulation and need a sex partner for satisfaction. Orgasm is such a unique and strong experience for the male animal that he will fight for the opportunity. Fighting for the opportunity for orgasm causes the competition in the animal world. The strongest male wins this competition and creates offsprings in his image with strong uniformity within species. Sexuality in animals is an instinct for propagation of an offspring with the best chance to survive.

(1415) The modern human male reaches sexual maturity between 14-17 years of age. His animal instincts are awaken with a thirst for female pursuit. He starts to look at pictures, read and learn about his own and the female sex organ and fantasizes about copulation. Males at this age are not ready for the consequences of unlimited intercourse. Most boys need another five, if not more, years before they have enough education to pursue a career and can take responsibility for a child.

(1416) A girl reaches puberty with a first menstruation between the age of 12-13, about two years before the boy. She will now have to care for her menstrual cycle for some 40 years. A teenaged girl could care for a child within the simple and family supported tribal life but is not ready for this responsibility in the complicated life of the modern female world. Most modern young females need, and want, at least five more years of education and their own occupation in order to secure a home for her children.

(1417) Both females and males have a period of at least five years with mature sex life but with a society not ready to accommodate them as they are. This period of social maturing has to be addressed and bridged with intensive sex and moral education.

(1418) Connections between two people, their children and their society through a lifetime and beyond can be, and very often is, a very complicated challenge for everybody. In tribal life, where life is fairly simple and the world is very small, most is community owned, most of the people know each other, the Golden Rule is the unwritten law and where forgiveness usually smoothers over most conflicts. Life during agricultural and industrial time is much more complicated.

(1419) During agricultural time the passing of property to the second generation became important. The parents would have great influence in selecting partners for their offspring and virginity was assuring. In the old cultures of the Far and Middle East the tradition of a prime wife, and for those who could afford it, secondary wives evolved. The inheritance rights would usually stay with the prime wife. If a woman became a widow another male in the family would adopt her. Some females may have to survive by serving the surplus single men. This was the start of one of the oldest occupations.

(1420) Prostitution became recognized as a necessary evil of society all through agricultural time and continued in modern industrial time. Pimps, semiprofessional entrepreneurs in this business, often abuse women who ended up in this occupation. These women can also be a risky exposure for sexually transmitted diseases. HIV infection has killed millions of young males, females and their children since it was first discovered in 1981. Modern society discourages such temporary sexual connections and has made the business of prostitution illegal.

(1421) It still should be noted that when prostitution is legalized, medically supervised and the prostitutes are paid according to their market value, the involved women are not abused and will make a good and secure living for themselves in the adult, mutual agreed sexual exchange. It is only when prostitution is illegal that women are abused.

(1422) Prostitution is legal in Nevada and in Holland and has not caused any social problems there. Prostitution was legal in San Francisco in the early 1900s. An early madam with a popular bordello on Pine Street retired as elected Mayor in Sausalito, a sign of the respect she accumulated from her earlier business.

(1423) In our modern society, the early animal urge for sex has to be controlled with social or religious rules. The transit period from puberty to family maturity for both males and females needs to be prepared for adult family life with sexual education, addressing the birth control, the moral responsibility for childbearing, and the risk for disease in occasional sexual encounters. Such sexual education may come from their families but should also be covered as a part of early public education in schools.

## Female Versus Male Role in Society

(1424) During the tribal time, males and females were both important partners in caring for the family. Females, despite their menstruation, pregnancy and childcare responsibilities, collected 70% of the calories. Males stood for hunt and security. The female's family influence was intimate and essentially on level with her male life partner. Lifetime for both sexes was short, often no more than 30 years for most males and females.

(1425) During agriculture time, the work of the ground required heavy metal tools. Men had to make these tools and do the heavy work on the farm. We are now entering the first Bronze Age from -3500 through -1000, followed by the Iron Period (-1000 through -700.)

(1426) Agriculture produced a surplus of food. The owner of the ground and its surplus made it possible for the male property owner/farmer to build a nicer, stationary shelter. A rich male farm-property-ownership evolved. The owner/farmer hired male workers for the fieldwork, male soldiers for its defense, and employed extra female workers for his large household.

(1427) He, the property owner/farmer, became a political heavyweight. He set the social and religious rules. The transcendent, religious creator became a male image and the most successful farmer became an anointed king. Originally the anointed king was a successful farmer who conquered, controlled and defended a big part of the farmland. The anointed king usually passed his land to his immediate family.

(1428) All through agricultural time the female usually played a small, if any, political role in the society. In the earliest and highly populated agricultural areas the landowner could own many women and really women became a property of the landowner.

(1429) The married male landowner imitated the sexual behavior of the in-herd-living animal. The religious rules evolved into a multi-wife society. Both early Veda/Brahma/Hinduism and the religions derived from Abraham, the early Judaism, Christianity and Islam had many wives or concubines. This patriarchal picture of society was typical for Middle East, Far East, Japan and the Americas for at least 6000 years of agricultural time. Salomon in Jerusalem was supposed to have 700 wives and 399 concubines and, in the 1400s when the Portuguese arrived on the West Coast of India, the local king was said to have 1000 wives. The king kept the pretty wives from his harem to give birth to many children in his image; the not-so-pretty ones were employed as housemaids. The unmarried males and the widows were left out in the cold and had to take up prostitution or homosexual relationships.

(1430) In the first part of the book it was suggested to divide history into three cultural periods, each one depending on the three ways of food transport: hand, cart and machine transport. The three-part division of the feminine rights through history parallels and supports the three-part cultural division of history. The female had equal rights to the man during the long tribal time, no rights during agricultural time, and is now winning back her equality during industrial time.

(1431) So far this has been a generic review of the social history of sexuality. The purpose of this addition to the Nine Pillars of History is to examine how each religious culture is coping with present transition from agricultural to industrial time. The movement is worldwide. It touches on flock or tribal memberships of the male.

## Flock or Tribe Member

(1432) With human's richer ability to communicate they formed tribal societies with an intellectual dimension, a "transcendent connection" between individuals and tribal life. This was different from other in group-living animals. This human transcendence involved different areas of the society with three areas of tribal life noteworthy in this context:

(1433) First, it evolved into a long lasting, individual relationship between two humans with an exclusive, sexually and emotionally expressed bond, in other words, into a Promise for Love and lifelong mutual support between a male and a female.

(1434) Second, it evolved into a relationship between members of the tribe, a Group-Morality with a group-subconscious experience eventually perceived and formulated as the "Golden Rule."

(1435) Third, man's dependence on nature and its powers led to a ritualistic relationship between man and the "creator" of man's world. The spiritual connection between an individual and his creator had reality only on the human side. The material world of humans communicated with god's transcendental world through mythological stories, rites and pictures relayed by the religious leaders. Words describing rites and symbolic material expressed this transcendental concept and became spiritual words or thoughts. A prayer focused towards a picture, a statue or a stone became a holy connection between the one who prayed and what the stone or the picture symbolized.

(1436) A ritual tradition was eventually written down in mid-agricultural time, first some 5000 years ago. The text became canonized and formed the social background to our different religious cultures.

(1437) Our family tradition communicated with religion and created a transcendental, moral "eternal life", mimicking the life around us. According to the religious knowledge of the time the communication was basically a hope for the best chance for survival for the tribe and the individual tribal member. The spiritual text describing this transcendental spiritual connection was based on the common community knowledge at the time. If no new knowledge entered society, this same connection could last for a long time, thousands of years. In modern time new knowledge is spreading fast through social media and the Internet. New knowledge has a very large public. Some Sumeric countries are hindering knowledge to spread.

(1438) We are entering the conflict area between the natural maturing process of the sexual organs with its male animal's instinct of hoarding females and the male's maturing process into a responsible member of the tribal society. The male had to mature within a transcendental connection between him and his selected female partner, that is, to develop a lifetime partnership based on love, but also to mature as a partner with the social consciousness of the multi-couple-society.

(1439) The early animal urge for sex had to be controlled with social and/or religious rules. This transit period from puberty to family maturity for both male and females had to be prepared with sexual education, addressing the birth control, the moral responsibility for child bearing and the risk for disease in occasional sex encounters. Such sexual education came primarily from the church and the family but is nowadays also covered as part of education in public schools, at least in industrialized, democratic nations.

(1440) Public education has been in the hands of different church organizations during much of history. The church set the moral code in general but also specifically for sexuality. This led to different local cultures all through agricultural time. The old agricultural traditions are still strong in many areas of the world.

(1441) How individuals experience transcendental rites was, and is, many times dependent on education. Buddha, with his message of an Educated Reality, was one of the first to break away from the very ritualistic Hinduism. The modern, educated society has in the same way often personalized its religious experience and distanced itself from religious, ritualistic extremism.

(1442) In tribal life, where the world was very small and local, social life was fairly simple; most was community owned, most of the people knew each other and forgiveness usually smoothed over most conflicts because the Golden Rule was the unwritten law. Life during agricultural and industrial time was, and usually is, much more complicated.

(1443) The agricultural time was typically patriarchal. The women played politically subordinated roles, no matter which religion dominated the society. This part of history is rather stationary from the standpoint of female rights.

(1444) A real and major change in the patriarchal society began when society entered the industrial time. Women were given back their personal, non-sexual identities. This did not happen quickly or easily. In the beginning of the industrialization period, women together with men, who were replaced by farm machinery, made up a pool of cheap labor. The more of them that were competing for jobs in the cities, the less they were paid, women and children the least.

(1445) Factories sprang up quickly. An acute need for energy to power the machines replaced manpower. Coal miners in England challenged this elimination of jobs and organized a strike in the 1800s. Other labor unions followed the example and showed the strength of community support, the "Sixth Pillar" need. Organized labor in Scandinavian and Anglo-Saxon countries started political labor parties. This eventually led to voting and property rights, first for men and later, through the suffrage movement, for women. Permanent voting rights without income modification for women were first instituted in Sweden in 1909, the USA in 1920, and England in 1928. The female would slowly regain her non-sexual individuality and become a politically equal partner to men in society. This feminism movement is now slowly consolidating its power within the modern society and spreading to other parts of the world. Women hold very responsible positions in government and the private sector today. Iceland and Finland have had female presidents, Norway and

England have had female prime ministers and USA had a female presidential candidate at the time of this writing.

(1446) The modern feminine movement strives to give the women the identity they had during the 190,000-year-long tribal time but lost during the 9800-year-long patriarchal agricultural time and is now recovering in the only 200 year-old modern industrial time.

(1447) The sexual urge of young males has, for many centuries, caused a major social complication in teenage pregnancies. The social stigma of such an event created lifetime hardships for the girl or fed an illegal abortion business that could cause death for the girl. Sweden was early in addressing this social problem. During the early 1950s Sweden started a state supported youth and school education program for birth control. The social government considered teenage pregnancies essentially as a social disease. Abortion could be offered if two doctors and a social worker agreed that the girl was exposed to social hardship.

(1448) The birth control pill was invented in about this time. Together, easy access to birth control and general sex education had an unexpected consequence: a casual attitude toward sexual activity. Pornographic literature flooded the market. Sexual freedom spread to Europe and USA and the divorce rate increased to end at least 50% of all marriages. This sexual revolution happened while I was growing up and going to medical school in Sweden and the United States. The Vietnam War was waged with a conscripted military force. Young people talked about what they experienced during the sexual revolution and their chance of being drafted. This affected everybody young—male or female. Many demonstrated against the war in Vietnam: "Make love, not war." The Vietnam War also greatly expanded the drug culture by the military forces becoming involved in the use of drugs and by the "hippies" using drugs as another weapon against the "establishment." The economical reality of it was that pornography and drug usage explored the sex drive of young males to such a degree that many young people felt no responsibility for the duty that males and females always have had to each other, to their children and to society.

(1449) Both males and females need to be educated about their sexual maturing process. This education needs to be addressed differently depending of the age of the child, but needs to started early in life, addressing each step in their maturing process appropriately. Children will mature very quickly with their access to the Internet. Starting a very close and open communication between parents and their children has to be the platform from which to build family security. Parents in every neighborhood may need to form a "tribe" to support each other. The neighborhood needs to help young people to build bonds safely.

(1450) So far this has been a physiological and anthropological review of the history of sexuality. The purpose of this addition to *The Nine Pillars of History* is to examine how each religious culture has been, and is, coping with the present transition from agricultural to industrial time. The movement is worldwide. It touches on different agendas: social, economical and religious. Even within each cultural society the changes may need to move at different speed, depending on the educational background of the general population.

(1451) The culture derived from each of the five world religions has had to mediate the eagerness for the human male to have sex and the female to enjoy her sex but still maintain control over her number of pregnancies and the moral maturing process of their children within the society.

## Veda/Brahma/Hinduism

(1452) Veda/Brahma/Hinduism is the oldest of the five religious cultures and offers some unique aspects to the history of femininity and sexuality. Its dogma originated from its oral Arian tradition and was written down in the old Veda books as well as in the large religious literature that followed over time. Without a unifying prophet, important cultural influences came from the Buddha movement for 1300 years, from the 1000 years of Islamic occupation (800-1850) and from the last 100 years of English occupation until India's independence in 1947.

(1453) In India a few Hindu traditions set it apart. Before independence and democracy female education was of very low priority. A family Hindu-man believed that he could not reach Nirvana unless he had a son. This belief is probably based on the agrarian heritage as noted in the introduction above and has had enormous social consequences. Marriage was, and often still is, arranged by the adult parents in order to secure parent's own old age and a continuity of the family fortune.

(1454) The security bond in ownership of farmland dominated agrarian culture before the industrial time. A girl was married at an early age and lived with her future in-laws. She would be of no value until she had produced a son. Sex for procreation rather than for transcendental love dominated prearranged marriages. A multi-wife society evolved with low individual female esteem. The Shiva sect even worships statues of the penis itself, as it stands surrounded by vaginal lips.

(1455) A feminine movement is a modern European idea within the independent, democratic India. It has strived for female-general and female-specific sex education and might eventually lead to true equality between the two sexes. With a very old belief system and traditions to overcome it might require time and financial efforts before females within Hinduism in India have equal rights to their male partners.

## Buddhism

(1456) Buddha, living in the -500s, reacted to the Hindu tradition of a social caste system and to basic religious acceptance of inherited rights. Buddha offered everyone, including females and untouchables, partnership in his reformation of the Hindu religion. According to Buddha, anyone can reach Reality, Buddha Pure Land, or Nirvana through his four Noble Truths and eight rules to live by.

(1457) Buddha and his followers set up some three hundred rules for a monk organization to spread the message. Buddha was asked to start a similar organization for females. According to historical tradition Buddha himself hesitated but Buddha's mother added a female nun-organization. The nun-movement grew parallel with the monk organization but has always been secondary. The feminine movement still separated Buddhism from Hinduism.

(1458) The Buddhism moral message is non-political and is independent from royal or central secular powers. It spread easily all over East Asia. In modern times Buddhism was eradicated from China when the Chinese Communist Party took over the central power. Just as in the former Soviet Union. The communist dogma did not allow any parallel religious dogma to compete. According to Marx religious dogmas were bourgeois relics. Communistic China, even without Buddhism, has not allowed a feministic movement. Abortions are used as birth control. Central edicts, allowing only one child, to control population growth have resulted in too many males. The scarcity of females and the modern rapid industrialization might lead to specific female, sexual education and eventually to female access to central power.

## Judaism

(1459) The Jews have since the second Diaspora in the year 134 and until the recognition of the independent Israel in 1948 never been part of an independen political power. The relative recognition of the female role is therefore limited to within the church organization. In rabinnical Judaism the female was a secondary citizen separated from the men. In modern time, within reformed Judaism, the old traditions are eliminated and the religious service is very similar to the reformed Christian service. Female in Israel have been serving in the military since the beginning of statehood and have served in many responsible positions including the role of Prime Minister.

## Christianity

(1460) Christianity, as a religion, had to give up political power with the advance of democracy but the patriarchal image of the agrarian culture is still spot wise alive in the industrial Christian culture. The Roman and the Greek Orthodox societies are still preoccupied with the ancient perception that females are "unclean" while having the perfectly normal "excretions" from their sexual organs, the monthly bleeding or a newborn child. The reformed movements within Christianity have left these issues aside but even some 80 years after women's suffrage, females are not always allowed to assume priesthood.

(1461) While these old traditions are changing, the female is rapidly gaining in equality to the male in personal identity. This is expressed in freedom from male domination in the home, workplace and the society. With the freedom has come personal responsibility for her home, her career and political influence. This is slowly being reflected in changing community laws. The purpose of these laws is to secure the female in her home with her children, the Second Historical Pillar.

(1462) One controversial result of the transcendental imagination of humans is the sexual experience by imagination. For the last 500 years, or since the invention of the printer, it has resulted in explicit pornographic mass literature, pornographic pictures, movies and recently in Internet dating and "dirty" talk through computers or phones. The business of pornography rests on the fundamental law of freedom of communication, the Sixth Historical Pillar. This business (in the West) has grown into a very large worldwide enterprise. It markets itself mainly to the to the 15 to 35-year-old male, the one at his peak hoarding age. The movement has to be seen as an immature outlet of the animal sexual instinct. There is a great need for a place or a way for single people to meet safely. In my youth it was music and pairs dancing in the home that brought people together. Dancing is a natural and, if supervised, safe way of meeting the opposite sex ever since tribal time.

# Islam

(1463) The large Arabian Empire, which thrived between 600 and 1600, declined during the following centuries. At its peak, the empire stretched from West Africa to East India. At that time, it was a too large to keep under central political control but the Muslim culture remained strong within this large area.

(1464) Islam is the only religion that maintains a close bond to the secular, political powers and may even dominate them. Traditional madrasahs (religious schools) have continued to educate young boys. Young males were taught Arabic in order to understand and read the Quran and many learned the text by heart. The Quran text was, and still can be, the sole male education or even the only formal education available to the general population outside the home. Islamic religious reading provided a common transcendental focus on the holy Ka'bah stone in Mecca. This gave a sense of religious, cultural unity for the whole area.

(1465) The canonization of the curia and the canonization of the Quran took place together with Christanity in parallel medieval time. They were both competing with each other for control over souls and taxes and expressed this in their laws by making defections from their own religion a mortal sin.

(1466) Islamic leaders wrote the books of Hadith in order to organize social traditions and the Sharia law to enforce them. The 40th Hadith is the first text that refers to the Golden-Rule-concept. Quran, Hadith and the Sharia Law together set the base for the very selective Muslim culture. Mohammed from the very beginning stressed the discipline within Islam. He gave his movement the name "Islam" actually meaning submit. The society has indeed remained a very selective and closed society, once a Muslim, always a Muslim with the rest of society all heathen.

(1467) The Muslim culture by itself rested on the early agrarian culture inherited from Abraham or, in other words, was a patriarchal tradition with the perception of the female as unclean during her natural "excretions" of childbirth and menstruation. The original sexual instinct of hoarding and marking the females as theirs was also present within all the social rules. Socially, women could be horded, and were not allowed to show any skin or secondary sexual signs outside the home. This was a very definite way of marking the female as spoken for.

(1468) Mohammed had nine wives but advised his followers to limit themselves to four, provided each wife had her own living quarters. These rules were modified for those who could afford it. Kings could have hundreds, if not thousands. The Quran does not allow homosexuality or prostitution. The female hoarding created a lack of females and opened a need for female enterprise located at the edge of towns or at the border of the country.

(1469) The Quran, Hadith and the Sharia law created a close agrarian society for 1500 years. In the 1920s, the technically attuned West came knocking on the door and discovered oil. Oil is one of the basic pillars, the one for survival from energy. Suddenly, there was an influx of both money and new ideas from the industrial West. The clash went particularly deep when it touched on modern education of women. Here is where we are today with the Al-Quada and the Taliban jihad movement clinging to the old times and clashing with the West.

(1470) With a Golden Rule only refered to in the Hadith various Muslim societies have destroyed each other's holy temples and even killed each other for 1500 years. In present days some parts of Africa's entire social structure is fallen apart. Some of the worst experiences of human history are repeating themselves today with Islamic religious extremists attacking democratic countries with terror.

## Conclusion

(1471) The Nine Pillars of History offers common denominators for the analysis of the powers that drive society. This insight hopefully offers possibility for a better understanding between different cultures. The eternal Golden Rule: Always treat others, as you like others to treat you" is the keystone for any social life.

(1472) After this historical and religious review I am compelled to recognize Jesus Christ as the first human who, through his life, exemplified the Golden Rule. Jesus bridges social history together with his spiritual belief and points to Our Heavenly Father as its origin.

(1473) **Is the Golden Rule the keystone for all religions and social lives to reach eternal peace?**

## An Alternative Way of Presenting the Manuscript

(1474) Knowing what we now know of the Nine Historical Pillars and looking back through the manuscript offers another way of presenting this review. We could have started with the animal instinct of propagation, it being as old as hunger. To this was added the transcendental dimension of life that followed the ability to speak. The ability to talk during the Hunting and Gathering era evolved into the bond between a male and a female, a bond between tribe members based on the Golden Rule and a bond to a higher power of Nature, a religion. Socially each tribal member became an equal part in the common decisions, the beginning of democracy.

(1475) Starting with agricultural time the physically strong male came to dominate social life. The richest farmer became a king, who still had a transcendental connection with Nature's higher powers. He made use of this connection to dogmatically dominate land and people, including his female partner. Ten thousand years of wars followed.

(1476) With the start of the industrial time followed an acute need for workers and energy. Each one of these evolved into independent powers that are trying to dogmatically control present societies. China is bonding with dogmatic communism for control of its population and the Arabic oil cartel is bonding with the dogmatic religion of Islam. Both movements can be intreperted as threats to their neighbors. Dogmatism remains a global destabilization factor, as it has been for 10,000 years.

# References

(1477) *The Second Sex* by Simone De Beauvoir, Bantham Books 1952.

(1478) *Hinduism, Past and Present* by Axel Michaels, Princeton University Press, 2002, ISBN 0-691-08952-3.

(1479) *Buddhism, Sexuality and Gender*, edited by Jose Ignatio Cabezon, State University of New York Press, 1992, ISBN 0-79144-0757-8.

(1480) *The Changing Nature of Man* by J.H. van den Berg, Delta Book, 1961.

(1481) *The History of Sexuality, Volume I* by Michel Foucault, Vintage Books, ISBN 0-679-72469-9.

(1482) *Making Sex* by Thomas Laqueur, Harvard University Press, 1990, ISBN 0-674-54349-1.

(1483) *Women in World Religions, Volume VI*, Executive Editors, Arvind Sharma and Katherine K. Young, State University of New York Press, 2002, ISBN 0-7914-5426-6.

(1484) *They Two Shall Be One* by Susan Dowell, Collins Publishing Group, 1990.

(1485) *The History of Prostitution* by William W. Sanger, M.G. Fredonia Books, 2002, ISBN 1 -58963-762-3.

(1486) *The Private Life of Chairman Mao* by Dr. Li Zhisui, Random House, 1994, ISBN 0-679-40035-4.

# E. Economics

# Introduction

(1487) To start with, I should emphasize that opinions and conclusions expressed here are of my own as drawn from my understanding of the Nine Pillars of History. As examples, I draw some of my conclusions from my experiences as a farmer, a physician, and a retired citizen from past activity in both Sweden and the U.S.

(1488) In pursuing the subject of the Nine Pillars of History our book now covers five major branches of academia: medicine, history, anthropology, religion, and finally economics. I have found that these five branches of academia exchange very little knowledge among them despite that they all touch on man's basic needs for survival and security. My hope is that *The Nine Pillars of History* will bridge each of these academic branches for the good of humanity.

(1489) No matter which social or economic theory is the basis for a nation's political and economic policy, I am sure that all have in mind the citizen's need for security from the Nine Pillars of History. It is the hope that the following historical analysis will be of some guidance.

(1490) I know I am repeating much of what I say under each pillar need because everything is coming together under the all-encompassing economy of society. *The economy is indeed the common facilitator of the Nine Pillars of History.* (Erickson)

(1491) Because of my background in the economies of Sweden and the U.S., Professor James Sheehan suggested that I compare the Swedish economy, and specifically its medical delivery system, with that in the USA. Sweden has had a national health delivery system for some 50 years. The U.S. is presently in the process of implimenting a national medical delivery system. Medical access is the Eighth Historical Pillar and therefore has given consequences. I will discuss how these consequences will affect the medical delivery in Sweden and the U.S. and actually the whole societies of both countries.

(1492) Like all professional literature, economics has its professional vocabulary. The websites of the journals *The Economist* and *Forbes* have an extensive list of definitions of economy:

(1493) economist.com/research/economics

(1494) forbes.com/tools/glossary/index.jhtml

## Historical Background

(1495) In his 2008 book *"The Ascent of Money"* professor Niall Ferguson of Harvard University and Stanford Hoover institute reviewed the historical evolution of present day economy. I will just narrate what I need in order to prove the relationship of the Nine Pillars of History to economics.

(1496)  The Ninth Historical Pillar, the one for free trade, started in tribal time as an effort to improve the security of life and the pursuit of happiness of family and tribal life and has continued until today and will continue forever.

(1497)  The first effort at a formal trade took place in Mesopotamia through contracts written on clay tablets.

(1498)  *A **contract** has three essential ingredients that are the basis for all trades: it rests on a rule of **trust** between two individuals and stands for a **commitment** for an exchange of service or things that is an offer and acceptance of an exchange of value (Ericson) within a given **time**.*

(1499)  The time could be immediate for an exchange of cash or for taking place after some time in the future as stated in the contract. The two parties signing the contract must have trust, or credentials, in each other to fulfill the agreement of the contract. The word "credentials" is derived from the Latin word *credo* that actually means believable.

(1500)  These rules for contracts stand for the very first clay contracts in Mesopotamia 5000 years ago as well as for present day paper and now often paperless trades.

(1501)  The oldest archeology find of coins is from islands outside Greece and are from the -600s. The practical value of coins was that they represented a transportable value that still could be traded even if the place for the trade was changed. Coins were made of the most indestructible metal, gold, silver or copper. For a long time in history the amount of gold, silver and copper in a nation's treasury represented its total cash inventory for trade.

(1502)  Before the 1500s, Europe was always hungry for the basic metals to mint coins. Those in control of minting coins, usually royalty, would use all kind of tricks to dilute the metal to serve their agenda. Royal neighbors would often have some very flimsy excuses to raid their neighbor's treasury of coin metal.

(1503) **The first sudden and large expansion of this "gold standard" was Spain's discovery of Peru and its Potosi Mine.** Philip II, the Spanish ruler in the late 1500s had his conquistadores ship tons of gold and silver to Europe.

(1504) The gold would enter the European market through Philip's preoccupation with Roman Catholic missionary. Holland and England were pirating Philip's ships loaded with silver and gold. Philip saw with envy on the rich trade that went on in Holland at the river openings into the continent. He declared war on Holland and England. His official reason was to subdue the Protestants for their religious belief but at the same time he was eager to collect and take over their treasury and collect their taxes. He might have thought that he was taking back what was originally stolen from him. Any way, the sudden influx of much Peruvian gold and silver had started the first major food price inflation since Roman time. The price of food increased sevenfold in the 1500s and at the same time made the "standard" for gold no longer a standard but a negotiated exchange and a floating value.

(1505) An Italian from Pisa, Leonardo Fibonacci, had made himself familiar with the originally Hindu/Arab numerals. The Arabs conquered the Indian Subcontinent and saw the system in use. The Arabs took the system home to Baghdad, the Arab intellectual center at the end of the first millennium. **Fibonacci recognized the advantages in the system and published his book *Liber Abaci* in 1202. The system allowed easy calculation of fractions. This meant one could calculate the interest on capital, important for the local, budding banking business in Italy.** The Roman numerals retired to keeping track of the order of inherited royalty.

(1506) **A major enlargement of a nation's cash base, independent from its inventory of gold, was the printing of state bonds that paid interest and was underwritten by the receivers of the interest, the nation's citizens.** The system started in the independent city-states of Italy. The city leaders learned to calculate interest. They all became involved in banking and some became very rich.

(1507) **The citizens of Holland, and later also England, made the system a part of their defense industry. Their bond money proved stronger than Spain's Peruvian gold.** Spain went into insolvency 14 times between 1557 and 1696 and had to come to Holland to resolve its cash problems.

(1508) **North Western Europe's cash inventory outside their gold collection grew and created trading centers in London, Amsterdam and Stockholm.** The Holland bank, the Wisselbank was founded in 1609. It was the first bank to issue modern-time cheques and an inter currency exchange to facilitate easier payments among the many different national mints at the time. All three of these capitals introduced common stocks to form large venture capitals for the purpose of starting their East India Trading Companies.

(1509) **The Swedish national bank, the "Riksbanken," was founded in 1656. It introduced what is now known as *fractional reserve banking*, meaning that part of its deposits was used for loans.** The bank paid interest on its deposits. It received interest on its loans and used a large portion of its deposits to increase its loan business.

(1510) The "Bank of England" was formed in 1694. It was a stock company with government privileges' that is, it was allowed to issue banknotes, a form of government bills to pay for services to the government. The banknotes did not yield interest but could be used as cash deposits in other banks.

(1511) Banknotes and fractional reserve banking enlarged the currency base in the home country, again beyond its gold reserve.

(1512) It can be concluded that:

(1513) *Trust in banks expands the national capital base through facilitating trades. Eventually the trust in banks had to be enforced by regulations.*

(1514) *Trust in banks is an important fundamental in all business transactions.*

(1515) *Trust in stocks and venture capital enlarges the capital base of the country. The value of stocks is independent from that of gold.*

(1516) **Eventually everything has a floating market value that is based on demand.**

(1517) In the 1500s, 1600s and 1700s, France was the dominating country in Western Europe. France had raided Northern Italy with its rich banks and many small German states for their gold. It had also negotiated a tax free, privileged relationship with the Catholic Church and eventually forced the pope to live in Avignon to serve French royal interests.

(1518) The huge French court became a decadent model for all other major courts in Europe. **Slowly the rulers became desperate for cash to keep up their baroque lifestyle and taxed people for just about anything needed to make a paltry living. Eventually during the reign of Louis XVI it would lead to the bloody French revolution in 1789.** Before this tumultuous time, in the early 1700s, a Scott by the name of John Law entered the French court and offered his services to the royal house.

(1519) Mr. Law was the son of a banker and an addicted gambler. He had to flee England because he had killed somebody in a duel for his romantic interest in a married lady. He came to Holland and learned its new banking ideas. Specifically he was inspired by the introduction of modern cheques and the formation of venture capital through stocks. He recognized that a swap in **cash was just an expression for an exchange of trust and might as easily be replaced with a printed banknote.** As an addicted gambler, Mr. Law was not concerned about the trust the banknote represented.

(1520) Mr. Law presented his proposal to the court. King Louis XV was a minor. The Prince of Orleans, the king's uncle, acted as a regent for the king. The financial pressure on the court kept on climbing because no one was eager to give up his or her elaborate lifestyle drawn from the common tax base. After some minor concern of the consequences the "French Royal Bank" with Mr. Law as its president was formed in 1716.

(1521) Working within an autocratic system **Mr. Law soon had a monopoly for printing money and the right to collect all taxes for the state.** Mr. Law, in control of the printing machinery and money distribution, became one of the richest people in the country. Very soon Mr. Law owned prime property, both in Paris and in the countryside. **France, as a nation, entered the old Chinese game of printing paper money. The Chinese had invented paper money in the 900s. Marco Polo visited Kublai Khan in the 1200s. Marco told the stories about how the Emperor of China papered his palaces with gold.**

(1522) Mr. Law was full of ideas for making the king rich. France owned the Louisiana Territory, its colony on the new American continent. Mr. Law proposed to form a stock company to invest in the territory. A new city, named New Orleans for the Prince, would be built with French, German and Swiss pioneers. The income from all the products from Louisiana Territory would be split among the investors.

(1523) Hardly anyone had been to the site for the new city. The site was just a swamp full of sickness-spreading bugs. Soon most of the pioneers were dead or had left. The rumor of a disaster spread to Paris. The investors made a run for the bank. The *Trust* for the bank was broken and a first modern national bust of a financial bubble evolved very fast.

(1524) Mr. Law with his life demonstrated some important facts.

(1525) *Money has to be based on Trust and any form of business without Trust is a bubble.*

(1526) *The weakness with Trust is that it is an intellectual and emotional perception, just like Love and Faith.*

(1527) *The ultimate need for money is security for yourself and your family. The ultimate need for the Nine Pillars of History is also security for yourself and your family. Here the two join together for the same goal. The difference between the two is that the Nine Pillars of History is of lasting value, while the economic concept of value is a floating value, different for different circumstances. In a negotiated trade the market itself determines its value.*

(1528) *The variable value of any trade makes market economy superior to a centrally planned economy.*

(1529) *A centrally planned economy can never in the long run recognize the variability in the market.*

(1530) A master in recognizing the psychology of a boom and bust situation in modern time has been George Soros. Mr.Soros used his insight as an investment possibility and created in a short time one of the world's largest private fortunes. Luckily for the world, George Soros invested part of his fortune in promoting a free and open democratic society in Eastern Europe. His donations to free education contributed much to the fall of the Soviet Union.

(1531) Here I will deviate from the main theme of economy and define three important concepts still pertinent to the economy of a civilized society.

(1532) The three words—*Trust, Love* and *Faith* are based on the transcendental connection between people. By "transcendental" what is meant is "beyond ordinary range of perception," meaning you cannot touch it but there is still a social bond binding people together. Society has introduced enforcements or institutions for each of these transcendental concepts. The enforcement is the glue that holds transcendental connections, and therefore our society together in a civilized way. An economy in a civilized format cannot exist without these enforcements.

## Trust

(1533) Trust applies to contracts between people. Criminal and business laws and a whole profession of lawyers enforce trust-connections between people. It is beyond the purpose of this publication to go into details of laws enforcing trust in contracts. I will only mention one abuse that stands out because of its enormity is the recent case of Mr. Bernard Madoff. Mr. Madoff used to be a director in the Securities and Exchange Commission (SEC), the federal organization given the authority to examine fraud in stock trades! In an uninterrupted 16-year Ponzi scheme, Mr. Madoff swindled his trusting clients of some $80 billion, money set-aside for their secure retirement. His possible involvement of swindling money was pointed out to the SEC organization but his past inside connections saved him from further scrutiny. In dealing with cash people will find all kinds of tricks to cheat the public. The Enron story and their Andersen accounting firm is another such example. **An enforcement organization needs to be *absolutely independent* from the people they examine, both economically and socially.**

# Faith

(1534) Faith is best described as submitting to a higher power as you perceive your higher power to be, a generic religious power-concept beyond a specific religion but morally very close to the Golder Rule of tribal time.

(1535) All religions must be subjugated to the ultimate, fundamental social rule, the Golden Rule: Love your neighbor as yourself. From the standpoint of the *Nine Pillars of History* no religion can claim moral superiority to and power over members of other religions. All religions rest on much younger concepts than the Golden Rule. Religions not committed to the Golden Rule are just warped expressions for personal power grabs. This fact is certainly true for any religion connected to a dogmatically ruling power. The historical review of agricultural time and even spot wise in our modern industrial time confirms the truth for this statement.

(1536) The many social atrocities in our history require further analysis of this social behavior. I will again have to go back to tribal time and analyse thought provoking words in my first language Swedish. Swedish is a language that has evolved itself on the sideline of major cultures. In Swedish there is a compound word "ödmjuk." It is composed of the word "öde" which means destiny and "mjuk" which means soft or gentle. "Ödmjuk" means to be gentle in your destiny. Other Swedish words such as "Stel, Stor and Stark" mean stiff, big and strong. "Stolt" is translated to proud or pride. Pride covers a large spectrum of emotions from socially healthy and accommodating to socially sickly and discriminating. Your pride needs to be controlled by the Golden Rule. If pride causes social abuse such as haughtiness, the Swedes have a pragmatic word for it, "stollig." A "stollig" behavior can characterize political and religious dogmatism that have ended in social atrocities throughout the last 10,000 years.

(1537) Faith is needed for the individual and is indeed a source for comfort to overcome many of life's challenges. By placing one's faith in God or a Higher Power, the individual is allowing faith to control the outcome of daily plans and worries. Thereby faith releases the individual to focus on positive thoughts and emotions. It gives the individual a chance to focus on happiness and the fulfillment and your own future.

## Love

(1538) Love rests on the transcendental bond between two people. Society has introduced different procedures to enforce this social commitment. To make it official all pairs in love have to sign a social contract, a marriage contract, in front of a state official. Up to recent time a marriage was the commitment between two people of opposite sex, mainly for the propagation of the family and ultimately the species. In the marriage procedure the two in love promise to stay faithful to each other in front of their social group so that none present would interfere or try to break their commitment. Lawyers need to mitigate any break-up to assure the safe care of any children of the marriage. If one member of the marriage commitment dies social benefits may continue and assist the surviving part of the family.

(1539) Homosexual partnerships are asking for similar social rights as in traditional marriage. The Golden Rule allows this expansion of the definition of marriage. The Golden Rule relies on the transcendental bond between two humans indifferent of their sex.

(1540) Our brain is the result of the human evolution from reptiles through apes to modern Homo sapiens living by the Golden Rule. In its evolutionary wake the brain still carries with it its reptilian functions. The reptilian portion of our brain is anatomically located in the highest portion of the brainstem. Above this brainstem is the limbic (Latin for border) system and capping the limbic system is the cortex, the gray surface of the brain. One may describe the brain as a big mushroom sitting on a stem, the top of the stem being the limbic system (white) and the gray area, cortex, capping it all. The limbic system contains many emotional, neural and hormonal controls like our sex and eating instincts. Each of these two areas may be subject of compulsive, selfcentered behavior if not controlled with cortical selfmonitoring. Complusive sexual behavior can replace the transcendental bond of love with pornography; compulsive eating behaviors can replace healthy hunger feeling. The prefrontal cortex is the area that contains what we can train and learn. The whole brain, the stem, the white limbic, and the gray cortex are all folded and tightly packed inside the boned skull for protection.

(1541) The connection between the cortical and limbic part of the brain may break down through any number of mindaltering drugs. An addictive breakdown will lead to self-centered social misconduct. Addictive behaviors can lead to any number of social harms from divorce, automobile accidents and ultimately suicide. Addictive behavior can be treated with behavior modification of the prefrontal cortex. The most successful model for this group therapy is the 12-Step program of Alcoholic Anonymous or "AA." The AA model offers a **voluntary** group support program to help the affected to recognize his or her disease. The process only works if the addict or alcoholic participates by admitting that they are powerless in their addiction and that their lives have become unmanageable.

(1542) The format and structure of AA's 12-step program can work for almost all cumpulsive behaviors, such as gambling, sex addiction, food addiction and countless others. Addiction in all its forms is classified as a medical disease by the American Medical Association within Obsessive Complusive Disorders of mental illness.

(1543) The social problems caused by addiction are as old as human society and should not be regulated through law enforcement. In the last 100 years the U.S. has tried to control mind-altering drugs through criminal enforcement. These efforts have been well intentioned. However, unintended consequences has lead to the creation of an illegal blackmarket subculture that has no tax benefits while incarceration of alcoholics and addicts creat huge tax burdens on public budgets. My old friend, Dr. Wesley Alles, the leader of Stanford University's Health Improvement Program, pointed out that a healthy and undisturbed cerebral cortex is the source of empathy and caring for our fellow citizens. All modern democratic nations have welfare programs that provide assistance to citizens. However, federal or national initiatives are often inadequate to meet the needs. These programs are often designed to be partnered with the private sector or a religious based charitable program. Alexis de Tocqueville in his 1835 classic review of the American culture thought that charitable cultures were unique for the newly founded U.S. In today's modern world, many countries look to the U.S. tax code for leadership in developing public/private partnership programs.

Now we can return to the specific history of economics and its specific relationship to the Nine Pillars of History.

## Insurance

(1544) Professor Niall Ferguson of Harvard Univercity and the Hoover Institute of Stanford reviewed the evolution of coins into the banking with bonds, stocks for venture capital and non-cash paper cheques and bills and how they all expanded the cash base of a nation, independent from its gold base. He documented that all forms of money rest on trust. Trust, as shown in our short insert above, needs a non-transcendental assurance; something to be signed on a permanent paper and that can take the place of a contract and that can be enforced by laws if something unexpected interferes. Here we come to the concept of insuring a contract originally based on trust.

(1545) Insurance, as we now know it, started in Scotland with two ministers concerned with what happened to widows of Protestant "priests" (often a generic term for an official of a church). From the 400s Roman Catholic priests were obliged to stay unmarried. The same tradition was also imposed on Greek Orthodox Bishops. Protestant priests from Luther (1500s) and forward were married and had children. With the Catholic tradition in place for some 1300 years, no one had thought of what happened to the widows of Protestant priests. If not independently wealthy the widows of Protestant ministers had nothing to support them. At the time there would be very little social support for widows in general. Widows of ministers would land in the poor house with their children.

(1546) Two Protestant ministers, Robert Wallace and Alexander Webster, joined a good friend, a professor in mathematics, Colin Maclaurin. Together the three of them worked out actuary tables showing the risk for the death each year of a Protestant minister.

(1547) The three men proposed that the Protestant ministers pool a small contribution to form an insurance fund. The fund would be invested with a percentage yield large enough to support eventual protestant widows and their children. This, the first life insurance fund, was born in 1776. The "Scottish Widows Insurance Fund" grew to the largest life insurance company of the country and became a model for life insurance companies in all of England and eventually the rest of the world.

(1548) **The generic concept of pooling and dividing the cost for paying for a common risk could be applied to a variety of situations,** such as our risk for sickness and unemployment, the risk for fire and weather damage to our homes, for our cars, property, for our loans and savings in our banks and so on. The insurance business turned out to be highly profitable.

(1549) Insurance funds were later allowed to invest their funds in the stock market. They eventually grew to the largest holders of equities, again enlarging a nation's cash base far beyond its gold storage.

(1550) *From the insurance concept we can conclude that in the psychological eagerness to pursue security, people will create a monetary value that can be transformed and expanded for further build of the Nine Pillars of History.*

(1551) The same technique can be expanded to cover national disasters like the Katrina storm in US in August of 2005. With tax credits for citizens living in exposed areas, such insurance funds would grow very fast to cover the cost for recovery provided politicians would agree to let the fund remain politically independent and untouched.

(1552) The same technique could also apply to insurance for farmers' harvests. It would require many small farmers to come together and pool their resources. Right now the government takes the farmers' income and allows some of their taxes to come back as low-interest disaster relief loans. For the farmers it may be cheaper to keep their tax credit and to build a fund for their own risk assessment. (This is just a farmer-to-farmer remark.)

(1553) The same technique can also be used to insure local banks instead of having the Federal Government insure them.

(1554) We have so far seen how a nation's value base could expand beyond its collection of gold, thanks to the expansion of its "trust base." Can a nation's trust base run out of resource? **Here we come to another economic concept as old as agriculture, the "Tragedy of Commons."**

(1555) The Tragedy of Commons was first experienced in farming in ancient time when the Commons was grazed down to bare ground by sheep, with no grass left for tribe members owning other animals. The Tragedy of Commons may lead to enormous tragedies like:

(1556) *For the large oceans that nobody owns: depletion from over-fishing and pollution from waste dumping.*

(1557) *For the underground Commons aquifer: the California Imperial Valley has sunk 10 feet from the over draft use and made its remaining ground water too salty for people to drink and food to be produced.*

(1558) *For air: the Los Angeles basin has become so populated and polluted that people have trouble breathing and seeing. This is true for many large metropolises all over the world.*

(1559) All these disasters are examples of what happens when everybody owns the Commons, but nobody steps up to the responsibility for the Commons.

(1560) Investments into the Commons will require a getting together for the common good. This is difficult with the Commons reaching into many different interests.

(1561) A nation's defense is a Commons. Defense is also a part of the Sixth Historical Pillar for community support and is crucial to a nation's survival. Any contracts to the Commons have to be submitted in competition with proposals from other contracts or the cost would be unlimited. The same is true for contracts to a state's Commons for transportation, roads and bridges. Some expenses to the Commons are so out of this world that nobody could or would know the cost. In such cases the contract has to be so called "cost plus a service fee." Many of the space program contracts have been this type.

(1562) Here we must ask ourselves: *Is not the total tax-base just a Commons and therefore subject to the tragedy of the Commons if not controlled by competition in bids for services from the Commons?*

(1563) **I have come to realize that the concept of the "Commons" has a very long and important history.**

(1564) *From my experience in reviewing history I have learned that what many own, nobody owns. The Commons has two sides, one side that is good for everybody and one side that may be abused for special interests. The good side is the creation of a community infrastructure. The bad side is what economists call "Tragedy of the Commons." The tragedy is that those in administrative power together with their service people may use their inside positions for personal gains. This is true for the administration of:*

(1565) *1) Countries.*

(1566) *2) Corporations.*

(1567) *3) Cooperatives.*

(1568) 1) In regard to countries, we have all experienced how personalized agenda in all the dogmatically controlled countries has led to war or economic disasters for the general population. We showed this in our review of political history. Abusive leadership started at the end of the first millennium with a feudal system and culminated in the 1700s with the baroque courts of Louis-kings in France. It ended when people took charge of the tax base in the People's Revolution first in England 1689, and 100 years later in the French Revolution 1789. The charismatic Napoleon declared himself a man of the people and made himself emperor with dogmatic power over the tax base. Napoleon built the world's largest army and caused the world's largest disaster until then. Hitler successfully doubled Napoleon's deed. Having reviewed world history I believe I can justify a sweeping statement:

(1569) *Ten thousand years of wars during agricultural time was actually due to the Tragedy of the Commons.*

(1570) The history of the Commons also has a successful side. (The Commons in this contest is spelled with capital C and with an s on its tail.) In democratic countries representatives from the people come to the Commons tax capital and through voting decide how they will spend their Commons tax-base for infrastructure for the Commons' good. Service people have to bid for building this infrastructure in competition with other bidders in order to determine a **realistic** price.

(1571) **A special category is employees and politicians paid within the Commons. Their pay and benefits can only be controlled through negotiations.**

(1572) **2)** In regard to corporations, its stocks, if very large can be seen as a Commons. We have all recently experienced how banks and their executives abused their close and unregulated relationship with rent-money to pocket large salaries and bonuses despite disastrous and irresponsible leadership. Uncontrolled money accumulation caused the world's second largest economic contraction in 2007.

(1573) **The purpose of banks is to facilitate risk, not to use their deposits to participate in risk-taking. Mr. Paul Volcker, retired Chairman of the U.S. Federal Reserve Bank, commented in 2007 in the *Wall Street Journal* on banks having their own derivative investment enterprises. Mr. Volcker noted that banks as derivative investors did not create work or, on our terms, access to the Nine Pillar-needs for society.** Derivative investments are always very large but create only capital in-transit, or so called "rent" money. Rent capital was not up till 2007 regulated. Some bank executives in control of the distribution from deposits and using deposits for investment in rent capital are in a tempting but also dangerous conflict of common interest. The bank's reserve can only cover so many risky loans.

(1574) The founder of the large investment group, The Vanguard Group, John C. Bogle, reviewed trends in fiduciary responsibilities of leaders in finance and industry in the *Wall Street Journal* from January 19, 2010. Mr. Bogle noted that in 1980 executive pay used to be about 40 times the average worker pay; it was now closing in on 400 times that pay in a typical U.S. corporation.

(1575) 3) Cooperatives are marketing organizations that are started and financed by participating farmers, using the farmers' credit and cash. In offering an economy of scale cooperatives are servicing the family farm in processing its commodities on a large scale, reaching national and even global markets and offering lower prices for the benefit of everybody.

(1576) Cooperatives leadership constitutes a Commons that has the potential to be abused. It is very important that the board of such organizations understand the workings of economy and not jeopardizing the organization.

(1577) Sweden submitted its cost for access to medicine to the Commons' tax-base in the 1950s. With union organization traditionally very strong in Sweden, all workers within health delivery, including doctors, organized and required work contracts corresponding to work contracts for industrial labor.

(1578) Health workers work 24/7 shifts and require a very large work pool. Sweden opened two more medical schools and besides allowed for many immigrants to work in the health industry. All this is to meet the need of the Eighth Historical Pillar but different pillar need had to compete with access to medicine from their tax-based support.

(1579) The first to let go from the tax-based support was the state church. The Lutheran Church had been an integral part of the government since the reformation in the 1500s. The church was let go in the year 2000. Today the cost for defense is under scrutiny. This can be dangerous gambling for a small country.

(1580) Milton Friedman, with his wife Rose D. Friedman, formed the most respected and influential economist team in modern time. Milton Friedman was honored with the Nobel Prize in Economy in 1976. Dr. Friedman first demonstrated his practical solutions as an adviser to Chile in the 1990s. Chile became a model for many modern national economies, among others, Sweden's.

(1581) Dr. Friedman addressed and defined the thousand-year-old observation of inflation as due to a government's policy to turn debt into cash too fast thereby flooding the market with printed cash and causing prices to rise.

(1582) Tax revenue and GNP are always changing but the speed of change needs to be similar and in the same direction according to Dr. Friedman.

(1583) If the GNP is not growing in pace with government obligations, such as commitments for salaries, pensions, social programs, defense and infrastructures, the deficit has to be covered with printed bills or treasury bonds. When governments do this without supporting its loan commitments, then a lot of loose, non-backed cash bills enter the home market. **Loosely printed non-backed money results in price inflation.**

(1584) The right way for cash to enter the market is by offering treasury bonds to an open, international market and for the country to show it is committed to pay the interest the nation has in its bonds. This will demonstrate that the country is serious to maintain trust in its economy.

(1585) The buyer of a state bond will look at the credit record of the bondholder, in this case the state, how well he/she can *trust* being paid the interest within the stipulated time.

(1586) There are short-term and long-term bonds. For long-term bonds the buyer must be assured that the buy-value of the bond and its interest is not eaten up by inflation. The interest on these bonds may need to be higher than on the short-term bonds. The interest on a nation's ten-year bond is considered nominal. The ten-year bond interest rate indicates the risk premium for the nation's inflation rate.

(1587) In all financial transactions timing is critical because values are always floating or changing. Timing is particularly critical during inflation because the buying power of the currency is declining unusually fast.

(1588) During inflation there are winners and losers. The winners are the people with income adjusting for inflation. The winners tend to be labor unions, particularly within state enterprises, and state employees who often sit close to policymakers and money distributors. When they have bought something with lasting value, like a home, and pay with a loan with locked-in interest, the loan is paid off with ease with their increased income from the inflation. On the other hand, the people living off a locked-in income, such as pensions or from an income not adjusted for inflation, will have a harder and harder time making a living. Their buy-value off the pension will decrease. Those who have loans with variable interest will of course have trouble with the increased payments for their loans changing.

(1589) There is another economic term in connection with inflation and that is "hyperinflation." Hyperinflation happens when governments purposely decide to flood the market with cash and prices increase with double or even triple rate inflation without corresponding growth in the Gross Domestic Product of the country, its GNP. In recent history the Weimar Government in Germany introduced hyperinflation after World War I in order to clean up Germany's war debts, in Russia/Soviet Union in order to clean up the debt left by the communists, and in Argentina in 1990 to clean up after President Peron's unlimited salary spirals. In each case the government had to declare bankruptcy and start over with a new currency, locked to an international standard like the dollar. Hyperinflation is very hard on a public that does not sit close to something of real value or have access to real money. Their saved economical efforts can disappear in a blink of an eye.

(1590) The international monetary standard used to be gold but modern markets are so large there is not enough gold to represent its values. **In 1924 the economist John Maynard Keynes declared the gold standard as a relic.** Gold still has an intrinsic value but not as a currency standard.

(1591) President Roosevelt took the U.S. dollar off from the gold standard in 1933. The Europeans within EU have started what they called ERM, an Exchange Rate Mechanism, or an interest-band outside which they would not allow their different currencies to vary. This would eventually lead to the creation of the euro currency in the year 2000. The euro has since become one of the international standards.

(1592) The euro would not be linked to gold or to the dollar. The European currencies would link together in the euro. The German mark came to dominate the euro because its national bank kept the interest on its bond higher than the bonds of the other currencies and actually, some of the EU-nations have used the lack of control of the ERM to print money. This has caused present concern about the EU sustainability.

(1593) Sweden was never able to join the ERM because of its earlier salary spirals. Sweden was afraid that joining euro base would cause its GNP products to become too expensive.

(1594) A salary spiral from the agenda of a specific political party can cause the production cost to climb so that nobody wants to buy the nation's products. This can be one cause of unemployment. To avoid political control of the national interest rate, nations place the control of their basic national interest rate in the hands of an agency that is totally independent from the winds of national political agendas. In the U.S., the Federal Reserve Bank controls the interest rate solely on how well the U.S. can sell its bonds on the international market.

(1595) Local banks borrow from larger national and international banks. The interest on these inter-bank national loans is set daily in what is called LIBOR market (London Interbank Offered Rate). The large banks lend to governments by buying government bonds. Governments set the interest on their loans through the interest it has to pay for selling its bonds on the open international LIBOR market.

Here the *Trust* of the whole world regulates the individual nation's bond rate. It is an interesting note to history that even the LIBOR market was recently (2012), subject for fraudulent manipulation. One of its trusties had used his personal influence for personal gain.

(1596) Deflation is the condition when price declines such that people refuse to sell or invest in their businesses. This will cause unemployment. Unemployment will be a rising cost to the national tax base and is the ultimate bottom for any economy.

(1597) Another cause of unemployment is credit contraction or when banks with poor judgment have lent money so that their own credibility comes into question. This is what happened in the U.S. and led to the bank crash of 2008. Here people were still willing to work, buy products and invest, but banks had lost trust in fellow banks. None were willing to lend to other banks, not knowing how many NINJA (no income, no job, no assets) loans the bank had on their books. This revealed another conflict of interest: the connection of a rating agency for loans at banks and insurance companies. Further extension of this subject is beyond the purpose of this book and I refer the reader to *All the Devils Are Here: The Hidden History of the Financial Crisis* (Bethany McLean, Joe Nocera, 2010, Portfolio/ Penguin).

(1598) President Obama and his economic team acted very decisively and sold large sums of U.S. bonds to the international market. The U.S. treasury collected a lot of cash and helped banks with their book value so banks could again start lending money and avoid unemployment. People were still willing to work both within government and the private sector. With people working they would be shopping and wheels would start turning again.

(1599) Thanks to the rapid response of the chairman of the Federal Reserve Bank the impact of this 2007-2008 contraction may not be as deep and long lasting as the one in the 1930s. At that time 89% of the equity market value went up in smoke and unemployment went up to 20% and lasted until World War II.

(1600) Federal Reserve Chairman Ben Bernanke had studied the mistake of holding back cash infusion in the 1930s. Mr. Bernanke was determined not to repeat the mistake. Still, at the time of this writing, the unemployment in the U.S. is now about 5%. (2016) Within EU in some member countries unemployment at least double that; in Greese unemployment is 40% and on the boarder of bankrupsy. In fact the whole of Euro may break up. President Obama is this weeek talking to and defending the Euro concept. (March 2016)

(1601) Here we come to a fundamental creation of the modern time economics, the global society. We have large geographical distances between producers of products and buyers of the same products. Indeed distances between sellers and producers are global.

(1602) ***Worker-need for security rests globally on their pursuits for the Nine Historical Pillars. We have to act accordingly. Neither the basic need for the Nine Historical Pillars nor the control of environment have any national borders.***

(1603) People worry that the large cash infusion from the 2009 into the Recovery and Reinvestment Act into the U.S. economy may cause inflation in addition to unemployment.

(1604) One good thing is that both the value of the dollar and the euro has been floating with its market-regulated, international trade value. The U.S. has to pay for its acute need for cash to cover pressure in its commitments for Social Security and Medical Care, for involvement in ongoing wars, for the threat from religious terrorists and rogue countries such North Korea and from the social danger of what in the U.S. are illicit drugs. (See also my review of illicit drugs in *Add Years to Your life and Life to Your Years, Part II. Family and Work Environment.* Here I address my experience with drug abuse as a medical director of a large U.S. corporation.)

(1605) The U.S. Government has supported its acute need for cash by selling government bonds on the open market and has thereby not induced inflation in the home market. The major buyers of U.S. bonds have been OPEC countries, China, Japan and the Organization of Petroleum Exporting Countries. These countries will earn interest on their investment and stabilize their currency vs. the dollar.

(1606) The communist government in China does not allow any organized labor unions and thereby controls labor cost. Low labor cost in China replaces the high-energy cost of producing the same product in the U.S. The cheaper labor cost has given China a huge surplus of trade with the U.S. and has thereby secured access to work and salaries for their workers that produce products sold to the U.S. The saving gives China a chance to offer their workers access to more of their Nine Pillar social needs, both from investments in the country's infrastructure and the opportunity for their citizens to pursue their personal Nine Pillar needs. China does not have many of the social networks that unions have achieved in the U.S. Chinese workers can now save for their old age, medical care, and housing or their own Nine Pillar-needs.

(1607) The China investment in U.S. treasuries will secure China's economic future. All evolving economies with cheap labor cost will need to place their surplus cash in some secure government's treasury bonds or stocks. Secure U.S. treasury bonds appear most secure against inflation and political conflicts even in present global political turmoil because of the more than 200+ years of U.S. freedom, democracy, and a strong defense. Certainly China and the U.S. are now dependent on each other. Professor Niall Ferguson has baptized the connection as "Chimerica."

(1608) The ultimate bottom for a modern country is lack of access to work that can be exchanged for our nine-pillar needs. We have already addressed the social safety net necessary to fill this need in democratic countries. We have also to address the over all political forces in spreading this access need. Here some forces have resently become very clear. **Underdeveloped countries don't need handouts; they need access to work and untampered democracy.**

(1609) Communication is key to reach access to work. In order to take part in the global exchange of the nine-pillar need everybody needs to communicate with each other.

(1610) **I suggest using English as the common international language. English has the longest history of democracy, has a common law vocabulary and is already an international language for trade.**

(1611) Another unique situation limited to democratic nations is the relationship between the representative leadership and its beurocratic labour support. The relationship is apt to become very warm and may include some personal agendas with no end in taxing the public. Here I come to the double taxing some streams of capital that passes through lawmaking hands.

(1612) Here I come to the question of taxing work creating situations. Situations that create work serve the workers as well as the work owners. They all live off the same "tribal ground." Worker and work owners should all be taxed as individuals because it is as individuals they commit to the common infrastructure. A company should be left alone and to have free hand to create more work and work situations.

(1613) There are probably some other double tax situations or double fee situations that should be cleaned up. The estate tax in the U.S. comes to mind. Sweden has done away with its estate tax. Estate tax is regarded in Sweden as double taxation.

(1614) After this historical introduction to modern finance we may be ready to address the economics of each specific Nine Pillars of History.

## The First Historical Pillar: Survival— Food, Water, Air, Energy and Sex

(1615) The First Historical Pillar is a collection of five needs that are fundamental for human life but basically independent of society. Individual humans have always come back to fill these needs for themselves to survive. We cannot live without them for more than a very short time. Here, we are talking sometimes of hours, days or maximum weeks.

(1616) **Food:** The basic industry for food is, of course, agriculture. Ever since the beginning of Augustus' time in Rome the farmers' life has been on the borderline of survival and subject to the haphazard agenda of the privileged nobility, who were closer to the rulers or, in modern terms, closer to the connection between government and the administration of corporations.

(1617) A farmers' income is an open book because his per acre income is a published fact. When the price on a commodity goes up all the suppliers or handlers of farm products increase their charges for their services.

(1618) The cost for farming remains steadily high and cash demanding for a full year, while the farmers' income depends on the weather during each year. This uneven risk for the farmers' income always puts the farmer in an "underdog" situation.

(1619) With weather being unpredictable a farmer is never secure of a good harvest. Farmers' insecurity used to keep church collections full. If this year's harvest is destroyed the farmer will have to cover his loss and his cost of living with saved capital for a full year. If he is an orchard farmer and loses his orchard in a storm, he has to cover his living for six years while paying for a new tree planting and waiting for the young orchard to grow back. If his harvest is lumber and he loses his forest in a storm, to a fire or insect infestation, the farmer has to look for another job until his son or daughter has grown up and is able to harvest the forest. A farmer is seldom able to recover from weather disasters by himself. He must always cover his harvest with insurance, if available.

(1620) In 1995 a big storm hit orchards in Northern California. The Federal Government stepped in, hedged the risk and helped the small farmer with low interest loans for replanting, provided he could not get a loan through regular channels. It takes six years to re-grow an orchard. Also a farmer needs food and housing every day.

(1621) In 2005 the Gudrun storm came in over Southern Sweden and blew down much of its hundred-year-old forest. The Swedish Government stepped in. After a six-month long negotiation, the government offered some help. In the meantime some farmers, who had planned to live off their old forest, committed suicide.

(1622) Industrial labor represents 98% of the population in both the U.S. and in Sweden. Many laborers have secured their Nine Pillar needs with union contracts. Industrial workers don't have time to grow food and don't want high food prices. In many industrial countries industrial unions can regulate food prices through their influence over government. Suppliers to the farms from the industrial part of society outnumber the farmer and insure that food prices stay within the inflationary index.

(1623) It is an interesting observation that the greatest threat for labor security in the mature industrialized world, both in the U.S. and Europe with the countries within the Organization for Economic Co-operation and Development (OECD), is communist China that does not allow the formation of labor unions. In China farmers' voting power is only one eighth (1/8) of the vote of that for an industrial worker.

(1624) China has had many famines throughout its long history. Access to food for the whole world cannot be left out in these negotiations. **Food is a common denominator for everybody's fundamental need of the Nine Historical Pillars.**

(1625) **Water:** Water has three main functions in society. It is necessary for human consumption, for food and for energy production. Water is usually, but not always, community owned and rates thereby controlled by politically appointed commissioners in a public utility board. The administrator for a water company asks the tax-paid board for a budget. If the budget is reasonable the request will be approved. This is a very simple procedure. An employment in a water department is more or less permanent with good benefits and a secure paid retirement.

(1626) In recent time there has been much improvement in the recording of individual water use and billings. In Europe some private corporations have taken notice of this fact and are proposing automated cheaper administration costs for communities. The politically appointed community administration has to take a stand according to their budgets and connections.

(1627) Fresh water for human consumption can be produced by salt water through osmotic techniques but the technique is so far relatively expensive. Processed water has to compete with re-circulated and collected sweet water from dams and private wells.

(1628) The cost of private wells depends on the cost of energy to pump the water from the ground water. The cost of energy to pump water in the U.S. has tripled in the last couple of years. The food-producing farmer is the main person paying for the increased cost of energy. Food being a pillar need assures the cost is paid for.

(1629) As noted already above under food production, the San Joaquin River has become dry from diverted water and does not re-supply the ground water pool in the Middle and Southern California. The ground water pool itself all through California has become shallower and requires deeper wells and is getting too salty even for farming. Actually the whole ground of the San Joaquin Valley of California has sunk 30 feet or 10 meters from all the removed ground water.

(1630) Water for the population in the dry Los Angeles basin has grown beyond expectations. Fresh water support for L.A. is at a critical level. (See also the paragraphs devoted to Industrial Time and The Nine Historical Pillars.)

(1631) Populations will follow work opportunities. Northern California has the water. It would be a lot cheaper to open work opportunities closer to water than to move water south. The central canal that was built for the transport of water south is already stressing the environment in the Northern California. To move work out of the dry L.A. basin would save both water losses in water transit to L.A. and energy cost for long distance L.A. commuters. Collecting more of the surface water may no longer be an option if we wish to still keep Northern California as a populated area.

(1632) L.A. has a lot of political power through its number of votes. Only courts can stop further drain of Northern California water. If courts could save water for the sake of a fish it ought to be possible to stop further water transfer for the good of the people in all of California. I cannot see any harm in that both work and people move away from the 1 to 2+ hour commuter life in the L.A. basin. **Water is a common denominator to everybody's fundamental need of the Nine Historical Pillars.**

(1633) **Energy:** Original energy on our earth comes from only a few resources: the sun, the earth itself, hydrocarbons, and nuclear.

(1634) The sun gives energy to wind, light and water, each of which can be converted to electricity with the help of windmills, water or electronic light panels, from water turbines in waterfalls, and of course, to all living life through its food production.

(1635) The earth's energy can be harvested from heat exchangers in the ocean or by drilling into the earth, which by itself is 15°C or 59°F. This is done for a lot of private houses in Sweden. My family drilled a 160-meter deep hole in the granite ground and used it for energy exchange. The heat recovered is two-thirds cheaper than heat from hydrocarbon despite the cost for pumping. Natural, warm wells in Iceland and in California do make a significant but mostly just local energy contribution.

(1636) Competition within different energy production is critical because we are addressing a pillar need. Large U.S. energy companies are controlling the harvesting of *most of* the different kinds of energy resources and selling them to the market. A Public Utility Board and a customer's selection between natural gas, oil, electricity or gasoline influence the price of energy sold to the public.

(1637) Nuclear energy can be used for an unlimited energy production. The storage of the radioactive ashes does cause some concern. This concern in my opinion is just a technical problem and, I am sure, can be solved if opened for competing contracts.

(1638) Newspapers like to play on the anxiety for nuclear accidents. The chance for a nuclear accident is very slim and recognized in the professional environmental review of the construction of nuclear plants. Only two major nuclear accidents have occurred so far. One was the accident that happened in the former Soviet Union. The Chernobyl Nuclear Plant was constructed under communistic administration with very little public responsibility. The second accident happened after an earthquake in the ocean floor outside Japan. It caused a tsunami along the eastern cost of Japan and considerable damage to a nuclear plant but the damage was mitigated by the rapid local emergency response. Japan had a lesson to learn but no greater catastrophy. In Germany, France, Japan and Sweden nuclear energy has supplied a large portion of the energy need without any serious negative consequences for some 30 years.

(1639) Nuclear plants need water for cooling and are often located close to population centers. Electricity transportation is cheap compared to exposing population centers to remote, but still, possible radiation exposure.

(1640) There is a shift from hydrocarbon to electricity for driving a car. This will place new demands on electricity. Nuclear is probably the only energy source that can meet the big demand that electric cars would require.

(1641) Hydrocarbons have so far been the cheapest energy to harvest. Car transportation is now growing very fast in the emerging countries, like China and India, causing the price of this energy to increase very fast.

(1642) Access to hydrocarbon is unevenly distributed on the earth. In places where it is found leaders have recognized their new political and economic power and are mixing their sudden economic good fortune with spreading old fashioned, dogmatic religious messages. This might delay democratic evolution based on the Nine Historical Pillars and cause different conflicts. It can be expected that the politically controlled hydrocarbon cartel will counter any effort to make society independent of hydrocarbon. Saudi Arabia has already stated it expects to be compensated for any replacement of hydrocarbon dependency.

(1643) In the last six to seven decades the rise in energy cost has caused mass industrial production to move into low labor cost countries. Cheap labor in communist countries or where labor is not allowed to organize, is essentially replacing expensive hydrocarbon for energy. Cheap labor countries are causing organized labor in democratic countries to lose their work security. This leads to large capital transfers to China and other low labor cost countries and for them to open their economy to a capital market and meet their labor pillar need.

(1644) This reminds me of when U.S. in the 1600-1800s was a slave country with a low labor cost. U.S. stayed a low salary country until workers organized in the early 1900s and eventually labor unions took over and determined the cost of production in their effort to meet their members' pillar need.

(1645) **Here it is important to remember: Without competition there is no limit to the cost for a historical pillar.**

(1646) Presently, the cost of oil dominates the cost of production. The cost of energy is the basic common denominator for the whole world's production efforts and is in this way a common denominator for workers' Ninth Historical Pillar need. All over the world a worker has to produce something that can be transported and sold to a buyer somewhere on the globe to fill that buyer's need and at the same time allowing the producing laborer to earn a living and to fill his or her own pillar need.

(1647) **Each producer needs a user.** Nations need to recognize this in their banking system. Banking cannot be allowed to arbitrarily close because of poor central political policies. Citizens need to be informed of logical regulations of currencies for banks and insurance companies so their efforts to pursue their Nine Historical Pillars are not jeopardized. **Such regulations do not hinder the growth in the value of currencies, banks or insurance companies but help them grow within the limits set by improving everybody's need for the Nine Historical Pillars.**

(1648) The subject of sex has been thoroughly discussed in Part D.

## The Second Historical Pillar: Dwelling

(1649) The economic crisis crossing the whole world at the present (2010) had its origin in the Second Historical Pillar, the urge or wish for a private dwelling. The facilitator for this exchange is the internationally regulated banking system.

(1650) Local banks used dweller-need and a deregulated finance system to sell sub-prime loans. The sub-prime loans are popularly called NINJA loans (No Income, No Job, no Assets). NINJA loans were mixed with loans with good security and re-sold to wholesale bankers, who, in turn, made larger packages and resold these packages to insurance companies. The insurance companies turned such super packages into security bonds with triple A-rated security because home loans had always been very secure. Nobody could check the quality of the security in these *super packages.*

(1651) The housing market had had inflation in housing prices for the past 100 years. Dweller need seemed to be insatiable. Dweller need is indeed insatiable, because it rests on the "Second Pillar," the need for security for you and your family.

(1652) Banks counted on rising house prices within the cities as the result of the rapid industrializing.

(1653) Modern banks were also flush with cash from the new inventions for creating capital through hedge funds.

(1654) Hedge funds invest in the stock market using computer techniques and follow the market's cyclical trends around a moving average. The computer would automatically buy or place a "call order" and place a "sell order" or "put order" around a five-year moving average. No human could do this as effectively as a computer. The computer was an automatic capital-making machine.

(1655) The inventors of the first hedge fund program, Robert Merton and Myron Scholes, received the Nobel Prize in Economy in 1997. Eventually they started their own hedge fund and became very rich, as did most hedge managers. This went on until something happened that was beyond the five-year average.

(1656) In Detroit car manufacturers were under contract for union workers' need for security. Car prices were raised to cover for the workers' benefit demand. Cars were produced mainly for the North American market where the cost of gasoline was a quarter of what it was in the heavy taxed gasoline markets in Europe and Asia. Some Asian countries had even subsidized fuel.

(1657) The European and the Asian car manufacturers were building small energy efficient cars for their expensive gasoline market.

(1658) The Arab cartel decided to raise gasoline prices. Suddenly there was no market for American cars in either U.S. or abroad. Suddenly union workers in Detroit were laid off and could not pay for their house loans. Suddenly banks working with fractional reserve banking were required to keep larger reserves. Suddenly income from hedge funds based on a five-year moving average dried up. Suddenly the insurance for NINJA loans in the local and large banks ran out of money. Suddenly all commercial activity stopped because banks and insurance companies did not know if they really had any secured value to base their loans on.

(1659) The Federal Government had to step in, very rapidly; that is, over a weekend, and issue treasury bills for $800 billion to cover the lack of cash. The government had to provide help: first to AIG that insured large insurance companies, then big banks, and finally gave some cash loans to the local banks. The overriding necessity was to save the production economy and workers from unemployment thereby possibly losing their homes and starving, both Nine Pillar needs.

(1660) The financial crisis hit the U.S. market first, but reached the global market second—because if the American worker could not buy things for his pillar need, the worker in China would not have work for his Nine Pillar need and so on and so on. The scenery repeated itself in Western Europe, Japan, and China.

(1661) Workers all over the world are dependent on their consumers being able to buy what they produce. They are all locked together in their pursuit for a better and secured living.

(1662) **The sudden collapse of the insurance and banking business demonstrated its need for regulation and its importance for keeping people working and earning a living for the fulfillment of workers' need for security in the Nine Historical Pillars.**

## The Third Historical Pillar: Cleanliness

(1663) The need for products improving cleanliness, hygiene and personal beauty is a growing market all over the world. There seems

344

to be enough competition to control the prices for what is used in our homes and for our personal hygiene and beauty.

(1664) The hygiene in food handling and hygiene in living spaces has had public pressure for control, at least, in industrialized countries. The U.S. and Western Europe are all collecting, returning, and controlling what happens to their waste products from their homes.

(1665) The consumption to meet our Nine Pillar need causes what economists call **negative or positive external effects**. The big question is—what happens to the Commons of air, water and global temperature? Nobody is owner of or solely responsible for these Commons. I will limit myself to make a few comments on the negative external effects on air, water and global temperature relative to how the changes in these Commons affect the Nine Pillar need of society and the challenges a lack of control raises for the world.

(1666) First it is necessary to set some premises.

(1667) Production and recirculation of waste are all dependent on the size of the population and the public's education. In industrialized, democratic countries with large populations, with public education free from political and religious dogmas, the political recognition of negative effects on the Commons from waste were early and spontaneously recognized. Public pressure created an early infrastructure for local controls of negativities. The awareness of a need for control of waste has now spread to large populations that have not had and do not have the same degree of education and democratization as mature democracies.

(1668) Developing countries are asking for mature democracies to pay for the gap they have created.

(1669) The price for a product or service is never a given number. A market or a demand determines the price in any situation. What is the cost of the negative external effect on the Commons of environment? The price for external effects in manufacturing will cause greater production cost and give an advantage to countries that do not care about environments. Have we come any further for global environmental control if not all participate and those who don't care continue to spew pollutants? Can results really be measured and monitored? These are the questions raised at the Climate Conference in Copenhagen in 2009. The meeting opened discussions for premises but that was all.

(1670) The problem of environmental control has further complications. The manufacturing and waste-recirculation are connected to worker's access to their personal Nine Pillar need. These needs, being pillar needs, tend to forego any need of the Commons.

(1671) The most densely populated countries, India and China, are now going through public education and democratizing. Democracy and free education have been late in coming to these countries. Some other countries control or even forbid public education just like Western countries did in the early 1800s. An uneducated public in underdeveloped countries with primitive infrastructure are now causing large negative external effects in manufacturing and public waste.

(1672) Can a complicated pollution program be accomplished without democracy and public education in developing countries?

(1673) Money exchanged between different countries does not always end up where it is supposed to go. Even in countries with large incomes from oil, such as Iran, Iraq and Nigeria, people kill each other for access to the oil income. In these countries very little money from oil income is left for citizens' Nine Pillar needs and for free education, and is last given to environmental impact of oil manufacturing or public waste. Like always, money tends to stay close to people in control of money distribution.

(1674) The commissioner to the EU from Sweden has been in charge of environmental issues within the EU. Attendance for each commissioner's work has been published. Meetings for environmental control were hardly attended, at least in 2005.

(1675) Control of waste *within* a country has the greatest chance to make an immediate impact. The industrialized nations have offered two different political solutions to cover the cost of negative external effects specifically for the control of carbon dioxide for global temperature control. One solution is based on a carbon tax and one is based on administrative solutions setting an administrative cap on emissions. Emissions would be traded between companies with more or less positive external effects, a cap and trade solution.

(1676) Some 25 years ago the EU started with a cap and trade policy for sulfur pollution from the Ruhr Area in Germany. Ruhr caused acid rain in areas north of Ruhr including Sweden, causing acidity in water, possibly affecting fish life and possibly deforesting Sweden.

(1677) The publicly owned Swedish forest pays for much of Sweden's medical and social support and is always of great concern. Germany neutralized its sulfur output locally and helped pay for neutralizing water resources in Sweden. The forest was actually fertilized and grew faster, a positive effect. Sweden has by itself cleaned all its waters by controlling the waste that Swedes used to dump into its rivers and lakes. Wildlife returned rapidly to normal in both lakes and rivers. Now people can bathe and fish right in downtown Stockholm. The Commons of the Baltic and North Sea surrounding the Swedish Peninsula are still suffering from over-fishing. Some of the old Soviet Bloc countries are still dumping waste into the Baltic Sea.

(1678) Our global world has to accommodate at least half a billion additional people <u>every ten years</u> before the present six billion population supposedly levels off at about nine billion in the 2050s. To meet the demand and waste for the Nine Historical Pillars of nine billion people should easily keep everybody busy in a prosperous, commercial exchange to make global life sustainable. The U.S. has said it is willing to participate provided results are monitored, verified, and all manufacturing nations are taking part.

## The Fourth Historical Pillar: Art

(1679) Art cannot be regulated. Controls happen most often within the soft and tender Historical Pillars "Five and Seven," communication and religion. **The society becomes a mental prison of an idea when communication and religion are regulated.**

(1680) The strength of the need for art is demonstrated in the price paid for art and its artists, art's eternal life and wide distribution.

(1681) The strength is also shown in the great effort dogmatic organizations put into its control. Many artists have paid with their life for challenging status quo.

(1682) Artistic freedom is indeed a pillar need for society and part of its economic web. Art responds to everybody's pursuit of the Nine Pillars of History.

## The Fifth Historical Pillar: Communication

(1683) Communication is the linkage of all economies. Access to the global Internet provides an equalizer for everybody in the pursuit of knowledge. The Internet reaches citizens of all countries despite that some dogmatic regimes make major efforts to keep their public in the dark.

(1684) The pillar stone in communication is *Truth*. Truth can be in the eyes of the beholder and can be difficult to recognize with everybody also having a say. **For the good of everybody the Nine Pillars of History help in defining and finding the Truth in society. Their 200.000 years of history assures their Truth.**

## The Sixth Historical Pillar: Community
## Freedom to Assemble for Group Support

(1685) The originator of national social programs was Germany's "steel" counselor Otto von Bismarck. He introduced a social support program, including old age pension, for the sole purpose of creating a homogeneous support base for a national army. With a national social system each citizen who spoke German got emotionally involved in defending and enlarging the nation. After a few short and very effective wars his Prussia defeated France and founded a united Germany in 1870.

(1686) Hitler's Germany after World War I was a national-socialist (Nazi) party nation. The party name "national" and "social" said that the program was based on Bismarck's national, socialistic program. The party program rebuilt Germany after the First World War. Hitler made the program dogmatic under his totalitarian leadership and started a most effective war machine. Nebuchadnezzar, Alexander, Napoleon and Hitler did not care about the Nine Pillar need; all dreamed of conquering the world with the "sword."

(1687) The post World War II democratic Germany was rebuilt a second time from a physically totally demolished society.

(1688) With U.S. support, a new democratic Germany, was created. With 50 years of peaceful growth Germany has grown to a major world economy and this time without any expansive land and people conquering policy.

(1689) Japan, impressed with Germany, started the national, socialist programs and mobilized a national war machine to conquer neighboring countries like Manchuria and China. (See Japan's history.)

(1690) With the help from the U.S. the post World War II democratic Japan rebuilt a physically totally demolished society and became a world economical power without any expansive land policy.

(1691) Feudal time placed a lot of weight on owning land because it placed the prince in control of the production source for food, the land. This was at a time when both transportation and trade were local and limited in size. **To fight for land in modern time, with a global economy, the control of land for this reason is hardly worth a drop of blood and certainly not worth dying for.**

(1692) The EU really used to be a bunch of nationalistic prince states fighting for taxes from commerce. A freely negotiated commerce solution does this much more effectively without anybody being hurt.

(1693) A goal for the people's common Nine Historical Pillars unites the stoutest historical enemies like France and Germany. Here I point also to the unification of the EU and the converging trade agreements all across the world.

## The Seventh Historical Pillar: Religion

(1694) The concept of religion evolved from our ability to talk. The words expressing religious concepts can be explained and followed through philology in comparing some critical words in Sanskrit with those of the same meaning in Swedish, English, Hebrew and Latin.

(1695) Religion took charge of educating the animal, *Homo sapiens,* originally a human flock member, and made him and her into a responsible tribal member of a society ruled by the Golden Rule:

(1696) *Always treat others as you would like them to treat you.*

(1697) The Golden Rule is still eternal in any society and basis for everybody's socialized pursuit of her and his own Nine Historical Pillars. To exemplify, five world religions were analyzed relative to the Golden Rule and the Nine Historical Pillars in Part V.

(1698) **Faith in the USA flowers like nowhere else in the world by being free and not taxed at all.** Nobody in the U.S. is forced to attend church or give a collection to the church and the church is not receiving any support from the Commons tax base. On weekends the churches (generic for any religious assembly) in the U.S. are filled several times a day. Such voluntary high attendance happens in no other country in the world. The voluntary attendance in U.S. churches of all different denominations proves a religious and moral belief is a fundamental need, indeed the "Seventh Historical Pillar."

## The Eighth Historical Pillar: Medicine

(1699) In 2012, the U.S. was trying to expand medical coverage to include some 46 million non-insured people out of a total population of some 307 million.

(1700) Access to a personalized quality medical care as perceived by the individual is the "Eighth Historical Pillar." Many of the people in the U.S. without medical coverage are foreigners. If people are working legally and paying tax they should be able to have access to medical care as all legally working people. Everybody should have access. The basic question is—Who pays for access? The majorities of working U.S. citizens pay by themselves for their access or have access through their employers paying from a worker/salary plan.

(1701) The cost of the medical coverage for people in the U.S. with access to medical care has recently increased by 16% a year. This means that it doubles about every fifth year according to the 70-rule (70 ÷ 16 is 4.375). Such an increase in cost will overwhelm any economy that underwrites it.

(1702) An enterprise making such earning increases is interested in growing and defending its position. This could be true also here. To find out the truth it is necessary to examine the medical profession and all its support systems using the Nine Pillars of History.

(1703) History has shown that any monopoly power will destroy a society, be it dogmatic religious or dogmatic political. A medical need, a life or death situation, can be interpreted as a situation for a monopolized need and access to medicine is indeed a pillar need, the Eighth. Some university professors, when I went to medical school in Sweden, were looked at, and looked at themselves, as gods.

(1704) My mentor for *The Nine Pillars,* Professor James Sheehan, encouraged me to write about the "Swedish system." I lived through its inception; I have worked for it at times, and both my wife and I have used it as patients. We worked and paid taxes for it during several short vacations from our university appointments in the U.S. and both of us have a small social security pension from the Swedish Government.

(1705) I have also had some experience from the U.S. system, both as a medical provider working as a doctor, as well as an insurer working as a medical director for a large corporation. In old age my wife and I have been medical consumers. We have worked the major portion of our lives in the U.S., are U.S. citizens, and receive a social security pension from the U.S. Government and retirement pensions from our employers.

(1706) Sweden is physically the size of California, but has only a quarter of California's population, or nine million. Like in California most people live in the southern quarter of the land. Originally, before World War II, 90% of the population was homogenously born Swedes, 99% Lutheran, all speaking Swedish, an old Germanic language, just like English. For access to higher education in the 1940s I had to have five years of English, three years of German and three years of French. To get accepted to medical school I had to have top grades in all academic subjects. Sweden at that time had three medical schools and graduated some 150 doctors a year.

(1707) Now the Swedish population consists of 20% immigrants, now many refugees from abusive Muslim countries. The government recognizes that many do not speak Swedish and offers schooling for foreigners and often helps them with translators at times of their critical life decisions. Sweden now has five medical schools and graduates some 300 doctors a year.

(1708) Access to medical care in Sweden has been going through an evolution. It started with a voluntary insurance before World War II. The socialist government after the war compelled Swedes to pay for medical coverage through their local income taxes. Every citizen became a child whose security depended on government support. **With the addition of young people the government added a large group who paid taxes but did not use the system**. Eventually the socialist government built a total medical and social access enterprise system with all medical and social support personnel and hospitals paid for through a *local*, county wide, regulated tax program, supplemented from the Commons national tax base. Salaries are regulated within one set national frame but negotiated locally similar to all labor union work contracts.

(1709) Before the doctors were placed on salary they were accused of abusing the national insurance just as is happening in the U.S. today. Doctors were accused of bolstering their fees and requesting many unnecessary tests. Much of doctors' bread and butter came from many unnecessary ECG tests at each doctor visit and a routine chest x-ray for every hospital admission.

(1710) The socialist party saw in the national medical society a last stronghold of the bourgeois society. In the 1950s the press attacked individual doctors for tax evasion. The press attacks were very rough. My wife and medical colleague and I thought it reminded us of Nazi

Germany. We had both paid for our chosen profession ourselves and were ready to start working after seven years of hard studies. If both of us were working, the after-tax net salaries would hardly cover the salary for household help. My wife and I were offered to rent a two-room apartment in a Stockholm suburb but we had to wait for at least two years before we could move in. If my wife would be pregnant we could count on an extra room. When an opportunity opened we left Sweden for a future in the U.S.

(1711) Since I left Sweden the medical education and working condition for doctors is very much different. Nowadays the government pays for all higher education and studies are supplemented with salary during the study time.

(1712) Doctors in Sweden work under a work contract. The doctor works for eight hours and receives six weeks vacation, as does any worker. The doctor receives extra pay for working during undesirable hours, such as nights and weekends, and has specified sick leave and old age pension.

(1713) The system claims it cannot pay in cash for all the on-duty time. The county compensates this with free time. The system is always short of doctors.

(1714) In the U.S. the warm climate of California, Florida and Hawaii attracts and are overpopulated with doctors. The EU has a basic law of free movement of people, capital and goods. Swedish educated doctors are popular in the rest of the EU. The same migration to warmer climate takes place in both Sweden and the U.S., causing a shortage of doctors in areas with colder climate.

(1715) Swedish doctor positions are filled with foreign doctors who have to learn to speak and understand Swedish in a short crash course. Language is no problem for doctors coming from Norway or Denmark. Doctors coming from the Middle East and Latin countries often have difficulties communicating with their patients.

(1716) The U.S. also has many foreign doctors. With English being an internationally accepted language for higher education in many countries, assimilation of them into the American society is easier than into the Swedish. The standard of living for doctors in Sweden is now essentially the same as in the U.S.

(1717) What do the Swedes get in their tax-paid medical and social support enterprise? Swedes get:

(1718) Tax-paid prenatal care, free child delivery, and one year off from work for parents, split between mother and father.

(1719) Tax-paid preschool, grade school and high school with child support up to age 18. Free higher education including salary during academic studies.

(1720) In regard to medical care it should first be noted that employers through a premium charged to every corporation in both Sweden and the U.S. pay for all injuries or diseases caused by employment. In Sweden the government charges a fee to every company to cover the cost. In the U.S. corporations and every employer contract with independent insurance companies pay and track costs for employment-related medical care.

(1721) In Sweden a local tax supplemented with a national tax pays for the cost of medical care. This includes acute and long-term care in acute or chronic care hospitals, in nursing homes, or for at-home care with a visiting nurse who helps with personal hygiene, food and housecleaning if needed. The same single-payer pays for the cost of psychiatric and drug abuse care in hospitals or ambulatory cares dependent on personal need.

(1722) A nominal cost of $20 supplements the cost of outpatient visits, compensation for travel or free taxi and may include ambulance service if needed.

(1723) National taxes pay for basic old age pension from age 67, which is smaller but similar to the U.S. social security, and is complemented with a personalized pension based on points for years of working service. Many buy a complementary pension to make up for loss in buying power during inflation. Retired people may be given assistance for apartment rent, heat and food if needed.

(1724) Tax may help to pay for basic funeral costs.

(1725) Tax pays for medications all through life with a nominal yearly self-risk. The self-risk has been growing from zero to now about $300 (2100 SEK).

(1726) Swedes are now the highest taxed people in the world. The taxes are collected from 18% sales tax on food, 24% sales tax on everything else, double the cost on all public services such as postage and telephone, and four times the cost of gasoline vs. the U.S. Also, a 24% value added tax (VAT) on any work like repairs in the household, an exponential increase of up to 50% tax maximum on work-related income. To view public TV costs some $300 per year. Traffic penalties are based on the income of the accused and can therefore be very large. Recently Sweden has removed its inheritance tax in order to help farms and other family enterprises.

(1727) The medical profession has to admit it is limited in making a definite diagnosis in some medical conditions, particularly for mental stress and for muscle and skeletal pains. Here the system can be overused. Both pain and stress can be claimed, but the doctor has very limited means to verify that the claim is justified. The doctor is usually apt to go along with the claim. Medical disability in Sweden is relatively common as compared with disabilities in the U.S., but fair comparison can only be done with medical disabilities from federal, state and city employment that are also paid from the Commons tax base.

(1728) Both Sweden and the U.S. have excellent quality medical care from birth to death. The cost should be similar but it is not.

(1729) The Kaiser Family Foundation (KFF) follows the cost for medical care in many countries and standardizes the cost according to currency and its Purchasing Power Parity (PPP). Bianca DiJulio, from the KFF has reviewed my quoted statistics and has even updated the numbers.

(1730) Between 2000 and 2010 the per capita medical cost in Sweden has been half that in the USA. A comparison of the cost in the two countries from 1970 to 2010 is shown in the tables below. The numbers are offered from member countries within the Organization for Economic Co-operation and Development (OECD) and provided by the non-political Kaiser Family Foundation (KFF).

## Annual per Capita Cost of Medical Care

| $ | 1970 | 1980 | 1990 | 2000 | 2005 | 2006 | 2007 | 2008 | 2009 | 2010 |
|---|------|------|------|------|------|------|------|------|------|------|
| Sweden | 311 | 943 | 1594 | 2287 | 2963 | 3195 | 3431 | 3656 | 3710 | 3758 |
| U.S. | 356 | 1102 | 2851 | 4791 | 6728 | 7107 | 7482 | 7760 | 7990 | 8233 |

## Annual Spending as Share of GNP

| % | 1970 | 1980 | 1990 | 2000 | 2005 | 2006 | 2007 | 2008 | 2009 | 2010 |
|---|------|------|------|------|------|------|------|------|------|------|
| Sweden | 6.8 | 8.9 | 8.3 | 8.2 | 9.1 | 9.0 | 9.0 | 9.2 | 10.1 | 9.6 |
| U.S. | 7.1 | 9.1 | 12.4 | 13.7 | 15.9 | 15.9 | 16.2 | 16.6 | 17.7 | 17.7 |

(1731) The survival rate of newborn and longevity of life are often used to compare effectiveness of different medical delivery systems.

(1732) The success of the Swedish medical and social enterprise is verified by the fact that Sweden has one of the lowest rates of newborn child death (Sweden 2%, U.S. 6%) and the highest rates of longevity in the world (Sweden 80 years, U.S. 77 years).

(1733) The annual growth rate of medical costs as percent of the GNP shows that the health cost does indeed weigh down on the Sweden's GNP but it does so even more in the USA. The Swedish system has a single payer, the taxpayer. The U.S. public tax supported health-spending accounts for only 46% of the population; the rest is paid by private insurance or donations. A comparison of health delivery in Sweden vs. the U.S., as I have experienced it, might be informative.

(1734) As earlier stated, in Sweden doctors are placed on salary. There are very few doctors in private practice in Sweden. The system in Sweden is similar to that for U.S. veterans; however, care covers not just veterans but the total family. As in the VA Hospital, each hospital has an inpatient and an outpatient care with the diagnostic support machinery and personnel serving both parts of the hospital. The VA organization is paid from the distant Washington federal budget.

(1735) In Sweden the *local* government pays for both the building and the maintenance of the hospitals and medical personnel. This makes salaries official and community approved. Actually, many salaries are publicized in the local paper. Communities become immediate buyers of not only doctors, but also buyers of medicine, medical supplies, the building of hospitals, as well as extended medical care facilities, and childcare. The local community feels protective about its medical and social support system because it serves the local public; the local medical support system is all theirs and the local population is using it.

(1736) In medicine it is impossible to please everybody. Particularly surgery is a risky business. In the U.S. lawyers use this fact to encourage their clients to sue their doctors for negligence or malpractice. Lawyers know that most suits are settled before going into an expensive U.S. court system. Lawyers therefore encourage people to come to them for an opportunity to sue the doctor and the hospital. Lawyers will not even charge anything for their service, but will keep half or a third of the settlement. Both the client and the lawyer are happy after pocketing the out-of-court settlement, usually just after some routine negotiating with the medical insurance company. In 2008 doctors paid $11 billion insuring themselves against lawsuits for malpractice according to *The Economist*, January 16, 2010, page 94. Malpractice expenditure can probably explain some differences between U.S. medical cost and the cost in the rest of the Western world.

(1737) **The malpractice insurance companies are aware of the game and charge large malpractice fees from the doctor and the hospital. The physician is essentially just a game pawn.**

(1738) This type of insurance company does not have much incentive to control the abuse because the medical need is a pillar need (the Eighth) and will always in some way be compensated with higher fees to the doctors and hospitals. Doctors' costs for malpractice insurance may be larger than the living cost for the doctor. The cost of malpractice forces many young doctors to sign up and limit their work to hospital salary employment, where the hospital helps with malpractice costs.

(1739) A possible, at least partial, solution to the malpractice game would be a general and mandatory arbitration. Some doctors and hospitals have arbitration written in the contract covering their services. Some U.S. states have issued tort reform to control the abuse. These states limit the amount of money that can be awarded in malpractice suits.

(1740) The malpractice game destroys the doctor/patient relationship. Already the father of medicine, Hippocrates, warned against talking bad about colleagues and had newly licensed doctors promise not to talk bad about each other. But, of course, lawyers never made such a promise and live off controversy. The "law making" part of government has more lawyers than doctors, "making sure that patients' rights cannot be compromised"—and the malpractice game to continue.

(1741) In both Sweden and the U.S., all medical malpractice claims are submitted to a state medical peer review with eventual warnings to the doctor and, if major, with license restrictions. A group of peers are professionally objective in judging doctors' work, have no personal financial incentive, and still have the good of the patient in mind. Large financial claims are very few in Sweden. I would think the medical malpractice game played in the U.S. explains some of the difference between the cost of medicine in the U.S. and the rest of the OECD world.

(1742) Another possible explanation to the difference in medical cost in Sweden vs. the U.S. is that the government is in control of its large national market. The buying power of a state has more negotiating strength than individual doctors and hospitals. Also in Canada with socialized medicine, the cost of medicine is cheaper than in the U.S. The government can, **at times,** be a smarter buyer of medicine and medical equipment.

(1743) The way hospitals are run in Sweden vs. the U.S. is also very different. Doctors using hospitals in Sweden are full-time employees of the hospital, just as doctors are within the VA or at the Kaiser Hospital organization, but this is not typical for the U.S.

(1744)  In the U.S., hospitals are surrounded with private practicing physicians or group practices that maintain the care of their patients both outside and inside the hospital. The doctor in his private practice may use the hospital both for the daily care and for special procedures done by a specialist, such as for an x-ray or for nuclear medicine. The hospital may own the equipment or not. The hospital is paid mainly for its nursing care, room and board, and for the use of the equipment dependent of who owns the equipment. Emergency room care is charged for separately and is usually done under separate and specialty-doctor contracts. If a doctor has invested in a medical laboratory or major diagnostic equipment it can be an opportunity for conflict of interest.

(1745)  U.S. rehabilitative medical care is provided for in separate facilities that are devoted to such care. The patient's private doctor may follow the care of his patient but an in-house doctor paid by that facility might take over the care.

(1746)  Paying for health care in the U.S. is a labyrinth system of individual, group, state and federal resources. Two separate armies of people execute bills—one army that writes the bills and another pays the bills. Individuals or a myriad of more or less comprehensive group plans plus state-run "Medicaid"—or federal run U.S "Medicare" pays for the bills.

(1747)  "Medicaid" is a singular state program that pays some 50% of the medical cost for those who, for one reason or another, can prove that he or she is unable to pay. The U.S federal overnment supports the state for the second half of Medicaid.

(1748)  "Medicare" is a U.S. federally administered program to which all workers have paid in capital drawn from their federal tax. Medicare coverage has four parts: "Part A" pays for hospital care, "Part B" for doctor bills, and "Part D" for drug needs. "Part C" pays for all A, B and C services but only for designated providers; that is, "Part C" covers a greater part of the cost but has no free choice of services.

(1749)  Parts A and B usually pay about 80% of cost. Most people pay for a complementary insurance that covers 80% of the 20% gap that Medicare leaves uncovered. The patient pays for this remaining portion.

(1750) This Medicare complementary insurance has, for many workers in the past, been part of their employment benefit. This benefit is no longer as common because companies can no longer afford to cover the cost. The cost of complementary medical insurance was a part of the U.S. car company's financial difficulties.

(1751) Private, luxurious retirement communities along with long-term adult and final care for old age in the U.S. require special private investments. The private investment is for most people accomplished by selling their equity in their family home. In this case, the attached medical care is again paid for from federal Medicare plus private insurance.

(1752) Swedish retirees are offered an apartment mixed in with people still of working age. People with sufficient retirement tend to stay in their homes or apartments until they are no longer able to care for themselves. In such cases they are offered a small one-room apartment with access to a community kitchen and attached long-term nursing care. The physical quality of these facilities is indeed very fine. The cultural and educational difference of people mixed together in these homes may eventually be traumatic experiences during people's final days.

(1753) In the U.S. retired people also try to stay in their home as long as they physically can. Both Medicare and Medicaid help pay for care in the home and different home services for 100-day-care each year. For details, search the Internet for Medicare or Medicaid.

(1754) I recently attended the opening of the enlarged El Camino Hospital in Mountain View, California. Local city tax and donations had financed the building of the hospital that therefore is an independent, 300-bed hospital. A trade journal recently recognized the El Camino Hospital as technically the most advanced hospital in the world. My old friend, Wesley Alles, was the Chairman of the Board at the time. He gave me a private showing.

(1755) The hospital rooms are all private rooms with beds automatically recording the weight and pulse and adjustable into numerous positions. Patients have transport channels separated from the public. Equipment includes top model electromagnetic image scanners, x-ray, and for treatment remote controlled surgery. All medical communication is electronically communicated and stored. Food may be adjusted to the patient's need but also taste-corrected according to cultural background. Nineteen "TUG" Robots for food and medicine transport contribute to a cleaner environment. Accuracy and safety are also improved as the robots move independently throughout the hospital carrying medical supplies and patient meals. In other words, the robots optimize staff time to patient care. A special area is set-aside for meditation. Religious officials from any religion have access to patients any time. The cost for admittance to El Camino Hospital is not more expensive than the cost in for-profit hispitals.

(1756) The cost for long-term medical nursing care in the U.S. causes elderly their most anxiety. Regular medical insurance has smartly left out the cost of long-term insurance in their regular medical care contracts. If the final years of one's life end up to be a patient with the syndrome of Alzheimer's, the cost for years of total nursing care will ruin the finances of most families in the U.S. Many families have no insurance for such long-term final care. The family impact for long-term medical care in Sweden is mitigated by the state. In the U.S. the single-family burden or such long-term medical care may be catastrophic.

(1757) The insurance system in the U.S. gives work to an army of insurance processors beyond the personnel caring for the patient. The cost of this administrative insurance expense can easily amount to 30% of the medical coverage. Again, insurance cost will be recovered, but never controlled, because the need rests ultimately on a pillar need.

(1758) In Sweden all social and medical personnel are unionized. The cost of this state enterprise, which rests on a pillar need, pushes other national programs aside. Specifically for Sweden, the cost of defense, another pillar need for a free nation, has been cut back. This may not feel very threatening to a nation that has always been free and not seriously threatened since Napoleon-time. The U.S. has had to defend itself, plus has helped many democratic nations from aggressive dogmatically misled neighbors, all through the 1900s. Dogmatically religiously warped extremists attacked the U.S. Homeland in 2001. In the U.S. the community need for defense is a very important part of its pillar need, the Sixth, and cannot be compromised.

(1759) Hospitals in the U.S. can be community supported, as it is for the El Camino Hospital, but are often <u>for-profit</u> organizations that hire doctors for a smaller salary. These hospitals give out contracts for more expensive special care like for emergency care and radiology. Some of these special care facilities require large investments, over a million dollars, as for an EMR, electromagnetic radiation scanner. Such services may be started with a pooled venture capital, independent from a hospital.

(1760) Starting with childcare in the U.S., the prenatal care, birth, delivery, and childcare are covered by private insurance. The individual state tax program, Medicaid, covers for the cost of uninsured people and special-need patients. The patient must verify to the state that he or she needs the state to pay for their medical need.

(1761) The state also helps with raising the child through school age, or to age 18, and many states pay for school lunches and travel with school buses. Race integration between schools was forced when segregated abused was obvious in the 1960s.

(1762) Adult working people pay for their own medical insurance from their salary, but as it is voluntary, people may not. This is true and common for many young people, who think that nothing will happen to them, and is particularly common for drug addicts who certainly will have health problems, but who don't care. People without insurance are a burden for the state Medicaid system. Some doctors refuse to care for Medicaid patients but competition may make some doctors available.

(1763) Pharmacies are usually independent services. They may have contracts with hospitals, be small independent pharmacies, or very large corporate chains. Patients pay the cost of filling a 30 or 90-day prescription. Pharmacies charge $10 or more for filling a prescription. The cost of medicines is supported either from Medicaid or individual privately paid medical insurance or corporate sponsored insurance. After age 65 the cost of physicians, hospitals and medications are complemented with federal tax funded Medicare from Washington.

(1764) Swedish citizens are now the heaviest taxed people in the world and taxed for every human need except sex. They are getting service back *after* they have paid the salaries and the pensions for all the people administrating and delivering their social needs, all sitting closer to the control of citizens' earned money than citizens are themselves. A "tragedy of the Commons" may be the given consequence in the long run.

(1765) The U.S. and Sweden, or actually all of Western Europe, stand at a crossroads. Access to medical support is a pillar need. The basic question is—should the Commons tax base finance a pillar need that cannot be controlled without competition? The cost will take from other needs financed from the Commons fund and eventually affect the cost of all production and therefore jeopardize production-worker access to their Nine Pillar needs. Open, informed discussions within a democratic system have to decide the consequences to the effect on everybody's Commons.

## The Ninth Historical Pillar: Trade

(1766) We are right now living in a historic time. China is the only large communist country still standing. China is going through a peaceful reorganization, allowing investment for profit and recognizing property rights. The U.S., the staunch and largest capital economy in the world, is seeking a solution to meet the "Eighth Historical Pillar" need, the need for medical coverage. China and U.S. have become interdependent through their large trade exchange. This increases the probability for a peaceful solution to any conflict between them. Free reasonable global trade is indeed the best hope for a peaceful future for all nations. Both China and the U.S. are striving to satisfy their citizens' need for the security in the eternal truth of the Nine Pillars of History.

# References

(1767) Some books that have influenced my thinking specifically about American politics and economics.

(1768) *The Great Deformation: The corruption of Capitalism in America.* David A.Stockman, 2013. ISBN 978-1-58648-912-0.

(1769) *How the West was Lost: Fifty years of Economic Folly and the Stark Choices Ahead.* Dambisa Moyo, 2011. ISBN 978-0374-17325-8.

(1770) *It's Enough to Make You Sick: The Failure of American Health Care and the Prescription for the Cure.* Jefferey M. Loboskky, M.D., 2012. ISBN 978-1-4422-1462-0.

(1771) *Working It, the Rules have Changed.* Greg Hutchins, Quality Plus Engineering, 4052 NE Couch Portland, OR 97232, tel 503-233-1012.

(1772) *Economic Systems & Society.* Capitalism, Communism and the Third World. George Dalton, 1974. Penguin Education.

(1773) *Basic Economics, A Common Sence Guide to the Economics. Thomas* Sowell, 2007. ISBN -13:978-0-465-00260-3.

(1774) *Civilization and the Rest.* Niall Ferguson, 2011. ISBN 978-1-59420-305-3.

(1775) *From Plato to Nato.* David Gress, 1953. ISBN 0-684-82789-1.

(1776) *Lords of Finance: The Bankers Who Broke the World.* Liaquat Ahamed, 2009, ISBN 978-1-59420-182-0.

(1777) *Open Society, Reforming Global Capitalism.* George Soros, 2000. ISBN 1-58648-019-7.

(1778) *A Free Nation: The Financial Roots of Democracy.* James Macdonald, 2003. ISBN: 0-374-17143-2.

(1779) *The General Theory of Employment, Interest and Money. John Maynard Keynes,* 2008. BN Publishing.

(1780) *The Lever of Riches: Technological Creativity and Economics Progress.* Joel Mokyr, 1990. ISBN:-13 978-0-19-507477-2

*(1781)* *Journey of the Universe.* Brian Thomas Swimme, Mary Evelyn Tucker, 2011. ISBN: 978-0-300-17190-7.

*(1782)* *Information Rules: A Strategic Guide to Network Economy.* Carl Shapiro, Hal. R. Varian, 1999. ISBN: 0-87584-863-X.

*(1783)* *The New York Bublic Library Book of Chronologies, The Ultimate One-Volume Collection of Dates, Events, People, Places and Pastimes.* Bruce Wetterau, 1990. ISBN: 0-13-620451-1.

*(1784)* *Vår Economi, En introduktion till samhälllsekonomin.* Klas Eklund, 1993. ISBN 91-550-4051-9.

*(1785)* *Hur Mycket politik tål ekonomin? Högskattesamhällets problem.* Assar Lindbeck, 1986. ISBN: 91-34-50817-1.

*(1786)* *Democracy the Swedish Way: Report from the Democratic Audit of Sweden.* Olof Petersson, Klaus von Beyme, Lauri Karvonen, Birgitta Nedelmann Eivind Smith, 1999. ISBN 91-7150-761-2.

*(1787)* *Nyckel till Frankrike.* Gunnar Bjerrome, Ulla Keyling, 1975. ISBN: 91-528-0084-9.

*(1788)* *Freds-och konfliktkunskap.* Svante Karlsson. ISBN 91-44-00598-9.

*(1789)* *International Regimes,* Edited by Stephen D. Krasner, 1983. ISBN: 0-8014-1550-0.

## A Personal Final Word

*(1790)* This text has taken me more than 12 years to accomplish. The text has required seven printings, each with an expanded text in order to cover the enormous scope of the Nine Pillars of History.

*(1791)* The Nine Historical Pillars were inspired from the hunting and gathering time. They were shown to be eternal, interdependent and were used as non-political denominators to assess past and present political history. A generic religion was identified from the philology of word concepts. The female role in a society together with five world religions were analyzed relative to the Golden Rule and the Nine Pillars of History. The evolution of economy was followed up to present days and shown to have the same goal as the Nine Historical Pillars; that is, the security for us and our family.

*Gunnar Sevelius MD*

(1792) I promised to repeat the "one-page" history from the start of the manuscript in order to challenge the reader: Now, when you have read the history of the Nine Pillar concept: Is this "one-page" history the ultimate truth? You can be the judge. See also:

Blog: www.ninepillars.com

(1793) **The discovery of nine common denominators through 200,000 years of history yields compelling hypotheses for their anthropological scope and present social relevance.**

## The Nine Pillars of History are:

1) Survival (food, water, air, energy, sex)
2) Shelter
3) Cleanliness
4) Art
5) Communication
6) Community (freedom to assemble for group support)
7) Religion
8) Medicine
9) Trade

**Food transport defines three historical time periods:**

- **Hand** transport for tribal time from 200,000-10,000 years ago.
- **Animal** transport for agricultural time: 10,000-1826 (steam-engine).
- **Machine** food transport for industrial time: 1826 - forward.

The female role in society parallels the periods of food transport:

- **In tribal time** the female was as important as the male, contributing 70% of calories to the tribe.
- **In agricultural time**, she was essentially politically powerless.
- **In industrial time** she is recovering her individual and political identity.

**The Nine Pillars of History recognize only two kinds of social leadership, one leading to conflicts:**

1) **Democratic,** based on the also 200,000 year old Golden Rule (because no society is sustainable without the Golden Rule).
2) **Dogmatic,** based on political or religious dogma, **often connected with war conflicts.**

**The Nine Historical Pillars have three inevitable traits:**

1) They are eternal.
2) They must be sustainable.
3) Their cost can only be controlled through free market forces.

**The present social fallout of the Nine Pillars of History are:**
**The Tragedy of the Commons (what many own, nobody owns):**
The Tragedy of the Commons from agricultural time will usually lead to selfish goals instead of for the public good with three predictable results:

1) **For countries**: royal, religious or political dogmatism leading to 10,000 years of war conflicts. **Democracy is the key to peace.**
2) **For corporations:** capital drifts to the top and stockholders lose control.
3) **For federal, state and local government:** personal agendas may lead to tax-waste and the public loses control.

**Medical cost, the 8th Pillar, compared to GNP is presently unsustainable**:

- Medical cost in the U.S. is 17% of the GNP and unsustainable.
- Medical cost in the in EU is 9% of the GNP but still unsustainable.
- Medical cost limits access to the remaining eight Pillars of History.

**The Nine Pillars of History might have a solution for runaway medical cost control**:

- Analyzing computerized medical records for medical efficacy.
- Comparing for-profit and not for-profit medical delivery systems for cost and medical efficiency.
- Mitigating medical conflicts through peer reviews instead of through litigations.
- Single and local control of payer system is likely to be the most efficient insurance system.

My wish is that the observation of the "Nine Historical Pillars" gives you, dear friend and reader, peace, security, dignity and hope for freedom. So, if I may respectfully borrow President Lincoln's words, *"that governments of the people, by the people and for the people, shall not perish from the earth."*

Gunnar Sevelius MD

Printed in the United States
By Bookmasters